D1519240

DANIEL MODE

THE TRAVELERS WITHIN

The Travelers Within is a travel adventure fiction series from author Daniel Mode. Inspired by extraordinary, real locations and remarkable stories from the road, *The Travelers Within* is a journey beyond all limits.

www.thetravelerswithin.com

THE TRAVELERS WITHIN
INTO THE UNKNOWN

A NOVEL BY

DANIEL MODE

For more information, address:
info@thetravelerswithin.com

FIRST EDITION 2020

ISBN 979-8-6639748-8-2 (paperback)

www.thetravelerswithin.com

Acknowledgments

My sincerest thanks to:

My dear friend, travel buddy and co-editor, Michael Thomas, for his tireless work and good humor in helping me complete this lengthy project. You were right all along, Michael; perfection IS the enemy of completion.

My co-editor Sue Paulson in England, for always adding the letter "u" to words like colour and favourite, which I later had to remove.

My "brothers from other mothers," Gabriel and Blair, for their undying support and reassurances.

My loving family Carol, Bob & Emily Mode for their boundless energy and encouragements.

My friends Jillian Pettit and Mathew Townsley for their help along the way.

And above all others, to my beloved partner in life, Laura. My sage counsel. My inspirer. My Muse. The one who encouraged me for years as I worked on this without hesitation. For her patience throughout the writing process. For her love. For everything.

🍍

INTO THE UNKNOWN

"I soon realized that no journey carries one far unless, as it extends into the world around us, it goes an equal distance into the world within."

- Lillian Smith

Chapter 1

April watched quietly from her desk. Across the room, the uniformed *SENAFRONT* officer escorted the strange man through the front door and into the central office.

Well, there he is... she thought. Though she'd been made aware of the stranger's forthcoming arrival, the circumstances which had brought him here still left so many questions unanswered.

Earlier that morning, the Panamanian paramilitary group tasked with patrolling the wild, war-torn border between Panama and Colombia, the *Servicio Nacional de Fronteras*, had picked the man up on a country road along the smuggler's jungle's edge.

April gazed on as the soldier reluctantly handed over his captive to the awaiting U.S. security personnel and then stormed from the building in a bluster. April's jaw tensed.

The disheveled stranger, a caucasian man in his late thirties, carried with him a black duffel bag, and appeared both feral and tamed to her in the same thought. His pleated slacks and button-up shirt were heavily soiled, stained and tattered, and seemed oversized for his stature, hanging and drooping from his frame like a carnival barker. His matted hair and beard were long and bedraggled, and his skin was dark and leathery from the sun. He looked like he'd been raised by wolves, yet there was something noticeably civilized, almost dignified in his mannerisms.

Who the hell is this guy?

As the peculiar man's inspection concluded, the security officer raised a pointed finger towards April's desk. The stranger turned to face her across the busy room.

Air trickled through April's teeth.

The young consulate clerk straightened in her chair in preparation for their impending meeting, pausing as the two's eyes suddenly locked. Though she'd been expecting him all day, now that he was finally here, she found herself unexpectedly beguiled by his appearance.

The man took a seat across from her, and an odorous waft of sweat and Right Guard floated into April's nostrils. In the three-plus years she'd endured at the U.S. Consulate in Panama City, two distinct types of men typically came to her desk. Hungover American businessmen who'd lost their passports in nightclubs or taxis during the previous night's company card fueled bender. Or, U.S. contract workers from the Canal Zone who'd found themselves in trouble with local authorities due to overzealous partaking of the rampant drugs and prostitution in the area. These were the men she knew from her time here. The men she "understood" and, more importantly, could easily handle.

The gentleman now sitting across from her, however... April wasn't sure just what he was.

A courteous smile curled from her lips as her thin, toned hand extended across the desk. "May I please see your passport, Mr. Hill?" she asked.

A simple request, yet the man's unflinching gaze remained on April. His hazel-green eyes peering below a dusty brow, transfixed on her in a trancelike state.

April began to fidget in her seat. "Excuse me, sir, can I please see your passport?" she insisted yet again, raising her voice a notch to feign increased authority.

Again, the stranger offered neither response nor reaction.

A lengthy silence and the distant clatter of office sounds filled the void between them. April settled back into her seat. *What the hell?* She mulled.

The young woman from Virginia was no stranger to self-reflection and deemed herself in possession of a great many positive traits, patience indeed being one of them. But patience in the face of being ignored was something altogether different.

Before she had a chance to bite her lip, a frustrated yawp suddenly burst from April's lips. "Hello! Mr. Hill!" she barked. Her loud bellow wrenching the mysterious man from his catatonic gaze and attracting more than a few glares from the surrounding office clerks.

The man jolted upright in his chair as if struck by lightning. Pigpen-esque micro clouds of dust springing from his shoulders. "What?!... What's that now?" he stammered.

"Your passport?!" she demanded again.

The man's eyes followed April's glaring pupils downward to find her palm outstretched on the desk before him. "Oh yes, of course," he mumbled, fumbling through his pockets and handing April the passport. "Sorry about that."

Grasping it from his fingers, April opened the worn blue booklet and proceeded to commence her inquiry. "Mr. Hill, where exactly have you been for the last—"

Suddenly, April's voice faltered. Her eyes lingered, transfixed, on an oddity immediately visible in the glossy booklet in her hand. In the next few prolonged seconds, her face gradually transformed. Annoyance... Shock... Puzzlement.

What the hell? She thought yet again.

April raised her gaze back to the man and squinted. "Mr. Hill...is this...is this an old picture?" she muttered.

"No... not really. Why do you ask?" he replied.

April contemplated his response but was incapable of articulating a polite retort. Instead, she continued to survey the man from beard to belt. "No reason," she answered.

Turning her eyes back down to the passport in her hands, the clean-cut man in the photograph stared up from the lustrous page, challenging her to recognize him. His round face was pale, chubby and clean-shaven. He smiled awkwardly and toothily from below a humdrum ten-dollar haircut, and his double chin poked out above his buttoned collar. His cherubic cheeks were rosy and bulbous. He was average looking in nearly every way.

April glanced back up at the rugged man across the desk from her, his hair hanging to his bearded chin, his arms dark and sinewy. He bore a marginal, but unmistakable resemblance to the person in the picture, but April couldn't fathom that they were one and the same. She glimpsed at the Date of Issue on the passport, and her stomach sank.

It's only seven months old. What in the world happened to this guy?

April felt dazed. "Mr. Hill…" was all she could muster. Words which had always been there for her, now felt lost beneath a sea of questions and theories sloshing around in her head. "I just… I just need to know two things from you right now," she began. "Do you think you can help me understand some things here?"

"I can certainly try," he replied.

The young woman slid her brown hair behind her ears, squared her shoulders and straightened in her seat. *Get it together, April.*

She placed the passport on the desk and eyed the man with newfound earnestness. "Well. Mr. Hill… the first thing I need to know, really, is… how did you end up way down here at the Colombian border in the first place? This is a long way from Texas," she finished with a sigh.

The man offered a half-grin of understanding. "It is now, isn't it," he muttered.

April took a sip of water from the glass on her desk. Though she was relieved she'd been able to vaguely articulate the first of her two pressing questions, she was well aware that the next was far more significant

And carried vastly darker implications.

She braced herself and began. "Also, Mr. Hill …" she faltered, "and more importantly… Can you please tell me anything about a missing young man from the U.S. named Jonah Shaughnessy? From what I gather, you were the last known person to be seen traveling with him. But that was nearly a month ago."

April watched her interviewee closely. Time seemed unmoving, anxiously anticipating his reaction. Barely breathing.

The man casually slumped back in his chair and locked eyes with the young woman. His lips formed into an unexpected grin. "Well, April, do you want the long version or the short?"

CHAPTER 2

Simon Hill was a sensible, rather ordinary man. As a young boy growing up in Odessa, Texas, his quintessential dream, like that of just about every other boy in the Lone Star state, was to one day become a cowboy. Wearing a ten-gallon hat or a silver helmet adorned with a blue star didn't matter one bit. Both carried equal levels of respect about town. So, when at age 10, Simon's father Kyle gave him and his older brother Jonathan a football signed by legendary Dallas Cowboy Roger Staubach, and the three threw it together for hours in his back yard—young Simon's dream had felt somehow fulfilled.

A few years passed, and after a series of unforeseen events had left the young man traumatized and weakened, his next goal evolved into something far more immediate: to get the hell out of Odessa and away from the woman he'd spent his entire youth growing to despise. His mother, Madeline— "The Ghost" as he'd come to call her.

Thank God! he rejoiced upon reading his acceptance letter to Texas Tech. And spared little time packing up his few belongings—forever leaving behind Odessa, Madeline Hill and the toxic memories of his painful high school years. The moment he walked into his dorm room in Lubbock, Simon let out a deep sigh of relief—and that goal too felt accomplished.

Time went on, as it does, and for Simon, graduating college and getting a good job took center stage. Always a methodical and persistent young man, he attacked this new purpose with calculated vigor. And four years later, Simon took his first job as a young suburban professional—a writer of heavy machinery user manuals for a co-op of farm equipment suppliers in the area.

Inherently systematic and precise, traits which made him a natural at technical writing, Simon had always been a mundane master at organizing information, and by extension, his personal life, into neat and tidy achievable steps. Finding great initial success at his new job, Simon believed the future to be lining up exactly as planned. A home and a family were the logical next chapters in Simon's *User's Guide to the American Dream*.

But at age twenty-five, Simon hadn't yet found a life partner, and a tingle of worry began to gnaw in his belly. When he reached thirty, a series of failed relationships had left his confidence worn and decimated, and Simon began to wonder if he'd ever meet the right woman. By thirty-five, he felt fairly certain that he never would.

Now, at thirty-eight, Simon hadn't tasted triumph in life nor the joys of success in nearly two decades. And, in the face of his life's seemingly inexorable decline, Simon had given up on striving for anything long ago, turning instead to a steady diet of antidepressants and anti-anxiety meds to help ease the surrender.

But all that began to change one morning in early May at the Redding & Co. central offices in San Antonio.

A light rain fell outside as the pallid, hefty man arrived for work at 7:30 a.m., just as he'd done the 4,423 workdays prior. And exactly as he'd done the 4,423 workdays prior, he sat down in his grey cubicle, switched on his computer, and placed his paper coffee cup in the upper right-hand corner of his desk. He stared at the screen as it booted up, slowly transitioning from black... to blue... to the Redding & Co. corporate logo.

Precisely as it'd done the 4,423 workdays prior.

Reaching into his drawer, Simon retrieved from it a long pink rubberized ladies' *personal massage wand* and began to fondle it in his hands deep in thought. Several nearby coworkers started to snicker at the sight. Yet, Simon remained oblivious, focused on the array of settings available on the waterproof device's handle, and the inconspicuous, well-conceived, USB charging port near its base. He switched it on, and the internal vibration motor whirred to life, sending both a loud humming buzz through the office and his observing coworkers into subdued giggles.

Simon's eyes veered to the surrounding cubicles, but found everyone working diligently on their own tasks. The woman nearest him clicked away on her computer keyboard. A man across the aisle held a phone receiver to his ear. Simon wondered if maybe he'd just imagined the sounds of laughter. With little in the way of friends or family to speak of, the lonesome Texan often found himself filling conversational hollows with imaginations of hushed whispers directed his way.

Maybe it was paranoia, he considered… or maybe it just made him a little less lonely in the world. He checked his watch. Three more hours till he could take his next Ativan.

In seventeen years in the workforce, Simon had written nearly a thousand user manuals and instruction guides for everything from pasta makers to jet-skis, toy robots and hunting rifles. It was a detail-oriented and solitary job, and Simon spent countless hours at his desk reviewing products, perusing engineering reports, and formatting simplified renditions of manufacturer spec sheets. On occasion, he'd speak on the phone with a product engineer or two, but Simon rarely had any face to face interactions in his daily routine. Even his technical illustrator, Danny, worked in a different wing of the building, and their correspondence was typically through the network.

A vague presence of a man, Simon found it easy to pass through the office as imperceptibly as a phantom. Few of the staff knew his name, and he knew even fewer yet, having years ago given up on office camaraderie. Instead, he chose to come and go with little to no human interaction, hiding himself in the droning babel and the homogenous sea of taupe and tan. It was a routine that had become such an integral part of his adult life that Simon had started to find a peculiar solace in his isolation. It felt easy and free of complications. Besides, his social skills had been left to decay for years.

***

At 7:53 a.m., Carly entered through the front doors of Redding & Co. and walked into the bullpen. A rotund, rather homely woman, Carly was just another of the countless office strangers to whom Simon had never given a second thought. Her affinity for neutral tone muumuus, hanging from her ample bosom straight to the floor, gave her a boxy, formless profile, allowing her to blend seamlessly into the surrounding office furniture. If one were to scan the office taking inventory, they'd likely say "cubicle, cubicle, copy machine—wait, no, that's Carly—cubicle, cubicle…"

But today, something about her was different. Grey, navy, beige, all of her go-to *colors* had been replaced with an atypically vibrant yellow and orange sundress. And as the large woman made her way through the bullpen, it proved remarkably difficult for people *not* to take notice. Her hefty stature and flowing, bright yellow skirt tails giving her the striking appearance of a blazing comet passing through the office.

As was typical in the banal world of Simon's white-collar workplace, the slightest idiosyncrasy or abnormality in the daily routine could quickly spiral into full bore pandemonium. Comet Carly was no exception. Like her near physical twin, the Sun, she exuded, on this particular morning, a gravitational pull that soon had the normally indifferent office drones locked into her orbit. Even Simon found his position amid the swirling trajectories converging at Carly's desk.

"What's happening?" he asked a passing Jane Doe, on course to its epicenter.

"Carly is showing everyone pictures from her honeymoon in Belize!" she beamed, before swerving to avoid a collision with others in the undulating corona.

Belize?

The name sounded oddly familiar to Simon but, amidst the extraordinary hullabaloo now permeating the sea of cubicles, he couldn't recall why. Nevertheless, he approached the woman's desk with a morbid curiosity, concealing himself in the back as always, and peeking over the shoulders of the dozen onlookers huddled around her.

Let's see what kind of man would marry Carly.

However, as Simon caught his first glimpse of the photograph displayed across Carly's glowing computer screen, the amorphous characters in the foreground, as weighty as they were, became transparent against the alluring tropical vista behind them.

Simon would later say that he never even saw the groom. Sure, the man was there, likely in at least half of the pictures. But Simon's eyes instantly abandoned focus on the wedded pair, riveted instead to the entrancing, polychromatic paradise beyond the two humans. It was unlike anything he'd ever seen before. *That ain't Galveston*

Simon's thoughts flickered back to the only beach he'd ever experienced: the gritty shore of the East Texas town where, five years earlier, he'd made a pilgrimage to see the ocean where his father had died. Simon recalled how grey and littered with garbage the sand had been. The murky seawater had been rippling and rank, the smell so offensive it made his nostrils burn just thinking about it.

The scene displayed on Carly's computer was decidedly different, however. The white sand, the turquoise sea, the verdant palms. Simon felt enraptured at once by their stunning, multi-hued vibrancy. And as the images continued to scroll across the screen, he grew so grossly hypnotized by their beauty, that if someone had told him to cluck like a chicken just then, he'd almost certainly have obeyed. Carly, meanwhile, continued to jabber on about her magical week of bliss, the squawking of her voice sounding increasingly like chicken clucking itself.

Then, as if a bolt of electricity shot through Simon's body, paralyzing him where he stood, the awestruck man abruptly recalled why the name "Belize" had sounded so familiar to him.

Dad.

***

That evening, Simon burst through the front door of his duplex apartment, charging straight to his home office. He'd barely made it through the day, counting the seconds till he could wrestle away from work and head home to see if *it* was still there.

An avid to-do lister with an equally powerful aversion to clutter, Simon had long ago developed a rather bad habit of placing papers and incomplete to-do lists into a special drawer in his filing cabinets. Out of sight, out of mind.

Thrusting open the drawer now, he pulled from it a veritable lifetime's worth of unfinished lists and proceeded to spread them out across his dining room table in a paper and stickum, color-checkered quilt. Most bore an unchecked box or two— "go to the gym" or "buy a new pillow"— but after a few minutes of frantic searching, Simon finally located the one he'd been looking for. It was a list he'd written when he was just twelve years old, a mere month after his father had unexpectedly passed away. He looked at it now, having not seen it in decades, in awe that it still existed.

1. Leave Odessa

2. Get a house with Jonathan

3. Go to Belize

Simon read the second item on the list and chuckled at the ridiculous notion of a twelve-year-old boy's idolization of his older brother. He recalled a time, way back, when his brother Jonathan and he had been practically inseparable. And Simon had genuinely believed the two would always be together.

But that was a lifetime ago.

Simon squinted, putting the thought out of his mind, and read the third item.

Go to Belize...

As the memory of this entry's origin rushed forward, Simon's heart constricted, water swelling in the edges of his eyes. Standing in the hollow of his empty dining room, Simon recalled a night by a campfire, long ago. A night when his father, Kyle, had regaled his two sons with whimsical tales of an adventure he'd taken well before they were born. Part of an offshore oil exploratory mission in the distant Central American land, Kyle Hill had set his boys imaginations alight with breathtaking accounts of white sand beaches, coconut palms and seawater as blue as sapphires.

Belize

Simon recognized this fond memory as one of the last genuinely happy moments in his life. Two weeks later, his father, Kyle, would pass away unexpectedly, and Simon's family life would die along with him. But again, that was long, long ago.

Simon took a seat and stared at the list in silence. That night, even sedated with a double dose of sleeping pills, he could barely sleep.

***

Over the following weeks, Simon's mind lingered on this place to which he'd never been. Each time Carly stepped away from her desk, Simon would meander past her cubicle, trying to catch a glimpse of the photographs now cycling as a screen saver on her widescreen monitor. On several occasions, he'd been caught staring, and he began to worry people might think he was stalking his coworker in the photographs. But it was something else entirely that now consumed him.

The near-magical, tropical paradise in Carly's images…

Long dormant memories of his lost father…

And an unexpected longing for something he was struggling to grasp.

CHAPTER 3

Jonah Shaughnessy fiddled with the last bits of food remaining on his plate, poking them around with his fork, lost in thought. As always, the wiry young man's Detroit Tigers baseball cap sat low over his chin-length brown hair, hiding his eyes in its shadow. His father Jim, a stolid man, as former military officers often are, stared across the dining room table at his son, wondering if Jonah was ever going to eat that last damn bite of eggs.

"So, what are you going to do today, Jonah?" he asked with a particular sort of obligatory parental interest.

Jonah's mother, Susan, glanced up from her plate, plastering her usual broad smile across her face in eager anticipation of her son's response. Jonah looked up at his father, then to his mother —*Why can't they just let me think in peace*— then turned back to his plate, saying nothing as the machinations in his mind churned back to work.

"Well, that sounds just great. Good luck with that," barked Jim, dropping his fork to his dish with a clank. Susan's smile faltered. Returning her eyes to her plate, she continued to eat her breakfast in silence. Jim's maddened eyes remained on his son.

"I'm going to my room," Jonah mumbled, excusing himself from the table.

"Do you need some help?" huffed Jim.

Jonah turned to him with a scowl. "I'm twenty-three years old. I think I can handle it," he replied.

"Goodbye, Jonah, honey," Susan called out quietly. "Thanks for joining us for breakfast."

***

Jonah entered his room and, as had become his custom, latched the door behind him and headed straight to his desk.

Finally.

For four years, this had been his routine. Jonah was well aware that the future path he'd chosen for himself would test every ounce of his knowledge, strength and determination. He needed to prepare. Unlocking a cabinet below the battered oak desktop, the young man pulled from it his collection of materials and laid everything out in front of him. Stacks of papers and charts. Cobbled together maps. And several worn-out dog-eared books.

The U.S. Department of Commerce's Kidnaping and Hostage Situation Survival Guide.

The US Marine Corps Manual for Land Navigation.

The SAS Survival Handbook.

Five months to departure and Jonah's preparations were nearly complete. *I need my laptop.* Jonah unlocked the brakes on his wheelchair and rolled to his bedside table to fetch it.

CHAPTER 4

Simon and sunshine had become estranged long ago—a relationship his milk-white complexion all too readily revealed. For fifteen years now, the pulsing glow of office fluorescents had provided his sole source of Vitamin D. His only glimpses of the sun coming through the UV glass of his windshield on his twenty-minute morning commute—a meditative time he'd grown to savor more than any other part of the day.

At the conclusion of work each evening, Simon invariably found himself driving under a black night sky to his sparse suburban duplex, a fortress of solitude where he could feel warmed, not by the sun, but by the all too familiar incandescence of his 50-inch, 3D, flat-screen television.

Yet in the weeks since seeing Carly's pictures of Belize, something inside of him had begun to stir. His typically mundane existence had somehow been infiltrated by daydreams of a sun-filled place where the air was clean, and the leaves were always green. Where the stresses and routines controlling his life maybe, just possibly, no longer held dominion.

Soon, his mornings would change.

Galvanized by this inexplicable desire, Simon took to pulling over beside the road on his commute to work each day. He'd step outside of his car and look to the sky, soaking his pale face in the hot sun. On that first day, he stopped for two minutes. The following day, for five. Then for ten. Closing his eyes tight, he'd attempt to teleport himself a thousand miles away to the Belizean coast. The whooshing sound of the freeway traffic nearby became waves crashing on a sandy shore. The pigeons chirping on the powerlines above were parrots and toucans eyeing him from coconut palms.

Simon didn't understand the deep desire that now penetrated him. *Why is Belize suddenly calling to me?* He wondered if, perhaps, it was merely nostalgia, a sentimental longing for that feeling of perfection he'd tasted when his father spoke of Belize that night long ago; a moment in time when he still had the love of his family, fanciful dreams of the future and a life wide open to infinite possibilities. Or maybe it truly *was* a desire for something else. A wanderlust that had always been there, buried beneath a lifetime of staying the course.

But why now? He'd always known there was a bigger world out there, after all. Movies and television had apprised him of such things. But, to Simon, the world beyond America wasn't a place for people like him. He was neither wealthy nor adventurous, and, as a Texan, one had to travel no further than New York City for a taste of the truly exotic.

Yet Carly had seen the world.

Fucking Carly?!

And if she could do it, well, that meant Simon could too.

It really was attainable.

And that…

Somehow…

Made it real.

CHAPTER 5

It was early on a Tuesday, and Jonah knew from experience that he'd likely have the place to himself. First through the door at opening time, he entered the Tropical Room of the University of Michigan Matthaei Botanical Gardens and the warm air at once thickened with humidity and the scent of damp leaves and earth. The 10,000 square-foot greenhouse, one of the largest in the United States, had been a weekly visit for the young man for years now—and Jonah had used his time there wisely.

As he rolled down the path slowly through the lush green environs of the simulated tropical rainforest, he stopped at each of the 476 plant species, one at a time.

"*Caladium Lindenni*... toxic

Dieffenbachia aurantiaca... toxic

Colocasia esculenta... edible."

Jonah was well aware of the tragic story of Chris McCandless—the young American adventurer who'd died in the Alaskan wilderness in 1992. Many had theorized that the young man had been killed from misidentifying seeds he'd foraged as edible. It was a mistake Jonah wouldn't possibly make.

Four months to departure and Jonah's preparations were nearly complete.

CHAPTER 6

It had been a month since that day at Carly's desk. A month since Simon's new dream—a real, actual, tangible goal—had finally arrived, and a dormant desire for action had begun to chug back to life inside him. It was a staggering development, and one Simon hoped would send him off his preordained timeline—slowly clicking away towards death—and into an alternate dimension where life could continue to get better. Where the world was unpredictable, and the extraordinary seemed possible.

So, he hatched a plan in his pajamas over cornflakes one morning.

A few days later, during his lunch break, he set the clandestine scheme into motion. Creeping from the office with the cunning prowess of a 215-

pound, pudgy white panther in business wear, Simon dexterously moved through the parking lot to his car, pounced inside and sped away through the endless field of Japanese sedans. As he pulled from the lot and off down the road, he glanced back repeatedly, hoping his unauthorized midday departure would go unnoticed and that he wouldn't be missed back at the office.

He wouldn't.

Fifteen minutes later, Simon reached the downtown San Antonio Federal Building. As he waited in the passport application line, he grew feverish with excitement and struggled to keep his legs still. The others in queue beside him, *world travelers* in his eyes, were part of an elite club Simon might soon actually be a part of. A month ago, he never would have dreamed he'd be standing here, but here he was. *Who ARE you right now, Simon?* He thought giddily. After years of mounting self-doubt and personal disappointment, the question itself brought him unfathomable joy.

***

In July, his passport finally arrived. Simon stared at the clean blue booklet for hours, its pages crisp and blank, waiting, craving the Belize stamp he hoped soon to get. From that moment forward, his *key to the world* went with him everywhere. He'd spend his lunch breaks in his office cubicle, holding it in his hands, rubbing it with his thumbs as he gazed at pictures online of the majestic Belizean coast dotted with colorful coral reefs, stilted cabanas and more. Tourist photos covered his screen each day of joyous smiling people splashing in the clear, blue waters and reveling in the sunshine. *Soon that will be me* he imagined.

Simon had already begun planning his visit, and in his typically methodical Simon fashion. He'd spent hours making detailed analytical tables of potential Belizean resorts and locales, and meticulously attributing values to everything from cuisine and amenities, to guest reviews and available activities. With a final score of 93.6, Simon eventually settled on a 1980's era white-walled gem dubbed the *Sunshine Bay Resort,* and spent each subsequent day memorizing everything from their lengthy resort activity list, to the grand buffet menu. As he read, researched and fantasized, his dream somehow felt closer with each passing moment, and less dream-like by the second.

***

August arrived, and with it came an unusual soreness in his abdomen one morning that began to fester. Throughout the day, Simon rubbed his side as the malady grew ever more painful. Though he struggled to work through it, by midday, there was no more denying its existence nor its severity. Something was terribly wrong. Simon limped to his car, buckled over the steering wheel, and drove himself to the ER. Within an hour, he'd received a diagnosis of appendicitis and was rolled into surgery.

Anesthetic... Relief... Darkness

That afternoon, as he slept, the hemorrhaging malefactor was removed, and two days later, the weary Simon returned home to recover. For a week, he languished in his empty house, alone. No family came to visit him. No friends called to check on him. No neighbors dropped by. Yet throughout his recovery, Simon managed to avoid loneliness via the flawless execution of his well-honed, tried and true technique: a blaring television relentlessly filled the house with chattering voices, applause and laughter—and an endless parade of food delivery drivers gave Simon a few fleeting seconds of daily conversation and a semblance of human interaction. The Zoloft and Vicodin helped to keep his *spirits high* as well.

After ten days, he was finally able to return to work. No cards were waiting for him there. No well-wishes were given. No one seemed to notice his absence whatsoever. The palpable weight of which briefly ached in his soul. So, he popped another Zoloft, and it was alright.

***

October arrived, and Halloween decorations began to appear on the leaf-strewn lawns of neighborhood front yards. Simon submitted his vacation request, triple-checking the forms before handing them to HR. His plan was a simple one: combine two weeks of his vacation time with the long Thanksgiving holiday to give himself almost three weeks in the Central American paradise.

For the past dozen Turkey-days or more, Simon had stayed in alone, graced only by the company of a supermarket rotisserie chicken, boxed stuffing, and the Macy's Thanksgiving Day Parade broadcast. Even Charlie Brown seemed to have a better Thanksgiving than him each year. A depressing thought.

But not this year!

The following days proved agonizing as Simon struggled to exercise patience, checking his mailbox and email accounts hourly in anticipation of the approval of his request. He hadn't taken a single vacation in the two years since he'd transferred to the Redding & Co. San Antonio office, working himself to the bone to become the "company man" that the upper echelon had desired. He'd done everything they'd asked of him, and now it was time to take a well-earned break. *Finally.*

Two excruciating weeks passed, and then, one ordinary morning, Simon arrived at the office and checked his mailbox., A letter from HR awaited him. *This is it!*

Snatching it from its box and tearing it open at once, Simon grinned ear to ear with jubilation. The plateaued path on which he'd plodded forward for countless years, now trembled beneath his feet, ready to crumble and give way to a magnificent spire, rising high to an unknown apex. *This is it!*

But the flurry of excitement was fleeting. Staring at the memo, the word printed in crimson at the top of the page suddenly burned against his eyes like the spit venom of a Mangshan pit viper. He stood motionless, frozen in disillusionment, running his fingers over it.

DENIED.

He hoped beyond reason that it was a joke, a gag, and that the word would just fall off the document at the glance of a fingernail. He scratched at it. But it remained. There were no hidden cameras. Suzanne Sommers wasn't about to pop out of hiding.

What is happening?

A wrenching knot twisted in his chest, and acid bubbled into his mouth. *Insufficient Vacation Time Available* were the only other words scrawled in red ink across the white sheet sitting heavy in his hand.

CHAPTER 7

It had always been Jonah's favorite place to get away from it all: close enough to Ann Arbor he could be there in under an hour, but far enough from his home and his family to feel free. As he drove down the dirt road into Pointe Mouillee State Game Area, the shore of Lake Eerie coming into view beside him, he rolled down his windows and felt the crisp October air fill his lungs. *Hallelujah.*

It was testing day. And, after numerous failed attempts, Jonah felt confident that he'd worked out all the kinks. *This time it has to work.*

Making his way to a desolate corner of the sprawling wetlands, he steered towards a remote boat launch oft frequented by surreptitious duck hunters during the off-season. As he arrived at the road's end, the young man gazed ahead at a sloping dirt ramp that sank gradually into the boggy channel—an eight-foot-wide, watery gash through browning grasslands that extended fifty feet out to the open lake water.

The sky was grey, as Michigan autumns often are, and a chill crept through Jonah as he inched the nose of his 4x4 van up to the ramp's zenith. Zipping up his coat, he pulled his hood over his Tigers cap and rolled down the passenger side window. Then, taking a long deep breath, he slowly began to drive forward into the water. *Here we go.*

Foot by foot, the van crept forward, ever deeper into the vast marsh. Soon, the front wheels were submerged below the surface, followed shortly by the bumper. He glanced down to the footwells. They were still dry. *So far, so good.*

Inch by inch, he proceeded, the water rising slowly over the fenders and up the outside door panels. He rechecked the footwells. Still dry. The engine snorkel chugged, rising from the hood alongside Jonah's windshield—air being desperately sucked in to feed the roaring V8 inside the slowly sinking sealed engine compartment.

Soon, water reached the exterior door handles. *Just a little bit further. . .* The brown liquid of Lake Eerie spilled over the hood, and Jonah eased off the gas, bringing the water line to just a few inches below his windshield. Only the top third of the vehicle now peeked out of the lake, like the eyes of a stalking crocodile. The engine rumbled loud below the water's surface. The sealed electrical system functioned properly.

Jonah knew this depth wouldn't be his only concern. He'd have to test this for longer. Much, much longer. Releasing several latches above the windshield, he folded down the hinged glass allowing a breeze from the lake to sweep across his face. He gathered a wool blanket from the passenger seat and pulled it up over him—settling in for the wait.

He checked his watch. *An hour oughta do it.*

Less than one week to departure and Jonah's preparations were nearly complete.

CHAPTER 8

For several interminable minutes, Simon simply stood, glaring at the letter in disbelief as the imperceptible blur of the office world continued to clatter on around him like a silent movie. When, eventually, his senses reset, Simon took a deep breath and walked hurriedly towards his supervisor's office.

His hand trembled as he knocked gently on the half-open door of his manager, Kathleen Harris. Through the two-inch crevice, he could see the woman seated at her desk, working diligently as always.

Few in the company moiled as hard as Ms. Harris. Few in the world, in fact, Simon thought. Though only a few years older than Simon, Kathleen Harris wore her age poorly, having achieved her superior status through an inhuman work ethic and an unrelenting dedication to efficiency and detail. Thin and gangly, with an affinity for navy blue polyester dress suits, everything about her served a calculated purpose, from her tidy bob haircut to her oversized eyeglasses. As Simon watched now, her focus remained squarely on the work spread before her, her arms whizzing about with the dervishian churning of an octopus.

Simon paused, deliberating whether to knock again. Then, suddenly, without even a glance up from her desk, Ms. Harris signaled him forward with a summoning wave from one of her tentacles.

Never the boat rocker, Simon realized in an instant exactly what he was about to do—and cowardice gripped him. Though Ms. Harris was known around the office as "tough but fair," it was a description Simon could neither confirm nor deny having rarely, if ever, spoken to her in person. Ms. Harris's preference had always been to give her subordinates their marching orders via email or through notes that appeared magically on their computers in the morning. A clear indication she had no time for personal interaction. Simon wondered if maybe she just wasn't a people person. Perhaps we could find some common ground there.

He slithered into her office and settled in the visitor's chair before her desk.

"M-Ms. Harris, I think there's been some sort of mistake," Simon sputtered. "I just received a letter denying my vacation request for next month?"

The woman's impenetrable gaze remained locked on her desk as she scribbled notes on forms and shuffled them into files with rhythmic efficiency. Without so much as an upward glance, she lifted a bony hand towards the paper in Simon's shaking hand. "Let's see," she muttered, snatching the letter and giving it a cursory look. "It says here you have insufficient vacation days, Mr. Hill. If you don't have the days, obviously you can't use them. I'm not sure what you're expecting me to do here," she said, handing Simon back his letter and continuing to go about her work.

Simon's legs weakened beneath him, and he began to feel queasy and disoriented.

Is this really happening?

"B-But Ms. Harris, I've never taken a vacation in the two years I've worked here," he replied. And then, raising his voice, perhaps one decibel higher than he should have, he continued. "There has to be some sort of a mistake!"

For the first time—maybe ever—Ms. Harris's furious hands halted. An exasperated sigh hissed through the room as folders fell to the desk. The woman's bespectacled eyes rose to meet Simon's, and though her acknowledgment of him was a small vindication, the vexed look upon her face convinced Simon he shouldn't be celebrating.

Simon smiled awkwardly.

Suddenly, a flash of recognition sparked from beyond the woman's thick lenses, "Didn't you just take a vacation last month?" she asked. "I remember doing the whole C33 Universal Remote user manual assigned to you while you were gone. It was days behind if I recall. You'd barely even started the Getting Started section!"

The anger in her voice was palpable and Simon's confusion equally so.

"Vacation?" he queried. But after a moment of thought, he understood. "Ooooooh, no, no, no . . . I didn't take a vacation. I had appendicitis and had to go to the hospital. I had surgery and was home recovering for a week after. I talked to you about it via email at the time. Don't you remember?"

Don't you remember? The words seemed innocuous enough to Simon.

But Kathleen Harris was in no mood to have her memory questioned. Before Simon could gather his breath from his final word, Ms. Harris tossed her pen down to the desk, sending Simon shuffling back in his seat.

Her eyes locked onto his with a penetrating scowl. He had clearly caught her on a bad day.

Oh, shit

"Look. Sick days. Vacation days. They're all the same to the company Mr. Hill. You say you never took a vacation last year? Well, we have a use it or lose it policy on vacation days that is clearly outlined in the fifty-two-page employee handbook you received when you began working here. If you didn't use them last year, unfortunately, that is your loss. We're under no obligation, either per your employee contract or under Texas state law, to notify you of their dissolution OR to reimburse you monetarily for days accrued. This isn't California, Mr. Hill. Now, what you just told me is that you used your two weeks of vacation this year to get some rest after your illness last month. THAT was your two-week vacation, Mr. Hill. You should have another two weeks accrued by this time next year and can take your vacation then . . . IF you're still with us," she added threateningly. "Now, please close the door behind you!"

And with that, her piercing eyes fell back to the work on her desk. Her hands once again setting to motion, shuffling color-tabbed folders like a croupier.

Simon, meanwhile, remained motionless and bewildered—dumbstruck by what had just transpired. Pulses of pain throbbed in his temples, and his fists clenched by his sides. How... did this happen? He questioned. Have I not done everything they've asked of me? He reasoned.

Yet as he attempted, in vain, to somehow come to terms with his situation, an all-too-familiar ember of rage suddenly sparked to a glow inside of him. Who the hell does she think she is?!

A veritable master of bottling up anger since childhood, Simon recognized now as yet another call to self-control. He slowly rose and exited the room—his pace quickening as he made his way through the office.

Upon reaching his desk, Simon unclenched his fists, the imprints of his fingernails leaving their usual lines in his palms. He threw open his desk drawer, hands frantically burrowing through the office bric-a-brac until he'd located the small brown bottles. Dry-swallowing a pair of pills without a second thought, Simon fell into his chair and stared at the floor gasping, sweating and waiting to be prescription-calmed. He prayed the cocktail of Sertraline and Lorazepam would soon reach his brain. A few minutes later, his heart rate began to slow.

That's it...

***

For the rest of the afternoon, Simon stared at the wall in a catatonic daze, replaying in his head all that had recently transpired to bring him to this point. He rubbed his fingers over his appendix removal scar and, though he wasn't a religious man, Simon found himself asking God, in his mind, why this had happened with such impossibly bad timing. Have I not always done everything I was supposed to do? Am I being punished for something?

The mere thought of toiling an entire year before taking a vacation felt like a Sisyphean task. Hopelessness began to settle in.

When five o'clock arrived, a time when most Redding & Co. employees typically left for the day, Simon didn't stay to put in the extra hours he'd done on each of the workdays that preceded this one. He questioned now how a thousand hours of unpaid overtime hadn't even earned him an ounce of human decency from Ms. Harris. It was time lost. Time he now wished he could take back.

As he prepared to depart the office for the day, he reached into his desk drawer and pulled from it his Belize guidebook and his passport, the sight of both nearly bringing him to tears. He bit his lip to keep from screaming. Fuuuuuuuuuuuuck!

***

The sun hung low in the sky, and Simon felt as though he was skipping school, driving home on time in the waning daylight. The scenery of San Antonio passed by as he took his daily route home, so familiar to him, and yet so different now illuminated by the early evening light.

As he drove on, he noticed the front gates of the Alamo historical monument passing beside him. Fond memories of a childhood visit with his father came rushing forward. He remembered his dad walking alongside him, holding his hand and telling him wild tales of the brave heroics of Davy Crockett and James Bowie. How the two men had fought for what they truly believed in, at all cost. How the Alamo was a relatively insignificant battle itself, but the courage of the men who had defended it was the real story. The stuff of legend.

Kyle Hill had loved stories like that... and Simon had loved listening to him tell them.

Simon began to imagine how Davie Crockett and Jim Bowie would have handled Ms. Harris. What would they have done if she'd spoken to them as she'd done to Simon earlier? He laughed, picturing how quickly their rifles would have come out, and the priceless look on her face as she stamped Approved hastily on their vacation request forms. They wouldn't take her guff!

The pain of the day's defeat ached in his body as he turned through the gates into his suburban development and the sprawl of indistinguishable duplex townhouses. He parked in his driveway and killed the engine, taking a few long breaths and fighting away moisture forming in the corners of his eyes. "You'll figure something out," he whispered to himself.

In the silence, his gaze began to wander throughout the quiet neighborhood aglow in the twilight. Down the block, some young boys kicked a soccer ball in their front yard. His neighbor raked orange leaves with his daughter, a few doors down. Simon remembered how much he'd wanted a family of his own when he was younger. I failed at that. Now I've failed again. Jesus, Simon.

As the sun dipped below the rows of rooftops, he soon found himself sitting in his car alone in the darkness of his driveway. The relentless assault of life having all but crushed the last battalions of optimism in his soul. A final defeat seemed inevitable. He'd always worn the white flag well.

Yet, as he eventually pulled the keys from the ignition and prepared to head inside, an unusual burning began to course through his body. It was a powerful consuming emotion unlike any he'd recognized before, and his senses sharpened as he became suddenly aware of its presence. What is this?

Simon summoned a memory of an article he'd read in a scientific magazine years ago. Something about how psychologists theorized that the broad spectrum of human emotions could be sorted into one of two specific categories: the innate emotions, which had been hardwired into human DNA through millions of years of evolution (anger, fear, sadness, joy) and the learned emotions, which we develop through experience and environmental stimuli (love, guilt, embarrassment, annoyance).

The article had made great sense to him at the time, and yet what he now sensed seemed to fall into a third heretofore unknown category. It was as seemingly inexplicable as it was exhilarating. Perhaps there was a break in his Venn diagram.

As if suddenly awakened, Simon switched on the dome light, pulled out his guidebook, and flipped to the map on which he'd marked the Sunshine Bay. Activating the GPS app on his phone, he typed in the name of the town nearest the resort.

A woman's voice echoed through the car. "Calculating Route."

That voice, so familiar, carried an entirely different significance for him in this hour. The sound of his breath and his beating heart filled the sensory vacuum of the dark car as he quietly anticipated the response. Soon, the numbers flickered onto the screen.

"One thousand, six hundred and eighty-four miles, thirty-one hours, twenty-six minutes." he read in a whisper. Less than two days from paradise.

***

That night Simon was incapable of sleep, his mind roiling with ruminations of a decade and a half of failures. Failed relationships, failed plans, failed everything.

Dammit, is my life always going to be a series of failures?

At 2:43 a.m., he decided that he couldn't let it. Everything was about to change.

CHAPTER 9

Jonah awoke with a gasp from his nightmare, as he'd done countless times since that cursed day six years ago. Lurching up quickly, he tossed the sheets aside and took a deep breath, wiping the sweat-soaked hair from his face. Around him lay nothing but darkness, and it took him a beat to realize just where he was. An inkling of light glimmered through the window, sending streaks of blue into the black room and slowly giving form to his bureau, his desk, his bed. He glanced at the clock on his bedside table. *It's only six-thirty.*

For a brief moment, Jonah debated going back to sleep… but then reasoned against it. *It's time to get to work.*

By 7:30 a.m., he was paddling down the Huron River, kayaking through the frigid water on a winding route towards Gallup. Around his neck dangled a timer, programmed to chime every five minutes. And, as had become procedure, each time it rang, Jonah marked on his kayak with a wax pencil his five-minute estimate of distance traveled. Correctly calculating how far he traveled over water in a given interval would be critical for his future success. Assessing the speed of the river current and the pace of his paddling had become nearly second nature to him in his training. He knew it was 17.38 km to Gallup.

When he finally arrived, three and a half hours later, Jonah tallied his calculations. *17.32 kilometers. Shit, I'm still 60 meters off.*

It would have to do.

Four days to departure and Jonah's preparation were nearly complete.

CHAPTER 10

Simon had been lying in bed for hours. The dreams floating through his head weren't the sort that carried spry sheep over picket fences, but rather the variety accompanied by open eyes and restlessness. Fantasies, perhaps.

As he'd done every day for years, Simon fried some bacon in the skillet, started the single-serving Nespresso machine, and poured himself a bowl of cornflakes. Taking a seat in the breakfast nook, he ate his food alone with the news blaring from his flat screen in the living room. They were saying something about a developing crisis somewhere or a political scandal or whatever. Simon couldn't concern himself with such things this morning.

After breakfast, he drove from his cul-de-sac and through the San Antonio streets as he'd done so many times before. Traffic was light, and pedestrians sauntered in and out of coffee shops along the roadside, preparing for a typical Tuesday morning hustle. Simon came to a red light and stopped. Thoughts swirled in his mind.

Sixteen blocks straight ahead lay the *Redding & Co.* office parking lot. From there, a short walk would take him through the lobby and into the bullpen—at this hour, undoubtedly alive with the semi-lucid chatter of groggy office workers, the ringing of telephones, the rustle of shuffling papers and the sporadic bangs of closing file cabinet drawers. Simon could already hear it in his head. A few more feet and he would be at his cubicle and taking a seat, staring at his computer screen and a post-it-note on its bezel bearing his daily "hit list."

Simon knew this—because *this is what life has always been.*

He turned on his blinker. When the light changed to green, Simon took a left onto the freeway on-ramp. Three and a half hours later, he arrived at the Mexican border crossing at Hidalgo, Texas.

CHAPTER 11

It was the last time Jonah had cried. He often had visions of that day. A life-changing moment, caged in his mind, still vivid down to the tiniest detail. The day a wheelchair became his loathsome permanent companion.

He could still feel his mother's arms wrapped around him as he wept in the hospital, the ball of her chin touching the back of his head, the warmth of her chest on his cheek, and the moistness of her tear-soaked blouse pressed against his face. And the look of disappointment in his father's eyes.

From that day on, Jonah never cried again in front of his father. To Jim Shaughnessy, crying equaled weakness, and Jonah couldn't allow his father to see him that way.

Now, six years later, Jonah began his morning workout as he always did. One hundred pull-ups in five minutes with Outkast's "B.O.B." booming in his earbuds. *The perfect five-minute workout song,* he often thought. With the arrival of his disability, the young man had made it his mission to create new abilities with the parts of him that still worked. Working tirelessly on his upper body, the young man now bore a chiseled physique and freakishly muscular arms.

After lunch, Jonah drove to the local hardware store carrying with him the excuse of picking up a bag of zip ties. Yet the truth was simpler than that. He longed to see old Tom McKinney one last time. Owner and proprietor of Leo's Hardware for nearly fifty years, the venerable Mr. McKinney was the closest thing to family Jonah had felt in ages. Once, long ago, Jonah had inquired why the store was named *Leo's* instead of *Tom's*—to which Mr. McKinney replied with a chuckle, "Well son, when I opened this place fifty years ago, the three biggest contractors in town were Abe Fischman, Howard Schwartz and Eli Levin... and to me, well, Leo just sounded like a good Jewish name."

Jonah had visited Tom at the store every week since.

"Jonah!" Tom rasped, as the young man entered the store. "Why, ever since Home Depot opened off the highway, I think you're the only one keeping me in business!" he decreed.

The line was one he'd used innumerable times to greet Jonah as he entered the musty establishment. And, right on cue, Jonah would call back: "Screw Home Depot!" from across the store, pausing to hear old Tom McKinney burst into fits of wheezing laughter.

Their weekly *bit* had become such a part of Jonah's life over the past four years, that now, as he perused Tom's shelves of aging hardware looking for something, anything, to purchase, he found himself struggling to formulate the words to say goodbye.

Or maybe, he just really didn't want to.

After a few minutes rolling his wheelchair through the aisles in contemplation, Jonah placed a dusty bag of zip ties by the register. "So, Tom..." he struggled, looking up at the smiling old man across the counter from him. "Well, Tom, so...so I'm going away in a few days... and well... well, I'm not sure when I'll be back this way again."

Jonah watched as Tom's normally jovial disposition changed in response. The old man gazed at Jonah through his aged eyes, the bags beneath them pale and drooping. The look he bore on his face was unmistakable.

Jonah, too, felt a bit heartbroken.

"Oh, okay there, Jonah," Tom stuttered with a crack in his voice. "Well, be safe out there," he continued.

Jonah's eyes lingered on Mr. McKinney. The silver-black hair thinning atop his head. The pencil perched as always in the top pocket of his brown overalls. The trusty tape measure at his hip. Jonah wanted so badly to pat him on the shoulder. Or give him a hug, even. Jonah knew, in that moment, that if he was going to tell anyone what he'd been up to, it would be Tom.

"You know, for years now Tom, I've been coming here every week and buying, well, a lot of pretty crazy stuff… and you've never once asked me what I've been up to with all of it. Aren't you a little curious?"

But the old man just furrowed his brow, pushed off the countertop to make himself taller, and spoke with a strength in his voice. "Well, I figure a man's business is his business alone," he said.

Jonah grinned wide. A *man's* business.

Though Jonah's parents continued to view him as just a child, Tom saw Jonah as more than that. The respect the two shared for each other was real, and something Jonah had relied on over the past few years— more than Tom would ever know.

"Well, Tom, I think this is goodbye," Jonah said, reluctantly. He extended his palm, and Tom McKinney grabbed it hard with a trembling hand, shaking it for nearly fifteen seconds before letting go.

Four days to departure and Jonah's preparations were nearly complete.

CHAPTER 12

What the hell am I doing?

Stacks of splintered wood crates sat piled high in the bed of the pick-up truck just a few feet ahead of Simon's bumper. He could hear the old truck's rattle through the windshield, and the smell of its exhaust began to trickle through his Corolla's air vents. Simon's heart lurched, sweat beading above his brow as he waited in queue at the Mexican border. He reached back to scratch his wet neck and leaned forward, allowing cooling air to pass between his clammy back and the sticky car seat. The traffic at the border was thick, but the air was hot and thicker. In Southern Texas, early fall still felt like the summer sometimes, and this October morning was just another one of those days.

But not for Simon.

Gazing at the *Leaving the United States* sign twenty feet ahead, he questioned his current situation with his usual push towards calculated caution. *Maybe I should just turn around?* The idea made so much more sense to him. Only four hours ago, he'd been eating breakfast in his air-conditioned San Antonio apartment. Now, here he was, inching closer and closer to leaving the United States for the first time in his heretofore uneventful life. He still languished in disbelief to its reality. *Maybe it's just a dream.*

Glancing at the passenger seat beside him, Simon spied his haphazardly packed, black duffle bag, and an alarm suddenly went off in his mind. In his groggy haste to leave his house earlier, he'd somehow forgotten something very, very dear to him. *Jesus, I forgot my pills!*

Simon pictured his little saviors still sitting in their brown cylinders on his bedside table. His morning dose of Ativan was wearing off, and a growing anxiety had already begun to gnaw beneath his skin. Ativan. Zoloft. Ambien. Simon realized he'd have to continue on this odyssey without them. *Oh god, this could get ugly.*

Looking back towards the windscreen, he spied a husky border guard a dozen feet ahead, beckoning his car forward. The tan-skinned guard clearly hailed from beyond the wall, and though Simon had lived his entire life just a few hours from Mexico, *the land on the other side of the fence* was a dark and foreboding place to him, conjuring images of rampant poverty, violence and chaos. There must be a reason why so many people risked their lives to try and cross the border into Texas, he figured. They had to be escaping something.

But now Simon felt like the one escaping. And the path to his distant destination ran straight through the country he feared most. He took a deep breath and focused.

Just relax, Simon. You can do this.

The Mexican border guard stepped up to his car. Simon rolled down his window, and the officer leaned in, speaking to him in a gruff, emotionless voice with foul breath that reeked of chaw. "Passport and destination, sir."

Simon thanked the stars that the man spoke English; his own Spanish being limited to *hola, si, con queso* and *no comprendo,* the latter having become his default response to the countless "Texicans" whose accents he couldn't fully understand back home.

It was typically greeted with an eye roll.

"Here you go," replied Simon, offering his passport with a trembling hand. "Destination is Belize," he continued. The words emanating from his mouth seeming disconnected and artificial. *Belize...Really?*

The guard thumbed through the crisp, unused blue book for what seemed an eternally long second before leaning in to look Simon over. Yellow sweat stains encircled the armpits of the podgy Texan's white Stafford dress shirt. His midriff bulged unflatteringly over his waist belt, testing the strength of the pearlescent plastic buttons holding his shirt together. Pleated grey slacks completed his uniform of the drab. Simon's pale disposition, round, ruddy cheeks and curving double chin only served to complement his attire in their extreme ordinariness. He was well aware that he appeared more like an out of shape office worker than a man on the verge of embarking on a thousand-mile journey through Mexico to Central America. He sensed the guard felt the same.

This can't be good, why is he taking so long? He's going to turn me back... or worse. Shit, I should have hidden my wallet! Wait! Why are you thinking that?

Finally, the guard spoke. And as he did so, his voice struck such a portentous tone that Simon shuddered. "After you cross the border, sir, lock your doors, and whatever you do, *don't* stop in any of the towns near here." He pointed ahead through the gate.

Simons arm hairs prickled to attention.

"In fact, don't stop for at least four hours from here. It ain't safe for guys like you out there," he continued.

The ominous dread in his voice carried with it one harsh and deliberate intention: to strike fear into the hearts of ill-prepared *gringos* who dared cross the border at this desolate junction.

Mission accomplished.

Simon feigned an awkward smile, thanked the guard for his guidance and proceeded through the gate.

What the hell am I doing? He thought yet again.

***

Ahead lay Route 97 and a stark, clouded landscape to the horizon. As the border post grew smaller and smaller against the scene disappearing in his rearview mirror, Simon finally wrenched open his clenched fingers. A deep pain ached in his palms and knuckles. It was just 11:26 a.m., but he already felt weary—the emotional exhaustion from the past thirty minutes released with a deep sigh that Simon had been storing up for at least an hour.

Maybe much, much longer.

Well, I made it through the border…

Torrents of emotions began to course through Simon's body. One of which was a particular fear he'd come to be all too familiar with. It was an emotion he'd been expecting all along and had been the guiding force for much of his life up until now.

A relentless fear of the unknown.

The feeling burned more strongly than it had in decades now.

But it wasn't alone.

Emerging from a place deep within, something unusual began to flood Simon's subconscious. He'd sensed it the moment he'd passed through the border gate and yet couldn't fathom why it existed amidst this trial of anguish and desperation. It was a feeling Simon hadn't felt in longer than he could remember. A feeling that was as un-Simon as the Sun is un-cold.

He felt excited.

Simon wrestled to understand the emotion, but neither reason nor rationality had a place in this internal dilemma.

But this was only the beginning.

The beginning of something significantly more substantial than Simon could even start to comprehend. And as he rambled further on down the highway, his future obscured by swirling memories of a series of events which had led to this moment, the only thing Simon knew for certain was that this sure as hell wasn't a dream. For better or for worse. *If Jonathan could see me now.*

Just then, his cell phone rang. He reached into the duffle, pulled out the device and stared at the caller ID.

Work.

The word glared back at him from the LCD display as Simon switched off the ringer and tossed the device back into his bag.

What the hell am I doing?

CHAPTER 13

Simon's older brother Jonathan had always been gregarious and naturally athletic when they were young. A crackerjack physical specimen, gifted with wit and charm, he was Simon's near-polar opposite in the universe. Though Jonathan was Simon's senior by a mere twenty months, by dint of his stout personality and two-foot height advantage, Jonathan had rightfully secured his position as the ringleader of the inseparable dyad from an early age. Simon, meanwhile, had lived in idolization of his older sibling as only a kid brother could. There was no step Jonathan could take, a word he could say or place he could go without his miniature kin following his feet, his words or his actions in near-perfect lockstep. "Polly want a cracker?" Jonathan often guffawed upon catching his zealous younger brother brazenly mimicking his every move—be it something as grandiose as a hand-flailing tantrum, or something as banal and tedious as spitting into the sink after every twentieth toothbrush stroke.

Yet despite Jonathan's dominant physical and social advantages, in his eyes, the two had always been equals. Simon was the other half of the *Hill Brothers* whole, the yin to his yang. And Jonathan would have done anything to protect his younger sibling.

But that was so, so long ago.

The boy's father, Kyle Hill, meanwhile, was what some would call a man's man. Others, well, they'd probably use less kind words. To Simon, however, the man was a near-mythical figure in his fading memory. An oil derrick worker in the Gulf of Mexico, Kyle worked tirelessly, only returning to Odessa for a week or two every few months—each time to the exuberant embrace of his loving boys. *The Three Musketeers* they'd often call themselves in jest, as they set about on their countless hunting and camping adventures into the great Texan outback, crying "All for one! And one for all!" from the windows of Kyle's rusted old pickup. In the finite universe of the two boy's Odessan childhood, Kyle had occupied a virtually infallible stature amidst the syzygy. He was the *paterfamilias*, the inspirer and the Athos to their Porthos and "Porthos *light.*" Though Simon had never taken to hunting the way his brother had, being more of a bird watcher himself, he savored the rare time spent with his dad and brother more than anything else in the world. He still reminisced about those days and never stopped yearning for the ability to go back and live them again.

But, again, that was long, long ago.

Then, there was "Milady de Winter." The unfortunate behind-the-back nickname, derived from the evil, plotting spy of Dumas's tales, that had been bestowed upon Simon's mother, Madeline Hill, by her *loving* husband, Kyle. Though the man found the nickname amusing and fitting, he was oblivious to how it fueled the fire of his boys' growing disdain for their mother. He knew very little of the dynamic between his wife and their children, having seldom spent a moment together with them as a *family*.

During the boy's wilderness escapades, Madeline was invariably left behind at home—and on the rare occasions that the four found themselves together in the house for a night, the constant yelling and fighting between the two parents made little sense to the boys. The only thing they knew for certain was that it was Madeline's fault.

But then everything changed. When Simon was twelve and Jonathan fourteen, their father drowned in an oil rig accident in the Gulf of Mexico, leaving the boys devastated and in mourning for weeks. Madeline, however, never seemed to shed a tear, and hadn't even bothered to host a memorial service.

The boys despised her for it.

From that point forward, Simon feared the sea, and his family never felt like a family again. Madeline continued to raise the boys as best she could, but something inside of her had clearly switched off. Jonathan soon began to lash out, battling anger as well as Madeline and the other children at school. Simon, more the introvert, was confused by his brother's behavior, and retreated into his own world of studies and working odd jobs to save money for college. The two brothers grew further and further apart as time passed on...and Simon grew more and more alone.

A week after graduating high school, Jonathan hastily moved to Houston, leaving Simon behind in Odessa, isolated with their mother.

For the next two years, the young boy resided with a woman so shut off to him and so detached that he felt as if she were a ghost haunting their home rather than his mother. A deep emptiness grew inside of him where the warmth and love of family had once resided. He hated his mother, though he never spoke of it, blaming her for all that had befallen the once-loving family. But soon, he would *be free,* he thought.

It wasn't long after he arrived in university that Simon realized such things have a way of not letting go. Just a few months into his freshman year, he began to find himself locked in his dorm room for days at a time. Debilitating waves of anxiety overwhelmed him with unexpected ferocity. Feelings that had remained bottled up for so many years began slowly crackling to the surface. During these self-imposed exiles, Simon inevitably missed classes, and his grades soon suffered. The mounting pressure he began to feel was only matched by a deep, unfillable darkness that huddled with him on his mattress those long, lonesome days and nights.

One afternoon, Simon grew so desperate to escape this destructive state that he visited his university's health department for help. An hour later, he emerged with a bottle of Valium and a pamphlet on seeking treatment for depression. The brochure would soon disappear into the wastebasket, but the Valium would become a crutch upon which Simon would lean for the better part of a decade. As time went on, a pleasing cocktail of Valium, Zoloft, Ativan and a good cup of Chamomile tea time and again had proven to be a surprisingly effective way of quashing his torrents of anxiety, depression and anger when they arrived. And they visited often.

Two months after Simon had left Odessa, Madeline sold the family home and moved to St. Luis. These days Simon rarely heard from the woman. She knew the unspoken truth of his feelings towards her and respectfully kept her distance. He'd long since stopped caring, though. She hadn't been there when he needed her, and he could never forgive that.

Simon did miss Jonathan, however. All the time.

He still tried to call Jonathan every Christmas. But the conversations were usually short and more courteous than warm or substantive, and they hadn't seen each other face to face in years. Simon felt renewed heartbreak each time he thought of how the two had grown so far apart.

CHAPTER 14

Several hours passed as Simon continued down the long, cracked highway heading south into eastern Mexico. Ramshackle town after ramshackle town seemed to rise out of nowhere amid the barren landscape. Rodolfo, La Purisma, Juan Antonio.

Simon glared uneasily through the dusty windshield towards the disappearing horizon. The broiling heat on the concrete far ahead, melting the road into a glistening sea of glass, reflecting the cerulean sky above. A distant blue ether beyond the grey and brown, calling to Simon but never getting any closer.

Simon struggled to stay focused. He needed to stay focused. The unmarked lane's dust-covered surface blended seamlessly into the sandy roadside shoulder, itself littered with an obstacle course of touts, scraggly dogs and the occasional free-roaming chicken, goat or pig. Simon strained to block out these unfamiliar and disquieting surroundings. He was neither rich, nor poor, and wouldn't diminish either if you asked, but he couldn't help but feel uncomfortable amid such poverty. The guard's words of warning hadn't helped much either.

Then there was the other recurring presence Simon found especially difficult to ignore. Gathered at the road's edge every few miles, stood posses of camo-clad soldiers brandishing assault rifles, grenade belts and heavy artillery. Together with the hulking Panhard VCR-TT armored military vehicles which passed him regularly along the highway, his brain throbbed trying to process the daunting world he now found himself in. *What on Earth am I doing here?* The question cycled through his mind every few minutes, and with every passing mile, Simon found himself further and further from the civilized world he'd spent thirty-eight years struggling to get comfortable in. But now he found himself an outsider in a bizarre realm where he could just as easily be killed by a stray bullet as a marauding goat running into the road. *This definitely isn't Texas anymore.*

Simon longed, once again, for a pill to take the worry away. Fear for his own survival grew inside of him with every catastrophic scenario his mind could conceive. *Jesus, what if I get a flat tire?! Or what if the police pull me over?!*

As dread and dark imaginings of his coming demise crushed heavy on his soul, Simon felt himself approaching a breaking point. He tightened his grip on the steering wheel, his knuckles going white. *If I turn around now, I could be home by tonight and still make it to work tomorrow.*

Simon would later say, that if he hadn't seen what he saw next, he quite possibly would have made a U-turn in retreat. A *flapping of butterfly wings* that would prove to change the course of his life forever. At that moment, just as all seemed lost and the journey ahead seemed overwhelming and impossible... a singular vision, far off in the distance, caught Simon's eye. As if the heavens parted and a ray of ethereal sunshine fell to the Earth, a beacon called out to him from the expanse, summoning him near. Simon squinted to make sure it was real. Was it a mirage? A figment of his imagination? As he grew closer, he realized no...

It actually is *a McDonalds!*

Simon's foot fell hard upon the accelerator. His mighty steed revved, fueled by his eagerness for the familiar—and his growling belly. He glanced over his shoulder to be sure the Mexican border guard he'd left behind 150 miles back wasn't somehow still keeping a watchful eye on him. *It's not technically stopping if I don't "technically" leave the car, right?*

With this loophole in mind, Simon approached the unicolor twin rainbows whispering muted prayers below his breath. *Please let there be a drive-thru. Please let there be a drive-thru.*

And there was.

Hallelujah!

But as he pulled into the parking lot, through the drive-thru lane and up to the menu board, all hope soon succumbed to a pounding thunderclap of dejection. *Shit, it's in Spanish!* It may as well have been hieroglyphics. Simon gawked at the indecipherable gobbledygook, thwarted. But inside him, a ferocious battle raged. In one corner stood the inclination to give up and keep on driving. In the other was a ravenous hunger for processed meat and fried potatoes. Simon froze, gripped with indecision. That is until he noticed something rather startling. Certain words like *hamburguesa,* sort of started making sense to him. *Is that enough to go on?* It was tenuous, indeed. But when Simon considered his other option, visiting an *actual* Mexican restaurant down the road, his decision was made. Simon ordered six *hamburguesas* and six *papas fritas,* an item which strongly resembled French fries in the picture on the menu board. The intercom crackled as the woman in the restaurant responded to Simon's broken Spanish with a few non-English questions of her own.

"*Si,*" Simon responded for some unknown reason, and drove forward to pay.

In the ten slow feet between the ordering intercom and the pickup window, something else occurred to Simon. He had only US dollars on him! Glancing ahead through the windshield, a car blocked his path forward. Looking over his shoulder, a vehicle sat behind him now as well. A wall stood to his right—the restaurant… on his left.

Trapped! Nowhere to run.

As his vehicle inched up to the window, the woman leaned out to repeat his order to him. *"Buenos días, señor. Seis hamburguesas y seis papas fritas, ciento veintidós pesos es todo."*

Simon stared at her blankly. She stared back at him equally blankly, waiting for a response. Eventually, one of them would have to give.

"One hundred twenty-two pesos sir," she repeated in a language that Simon found himself surprisingly understanding. For a split second, Simon wondered if he now miraculously understood Spanish. Visions flashed through his mind of countless documented instances of people acquiring extreme powers in extreme situations. A mother lifting a car off her trapped child, a surfer fighting off a twenty-foot Great White shark. *Could this be my new superpower?!*

"Sir, one hundred twenty-two pesos, please," she repeated with palpable annoyance.

Dammit, that was definitely English.

Simon reached into his pocket and began to pull US dollars from his wallet.

"Pesos o credit card, sir," she squawked, her frustration with the bumbling *gringo* growing by the second. Flustered, Simon handed over his card to the woman who processed it hurriedly before hustling him on out the lane.

Back on the road, Simon scarfed down the first of the comforting burgers and realized just how completely unprepared he was for traveling through Mexico. *At least by tomorrow afternoon, I'll be in English-speaking Belize.* The thought of arriving at his destination made him grin a ketchup-covered grin.

Reaching into his bag, Simon pulled out his phone to discover he'd missed six calls from work already. *Well, I guess they noticed I'm not there.* Checking his inbox, he found a message from Ms. Harris enquiring as to his whereabouts. As he drove, he sent her a two-word response that felt so fulfilling that he couldn't help but smirk. *Home sick.*

He slipped his phone back into his bag and smiled.

It was Tuesday, and Simon planned to drive to Belize, spend two days on the beach and then return to work by Monday. It was a crazy plan, but he felt confident the timeline could work. *This is really happening. I'm really doing this!*

Two months later... as Simon crouched in the dark jungle of Nicaragua's Moskito Coast... shrouded in the blackness of night, drenched with sweat and covered with mosquitos... Hiding from the flashlight beams of drug smugglers brandishing automatic rifles just a few feet from where he lay... There, as his heart threatened to burst from his clenched chest and a violent death seemed all too imminent... he would remember this moment, that first day driving into Mexico... as when it all truly began.

CHAPTER 15

A long, hot day became a long, hot night. Simon had stopped at a Texaco a few hours back and managed to withdraw pesos from an ATM, fill up his gas tank and buy two Red Bulls, all without actually speaking to anyone at the station. Simon considered this a great success in his mind. The less he interacted with the locals here, the better. An incognizant xenophobic notion that was constantly appearing as he passed through this foreign place.

The typically sedentary Simon was accustomed to sitting for twelve hours at a time in the office. But after seventeen hours on the road, his whole body now ached, and his eyes began to close involuntarily. *If I see a Holiday Inn, a Super 8, or any other American hotel chain, I have to stop.* Yet in this scarcely developed region of the country, he'd seen nothing of the sort—only the pale grey trapezoid in his headlights framed by black on all sides. Hours ticked onward, and the monotonous scene caused Simon to enter various states of delirium.

As midnight arrived, he was suddenly rescued.

Hilton Villahermosa, 60km ahead, the sign read.

Thank God.

Simon accelerated towards the capital of the Mexican state of Tabasco, the famously beautiful city of Villahermosa. But after eighteen hours of driving, Simon could see nothing but the billboards passing by the side of the road.

Hilton Villahermosa, 40km ahead...

Hilton Villahermosa, 20km ahead...

And so on, until he was in the parking lot and trudging zombie-like to the front reception desk. He made it to a room—barely—and collapsed.

***

Awakening to the harsh reality of a 7 a.m. wake-up call, Simon discovered he was still fully dressed and lying on top of his still made bed with his head on his duffel bag. *Well, at least I took off my shoes.*

After a hot shower, he strolled downstairs for a hearty American-style egg breakfast before getting back in the car by 8 a.m. *This is it! Tonight, I'll be on the shores of the Caribbean!*

Simon giggled with joy as he charged towards the border, forcing himself to ease off the accelerator every few minutes to maintain sanity.

Shortly after noon, he passed the turnoff to Chetumal, Mexico and soon thereafter arrived at the checkpoint gates to enter Belize. *Bienvenidos a Belice: Welcome to Belize.* The sign above him glowed like a double rainbow. *It's.... glorious.*

Soon he would have his pot of gold, too. When the circular, blue Belize stamp was pressed into his passport minutes later, Simon stared at it in awe of its magnitude. The inked words and numbers he'd coveted for so long seemed to actually smile back at him.

I really have it. I'm really freaking here. Triumph overwhelmed him. Victory was finally his.

Crossing the border into Belize, Simon at once realized just how different the neighboring countries were. The heavily armed soldiers and packs of emaciated stray dogs that had lined the Mexican highway just a few miles north, now gave way to manicured roadside beds of colorful flowers and arching canopies of tropical palms. The road itself was neither dusty nor cracked but, rather, freshly paved and clean. Even the sun seemed brighter, and the sky bluer, in Simon's eyes.

When he pulled over for gas and a quick lunch at Burger King, the local Belizean's spoke English. And Simon rejoiced. Their thick creole accents were unusual, but their words intelligible.

As Simon sped euphorically down the highway towards the coast, a warm breeze rushed across his cherubic face through the car's four open windows, flicking his hair into small brown waves. For two straight hours, he wore a smile as wide as the horizon until his teeth went dry. And when, in the late afternoon, he saw the sign beside the road, he chuckled with joy. *This is it!*

Sunshine Bay Resort it read as he pulled off the main highway and onto the sandy white dirt road. *This is really, really it!*

Quintessentially tropical, the wide, sand-strewn path ahead sat lined with coconut palms and dotted with colorful wooden signs. Proceeding down the immaculate white floored lane, past gardens and fountains, and through a green tunnel of trellises bestrewn with Orchids, Wisteria and other floral climbers, he stared up through the windshield at the colorful organic display engulfing him in sheer wonderment. "This is amazing," he whispered to himself. The words feeling meager in their gross understatement.

When Simon emerged from the flowered corridor, a glittering array of white walls and windows appeared before him, imposing in both breadth and grandeur. It was the Sunshine Bay Resort, and it was exactly as Simon had imagined.

Seconds later, his car came to rest in a sandy lot beside the hotel entrance. Simon sat for a long spell in disbelief at what he'd just accomplished and where he now was. He wished his father could see him now. *I'm here, Dad.*

Simon also longed to call his brother Jonathan to tell him how he'd finally made it here after all these years. *I did it, Jon.*

Stepping from the car, Simon stretched his arms wide and inhaled a deep breath of the salty, warm sea breeze billowing past his grin. The blue sky above him and the warm sunshine on his head and pasty arms embraced him wholly. He dug deep into his pocket and pulled from it the twenty-six-year-old piece of paper that had started this whole adventure. He unfolded it in the sunshine and took another long look.

3. Go to Belize . . .

He was so happy he nearly began to cry. "I'm really here," he whispered.

After hurriedly checking in to his room, a jubilant Simon dashed chortling across the resort's central lawn with the swimming pool locked dead in his sights. As he launched gracefully through the air and into the cool water with a thunderous splash, the mosaic of vivid, blue tiles rising around him filled Simon with a sense of joy and achievement unlike any he'd known in a long, long time. Sunbeams twinkled through the water as glistening air bubbles rolled out of his smiling mouth and made their way to the surface. When his head eventually emerged to a view of a sun-soaked white sand beach and the ocean beyond, that wide smile somehow grew even wider. Everything was just as wonderful as his father had described.

I've arrived.

CHAPTER 16

Jonah entered the bank and took a number. Parking himself in the waiting area, he picked up a US Weekly magazine from the table and began to flip through the glossy pages of celebrity news and gossip. He read such intriguing headlines as *Blah, Blah, Blah Shows Off Her Curves in this*

Bikini Selfie, and *Celebrity X and Celebrity Q Share a Kiss on the Ski Slopes: Could this be Love?*

Jonah couldn't help but think how different his life was from those of the smiling beautiful people splattered across the pages. He glanced down to his legs hanging over the edge of his wheelchair in his old grey cargo pants, and then back up to the pages. *Glad I'm not them,* he thought and tossed the magazine back onto the table.

A chime dinged, and Jonah looked up to see his number flashing on the screen. Making his way to the agent's desk, he began to slide the heavy customer chair out of his way. As he did, the agent across from him, an African American woman in a fitted red skirt suit, glanced up from her computer and realized what was happening. She sprung from her seat and dashed around the desk to help Jonah, pulling the chair from his grip.

"I've got it!" Jonah hollered, not realizing how his voice would carry through the quiet bank. The agent froze and released the chair at once. Jonah glanced up to find the woman staring down at him, mortified. Several people in the nearby teller line glared at him as well. "I'm sorry," he muttered.

"No, I'm sorry I assumed you needed help," the woman replied with a smile.

Jonah gave her an appreciative grin in return. Looking at her, he thought that she might have been middle-aged or possibly two decades older—but it was hard to tell because she looked so exhausted and bored with her job.

"So, what BANKING NEEDS can I help you with today?" she asked, taking her seat.

Jonah eased up to the desk and retrieved a piece of paper from his pocket. "It's a long list, so you might want to write this down."

"Sure thing," the woman replied, taking out a notepad.

"First, I would like to withdraw from my account $2,700 in US currency," he began.

"Okay."

"Then, I also need some foreign currency. $150 worth of Mexican pesos, and $50 each in Guatemalan quetzals, Honduran lempira & Costa Rican colons."

The bank agent continued to scribble Jonah's list on the pad in front of her, pausing, on occasion, to glance up at the young man, intrigued. Jonah continued.

"Next, I'll need all international fraud protection removed from my checking account. I'll be traveling for a while, and I can't afford to have my card suspended if I use it in a different country."

"What country will you be visiting?" the woman asked.

"That's of no concern," Jonah replied. "I need fraud protection removed from ALL countries." Then, without realizing it, he again raised his voice. "This is EXTREMELY important. I CANNOT have my card suspended!" he reiterated forcibly.

Across the desk, the woman seemed visibly shaken by his tone.

"I'm sorry I raised my voice," he muttered. "It's just really important."

"I understand, sir, I'll take care of it… Anything else?"

"Yes, after we take out the currency, I'd like to leave $500 only in my checking account and transfer the rest into my savings. Then I'd like to schedule an auto-transfer. I'd like to have $200 transferred from my savings account every month into my checking account."

"Every month or week?"

"Every month," Jonah replied.

"For how many months?"

"Two years," Jonah said quietly.

The bank agent glanced up at him, surprised. The two locked eyes, and Jonah could see her mind spinning. She glanced down to Jonah's legs again, and then catching herself, quickly averted her eyes back to her notebook.

***

Later that evening, Jonah sat in his room and laid out the currency on his desk. He put 2,000 dollars into his wallet and divided the remaining cash into twelve stacks on his desk: Seven in US dollars, two in Mexican *pesos* and one each for the *quetzals, lempira* and *colons*.

Once the stacks were ready, he pulled out his pouch laminator and ran each thin stack through the machine, sealing each pile in a waterproof plastic film. Jonah gathered the twelve stacks into his lap, moved to his bed and slid himself onto the mattress. Flipping his wheelchair upside down, he unclasped a hidden pocket he'd sewn into the bottom of its seat. Jonah slipped the money into the pocket and re-secured it, hiding the access point under the railing. He ran his hands over the bottom of the chair, proud of his handiwork. The pocket was completely invisible.

Three days to departure and Jonah's preparation were nearly complete.

CHAPTER 17

After a relaxing afternoon by the pool, Simon attacked the resort's grand buffet with ferocity, gobbling up more seafood than any one man should in a single sitting. *At $350 a night, I'm sure as hell getting my money's worth!* He thought.

It made logical sense. Simon loved to eat and was well seasoned in the art of the binge. Food gave him pleasure. Food gave him something to do with his time. Food gave him ninety percent of his social interactions. And food gave him his belly. Over the past twenty years, Simon had reluctantly updated his entire wardrobe three times. Medium to Large to XL to XXL. Though he pretended the battening was just part of growing older, the truth was undeniable. Still, this meal at the Sunshine Bay Resort brought with it a special satisfaction as he gorged himself into a stupor.

By eight o'clock, Simon was back in his luxurious white room, stretched out like a starfish atop his deluxe pillow-top mattress, staring up at the circling rattan fan and the mocha-colored exposed beams above. The flatscreen TV flickered on the wall as the faint sounds of Jimmy Buffet echoed from the pool bar outside, and the distant crashing of waves lulled him peacefully towards sleep. Everything felt absolutely perfect. His dreams that night were pleasant ones.

***

The Beach Boys *Kokomo* eased through the open window as Simon awoke. He sang along merrily from his blissful silk cocoon. "Erooba, jammama, come on pretty mamba…"

Simon swept open his blinds to discover a stunning view of the Caribbean Sea that nearly burst through the glass with its vividness. It was only 8 a.m., but the vast, turquoise expanse beyond was already speckled with the white lines of ski boats, and numerous black dots that Simon assumed were snorkelers. Or sharks. Hopefully, not both.

So many things to do today… But first… It's eating time.

Cheesy scrambled eggs with sausage. Check. Waffles with whipped cream. Check. Ham with mustard cream sauce. Check. After another gluttonous feasting, Simon rubbed his stomach affectionately as he made his way through the courtyard gardens towards the beach.

Constructed in classic 1980's era fashion, the imposing Sunshine Bay Resort stood like a great white monolith amidst the lush surrounding forest. Encircled on three sides by fifteen-foot high whitewashed walls, the horseshoe-shaped bulwark opened to the sea, cradling the U-form resort and its guests within. Green lawns flecked with colorful flowers and palms encompassed the central pool area like a garden paradise perched upon a pedestal above the sandy shore. There was nothing particularly *special* about the resort, but to Simon, it was Heaven on Earth.

As he moseyed down the stairs from the pool terrace, the towering outer walls of the resort eventually came to a dramatic end, allowing sweeping views of the bay from the sand below. "Wow…" he muttered to himself, awestruck. From his position near the center of the capacious bay, powder-white sand curled away on either side like the arched wings of a great sea bird. Lining the beach in both directions stretched a vast palm forest, and Simon was surprised to find no other manmade structures in sight—just a few wooden fishing boats beached at the far end of the bay.

The sand and waters around him, however, were alive with action. Throngs of happy resort goers were already splayed out on loungers beside him, the colors of their flesh spanning a gamut of pinks and reds as they flopped over and over, roasting themselves to a crisp in the rotisserie of the sun's rays. Ahead of him, the iridescent Caribbean waters teamed with life. Jet skis and paragliders buzzed around in the distance as snorkelers and swimmers floated nearby, in the shallows.

Simon paused to take it all in. Chubby Checker's *Limbo Rock* resonated from the pool bar across the sand. Simon had just begun to sway with the music, deep in contemplation, when a booming call echoed from behind him. "It's not a dream, it's Belize!" came the boisterous voice.

Simon swung around, startled to find an overly cheery hotel concierge approaching him with an eager smile. Clad in all white, the rambunctious man was closing in fast.

Uh oh…

Simon offered a half-smile as a courtesy, but soon realized what a mistake it had been.

"Welcome, sir, welcome, sir!" the man said as he arrived at Simon's side. "Which of our many activities can I help you with today?!"

Simon tried hurriedly to articulate a polite dismissal. Yet, before any words had a chance to exit his mouth, the man launched into a spiel so well-rehearsed that Simon felt sure he'd soon walk away with a new vacuum cleaner. "At the Sunshine Bay Resort, sir, we have so MANY wonderful activities available…"

Oh brother.

Simon gave in. Smiling and nodding politely as the man rambled on…and on… and then on some more. Simon had long ago memorized the hotel's activity list and scarcely needed a refresher, but he stood patiently waiting, continuing to soak up his surroundings all the while. Down the beach, a newlywed couple walked hand in hand, lost in each other's adoration. Nearby, a pair of young boys were burying their reluctant sister in the sand. A few feet away, two large, lobster-colored men lay sprawled out with gold chains resting on their oily black chest hair.

Simon's eyes wandered about the scene, dashing from one delightful morsel to the next. Until… amidst the hackneyed sea of ocean revelers and sun worshippers, littering the shoreline like a paisley blanket of flesh and plastic… he saw her.

Actually, it was her long, flowing red hair that first caught his eye. The alluring young woman strolled, smiling, across the sand a short distance down the beach, immediately capturing Simon's gaze. As he stared on entranced, the jabbering voice of the concierge grew hushed in Simon's ears.

The comely twenty-something sat down beside a young man lying atop a large, red sarong spread wide in the shade of a native palm. Her skin was taut, dusted with a deep layer of freckles, and her long, fiery red locks hung down to kiss her mid-back. A tiny green bikini hugged her fit body well, and Simon found her unusually tanned for a ginger. There was a hippie-ish natural beauty about her that Simon couldn't turn away from. She captivated him, and he stared on bewitched by her every subtle movement. As she laughed, Simon wondered, *is it her smile that I find so beautiful?*

But then again, maybe it was everything.

Her cohort was similar in age and style. Handsome, deeply tanned and wiry, the young man bore wavy brown hair to his shoulders and a bit of scruff at the tip of his chin. At his waist were a pair of worn black cargo shorts and a few bracelets on his wrists made of string and beads sat where his plastic resort wristband should have been. They had names for people like him in Texas Simon thought; *dirty hippie, freak, long hair, artist* or any one of a variety of negative expressions for people with alternative sexual orientations.

Simon's mind suddenly hearkened back to the *outsider* cliques of his high school years—*outsiders* in Odessa being anyone not easily defined as a jock, a bible thumper, a future farmer or an auto-mechanic.

The other one percent.

Yet within these rogue clans, there seemed to invariably be a ringleader character who somehow dated a girl that *everyone* in the school found attractive. The pudgy LARPer with his mousy yet perfectly proportioned elfin princess. The pale, lanky goth with his slender, raven-haired beauty. The geek with his bespectacled girlfriend who, if she'd just take out her ponytail, could probably date anyone in the school. And then there was the handsome hippy with his free-spirited, yet classically beautiful flower child. Simon could see that essence in this couple before him now. *He probably plays the guitar.*

As the couple sat talking and laughing, they exuded an authentic comfort and happiness that Simon found himself drawn to. And when they touched each other playfully but intimately, Simon just couldn't wrench his eyes away. He wished he were the one touching her soft skin. *Who are you people?* He wondered.

The pair were intriguing if for no other reason than they seemed so out of place here amidst the sunburned and spray-tanned resort crowd filling the beach.

"So, what would you like to do first!? Go for a swim?!" the concierge barked at Simon, tearing his gaze away from the young couple and jarring him back to the conversation.

"Um, oh... No, I'm actually terrified of the ocean..." Simon said, scrambling to access his memory. "I guess, I'll uuuuh...get a massage?" he stammered.

"Excellent choice, sir! Follow me to relaxation!"

And with that, the man grabbed Simon's arm and began to pull him towards a cluster of pagodas down the beach. Simon, unable to resist, glanced over his shoulder at the couple one last time. He wondered if he'd ever see them again.

***

For the remainder of the day, Simon pampered himself in the spa, attempted yoga for about five minutes and "snorkeled" while crouching in a shallow tidal pool down by the shoreline. When he returned to the resort in the late afternoon, he looked to the spot where the young couple had once been resting, but they were gone.

Attempting to purge them from his mind, Simon headed to the buffet and stuffed himself with half a pan of baked fish and a miniature mountain of gratin potatoes, washing it all down with a frozen margarita. *I should take a walk to digest.* At least that's what he told himself.

For half an hour, Simon meandered throughout the resort complex searching for the young couple, but to no avail. As he strolled through the gardens, he slowly realized how much of his day he'd been distracted by them, oddly curious about their story. *Why do you even care?* It was a question that had no clear answer.

Later that evening, Simon sat by the pool, his white belly having turned a rosy pink, and sipped on an oversized daiquiri in complete relaxation. Radio Margaritaville echoed on a seemingly endless loop across the terrace as an English cricket match played on a flat-screen behind the pool bar. Simon noticed a clock in the corner of the screen that read 6:30 p.m.

I'd probably still be at work if I were back in San Antonio right now. He smiled to himself, delighted at the thought.

For the next few hours, Simon continued to drink frozen cocktails without restraint. He exchanged occasional smiles and a few words with some of the other guests and the bartender but mostly watched sports highlights on the television. The other patrons were primarily couples and families, and Simon gradually began to feel out of place alone at the bar. So, he continued to drink.

By 10 o'clock, he stumbled back to his room and violently relieved his stomach of the half dozen cocktails he'd foolishly consumed. Crashing into bed, he stared up at the whirling ceiling fan, which quickly dizzied his pickled brain and forced him to shut his eyes. *Oh, God.*

As he lay in the darkness, Simon's mind once again turned to the couple on the beach and how happy they'd seemed together. *I want something like that.*

Rolling into the middle of the oversized bed in the center of the large dark room, Simon soon found himself in the company of an old companion he hadn't been forced to face in years—loneliness.

CHAPTER 18

The hangover was the worst Simon could remember, though, to be fair, his memory *was* a bit hazy. After splashing some cold water on his face, he lumbered, squinting, to the pool and planted himself beneath a gardenside umbrella to try and get his wits together. Simon knew he needed to call work. It had been more than three days already, yet he dreaded the idea. Checking the two new messages on his phone, he found both were from the office, and recognized with a certain sadness how nobody outside of work had called to find out where he was. There really *wasn't* anybody else in his life, though. The loneliness he'd begun to feel the night before had carried through to the morning, and once again, his old pal Zoloft was unavailable to comfort him.

Simon dialed the office number then pressed the button. Sixteen-hundred miles away in San Antonio, the phone rang. He shifted in his seat as he prepared to exploit his hungover state to mimic a convincing sick voice. The plan was to leave the following morning for the long journey home—a journey he already viewed as a green mile.

"Redding and Co., How can I direct your call?" hissed the receptionist's voice over the line.

"This is employee 2473. Please connect me to the HR department."

"One moment, please…"

Simon gazed around the pool, gradually being calmed by the smooth sounds of *muzak* coming through the cellphone speaker. A slow smile started to creep onto his face.

Then, rather abruptly, a voice blared through the earpiece like a fist to the jaw.

"This is Kathleen Harris. Where are you, Mr. Hill?!"

Simon's eyes nearly burst from their sockets. *Fuuuuuuuuuuuuuuuuck!*

The cyclonic fury in the woman's voice felt much, much closer than the sixteen-hundred miles that separated them. Simon quickly sat up in his seat and glanced over his shoulder. *She can't know I'm here… Can she?!*

"Ahem, hello" —he coughed— "Ms. Harris. It's Simon Hill. I'm at home still sick and just wanted to check in."

Swatting away his words like a fly, Ms. Harris began an eviscerating, five-minute tirade on the extra workload he'd given her and detailed her belief that he was faking his illness because of their prior conversation. When she eventually concluded her speech, Simon assured her he was, in fact, sick, which, in his hung-over state, wasn't technically a lie, and that he would be back in the office in a few days. The thought of which made his stomach burn.

"Let me REMIND YOU that you have NO remaining vacation days, Mr. Hill, so this will be both unpaid leave. AND noted as an 'unapproved absence' in your file!"

Simon bit his tongue. *THANK YOU FOR REMINDING ME THAT I HAVE NO VACATION DAYS, I'D COMPLETELY FORGOTTEN!*

His blood was searing, and his head throbbed deep in his temples. Simon knew that if he stayed on the phone any longer, he might say something he would regret. He already feared for his job and what would happen when he returned. Especially if the Wicked Witch of the South somehow found out where he actually was.

"Thank you, Ms. Harris. I'll see you soon," he said, using maximum possible restraint.

Simon clicked the hang-up button on his mobile and just managed to stop short of throwing his phone the fifty yards into the ocean. "Jesus, what a bitch," he said to the breeze.

The breeze billowed back with a warm breath of sympathy. The sun was shining, and the nearby flowers smelled fresh and fragrant. From his poolside roost, he looked out at the undulating sea. The waves were mesmerizing, and their rhythmic rolling began to calm him. The palms above him made flickering shadows on the patio at his feet. *I don't want to go home tomorrow.* The thought of it began to torture him. It felt increasingly like suicide. *I've come so far to get here, and I might not even have a job when I get back. What'll I do if I lose it!? Then again, what'll I do if I keep it!?*

For several interminable minutes, Simon pondered the myriad parallel universes he could steer his life towards at this moment. Gazing out into the ocean ahead and his future beyond that, Simon eventually crawled into the pool and lingered beneath the water for a spell, staring up at the sun shimmering through the surface in ablution. *This is what I want.*

When he made it back to his seat, he sat with his eyes closed in mindful contemplation. All he could hear was the wind, the sea, and the faint sounds of laughter. *This is what I want.*

And as he sat there, embraced by the radiance of the world around him and the prospect of returning to a self-created hell, Simon did something that he had only done once before in the past thirty-eight years. He made a completely irrational decision.

Going against all his natural instincts to head back to San Antonio with his tail between his legs, Simon decided to take a chance for once in his life. He would extend his trip for a few more days and see what happened. *Fuck it,* he thought to himself triumphantly.

Though he certainly didn't know it at the time, the decision would be the most significant of his life. In that moment, however, he just felt proud about his choice, and promptly sighed a long breath of relief. He laid back deep in his lounger and relaxed in a way that had hitherto been entirely foreign to him. Simon felt a subtle change coming over him. And he liked it. *This is what I want.*

CHAPTER 19

How do you say goodbye? Jonah stared at the blank piece of paper lying flat under the orange glow of his desk lamp. He tapped his pencil eraser on the hard surface, struggling to find the words to begin. *Maybe I should give them an explanation?* It seemed like the logical beginning, and so he began to write:

Dear Mom & Dad,

By the time you read this, you will likely have realized that I'm not where you thought I would be. I'm sorry I had to lie to you for so many years, but you never would have allowed me to go if you'd known the truth. I guess by now, there's nothing you can do to stop me, so I might as well share with you my plan…

When he'd finished his letter twenty minutes later, Jonah wiped the moisture away from his eyes, placed the paper in an envelope, sealed it and stuffed it in his bag. Zipping up the large backpack, he rested it on the floor and looked around his room. He stared at the door, now shut and locked—And recalled a time, prior to six years ago, when his father and mother would stop by to say 'hi' or just wave with a smile through the open door as they walked by. He stared at the bed—Where he'd spent nearly two years crying himself to sleep before finally hatching "the plan." He stared at the desk—Where for the past four years, he'd studied, plotted and prepared daily for the biggest and most challenging adventure of his life. A journey that would test him to his very limits.

Jonah looked at the room, and he couldn't believe that the time had finally arrived.

Twelve hours to departure and Jonah's preparations WERE complete.

***

The following morning, he emerged from his room at 7:30 a.m. and made his way to the kitchen. He was surprised to find his father and mother already sitting at the table waiting for him. They looked as though they'd been up for hours.

"There he is!" Susan Shaughnessy yelped and gave a broad smile as Jonah entered the room. "Honey, I have everything ready to make your favorite, a Denver omelet! One last home-cooked meal before you leave us for a few months." And with that, she jumped up and began to cook. Though she wore her usual smile, Jonah could tell she'd been crying, and was straining now to fight back the tears.

"Thanks, mom," Jonah replied.

"Come sit with me, son," Jim Shaughnessy said. The gentleness in his typically gruff voice was unrecognizable to Jonah. He poured Jonah a glass of juice as the young man came to his spot at the table. "So, are you all ready to go?" he asked.

"Yeah, I think I am," replied Jonah.

"Do you have all your clothes packed and your camping gear loaded up?"

"Yeah, dad, of course."

"Okay, okay. Do you have your National Parks Pass and know where you're going first?"

"Yeah, I have my pass, and I told you I'm headed north first to Voyageurs in Minnesota, then to Roosevelt, Yellowstone and Glacier before the winter gets going."

Jim let out a deep sigh. "I still don't understand why you're starting this in the fall, wouldn't it be safer to start in the spring?"

Jonah raised his voice in frustration "Dad! I've told you a hundred times! I have to leave in the fall so I can get campsites at all the parks without having to make reservations. If I went in the spring and summer, everything would be booked up!"

As Jonah finished, he realized how loudly he'd been speaking. He hated that he had to lie to his father. But even worse, he hated yelling lies at the man. He took a deep breath. "I'm sorry I raised my voice...I really don't want to fight with you."

Jim gave a restrained smile. "I don't want to fight with you either... As much as we don't see eye to eye on a lot of things... well...I'm gonna miss you while you're gone," he said. The sincerity in the normally stern man's voice made Jonah tremble.

"I'm gonna miss you too, dad."

***

After breakfast, Jonah loaded his bag into his vehicle and climbed into the driver's seat. His mother and father stepped to the window to say one final goodbye. Jonah wanted desperately to tell them the truth. That he wasn't going to Minnesota. That he wouldn't be back in two months. And that there was a very real possibility that they'd never see him again.

CHAPTER 20

For two days, Simon whiled away the hours eating, lounging by the pool, playing shuffleboard and, above all else, relaxing. On the third afternoon, while desperately clutching a banana-shaped inflatable flying at breakneck speed across the water, —*What was I thinking*! — Simon looked to the shore, and spied from a distance the young couple ambling down the beach, away from the resort. *It's them.*

Keeping his eyes fixed on the pair as best he could through the cloud of mist battering his face, Simon watched, fascinated, as they veered off the beach and onto a mysterious dirt road that sliced deep into the dense palm forest adjacent to the hotel grounds. Simon had no idea where the road led as it was invisible from the resort, shielded by the thick woods. The strange couple's use of it now piqued his intrigue. *Where are they going?*

Once safely back on the beach, Simon kissed the ground before scampering down the shoreline until he'd arrived at the threshold where the dirt road disappeared into the forest. In the failing light, the shrouded corridor into the trees appeared dark and foreboding. He stood on the beach, staring at it for some time. The chirping of crickets and the rustling of leaves were the only sounds emanating from within. *Where the hell does this go?*

After a few pensive minutes, he turned and retreated back to the resort, riddled with countless new questions.

***

Another day would go by before he would begin to find answers. The sun blazed down from on high as Simon lay by the pool humming along to UB40's *Red, Red, Wine,* when he spotted the couple walking by on the beach. Without thinking, he rose and scurried down to the sand in an effort to catch a glimpse of their destination. The red sarong sat nestled once again below the hanging palm in exactly the same place as it had been the week before. The couple, wet from a recent swim, sprawled out upon it, drying off in the hot sun. From where he was standing, Simon could see the water beading on the girl's well-formed body, and he found himself staring at her, once again hypnotized. So lost in thought was Simon, that he failed to realize that the girl had noticed his gawking and was now staring back at him, smiling. When his eyes finally drifted up and locked with hers, she waved at him and raised her eyebrows. *Oh shit!*

With the poise of a startled cat, Simon recoiled awkwardly and bounded back up the stairs towards the pool, placing space and, more importantly, the resort wall between him and the mystery girl. *Shit! Shit! Shit!!*

Skulking around the pool, he repeatedly glanced to the beach abutting edge of the wall, waiting breathlessly to see if the couple would come walking around it. *Please don't come up here!* He begged. But after his initial anguish had waned, he eventually sat down in a pool lounger to seethe with humiliation. *God, I must have looked like such a creep. What were you thinking, Simon?*

***

Several hours went by as he sat by the pool bar stewing and biding his time, terrified to head back down to the beach or even peek around the wall to see if they were still there. Finally, late afternoon arrived. *It's been hours, they must be gone by now,* he thought, and mustering up the little courage he possessed, Simon ambled his way back down to the beach, straining to look as casual as possible.

Emerging around the wall, he darted a hurried glance towards where the couple had been lying, and noticed that the pool of shade below the palm tree was now empty. The couple were nowhere in sight. Relieved to once again be able to venture onto the beach, Simon made his way towards the water's edge. A wave rolled in, and the sea glided up the sand and covered his feet. Simon looked out at the ocean and let out a deep sigh.

Suddenly, a girl's voice boomed from directly behind him. "Hello there!"

Buckling at the knees, Simon nearly fell over from shock, contorting his body around quickly to find the young woman and the man smiling widely and chuckling at his awkward reaction. His heart seemed to stop— *Busted*—as he forced a pained smile onto his alarmed face and tilted his eyes downward in the hopes of finding a hole in the sand to bury his head in.

The young man gave a wide grin. "How's it going?" he asked with a laugh.

Though Simon heard the cordial question, petrified organisms are typically incapable of speech. Simon was no different. A long awkward silence ensued before the girl politely decided to break the ice. "I'm Alice, and this is Jack," she said. A tenderness in her voice and the distinct presence of a slight Southern drawl consoled Simon, putting him somewhat at ease. She extended her freckled hand to shake Simon's, and after a confused pause, he took it, noticing how small and soft it was.

"I'm, uh, Simon," he struggled to say. *Why on Earth are you so nervous, Simon?! Calm down, man. Calm...down.*

Jack spoke with cheery confidence. "Nice to meet ya, Simon, where ya from?" he asked.

"Texas," replied Simon looking up, and then paused. "In the USA," he continued. "You two?"

"Well, I'm from Nashville, and Jack here's from New Hampshire," Alice said, pausing for a moment before broadening her smile. "In the USA," she continued with a chuckle.

Simon could sense she was poking good fun at him, and he grinned at her friendly teasing.

"So how long ya in Belize?" Jack asked.

"Oh, I don't know, maybe a few more days. And then I'm headed back up to Texas... How bout you?"

"Well, we also don't know. Been here a week already but thinkin' about stayin' anotha before we move on. We kinda love it here!" replied Jack. As he finished his sentence, the young man swung his arms out towards the beach. "I mean, look at this!" he belted.

Though only a few moments had passed, Simon felt comforted by the couple's laid back and affable nature. The expressiveness of Jack's mannerisms was also proving to be rather humorous to the comparatively deadpan Texan. Simon smiled, racking his brain for something—anything else—to talk to them about. "Yeah, it's a great resort, isn't it? The buffet is incredible, and the rooms are so nice, aren't they? Do you guys have a sea-view room?"

Alice gave Simon another coy smile and a little giggle before lifting her toned arm and pointing down the beach towards the dirt road. Simon's eyes followed across her smooth skin and off the tip of her finger without hesitation.

"Actually, we're not stayin' here, Simon, we're stayin' down that way. In a village about a kilometer down the beach. We just come over here cause the swimming's the best."

Simon's gaze down the beach lingered.

In his stupor, it took him a moment to absorb Alice's words and process. Finally, it clicked. *Did she just say, "a village"?* He realized that he'd never even considered what lay outside the walls of the resort. Much less within and beyond the palm forest that surrounded it. "A village?" he muttered. "What kind of village?"

"Oh, it's just a local fishing village down the way," Alice replied. "It's not much honestly, but the people are friendly, and the price is right. We're stayin' at a guesthouse there with a really great family."

A guesthouse? Simon mused.

"Oh, a B&B kinda thing?"

Alice and Jack smiled. "Yeah, kinda," she replied.

"I stayed at one of those with my folks when I was a kid," said Simon enthusiastically. "Didn't much care for it. Had to share a bathroom with the owners. An elderly couple. Do you have to share a bathroom?"

"Yeah, we do," Alice said, chuckling again.

Though Simon was oblivious to the effect he was having, he'd already begun to endear himself to the young woman.

"You know, now that I think about it, I did notice you two didn't have wristbands for the resort." Simon held up his wrist to show his plastic access bracelet.

Jack and Alice smiled.

"Oh yeah? Now that I think about it, I DID notice you were watchin' us earlier!" Alice responded mockingly.

Simon's face turned nearly as red as his belly.

"Yeah, well, see, I saw you two before, and I thought—well, I don't know what I thought, but I was thinkin' that... well, that doesn't sound right but—"

"Hey, don't worry about it, Simon. I'm just messin' with you!" Alice said, playfully shoving the shoulder of the fumbling Texan.

Jack, who'd been grinning at this whole interaction, began to laugh as well before chiming in with his boisterous voice. "Wait, partna! So you haven't left the fortress at all since you've been in Belize?!"

Simon was perplexed by the odd question and sensed from Jack's tone that it was a loaded one. "Well. . . No, not really. . . Why would I leave?"

Simon immediately attempted to rationalize his question, continuing to ramble as he did.

"I mean, I have everything I could want here. It's an all-inclusive resort, so there's no real point in going outside the walls, I think... I mean, everything is here. Food, drink... everything!"

As he concluded his rant, Simon gave a forced smile, feigning confidence in his own words. Oddly, though, he'd begun to question their validity. Certainly, their eloquence.

The young couple looked amused and flitted each other a glance, seemingly sharing a thought telepathically. They gazed again to Simon and smiled.

"Hey-a, strange question," Jack began. "But do you wanna join us for dinner in the village tonight?"

The inquiry, though rather unassuming, instantly befuddled Simon.

Did they just invite me to dinner?

"Dinner? In the village?" he stuttered.

"Hehe, yeah. There's a great place to eat over there." Jack chuckled.

A great place to eat? In the village?

Simon bit his lip, trying to wrap his head around the intriguing yet highly unexpected proposition. He debated not only *why* they would invite him to dinner, but what it might possibly be like—and more. A barrage of questions coursed through his brain. *Where is this village, and how would I get there and back? Would I have to walk through the woods? In the dark, even? Why would I pay for dinner when I could eat all I want for free at the buffet? What kind of food do they have? I don't even know these people—why are they inviting me to dinner?!*

Yet, as Simon frantically deliberated all the possible reasons for NOT doing something so audacious, Alice once again spoke, and with such an honest and warm tone that Simon instantly tossed his reservations and qualms aside.

"Please come," she said simply.

And he knew he would.

"Absolutely." The words spilled from Simon's mouth without another thought.

"Great!" Alice said, clapping her hands together with a smile. "Can you be ready to go in an hour or so?"

"Um, yeah, of course. I don't really have any nice clothes, though, so I hope it's not too fancy a place," he replied.

The concern over his personal appearance sent Jack and Alice into fits.

"Don't worry about it, what you're wearin' now is fine," Jack said, snickering. Then, tilting his head to the sky, he yelled wildly. "It's Belize, man!" and slapped Simon on the shoulder, laughing.

Simon played along, laughing as well though he'd already begun to sense that Jack was possibly a bit mad —*but certainly interesting.*

As the couple turned and meandered off down the beach towards the dirt road, Jack hollered over his shoulder, "We'll meet ya back here in an hour, okay, buddy?"

"Sounds good!" Simon yelled back, waving awkwardly before realizing what he was doing and thrusting his hands to his sides. As Simon watched the pair walk away, he finally unclenched his chest and released an exasperated breath. *I can't believe that just happened.*

Within seconds, Simon was dashing across the beach and up towards his room. The countless butterflies flapping in his belly nearly lifted him off the path and into the sky. He knew practically nothing about the two strangers but recognized that his feelings towards Alice were both profound and confusing. She was gorgeous, a southern sweetheart and, astoundingly, she seemed actually to want him to join them. *I think they both do.*

It was mortifying.

In as long as Simon could remember, no one had been this outwardly friendly towards him. *Especially not attractive, charming people like Jack and Alice.*

As the elevator to Simon's room crept quietly upwards, Simon stared through the glass, and suddenly an itch of that all too familiar paranoia once again wriggled inside of him. *What am I getting myself into?*

CHAPTER 21

"Heya bud, can I help you with something?" the man behind the counter asked.

Jonah glanced up at the camouflage hat on the man's head, emblazoned with the logo *Rebel Rules* on the front, and couldn't help but wonder what the hell it meant. *Does he mean rebels themselves rule?... Or are there a set of rules by which rebels must adhere? Kinda defeats the point of being a rebel, doesn't it?*

"Son, you alright?" the man asked from behind his goatee.

"Oh yeah, sorry," Jonah mumbled, pulling a piece of paper from his pocket. "I have a list... I'm hoping you can help me with some of this."

"Well, son, we're the biggest hunting and surplus supplier in the Midwest, like the sign out front says, so I betcha we can help you with a lot of that."

Jonah cracked a smile. *This guy is priceless.*

"Alright then... so I need three months of freeze-dried emergency food packets and six months of Survival tabs."

"Done," the man said, thumping his hand on the counter with a toothy smile. "What's next?"

Price-less.

"You guys have trapping gear?"

"You see that sign out front?"

Jonah chuckled. "Alright, stupid question. So, I need six 11/3-inch coil spring traps, three #11 double long springs, nine #110 body grip traps, and twelve 7x7 cable snares with slide locks."

"You want stakes or anchors for the snares?"

"Which is better?"

"You don't *know*?" the man joked in a half-mocking tone.

Jonah just stared at him.

The man guffawed. "Oh, I'm just messing with ya! Lighten up... You even know how to use this stuff?"

"I read about it... and watched some YouTube videos," Jonah replied.

"Haha—YouTube videos?... Well, bud, I'll tell you what. If you don't mind hangin' out for a bit, I go on break shortly and can take ya out back and show ya how to set these traps and snares."

Jonah pondered the proposal. *Jim Bob here wants to "take me out back." Why does that not sound like a good idea?*

"Names Kevin, by the way, but folks call me Kev," the man said, extending his hand.

Jonah stared at the hand for a moment and then shook it. "My name's Jonah... Yeah, sure, I'll wait for a bit. I appreciate it."

"No problem."

Twenty minutes later, Jonah followed Kevin around the building to a grassy plateau abutting a small patch of woods. "So, what are you looking to trap? Squirrels? Gophers?" asked Kevin.

"Mostly paca and agouti, maybe a capybara if I'm lucky," replied Jonah.

Kevin paused and darted him a squint. "Son, where the hell you goin'?!" he asked.

Jonah paused, then looked at Kevin. "Meh, nowhere," he replied with a wink.

Kevin laughed. "Say no more!"

CHAPTER 22

What on Earth will we talk about? Simon paced around his room, lamenting how boring Jack and Alice would probably find him to be. He tried desperately to conjure interesting stories from his life or any fascinating Simon tidbits he could share at dinner. But this train of thought quickly carried him towards the bleak conclusion that his journey down to Belize was the only exciting thing he'd done in the past twenty years. *Jesus, I better stick with asking them questions.*

Simon felt himself sweating. He recognized this sensation far too well. In recent years, he'd pushed himself into a series of internet dates back in San Antonio. A collection of contrived human interactions he'd blown epically. *What's to keep me from blowing this too? Just remember… it's not a date… Or is it?*

Time was up. It was time to leave.

Stopping at the pool bar on the way to the beach, Simon downed a frozen margarita in one colossal chug. The cocktail worked wonders to calm his agitated nerves, but also gave him the worst brain freeze he'd had since discovering Slushies when he was eight. He snickered through the pain now, remembering that fateful day.

Fifteen minutes passed as he stood on the beach, waiting for Jack and Alice to arrive. His brain had finally begun to thaw when he noticed them emerging from the forest and walking towards him in the fading daylight. Jack wore a loose-fitting beige button-up shirt that looked as if it were made of hemp or some other natural material, and the same cargo shorts and brown leather flip-flops he'd been wearing earlier. His wavy brown hair was up in a ponytail, and he looked ruggedly handsome, Simon thought. *For a skinny hippie.*

Alice was wearing a light cotton, baby-blue dress that came to her mid-thigh emblazoned with the word's *Sri Lanka* across it. The armholes were cut long and low down to her waist and revealed the whole side of her toned body and her bikini top inside. Her long red hair hung down behind her freckled shoulders. *Good God, she's beautiful.*

Simon glanced down to his grey slacks and the white button-up work shirt he was wearing and recognized at once that he needed to get some cooler clothes. At least he had his top two buttons unbuttoned casually, he thought, hurriedly rolling up his sleeves.

"You ready to go?" Alice asked chipperly as they strolled up.

"Yeah, definitely," Simon replied.

Here goes something.

The night was warm and clear as the three wandered away from the 'fortress,' as Jack not-so-lovingly referred to the resort. A hundred yards down the beach, they cut off through a clearing in the woods and onto the shadowy sand road Simon had seen before. The empty lane was dotted with patches of grass, and it glowed a cool blue in the twilight. The sounds of birds and insects filled the air, and the wind rustled through the palms above them. It felt oddly quiet and serene without the sound of the pool bar music now. Simon was surprised by how much he enjoyed it.

As the group walked onward through the tropical forest, Simon soon began to notice dilapidated shacks appearing along the path beside them. Nestled deep in the thicket, the small homes appeared to be made of scrap wood and were roofed with rusted sheets of corrugated steel. His pulse started to quicken. *Wheeeere are we going?*

Soon, they bore left onto a wider dirt road running parallel to the beach roughly fifty yards in. Simon could still hear the faint echo of waves in the distance through the woods—a sound he found oddly comforting.

Clustered rows of single and two-story concrete homes began to appear amidst the trees, poorly plastered and painted with flaking colors. Simon could smell wood smoke, and orange light flickered in the windows of many of the structures. The vegetation was still thick, and beside the greenery, Simon noticed some old, blue plastic barrels of stagnant water resting beside the road. As they walked past, a cloud of gnats and mosquitos swarmed, and Simon swatted at them ferociously before finally escaping their bites. A pair of somewhat disheveled, shirtless boys rode by on bicycles staring at them, as women hung clothes on lines strung between their homes and nearby trees.

To say that this was an alien world to Simon would be putting it far too lightly. He'd seen a few communities like this on his drive through Mexico but had always averted his eyes from the poverty. Though he'd questioned why he'd done so, the answer was simple to him. *Why would anyone want to look at this?*

"This is Brasilito!" Jack abruptly proclaimed, wresting Simon from his dreary thoughts. "The super cool village Alice and I are stayin' in," he added with a smile.

Simon's stomach sank a bit. *Is Jack being sarcastic?*

"We just need ta stop by our place real quick on the way to grab my wallet," Jack went on. "Sound good, partna?"

"Yeah, sure thing," Simon mumbled quietly, still struggling to take in his unfamiliar surroundings.

As they proceeded through the 'town,' Simon spotted several gatherings of weathered men unloading rolled nets and buckets from rickety wooden pushcarts throughout the village. As the men chatted away, roars of laughter would burst out repeatedly, each time making Simon inadvertently chuckle. They spoke a language Simon didn't recognize, yet he strained to try and make out their words. *These must be the fishermen, but why aren't they speaking English?*

A good many of the local villagers began to give friendly waves to the three Americans as they walked through the settlement. Simon, though a bit startled by this, felt compelled to wave back at each of them. A smile slowly began to grow on his face.

"Hallo!" a few children yelled to the passing strangers as they walked by, and Alice yelled, "Hello!" back in response, causing the kids to giggle and run away shyly. Alice and Simon laughed. *Everyone is so friendly in this town.* Simon wondered why he was so surprised by that.

Soon they reached a small green house and approached the front door. Alice and Jack entered through the low portal while Simon paused for a bit, noticing something rather peculiar about the structure. Though the front exterior wall was plastered and painted, the rest of the building was just exposed grey cinder block. He glanced back over his shoulder and was surprised to find that the whole village was built the same way.

"Come on in partna!" Jack yelled to him from inside.

Simon turned quickly to enter, and at once cracked his head with a thump on the top of the curiously low door frame. "Ah shit!" he hollered, rubbing his forehead as he ducked into the front room of the small home.

Once inside, Simon found the home's interior saturated with a thick humidity and reeking of mildew and mold. The air inside seemed ancient and unmoving, hanging there in a hot, viscous soup. Squinting around the small, dimly lit chamber, Simon was dumbfounded by how low the ceiling was. As he moved through the room, he had to bend repeatedly to keep from striking his head on the haphazard crossbeams. The only illumination came from a dangling white florescent bulb and a small, square window through which the last traces of twilight trickled in. The floor was painted concrete, and the furniture was tattered and filthy. An old, boxy CRT television sat in the corner and piles of heavily used toys lay against the wall. Jack and Alice were nowhere to be found, so Simon just stood there waiting. Sweating. Breathing deeply in the thick, warm air.

An impossibly long few seconds passed before Jack reentered into the living room through a doorway in the back wall. Following closely behind him was a squat, dark-skinned local woman donning an apron. She had a kind look upon her face. "This is Nina, the mother of the house," Jack said, introducing them. "Nina, this is Simon."

"*Hola,* Simon," Nina said to him with a gentle voice and a warm smile. She walked up to shake his hand.

"*Hola,* Nina," he replied, obliging her.

Simon had already noticed the apparent height difference between Americans and Belizeans, the knot now growing on his forehead bringing home the point, but the diminutive Nina was exceptionally small. She couldn't have been more than 4'10". *If that.*

"Do you wanna see our amazing, resort-like room?" asked Jack in jest.

"Sure," Simon replied, releasing the still smiling Nina's hand.

As he followed Jack through the door into the back half of the home, Simon found the area split into two separate rooms. One contained four beds and appeared packed with clothes, old furniture and children's things strewn about. The other, which Jack now led Simon into, was far tidier and mostly barren by comparison. A thin, double mattress sat along the back wall with a pair of backpacks lying at the foot of it. Beside the bed sat a frail end table that looked barely capable of supporting the lamp that sat atop it. A framed picture of the Virgin Mary, the room's only decoration, hung small on the wide, chipped cement wall.

Simon envisioned the double-thick pillow-top mattress and flat-screen TV waiting for him back in his hotel room, and he shuddered at the relative squalor Jack and Alice were living in. *Why are they here?*

"This is our place," Jack said with an exuberant smile, stretching his arms out wide. "It ain't much, but it's home, baby!"

Alice chuckled in the corner while zipping up her bag and securing her luggage lock. Simon, meanwhile, felt instantly remorseful for having spoken so braggartly of the buffet and the luxurious amenities he had back at the resort.

"So, the family all lives in the other room, and they rent out this one to gringos like us that come through here occasionally," said Alice. "The bathroom is in the hall if you need to use it before we go. The one at the restaurant is a liiiitle bit questionable," she added with a sinister laugh. Jack joined in the laughter, sounding almost maniacal.

What the hell are they laughing about?!

As the trio walked out of the house and into the village, the sky and the town around them had grown dark and still. In the faint glow of the rising moon, Simon could see Jack walking beside him, grinning.

"Why are you staying here instead of at a hotel by the beach?" Simon asked timidly.

Jack glanced at him. "How much do ya pay for that fancy hotel you're staying in?" he asked.

Simon felt guilty telling them he paid $350 a night.

"$300 a night," he replied.

Alice and Jack's eyes lit up, and they turned to each other with looks of astonishment. Alice glanced back to Simon—and in the pale moonlight, she spoke unequivocally. "We're payin' around $9 a night here for the two of us, and Nina makes us a homemade breakfast every mornin'. We get to eat with the family and talk about what we're all gettin' up to for the day, and they tell us all about life in Belize and the history of the village. It's really been amazing so far."

There was a confident insightfulness in the way she spoke of their experience. Simon was puzzled by how enthusiastic she seemed with the bizarre situation and walked in silence, pondering. *Well, of course, its nine dollars a night. It LOOKS like nine dollars a night. And why on Earth would they want to know about life in the village and what the locals are going to do for the day? Who really cares about that stuff?*

Simon couldn't wrap his head around any of it except the $9 a night part. *Obviously, Jack and Alice must be poor, and this is the only room they can afford.* He attempted to formulate a response to Alice but struggled to come up with anything that wouldn't sound insulting. Instead, he just continued to walk in silence.

When they finally arrived at the patchwork wooden door at the restaurant's entrance, the thumping hum of lively music resonated from within. Alice stepped through the door first.... and then Jack. Simon took a long, deep breath... *in we go*...and then pushed on the creaking door, ducking inside.

CHAPTER 23

After a half-hour of Kevin watching Jonah dexterously setting up snares and traps, the pair headed back towards the warehouse. "Damn, I stand corrected, I guess you CAN learn something on YouTube!" Kevin said, scratching his head.

Jonah laughed under his breath. "Yeah, I'm also just good with my hands," he replied.

The two made their way around the side of the building, and as they did, Jonah abruptly stopped beneath the shaded shelter of a plastic awning. "Hey Kev?" he asked.

Kevin stopped and turned to the young man. "What's up, Jonah?"

Jonah paused, taking a moment to scan their surroundings before looking back to Kevin. "Hey, you know where I can get a few guns?" he said softly.

Kevin smiled a toothy smile. "Well, whatcha looking for?"

"Maximum firepower that will fit into a space 14 inches by 17 inches by 5 inches."

Kevin chuckled. "Well, that's an odd request, but lemme see what I can figure."

CHAPTER 24

Ten feet wide and twice as deep, the 'restaurant' before Simon was little more than a slight hovel of a place in his widening eyes. Along the right-hand side, a timeworn and dusty bamboo bar sat with a brawny dreadlocked bartender cleaning up behind it. A collection of grubby, handwrought wooden tables hugged the left wall, where four or five locals sat in a group, chattering in grumbly voices that erupted into laughter every few seconds. The rhythmic drumming of Caribbean Soca music hopped loudly from a pair of crackling speakers on the far wall, causing the out-of-place Texan to smirk. An odd jumble of knick-knacks and instruments rested on the dirt floor in the back corner, and a tangle of fishing nets and shells hung from the ceiling throughout the cluttered place. Bright colors painted haphazardly on the walls now flaked from the age and humidity, and any charm the "beach shack" décor was intended to instill had long ago been lost to time. Yet there was something extraordinarily lively and comforting about the place that left Simon... well... enchanted. Oh my god, this place is amazing.

Across the room, the hulking bartender suddenly caught sight of the group gathered in the doorway. In an instant, his eyes lit up wide, and Simon felt the strong man's pupils piercing his very soul. Uh oh.

"Buiti Achuluruni!" the man roared loudly, extending his muscular arms out wide.

Simon took a step backward.

"Tuluuuuuuuu!" replied Jack, throwing his arms into the air wildly.

Simon's head darted back and forth between the two men.

Oh shit, what's happening here?

But he felt fairly positive he understood.

From the war cries of Diomedes to the howling Roman barritus, the raging flugelhorns of the Scottish Highlands or Tyr! of the Norse Vikings, the great battle cries of history have rallied courage into the hearts of those who have called upon them and weakened the knees of anyone in their path. At this moment... Simon's legs felt much like Play-doh beneath him. Shit, well, I guess this is happening...

As Simon cleared his voice and prepared to thrust his own barbaric yawp across the room—likely more SpongeBob than William Wallace—a huge smile suddenly and unexpectedly overtook the burly barkeeper's scruffy, bearded face. Simon froze, glaring, paralyzed, as Jack and Alice sauntered to the bar, leaned over and grabbed the dreaded barman in a strong embrace. Suddenly all became clear.

Ahaaaaaaa! They're friends. Okay, that makes a lot more sense.

A grin of relief passed across his face, and one thought penetrated deep into his consciousness. Of COURSE, they know the bartender. Damnit, they're cool.

Unclenching his cheeks, Simon rolled his sleeves up one more rung and casually made his way to the bar beside Jack.

Alice and the barkeep, Tulu, had their backs turned, exchanging kisses to each other's cheeks. "Shhhhh," Jack whispered to Simon, a finger pressed to his grinning mouth. Simon nodded in understanding and then watched breathlessly as Jack not-so-slyly leaned over the bar to try and surreptitiously finagle a bottle of rum from behind Tulu's back.

What... the hell... is he doing?

As Jack's fingers inched closer and closer to the flask, Simon's heart raced, until suddenly, Tulu's hand sprung from nowhere and smacked Jack's fingers away, sending Simon and the rest of the group into gasps of laughter.

"Ha ha ha, What da hell you tink yah doin' man!" Tulu hooted, his hearty Caribbean accent instantly leaving Simon smitten.

"I dunno!" Jack yelled, rolling his eyes with a chuckle and rubbing his sore hand.

Alice just shook her head. "Tulu, this is Simon... Simon, Tulu"

The jolly Tulu turned to Simon, hollering "Hallo Simon!" in a deep, booming voice that dominated the room. Reaching over the bar, he grabbed Simon's hand and shook it vigorously, the strength of his grip and the callousness of his paw, making Simon temporarily question his own manliness. Stupid desk job.

"Yah want some bee-ahs?!" queried the amicable barkeep as he continued to smile widely and shake Simon's hand wildly. Simon couldn't help but nod and laugh though his arm was starting to feel like jelly.

"Of course," Jack responded.

"Yes... please," begged Simon.

Releasing Simon from his clutches, Tulu reached into a cooler box behind the bar, pulled out three large, brown bottles of Belkin beer, popped the tops and handed the cold vessels to his three guests. The man's smile was infectious, and Simon noticed his own cheeks were now aching from following the Belizeans lead.

"Do yah like chicken and lobster Simon?!" Tulu asked loudly.

"Doesn't everybody?" Simon replied.

"Good answer!" Tulu howled, shooing the group over to one of the tables. "Well, grab a seat now!"

Simon was dazed, his head already swirling from the frenetic pace of the moment. And as he took his seat at a table beside the boisterous group of locals, a few of the more intoxicated of the old men reached over and slapped him on the back cordially. Though it startled him at first, Simon quickly realized the sentiment and smiled back kindly. People are so damn nice here.

"Cheers!" bellowed Jack to the sky, lifting his bottle high above the table. Alice and a still grinning Simon responded the same, and the three bottles met with a loud clink. The beer was ice cold and refreshing as it rushed down Simon's throat. Oh, that's good.

Jack leaned in to Simon. "This is Tulu's family's place," he said. "His mom and aunt cook in the back, and Tulu and his brother go out fishin' in the morning for lobster, conch and other seafood."

"Lobster fishing?! That sounds amazing. Are they gonna bring us some menus?" Simon asked eagerly.

Jack chuckled and stared at Simon for a second. "There's no menu here, man, just eat what they bring ya," he replied.

The notion seemed absurd, but in the moment, Simon was feeling inspired to go with the flow. He glanced to the table of locals beside him and found it bestrewn with countless beer bottles and plates littered with the scraps and shells of various sea creatures. He turned back towards the kitchen curtain and then surveyed the rest of the structure's squalid interior. Filthy by American standards, Simon would never, ever have jeopardized his stomach's health at a place like this back home. But in this moment… in this place…he couldn't wait for their food to hit the table.

Great comfort arose in Jack and Alice knowing the people here, and Simon looked across the table at the couple now with renewed reverence. He wondered how they knew Tulu and how they'd ended up in this place.

It occurred to him how little he knew of his two new acquaintances. "So, y'all are just down here for a week, huh? Did you fly down or drive?"

"Drive?!" Jack snorted. "What, are ya nuts?!"

Simon smiled wide, though he didn't get the question.

"No, we flew down to the Yucatan about two months ago. We've been workin' our way south, overland, ever since. Just crossed into Belize a couple weeks ago."

Wait, what was that?

Simon fought to comprehend Jack's statement. "Two months?!" he asked in dismay.

Jack laughed. "Yeah, more or less," he replied.

"Wow," said Simon. That's... um... a long time."

Two months seemed an inordinate amount of time to him. For several seconds, he wrestled with the concept in his mind, taking a beat to formulate an intelligent response.

"Where's the Yucatan?" he finally asked. Nice one.

"Oh, it's a bit north of here," replied Jack, pausing to take a long pull off his beer. "It's the big peninsula in Mexico on the Caribbean side... Where Cancun and Tulum are."

"Oh!" Simon responded excitedly. "I must have driven right through there, or maybe next to it anyway. Not really sure exactly," he laughed.

Yet before Simon finished his chuckle, he noticed Jack and Alice's faces changing abruptly. Their cool and confident grins were replaced by looks of outright shock. Darting each other one of their telepathic glances, the two turned back to Simon bearing faces of stunned disbelief.

"Wait, you DROVE down here?!" Jack said, aghast. "Through Tamaulipas and Veracruz?!"

Shit. Did I do something wrong?

"Yeah? I think so. I remember seeing a Veracruz sign, at least. Why?" Simon fretted.

Jack stared at him, slack-jawed, for what felt like eons.

This can't be good.

"Man, you are one crazy sonofabitch, Simon!" he finally belted. "You know you drove straight through Zetas country, right?" he continued, startling the reeling Texan.

What the hell is this guy talking about? Simon's voice trembled. "What's a Zetas?" he asked, fearful of the answer.

The couple across from him continued to stare with astonishment in their eyes. Finally, Jack chuckled and released a deep sigh. "The Zetas are the biggest drug cartel in Mexico, man. You HAVE heard there's a drug war goin' on there the last decade, right? Hundreds, maybe thousands of people are being kidnapped or murdered every year. I read that ten people were gunned down in the streets of Veracruz just a couple days ago!"

The vacant look on Simon's face revealed that the connection between these stark facts and his own journey was still escaping him.

"You just drove right through the heart of a war zone partna... You're lucky to be alive!" Jack hollered, slapping Simon on the back, laughing uproariously and taking a long pull off his beer. He sat back, grinning.

Simon paused, dumbfounded, for a few seconds taking it all in.

So THAT'S why the border guard told me not to stop.

"Oh shit," Simon muttered, finally putting it all together.

Jack and Alice burst into laughter at their doe-eyed compatriot. After a few seconds, even Simon joined in as he sensed the humor in his naiveté.

"To Simon's health!" Jack yelled, holding up his beer, "The most unwittingly brave man I know!"

"Here, here!" Alice added as the three of them raised their bottles and toasted once again. The drunk locals at the table next to them followed suit and lifted their bottles with a holler. Alice, Jack and Simon laughed even harder.

Though on the surface, he was attempting to shrug it all off as a humorous misadventure, Simon felt his troubled mind racing. A warzone!? Shit, I have to drive back up through there again in a few days! He considered his imminent return journey, and his pulse quickened behind his smile. He began to formulate a defensive strategy in his mind— something to do with purchasing a kitchen knife and a Mexican disguise.

But as his brain swirled, something across the room suddenly distracted him. An eclectic group of young local men and women had entered the restaurant and now sat at the bar across from Tulu. Many of them hugged the sociable barkeep, and as the group spoke with him and laughed, Simon began to forget his worries and felt a sense of warmth radiating among the local community.

"So, what made ya come to Belize?" asked Jack, fetching Simon back to the table.

It was a complicated question, and Simon struggled for a clear-cut answer. "I guess…," he began… "I guess it was just… just sort of calling to me… I don't know really," he said, smiling.

Jack and Alice grinned in reply, giving him nods of understanding. "Yeah, I know the feelin', amigo…" Jack said solemnly. "It's sort of like ya feel destined to go somewhere for no real reason, right?"

"Yeah… kinda like that," Simon replied.

Jack and Alice smiled again. Simon could see Jack's mind working hard to articulate a thought. When he had it, the young man spoke with a hallowed veneration that was unmistakable.

"Personally, man, I'm of the belief that there are travelers within all of us. That everyone, no matter who they are, feels that way at some point in their life. We all get this weird, unexplainable need to go somewhere we've never been before, for reasons we just can't fully understand…. And really, it could be just about anywhere. It could be a new steakhouse downtown… or the Empire State Building… or even a yurt horse camp on the plains of Mongolia!" he chuckled.

Simon laughed along, clueless as to what a yurt was.

"I think, really, the most important thing is what happens next," Jack continued. "What you do… AFTER you get that feeling? You know what I mean?"

Not really, thought Simon. "Yeah, I think so," he lied.

"I mean, do we follow that strange desire and go for what we want? Or do we just sit around thinkin': That's impossible! Places like that are for other people, not me!" Jack thumped his hand on the table.

Simon jumped in his seat.

"But ya know what's great?" Jack continued, intensely pointing at Simon.

What?! What's great?!

"Some of us… some of us actually get there eventually… Like you makin' it to Belize man…. and us makin' it here too." Jack sat back in his seat, raised his bottle and clinked the bottle in Simon's hand before going on. "But lots of people, man, the unlucky ones in my opinion… they don't ever even try to get there… and ya know what? They never do."

Alice had been listening mindfully to her beau and now picked up right where he left off. "Well, beyond THAT… what happens next?! I mean, what happens when, or if, you DO get there?" she asked Simon, who shrugged in response. "I mean for some people, when they get where they're goin'… when they achieve that goal… that's it!" she continued. "They reach their big objective, and then they're ready to head on home. Back to their life, back to their job. Back to what's comfortable."

Okay, that I understand.

"But for other people," she went on, smiling at the two men and putting one hand on Simon's shoulder and the other on Jack's arm, "they just wanna keep on goin'… and goin' and goin' and goin' further and further into the world... They wanna see more... They wanna feel more... For them… For us… goin' back really isn't an option. We're just wanderers by nature."

At this, Alice and Jack locked eyes and seemed instantly lost in their waxing poetic minds. Simon watched spellbound as the two languished in their apparent mutual understanding of each other and the cosmos. In their minds, the world was a vast universe demanding to be revealed—a riddle wrapped in an enigma, wrapped in 126 billion acres of earth, rock and water. Simon's mind worked a bit differently, however.

These two are a couple of freakin' beatniks, aren't they?!

Simon was straining mightily to take Alice and Jack seriously. Though he could sense an ounce of truth in their idealistic worldview, moreover, he was most surprised that they seemed to be including him in this latter group of people, the wanderers as they called themselves. Maybe they could see something in him that he'd never seen in himself. And though he certainly feared returning to his life in San Antonio, he just couldn't see any other apparent path forward.

"So, where are you compelled to go to next?" he eventually asked.

Jack smiled. "Everywhere," he responded casually.

Simon snickered at the very "Jack" response.

Just then, the curtain to the kitchen swooshed open.

In a flash, Tulu's aunt Isebei came barreling out towards them with her hands full of steaming plates. A heavyset, waddling woman, looking as Caribbean as they come, Isebei donned a stained red apron, a green handkerchief in her hair and a smile as wide as the horizon. "Here yah go!" she chortled and took special care in placing the hot plates on the table in front of her guests. "Ah know ya gonna like it!" she howled uproariously.

Simons looked down, his eyes nearly bursting from their sockets at the sight of the colorful spread before him. What IS this?! he swooned. And as he glanced up to the kindly woman with a childlike expression of joy and wonderment, Isebei burst into a deep and hearty laugh. "Hahaha, dear… Ah can see this one likes to eat!" she said, slapping Simon across the back.

Awe man.

"Okay, son, so ya see that thar is stewed chicken!" she said, pointing to a large piece of meat on Simon's plate, smothered in a fiery red and orange sauce. "It's a family recipe ah know yah gonna like," she exclaimed and paused to give Simon an emphatic smile and a wink.

Simon chuckled with delight.

"Then you have red beans wit' chili, cabbage, coconut rice and fried plantains… it's like assaaaa fried banana!" she sputtered, laughing and slapping Simon on the back again.

Her joyous hooting was so strikingly jolly, Simon couldn't help but join in. "This is great!" he squawked to a round of laughter. The pungent aromas of chilies, vinegar, roast chicken and coconut wafted across his face with an intensity that made his eyes tear and his mouth water. He looked back up at the woman with an eager smile, and once again, she burst into laughter and laid her hand on his shoulder warmly.

In the thirty seconds Simon had known her, Isebei had displayed a motherly presence such as Simon had never experienced in his life before. Why wasn't my family like that?! No wonder Tulu is always smiling!

"You kids enjoy now, okay?!" she beamed before heading back to the kitchen. The trio thanked her emphatically as she waddled away, still laughing. Mostly at Simon.

For ten minutes, the feasting was so voracious that the three barely spoke. The garlic and chili of the chicken, the creamy coconut rice and the cold beer united in a sumptuous explosion of flavor that sent Simons palate dancing. This is unbelievable.

When, eventually, Alice paused momentarily to glance up from her plate, a clownish ring of red hot sauce surrounded her lips, sending Simon and Jack into full-mouthed giggles, unaware that they, too, bore similar face adornments. Alice laughed to tears upon seeing them.

As the three cackled and snorted with stuffed mouths and saucy hands, Simon started to imagine what they must look like to outside observers. But before he had a chance to feel self-conscious, Tulu's mom burst from the kitchen, grinning ear to ear, with three more dishes in her hands. What?!

With a clunk, she plopped the plates down before them, and Simon's jaw dropped at the sight of the giant, grilled spiny lobsters in front of him.

"Caught em' mah-self dis morning!" Tulu yelled across the room.

Simon threw Tulu a hot-sauce-covered thumbs-up, and Tulu broke out laughing, giving Simon a thumbs-up in return.

Pulling out a chunk of lobster meat with his greasy fingers, Simon dipped it in the liquid butter bowl on the plate and tossed it in his mouth. "Oh, dear lord," he said, his eyes squinting in ecstasy.

Simon had eaten lobster before, specifically Red Lobster lobster back in San Antonio, but this... this was unlike anything he'd ever tasted before. "Unbelievable!" he hollered to Jack and Alice, who were already hard at work, tearing apart their crustaceans.

Alice glanced up at Simon for a second. "Yup," she said, smiling.

Simon grinned a saucy grin before continuing with the gormandizing, pausing only to take a necessary breath every few seconds.

As the trio wolfed down their food like a pack of starving dogs, Simon noticed that some of the young local men and women who'd entered the restaurant earlier had since headed over to the instrument corner. A few muted thumps rang out as a pair of men slapped on the drums with their hands for a bit, but Simon paid it little mind. His focus returning quickly to the home-cooked bounty before him.

Then, almost at once, the Soca music on the speakers cut out, and one of the young women standing in the corner began to bellow a loud, guttural, chant-like song in a language Simon couldn't ascertain. Immediately, his eyes darted up to see what was happening. As he did so, a roar of drumming began that seemed to shake the restaurant and the chair on which he sat. Whoooooa!

Two men sat on crates in the corner now, large drums resting between their legs, slapping at them furiously with both hands in an intense rhythm that began to fall in sync with the woman's singing and chanting.

Thump, thump, thump, th-th-thump, thump, thump

Another woman lingering at the bar then walked over, picked up a pair of hardened gourds on sticks, and began to shake them to the cadence. The dried seeds inside rattled wildly like a local type of maraca.

Sheechicka, sheechicka, sheechicka, sheechicka

As soon as she'd joined the rhythm, another man slowly approached from the bar, picked up a loop of rope laced through a sorted collection of turtle shells, draped the creation over his shoulder and began knocking the pieces with a round stick, making a hollow clinking sound to the beat.

Clank, clank, clank. Clank, clank cl-clank.

Simon grinned ear to ear, in stupefied awe at what was coming together.

Finally, the one man remaining at the bar finished his beer and sat down his empty bottle. Ambling over to the band, he picked up a large, spiraled conch shell and lifted it to his lips. Simon could see finger holes bored into its side as the man began to blow it like a flute, adding a beautiful echoing melody to the intense rhythm section and singing.

Alice smiled at Simon and nodded her head to the captivating beat. "They're Garifuna!" she hollered over the lively music.

He looked at her, overwhelmed by the moment.

"Descendants of African slaves brought to the Caribbean 400 years ago," she continued. "They live all over this region. This village is Garifuna. This is their local music," she said, giggling. "Idn't it great!?"

Simon smiled and nodded, his knee beginning to bounce up and down under the table. "It's incredible! This whole place is incredible!"

Jack and Alice sent him looks of affection, and he smiled graciously. Though the couple were so unlike anyone Simon could have ever pictured himself connecting with, he couldn't believe how close he felt to them already.

As Simon sat lost in thought for a few moments, watching the band playing in the corner, drinking his second large beer and finishing his lobster… it hit him that he was having possibly the best night of his entire life.

Just then, Alice grabbed his hand, yanking him up out of his seat and dragging him reluctantly with a dash to the back of the restaurant. When they came to a stop in front of the band, Alice began to gyrate and dance to the music, causing Simon to blush immediately and turn back towards the table in desperate retreat. But the young woman wasn't having it. She snatched him from behind and spun him back towards her, laughing and clasping his hands with hers.

Oh shit. Simon had no idea what to do. A dancer he was not, yet he now stood in the middle of the restaurant with what felt like a million eyes on him.

"Just relax," Alice said with a smile.

Simon looked deeply at her. At her eyes… at her smile… at her neck… at her breasts… at her rolling hips… at her feet moving just a few inches from his. Simon's skin went flushed, and he felt something burning inside of him. This is really happening. He slowly began to dance with her.

Alice was at least ten years younger than Simon, and feeling her body as they danced made his blood run hot and his arms quiver. The two laughed as she led him, swinging him around and shaking their legs to the music. Soon, however, Simon began to panic. Overwhelmed by Alice's sensuality and his own self-consciousness, his face glowed red as the devil, and he took off running towards his seat in surrender. Alice grabbed onto his shirt, trying riotously to keep him on the dance floor—but Simon just dragged her along behind him.

When finally he reached the safety of his chair, Simon let out a massive sigh of relief. Thank god, I made it.

Jack, who had since joined the table of locals and was in an animated conversation with them, was next on Alice's list. She yanked him up and pulled him happily to the back of the room, where the two began to dance. The local men at the table beside Simon patted him on the back, seemingly taking pity on him for his terrible dancing. Simon raised his bottle at them, and sat back, sweat-soaked with a strained laugh. As he watched Jack and Alice dance frenetically to the primal rhythm of the Garifuna music, Simon sipped easily on his beer and smiled, taking it all in. I can't believe I'm here right now.

A few minutes later, Jack broke away from Alice and thrust into a crazy, bird-like dance, flapping his arms wildly and strutting around the bar in circles, his craning head bobbing and pecking to the music. The band began to laugh at the crazy gringo, as did the locals sitting next to Simon. What an idiot! But Simon couldn't help but laugh along. Though he found Jack eminently childish and ridiculous in so many ways, the guy had an unbridled fearlessness about him that Simon and others couldn't help but appreciate. He's acting like a fool, but he doesn't look foolish… just happy.

Simon wished in his heart that he had the impulsiveness and confidence of a Jack, and bemoaned his own conservative, long-game approach to life. Maybe someday.

For a long while, Simon sat savoring the moment and the company he was in. He knew that this world was unlike any he'd ever experienced before, or maybe ever would again.

An hour later, the threesome stumbled from the bar, laughing and chatting as they made their way through the village. When they reached the beach and started walking back towards the resort, the moon shone above them, casting an icy blue glow across the sand. The halcyon waves lapped in white ripples beside them as Jack put his arm around a cock-eyed Simon. "Glad ya came out with us tonight, amigo," Jack said.

"I'm glad I came out too," replied Simon, stumbling a bit and putting his arm around Jack to stabilize himself. "Really glad."

"Hey, so you have a car, right?" asked Jack.

"Yeah, wrhy?" slurred Simon.

"You wanna go somewhere really, really… REALLY cool tomorrow?"

"Of course, man, I love really, really, really cool somewheres."

Simon faltered from under Jack's arm and nearly spilled onto the sand as the group approached the resort stairs. The smooth sounds of Jimmy Buffet echoed as always from the pool bar.

"Great! Meet us here at one o'clock then," Jack continued, chuckling.

"I think it's one now, man," Simon said, glancing at his watch.

Jack and Alice snickered at their sloshed friend, Simon joining in, too tipsy to realize why.

"Haha, okay man. Well, we'll see ya here at one IN THE AFTERNOON then? Bring your passport—you'll need ID. It's gonna be life-changing," Jack added, pointing at Simon and watching as Simon seemed to comprehend. More or less, anyway.

"Cool! See you then!" Simon hollered, slogging up the stairs. When he reached the halfway point, he turned and stumbled back down to hug Alice.

Unable to keep from laughing, she hugged him in return.

"Good night Alice," he said.

"Good night Simon," she replied with a smile.

Simon wobbled back up the stairs, past the few ogling guests lingering at the pool bar, and took the elevator up to his room. Barely. Within seconds he'd collapsed onto his bed in a heap, staring up at the ceiling, smiling and reveling in the night and his new friends.

"I can't believe I freakin' danced," he muttered to himself, laughing in the darkness.

Though he was drunker than Cooter Brown, Simon could barely sleep that night. Thoughts of all that had happened swirled in his head. And the room, regrettably, swirled around that.

CHAPTER 25

For hours, the sun glinted through the windows.

Crippled by a fogged mind and a parched palate, Simon eventually dragged himself from bed on a desperate expedition towards the toilet. A grueling and arduous ten-foot journey that nearly defeated him. This was his Everest. *I'm never drinking again…*

An hour later, after a good deal of staring in the mirror, trying to convince himself he had what it took, Simon summoned the courage to look death in the face and embark on an even greater and more daunting campaign. *You got this.*

When he finally reached the resort restaurant, he let out a deep sigh of relief. *I knew you had it in you.*

With his body on autopilot, Simon wearily replicated his ritual of the five mornings prior, robotically moving through the buffet assembly line, collecting a plate each of eggs, waffles and ham with cream sauce. Then, just as he'd done the five mornings prior, he set about shoveling the bounteous portions into his mouth at near breakneck speed.

Only this time, something was curiously different. *Why doesn't this taste as good?*

Simon took a few more calculated bites, holding the morsels in his mouth long enough to let his taste buds fully register the various flavors within. The eggs sure tasted like eggs. The waffles were indeed waffles, and the ham was undeniably ham.

Simon recalled with longing the glorious meal he'd eaten the previous night at Tulu's place. *That stewed chicken was outstanding. I wonder what the local people eat for breakfast? Lobster?... Coconut rice?... Those banana thingys?* His mouth salivated, just thinking about it. *I wonder if Tulu is off fishing for lobster right now? That would be SO incredible.*

The previous night had blazed an indelible imprint on Simon. For almost an hour, he sat in the restaurant, lost in thoughts of a distant world, less than a mile away, yet so vastly removed from the one he now resided in. He glanced at his watch. It was only 10:30 a.m. *Damnit.*

For the remainder of the morning, Simon tried valiantly to entertain himself, flipping through the TV channels, going for a stroll on the beach and dallying about the pool, all the while counting down the minutes until one o'clock.

When the hour of their rendezvous finally arrived, Simon hurried down to the beach, fervent with anticipation. He scoured the sand around the resort but soon realized Jack and Alice were nowhere to be found. *Just be patient. They'll come.* Simon wanted to believe it, but optimism had let him down far too many times. Taking a seat on the steps, he waited for thirty minutes with no sign of the young couple. After a while, his excitement waned, and a far too familiar feeling of rejection began to cloud his psyche. He had all but lost hope when he noticed a pair of people emerging from the woods down the beach and turning his way. Simon gave a wide smile. *It's Jack and Alice.* They were actually coming for him.

As the couple approached, Simon waved and walked briskly towards them.

"*Hola amigo*! Sorry, we're late," Jack hollered as he drew near.

"*Hola*, no problem," responded Simon, restraining how he really felt. He gave Alice a hug and Jack a handshake.

"Ready to go?" asked Jack, a backpack slung over his shoulder.

"Definitely."

As they began to walk towards the parking lot, Jack suddenly blurted out, "I'm drivin'!" and took off running across the sand, hollering with his arms waving in the air.

"What the hell?!" yelled Alice as she and Simon hooted and then bolted after him in hot pursuit.

It was only one, maybe two minutes long, but in that fleeting moment Simon spent with Alice, chasing Jack across the resort grounds… past the pool, past several gawking guests and through the courtyard…the three of them laughing hysterically in the aureate sunshine and the sea breeze… his heart nearly exploded with happiness. And ten minutes later, as they drifted westward down the Hummingbird Highway, the midday sky shining blue and bright above the open road ahead, Simon leaned back in the passenger seat, envisioning a mélange of potential destinations he might soon see with his new friends. Villages, beaches, mountains, the possibilities were endless. It didn't matter where they were going, as long as it was together.

"So, where are we heading?" asked Simon.

"You'll see when we get there. It's a secret," replied Jack with a devilish grin.

I can't believe I let Jack drive.

***

As the car rambled on down the road, Simon rattled off a myriad of questions to the couple about their lives back home and what had led them to Belize. He listened intently as Alice laid it all out for him: how over the summer, the pair had worked various part-time jobs in Colorado while fashioning a plan to travel throughout the fall and into the winter. As soon as they'd hit their target number, they'd hopped on the first plane they could find headed to Cancun and began their journey south.

Though the idea of working for the sole purpose of funding travel was a bizarre concept to Simon, he was fascinated by a life path so dissimilar to his own. They were not him—and he loved that about them. It wasn't long, however, before his inquisitive nature got the best of him. Through his incessant questioning of their "careers" and what they were going to do when they returned to civilization, Simon unknowingly struck a nerve.

"But, I mean, what is your plan long term?" he asked for the umpteenth time.

Finally, a supremely rankled Alice snapped. "We just had jobs, not careers Simon!" she asserted. "And we're not goin' back yet, so we'll figure that out when the time comes!"

Her exasperated words hit Simon like a hammer, and the car fell silent save for the hum of the tires on the tarmac below. Simon knew exactly how he must have sounded. Like a nagging parent. Regret stung in his belly like poison as he hastily tried to backtrack. "Wait, I didn't mean it like that," he sputtered. "I mean, I admire like crazy what y'all are doin' guys... Sorry... I'm SO sorry if it didn't sound that way...I really wish I could do what y'all are doing." The words emanating from his mouth felt feeble and inadequate. He hoped for a positive response, but none came. As the strained silence stretched on, finally, Jack came to his rescue.

"Simon, I think ya just have to look at the world a bit differently," he said. "There's a great quote by Tolkien, it's actually one of my personal faves. It goes, '*Not all those who wander are lost*'... and you know what? I believe that wholeheartedly, man...." Jack turned to Simon and smiled. "*Not all those who wander are lost*, my friend. Remember those words."

Simon stared at Jack and considered his words. Specifically, he considered them a bunch of hippie phooey. *Tolkien? Seriously, you're ACTUALLY quoting the Hobbit guy, now?*

It was the kind of thing the New Hampshire *long hair* had been spewing regularly, and though Simon liked Jack, he felt it was in his Southern heritage to ignore such malarkey. *Dad woulda certainly laughed at this man. And grandpa, whoa nelly, grandpa woulda...*

It was in that instant that something odd popped into Simon's brain. A vastly different quote, but one oddly relevant in the moment. *The enemy of my enemy is my friend.*

Throughout Simon's childhood, he'd grown to loath his grandfather. The man had scared the living hell out of him as a young boy, and Simon recalled how years after the old man's death, he'd finally realized the guy had just been a dyed-in-the-wool racist sonofabitch. Simon had dedicated himself to never becoming anything like him—and though he had succeeded, for the most part, somehow, sometimes the tempestuous old-timer's poisonous words of distrust and bigotry still occupied a dark corner in the deep recesses of Simon's mind. *The enemy of my enemy is my friend.* Simon hated the vitriolic old man almost as fiercely as the old man would have despised Jack and his romanticized outlook on life. Maybe that meant something. Simon decided then and there to try and start listening to Jack. Not just hearing him, but attempting, however difficult, to listen to him.

"Not all those who wander are lost, eh? Well, I guess that's a pretty interesting mantra." Biting his lip, Simon leaned over his shoulder and spoke softly to Alice. "I'm really sorry if I insulted you, Alice," he said.

She smiled her perfect smile at him and began to rub his shoulders from the back seat. "Oh, don't worry about it, Simon, we still love you," she said warmly.

Jack just laughed.

And yet, despite Alice's jesting tone, the words fell upon Simon with a profound impact. It had been an eternity, decades even since anyone had uttered such words to him. Though he was perfectly aware that Alice hadn't meant them literally, it filled him with emotion to hear them.

***

They entered the town of San Ignacio around 3 o'clock. *Cayo,* as the locals call it.

"Is this where we're headed?" asked Simon.

"Nope, just a little further," Jack replied, darting Simon a devious smile that made his skin crawl.

Contriving a smirk in return, Simon had begun to wonder with ever greater urgency *where* in fact, they were going. Glancing at his watch, he realized how quickly time had passed, and it occurred to him that he never would have let someone else drive his car before, so why had he done so now?

Twenty minutes later, as they arrived at a heavily militarized checkpoint at the Guatemala border, and several camo-clad soldiers approached their car windows, Simon's mild sense of curiosity and concern quickly turned into something a whole lot stronger indeed.

CHAPTER 26

"Hey Jonah, how are you, son?" Jim Shaughnessy's voice crackled through the earpiece.

"Hey dad, things are going just fine. Been a lot of driving but I'm getting used to it. How about you guys?"

"Oh, we're fine too, I'm giving a talk at the University tomorrow about trade sanctions, but besides that, same as usual. Where are you?"

"Hold on a second dad, let me pull over so we can talk."

Jonah swiftly steered his van to the road's edge and came to a stop. He sat his phone on the seat, frantically grabbing a map from the glove box and counting days on his fingers. He picked up the phone again. "Yeah, so I left Voyageurs this morning and just crossed into North Dakota…

Should make it to Roosevelt National Park by tonight and will spend a few days there before heading to Yellowstone. So far, so good." Jonah's head hung low.

"I heard you guys got quite a bit of snow up there yesterday. Your camping equipment holding up?"

Jonah paused. *Shit, I should have looked at the weather.* "Yeah, I'm fine. Freezing up here, though!" Jonah squinted and looked out of his open window. Outside, the sun was shining, and the temperature was a balmy seventy degrees. A green sign a few yards ahead welcomed him to *Norfork, Arkansas, Population 502.* Nearly a thousand miles south of where he was supposed to be. "Well, dad, I'm sorry to make this call so short, but I really gotta get going if I'm gonna get my tarp down and set up my tent by sundown."

"Okay, well, maybe we can talk again tomorrow, and you can chat with your mother?"

Jonah knew this wouldn't be a possibility. *Dammit, what do I say?* "So, dad… I'm…I'm probably going to be out of cell range for a few days, so why don't we just plan on talking next week, okay? I'll call you, okay?"

Jonah waited for a response.

After a short silence, Jim spoke. "Okay, Jonah, we'll talk next week… Sorry to bother you."

"Bye, dad," Jonah said, hanging up the phone with a deep sigh.

***

A few minutes later, Jonah crossed the boundary into Arkansas' Buffalo National River Wilderness Area. Together with the abutting Leatherwood Wilderness Area of the Ozark National Forest, the two vast tracts formed one of the largest and most remote wilderness systems in the eastern US. And as Jonah pressed on through the sprawling wooded terrain, he knew at once that his research had paid off. *This is perfect.* With just a smattering of maintained trails in the southernmost part of the region, Jonah could see that he'd have most of the 40,000 acres of woodlands to lose himself in. So, deeper into the wild, he drove.

A half-hour passed without him seeing another vehicle. After a while, Jonah pulled over and retrieved from his bag a laminated topo map on which he'd marked several roads and locations throughout the wilderness. He positioned himself on the map. *There we are.* And then still deeper into the backcountry, he went.

Soon, Jonah turned the steering wheel sharply and veered the van off onto an unmarked dirt road cutting through the forest towards his chosen destination. The leaves and branches scattered on the path reminded him why he'd selected this specific track when he'd discovered it on a Google satellite image months ago. Probably once an old logging or fire road, now the narrow route was essentially a road to nowhere. *Nobody goes this way... All according to plan.* He knew this was one of the most isolated parts of the Ozarks and the ideal location for his next test phase.

Twenty minutes later, he arrived at a set of coordinates he'd marked for himself on the map and steered off the "road" and into the forest.

***

Another hour later, and Jonah was ready. In the window of his locked van hung a sign reading *Back in 5-6 days. Off camping. Jonah. Nov. 3.*

He maneuvered into his all-terrain wheelchair and looked out at the sprawling forest in front of him. The chair, developed by MIT engineers for use in the third world, was made primarily of inexpensive mountain bike parts and required Jonah to push levers on the sides forward and backward to move, rather than grabbing onto traditional handrims. The ratcheting levers made for significantly higher torque to get over rough terrain or through mud, and vastly more speed on flat ground. Jonah had added several of his own modifications and refinements to the chair as well. On the back, he now hung his camping pack, a sealed food storage cylinder, and a custom quiver for easy access to his carbon-fiber telescoping pole saw—the "Pathmaker" as he'd affectionately come to call it. Bracketed to the sides of the seat sat a pair of high intensity LED flashlights and an umbrella mount for rainy days. A flip-out tray table, a waterproof document pocket and several other small storage pouches completed Jonah's masterpiece of engineering. *Four years in the making; let's see how she holds up.*

Jonah put away his GPS, flipped open the table and pulled out his laminated topo map, tritium lensatic compass and coordinate scale protractor. *Time to go old school.* Using the precision tools, he placed himself precisely on the map.

Okay, here we go.

CHAPTER 27

Simon began to panic as they approached the border gate, glaring up through the windshield at an armed soldier staring back at them from a watchtower. "Are we crossing the border?" he exclaimed.

"Yeah, ya brought ya passport, right?" Jack said with a nonchalant smirk.

"Yeah, but why the hell are we going into Guatemala?!"

"Well, then great!" replied Jack, ignoring Simon's question entirely and putting his hand on the spiraling Texan's shoulder.

Simon's mind erupted. *Isn't it dangerous in Guatemala? I remember that whole CIA guerilla war thing in the '90s, but are they still around? Are Jack and Alice kidnapping me?! I don't speak any Spanish! Where are we going?!*

Simon glanced over his shoulder and locked eyes with Alice in the back seat, dread on his face and perspiration dripping from his brow.

Reaching out, Alice put her arm on his shoulder. "Darling, just trust us," she said.

Her voice was calm and gentle, her touch soothing.

Simon grinned as best he could and turned back around.

The Guatemalan border guards just outside their windows wore heavy green fatigues and had automatic rifles draped low over their shoulders. As one of the men seized the passports from the three *gringos*, Jack spoke briefly to them in broken Spanish, his ability to communicate only mildly easing Simon's consternation. When the soldiers finally returned the booklets, Simon located the newest stamp in his passport and ran his fingers over it. *Guatemala? Unbelievable.*

"¡*Vamos*!" hollered the camo-clad guard, startling Simon and waving them through with a flick of the hand. Simon stared ahead through the glass, struggling to grasp the reality of the situation he now found himself in.

***

As Jack drove Simon's car onward through Belize's far less developed neighbor, it didn't take long for the world outside their windows to radically change. Simon's trepidation grew, as just a few miles after crossing the border, a shocking level of poverty pervaded the rolling, verdant countryside. *Good lord.*

Vaguely similar to what Simon had seen in Mexico, the landscape was lusher and far more mountainous. The corrugated steel shacks and dilapidated buildings scattered across the Guatemalan frontier revealed a hardship that made Simon shudder. Emaciated children in stained, tattered clothing sat on the muddy ground beside the road and stared up at Simon's car as they passed by. Scraggly dogs roamed in packs everywhere or slept half-dead in the shade of sapodilla trees. The car rolled past military post after military post as jeeps packed with rifle-toting soldiers passed them on the road. Simon stared out the window at the third world passing by and longed for an anti-anxietal to take the edge off. Or better yet, to be back in his hotel room at the Sunshine Bay. *What have I gotten myself into?*

Minutes stretched into hours as they continued on through the Guatemalan countryside—the sun setting over the hilltops, taking with it any final traces of Simon's dwindling patience. Alice was issuing meticulous directions to Jack from a map she'd spread out on the back seat, yet Simon still had no clue where they were headed and had long since given up broaching the subject. After a while, he decided to turn to the only thing he had left in his emotional quiver. Trust.

Shortly after dusk, Jack turned the car off the main highway and onto a dirt road, vanishing through the darkness into a dense jungle. As they crept forward, slowly, slowly, through the black, wooded trace, Simon's brain immediately turned to scenes from out of a horror movie. *They're going to kill me now. Bury me in this jungle and steal my identity. Maybe they're part of a cult or something. Guatemalan devil worshippers?!*

Just then, out of the seemingly impenetrable darkness, the distant outline of a small house emerged in a forest clearing ahead. A yellow lantern glowed dimly above the front door. Jack eased the car right up to the structure and then brought it to a lumbering halt in a small grassy field.

He killed the engine. Silence.

Glancing over to Simon in the shadows, he grinned. "I think we're here. Wait a minute."

The distraught Texan smiled awkwardly back at Jack, straining to appear cool and calm, though Jack's use of the words '*I think*' had started a new cascade of fear in Simon's mind.

The driver's door creaked as Jack stepped out into the night and walked slowly towards the front porch of the little house nestled in the dark jungle. Simon watched transfixed through the dusty windshield glass as Jack ambled past the headlight beams towards the front door. The silence in the car was agonizing.

What... is going... to happen...?

Jack stepped to the top-lit doorway and knocked.

Simons pulse quickened.

After a few moments, the door opened.

For several long seconds, Simon squinted, attempting to discern what was happening—yet the darkness and sooty glass obscured his vision.

A minute or two later, Jack returned. "Let's go," he said, snatching his bag from the back seat and motioning for Simon and Alice to follow.

Simon paused. *Fuck.*

As Simon stepped from the car into the hot black night, he couldn't help but fear the distinct possibility of an imminent hammer blow to the head, maneuvering himself into a position where he could keep an eye on both Jack and Alice.

Then, without warning, Jack killed the headlights.

Simon stood drowning in nebulous blackness, the sound of crickets surrounding him.

The car door shut nearby. *Oh shit.*

A flashlight clicked on a few feet ahead of him. "Follow me," said Jack.

The pounding of Simon's heart and the gasps of his rapid breathing joined the nocturnal sounds of the jungle around him. Following the ring of light across the clearing, he braced himself for an imminent attack. What a fool he'd been, he thought—following these two strangers out into the middle of the Guatemalan jungle. Using the beautiful Alice to lure him out here seemed so damn obvious now. Simon gritted his teeth and braced for it. *Just finish me quickly.*

Then, from out of the void, he heard Jack whispering something to Alice. Perhaps it was the go-ahead command for *OPERATION: MURDER SIMON AND LEAVE HIM IN THE GUATEMALAN JUNGLE,* he thought. But, after a second, he realized it sounded much more like: "She said we can stay here for the night."

Simon froze in his tracks. "Wait. What?! We're staying here?!" he whisper-yelled to Jack. "I thought we were just goin' somewhere for the day, Jack! What's going on?!"

"I never said that," Jack replied with a dry laugh from the pitch abyss. "Don't worry, though…" he whispered. "I'll pay for the room... It's only nine dollars!" And with that, Jack and Alice began to laugh wildly in the darkness.

Simon stood motionless, listening.

They were not going to kill him on this day.

Simon sarcastically joined in the laughter in response. "Ha, ha, ha, it's not that funny guys," he said, causing the couple to laugh even harder.

A few seconds later, the trio ducked through the door and into a modest home. "This is Anita," Jack said, introducing Alice and Simon to the woman of the house. The squat lady had a kind and hearty disposition, and her dark skin and round face told of indigenous heritage.

Giving a courteous nod, she led them through the room to the back of the structure. When they arrived at their bedroom, Simon winced at the meager and sparsely decorated lodgings. A thin double mattress and an even thinner twin mat lay on the floor of the empty, planked room. The only other object, an aged electric, oscillating fan, sat in the corner.

"Dibs on the big bed," Simon joked and launched himself with a thud onto the hard 'mattress'. A wave of unexpected pain shot through his side. "Oh my god, that's hard!" he exclaimed, sending the other two bursting into laughter as he rubbed his shoulder.

The room was more or less barren and hardly clean, but after a few moments, Simon began to feel surprisingly okay with it.

Anita prepared them a dinner of some beans and rice with tortillas and fried plantains, which they ate graciously at a table in the front room.

"She's not going to join us?" Simon asked.

"No, it's only six, and she'll eat dinner with her family when they get home later. We have to go to sleep soon though—we're gettin' up at 4 a.m. tonight," Jack said, shoveling a tortilla full of beans into his mouth.

"4 a.m.?!" Simon shouted, feigning anger but guffawing at the preposterousness of this affair. "I'm on vacation, man!" he chuckled, launching the three of them into fits yet again.

At dinner's conclusion, they helped Anita clear the table and retired to their room for the night. Simon crawled under the threadbare sheet atop the twin mat and rested his head upon the stiff pillow. As he lay there watching Jack and Alice getting into bed beside him, an unexpected feeling began to swell inside him. For some peculiar reason, even though he no longer had his sumptuous, pillow-top mattress, his 1,000 thread count bed sheets and his flat-screen television, Simon felt surprisingly comforted. More so even. Perhaps because he was no longer alone, here in this rustic room with his new friends. Or maybe, it was because he was off on a bizarre adventure to parts unknown. Or something else entirely. He wasn't sure *why* he felt so good, but it didn't matter. He just did.

As he, Jack and Alice chatted in the dark, Simon smiled happily, hidden in the blackness. He was reminded of a time long ago when he went camping as a child. When Simon, his brother and his father had lied huddled together in their tent, talking about the wilderness and telling wild stories and jokes, and inevitably ended up staying awake half the night. Now, in a small house in the jungles of Guatemala, he found himself laughing and joking with Alice and Jack and endeavoring to somehow fall asleep at 7 p.m. It was a situation as improbable as it was gratifying.

After an hour or two of Alice repeatedly chastising Jack and Simon and telling them to shut up so she could sleep, Simon finally closed his eyes and drifted off with a contented smile on his face, unlike any he'd known in years.

CHAPTER 28

At 4 a.m., the alarm began to blare—and by 4:15 a.m., they were in the car, once again driving through the black woods of northern Guatemala. Simon slept in the back seat, having barely made it to the car before collapsing. Alice, meanwhile, sat shotgun, her headlamp fixated on the map in her lap as she guided Jack through the lightless, winding backroads.

When Simon finally awoke, he lurched up, disoriented, and stared out the window at the dark forest surrounding him. The car was parked, and Jack and Alice were gone. *Where the hell am I?*

Clack! Clack! Clack! A loud knocking clapped from behind him, launching Simon from his seat with a high-pitched yelp. Spinning around, he found Jack and Alice outside the car's side window laughing at him through the glass. "Let's go, Simon!" Jack called to him. Simon offered his middle finger and a contemptuous smile in retort.

Stumbling from the car, listless and groggy, Simon made it to his feet and surveyed his peculiar surroundings. He found himself standing on the edge of a sprawling swath of cracked concrete, scarcely illuminated by the moon and the luminescence of a solitary streetlamp. The lot was separated from the surrounding forests by a tall wooden fence with an open steel gate nearby.

"What is this place?" he asked.

"This way," Jack hollered.

Glancing over, Simon found his friends already wandering through the gate and onto a path headed into the woods. *Seriously?!*

There is dark, and then there is *jungle dark,* Simon would soon discover. He had never experienced the latter until this moment. The faint light of the moon and stars were no match for the impenetrable, intertwining treetops that veiled the black landscape below. Simon followed the pair closely, dreadful of what might occur should he become separated from his friends out here. If it weren't for the amber glow of Alice's headlamp illuminating the dirt trail ahead, and the flickering circle of Jack's flashlight hitting the surrounding trees, Simon would be completely blind.

"So, are you going to tell me where we're going yet?" he asked.

"You'll see," Alice replied.

Slowly, Simon gathered his wits about him, and his senses gradually sharpened. As they pushed further into the forest, he started to delineate the vague outlines of large structures amidst the forest around him. *What are those?* He thought. Yet the pitch-black forest offered no answers. It's only response, the wild chorus of countless insects and animals emanating from the surrounding darkness. He hastened his pace to stay close to Jack and Alice.

The white noise cacophony of bug and bird sounds seemed to grow louder with every step, until suddenly, a collection of thundering, beast-like roars that cut through the jungle, striking fear deep in Simon's soul and stopping him dead in his tracks.

WHAT THE HELL WAS THAT?!

The horrid howls sounded some way off in the distance but were unlike anything Simon had ever heard before. His imagination raced through a myriad of bloodthirsty creatures, both real and fictitious, lurking, gathering strength in the darkness and preparing to pounce. He rushed ahead and placed himself between Alice and Jack. "Did you guys hear that?!" he begged.

No response.

I hate you people.

Five more minutes of slow marching through the jungle would pass before Alice turned back to Simon and whispered, "This is it."

Simon, growing weary of the games, erupted. "This is *what*?!" he belted. But again, he received no reply. Frustrated, he cast his eyes over Alice's shoulder and observed, ahead of them, the forest separating and allowing a pool of starlight to filter through the trees. Within this space sat a weathered wooden staircase, clinging to the side of a massive, vine-covered stone structure. As they approached, Simon looked up to see the stairs and the wall rising high above them and disappearing into the forest canopy. *Jesus Christ.*

The three began to climb. The stairs creaked as they wound their way up through the trees and into the dense foliage. Simon grew more and more anxious the higher they went, the squeaking boards under his feet calling into question the solidity of the rickety old stairway. *Death by plummet* seemed like a gloomy way to go.

As they climbed higher, Simon passed his hand along the stone structure beside him, and the aged rock felt rough and cold against his fingertips. He could tell whatever this was, it was ancient, yet in the glancing beam of Jack's flashlight, it was impossible to distinguish its shape or purpose.

Up, up, up they went. Rising high into the darkness.

After a draining, ten-minute ascent, they finally breached the tree canopy and reached the structure's zenith.

The sky above them glowed a deep indigo in the pre-dawn hour, speckled with hundreds of blue stars.

The three plopped down wearily upon a large stone slab and gazed out over the treetops in the first inklings of twilight. Simon squinted, trying to comprehend where he was and what he was perched atop. All he could distinguish, however, was the faint, growing impression of a distant horizon line.

A few solemn seconds passed, when suddenly, the roaring howls of the crepuscular creatures echoed through the night air once more. This time, they sounded much closer. Simon trembled with dread. "What in God's name is that?" he whispered to Jack—terrified to hear the reply. He was sure that Jack would say *lions* or *dragons* or something of similar malevolence.

"Sounds like demons, right?" Jack said with a smirk.

I hadn't thought of demons. Is it Demons?!

"Yeah… it's horrifying," replied Simon.

"Well, don't worry, it's not demons," Jack pronounced calmly and turned away.

Simon stared at him blankly, waiting for Jack to continue—but no more words were spoken.

I think I'm going to kill this guy.

Several more minutes passed, and as they sat there, the swelling sounds of the jungle hailed the dawn of a new day. The world around them began to glow scarlet with the first blush of morning, and the horizon seemed to foretell the sun's imminent arrival as a radiant fiery aurora undulated far off at the skyline.

It was at this moment that Simon noticed something bizarre emerging from the darkness. There, amidst the never-ending sea of treetops glinting gold in the morning glow, stood what appeared to be several giant black megaliths, towering over the trees below. "What are those?" he muttered to himself.

Jack and Alice remained silent. And as the sun finally breached the tree line, its warm beams illuminating Simon's face and the world, the massive structures burst ablaze with an orange luminosity. Simon immediately recognized what they were, and where he now was.

Oh my god, they're… pyramids!

In every direction, the monumental stone temples rose from the treetops like volcanic spires rising from a grassy plain.

"Ho…ly…shit," Simon breathed.

Glancing downwards towards his feet, he was stunned to find that he was sitting atop one of the ancient, stepped structures. Its massive, terraced stone base, hidden in the jungle far below him.

"Where… are we?" he whispered to Alice, quivering with awe and dumbfounded by the enormity of what he was witnessing.

"This is Tikal, the ancient city of the Mayas," she responded, smiling. "You're sittin' on a temple that was built two thousand years ago, man," she whispered, placing her hand on Simon's shoulder.

Simon looked down again at the carved stone structure below him with building reverence.

"Pretty cool, huh?" Jack added.

Simon glanced up and nodded, stunned. *Two THOUSAND years?* He could barely fathom such an ancient time. *The Alamo was the oldest thing I've ever seen, but shit, it's not even two HUNDRED years old.*

Simon rubbed his head in disbelief as the threesome sat quietly in the gleam of the dawning sun. Slowly, Simon's mind slipped off into daydream ideations of the ancient Mayan civilization that populated these lands two millennia ago. *Two thousand years ago.* He began to ponder: if he'd lived amongst the Maya two thousand years ago, what would he have been? Perhaps a high priest, tasked with charting the stars and the heavens and making groundbreaking astronomical calculations, changing humankind's celestial understanding of the universe forever.

Or, maybe he would have been a human sacrifice to the Gods because of his lack of physical size and strength.

He was leaning towards the latter but spent several minutes trying to convince himself of the former.

For the first time in his life, he began to question his own relevance in the universe. How, he wondered, could they have built something so extraordinary, so grandiose, so astounding, two thousand years before the discovery of electricity? They had no trucks to help them. No cranes or computers. Just their hands, their brains and their unyielding will to do something incredible. They had envisioned something so much grander than the world they lived in and had dedicated themselves to making it a reality. They had decided to do it... and so they did it. The revelation was deeply humbling for Simon. Tikal's magnificence made him feel small and insignificant in its presence. A mere scrap on the cutting room floor of history. *What have I ever built?*

The question rattled around in his brain and weighed heavily on his being. The answer was painfully obvious, though. *Absolutely fucking nothing.* Simon continued to scour his mind for a shred of something, some achievement to hang on to and grasp. But the truth was…he hadn't *built* anything. He hadn't built relationships with his family, women or friends. He hadn't built a home, a family of his own or even a life for himself outside of his work. And he sure as hell hadn't built a 300-foot-tall step pyramid in the middle of the jungle.

But then he saw it. A shard of splintered stone lying beside him on the slab he was sitting on. Picking it up, he held it in his hand and stared at it. *This piece of stone might have last been held by a Mayan worker. Now I'M holding it.* Though it weighed only a pittance, the significance of the small shard in his hand felt massive. *Maybe I am a part of history.*

Simon had never considered himself part of anything larger than his paltry life back in San Antonio. Never part of a world beyond Texas, or a time greater than the present. And yet, at that moment, sitting amidst the scattered remains of this once mighty civilization, he felt somehow attached to it. His mere presence here, both physically and emotionally, made him part of the same reality. Part of the same history. Part of the same world. And perhaps, by his presence alone, he might still have the capacity to change that world. *What COULD I build?*

At once, his mind churned with a profound burst of optimism and inspiration. As more loud howls echoed across the valley, Simon paid them no mind. Instead, he looked out at the vastness of the world from his perch atop the ancient pyramid, and felt the stirrings of a belief in a new and wide-open future growing within him. *If people without electricity could build this, anything is possible.*

"Howler monkeys," a voice suddenly said from behind him.

Simon turned as Jack walked over and wedged himself between Simon and Alice, putting an arm over their shoulders. "They're howler monkeys, Simon," he repeated.

Simon smiled. "Of course, they are." *I knew they weren't demons.*

"So, this is pretty great, huh?" asked Jack, with impeccably delivered understatement.

Simon smiled and put his arm around Jack and looked over at his two friends sitting beside him. "Thanks for bringing me here, guys," he said, his voice trembling with palpable earnestness.

Jack and Alice smiled back at him.

"Really," Simon continued.

The three of them sat for a while in silence, gazing out at the sunrise over the jungle and the remnants of the great Mayan civilization. For the rest of the morning, they wandered through the rocky ruins and, by midday, they had returned to Simon's car and were heading back towards Belize.

At sundown, with Simon driving and Jack and Alice passed out in the back seat of the car, they pulled up to the Sunshine Bay Resort. Simon parked in the sandy lot and turned off the ignition. Leaning over the seat, he looked back at the still dozing couple.

He didn't want to wake them up and say goodbye.

CHAPTER 29

That night, after a long hot shower, Simon made his way, once again, to the buffet. The previously satisfying food now tasted bland, and the atmosphere felt dull, repetitive and stale.

When he'd finished eating, he ventured down to the pool bar for a drink and sat for a few minutes taking stock of the hodgepodge of people milling about. Beside him sat two men, of about his age, discussing at length their upcoming family outings to Disney World, and whether upgrading their rooms to suites for an additional $400 a night would be worth it. They concluded that it was. Across the bar, a pair of women were arguing over who made the better handbags, Coach or Chanel, and engaging in quite the spirited debate about it. An older couple sat at a table by the pool in silence, their matching iPads illuminating their emotionless faces.

Simon had a growing suspicion that something was wrong with this scene, but he couldn't quite discern what it was. The smooth tunes of Radio Margaritaville were bringing him to the brink of madness as well.

After twenty minutes of quiet observation, he wandered back to his room and lay in bed, reminiscing about everything that had transpired in the previous forty-eight hours.

It had changed him. He knew it had, but he couldn't explain how.

As he eased off to sleep in the comforting embrace of his pillow-top mattress, the 1000 thread count sheets and the low glow of the flickering flat screen, he longed to be back on the floor of the small room in the little house in the jungle of Guatemala—joking, laughing and telling stories in the dark with his friends.

***

The next morning Simon awoke feeling like a different man. He lay in bed for more than an hour thinking back on his life in San Antonio, his menial job at the firm and the dearth of respect and satisfaction he'd received there. He recalled with profound disappointment how hard he'd labored for so many years. So much unnecessary time and effort, which could have been better used in building lasting friendships and relationships—building a fulfilling life.

He pondered with new clarity the few occasions when he'd met interesting people over the years and how, in the rare instances where there'd been an initial connection, his lack of confidence and fear of rejection had inevitably doomed him. Certainly, they would find something wrong with him, he believed, and that certainty caused him to put off plans with potential new friends until, eventually, the calls stopped altogether. Even his few college friends had long since given up on reaching out to him.

Then, there were his many failed attempts with women. How difficult it had always seemed to put forth a concerted effort into his relationships. *I tried* he'd always told himself, but deep down, he knew he never actually did. He had begun each date with one foot out the door, and had assumed the romance was destined to fail no matter how hard he tried. And so, it did.

He'd never blamed himself, though. His all-consuming job invariably became the scapegoat. The priority it had over the rest of his life controlled it. Yet now, in this lucid state, he realized that he'd been the one to give it that power. *What a fool I've been.*

Simon hadn't realized just how lonely he'd become—until now. The antidepressants and the excessive numbers of hours devoted to work had blinded him from seeing it. So many chances lost, opportunities to connect with women, friends, and maybe even… *his family* missed. He'd never understood the extent to which loneliness had chipped away at his soul. But he was beginning to. *What have I sacrificed so much of my life for?*

As he felt regret and frustration swelling inside him, he remembered the one thing he did have… Thirty-two thousand dollars in savings sitting in a bank account back in Texas. Simon was lousy at many things, but saving money had never been one of them. He'd put aside a chunk of his paycheck for the better part of a decade—all part of his master plan to buy a house and start a family. A dream that he had all but given up on these days.

Simon considered this now, and his mind burst alight with ideas and revelations. Things were changing. He was changing.

If there was ever going to be a time in his life to move in a different direction, this must surely be it. He was thirty-eight, but he still had enough good years left in which to turn things around. He damn sure had the money to make a go of it, and now he had Jack and Alice to show him the way.

***

After breakfast, Simon made his way to the business center in the lobby and drafted a formal letter of resignation. He composed an eloquent email to Ms. Harris that walked a subtle line between respect and disdain and attached his notice of departure. For a good long while, he sat there, staring at the email and began to consider, in his usual methodical way, the pros and cons of what he was doing. *Is this really a good idea?* He questioned. And then catching himself doing it, he grew furious. "Fuck pros and cons," he muttered under his breath and hit the send button with atypical assertion. A wave of relief, excitement and self-respect instantly swept over him like a maelstrom. Freedom mushroomed inside. Freedom to live again.

He stared at the words *MESSAGE SENT* on the screen for some time, smiling. *I really fucking did it. Holy shit, I REALLY FUCKING DID IT!*

There was no going back now.

Simon was about to depart the computer room in desperate need of oxygen when he decided to check his old social network page. He hadn't visited it in at least a year, and he now took a long, depressing look at it.

There wasn't much to see. His last post was dated nearly three years ago and read, "Moving to San Antonio today!" and had been liked by his brother, his mother and his old college friend, Charlie. Three of his 16 *friends*. He remembered how exciting that post had been to him at the time and how it was such important news in his world. Then, he wondered what his life would have been like had he never moved to San Antonio.

Struggling to conceive of any alternate realities beyond that one, he conceded that it had always been his natural path. Besides, it had gotten him to this point, so now wasn't the time for regrets.

Flipping back through previous posts, he found them all equally irrelevant to the universe he now was beginning to see. Simon began to type a new post, thinking, *this one will be a little more interesting.*

Greetings from Central America,

Yes, you read that correctly, and I don't mean the center of America. I'm not in Kansas. I'm in Belize. The little country just south of Mexico. Can you believe it!

Well, those of you who know me are going to read this email and immediately think I've gone crazy. Well let's just put one thing to rest, I'm not. In fact, I don't remember feeling this sane in a long time.

So, I guess I'll just start at the beginning. I know it doesn't sound like something I'd do, but a week ago, I left San Antonio and headed south, crossing the border into northern Mexico. For two days, I drove through a drug war zone, past military soldiers and run-down towns everywhere. I admit I was scared, though not as much as I probably should have been.

Eventually, I reached my destination, Sunshine Bay, Belize, where I spent several wonderful days having fun in the sun. It's so beautiful here I can't even describe it. A few days ago, I had the opportunity to visit a local Garifuna village. While there, I ate spicy chicken and lobster at an incredible restaurant and listened to an amazing local band play drums, conch and the turtle shells. It was unbelievable! Even more unbelievable, I got to dance with a beautiful woman that night. Yeah, you read that right, I danced! It was one of the best meals I've ever eaten and one of the best nights of my life.

The next day I crossed into Guatemala with some friends. While there, I watched the sunrise over the jungle from the top of a Mayan step pyramid in Tikal. It was life changing.

That was yesterday. Now, I have just quit my job. I have no idea what the future will bring, but I'm feeling surprisingly okay about that. I'm starting to think that maybe every day is only as good as you allow it to be, and they might all have the potential to be great ones. That's what I'm hoping anyway. If there's still time for me, I'm going to make the most of it.

All the best, Simon

He hit *post* and stared at the computer screen for a moment reveling in it. The most exciting two days of his life had been the last two, and that was a pretty amazing thing.

CHAPTER 30

Simon dashed from the computer room and hurried down to the beach in search of Jack and Alice. He desperately needed to share with them the news of his resignation and couldn't stop dreaming of where the threesome's adventures might take them next. The beach was humming with a mid-morning crowd, but as Simon wandered up and down, the young couple were nowhere to be found. After a short spell, he gave up in frustration and positioned himself up on the patio, perched beneath an umbrella, with a bird's-eye view of the sand below.

Hours went by, and as he sat poolside watching the day pass by. Encircled by the towering white fortress walls on three sides, Simon felt a peculiar sensation overtaking him. The massive walls surrounding the resort had begun to strike a different chord within him. Since the day he'd arrived, Simon had always felt secure, protected by their presence. Now, however, he found himself feeling trapped within their shelter. *I've got to get out of this place.*

As the sun set and dinnertime arrived, Simon trudged reluctantly back to the hotel's buffet, where he once again endured a heaping helping of humdrum. Though it no longer gave him pleasure, he scarfed down his fill before venturing back out to the beach to resume his search for Jack and

Alice. The moon was illuminating the sand now as the sounds of *Summer Breeze* drifted from the pool bar. Still, there was no sign of Jack or Alice. *Dammit, where could they be?*

Simon stood alone on the dark beach. The sound of the waves rolling in beside him did little to soothe his frustration. Thirty hours had gone by since he'd bid his friends farewell. The beach was desolate now, and he stared off in the direction of the dirt road, contemplating what to do next. After a few moments, he made a decision. *I have to do it.*

"It" was something drastic, something so perilous seeming he would never have dreamt of doing "it" just a few short days ago. He began the walk to Brasilito to see if Jack and Alice were home. Though it would only take fifteen-minutes, the sun had set, he was alone now, and he didn't speak a lick of Garifuna. The whole endeavor seemed daunting. *You can do this.*

Down the beach he traipsed. The further on he went, the darker it grew as the incandescent haze of the resort lighting dwindled behind him. *Maybe I should just turn back.*

Upon reaching the head of the dirt road, Simon turned to face it and stopped. The shadowy pathway ahead disappeared into blackness under the arched canopy of rattling palm leaves. Scattered patches of glowing blue sat like stepping stones where gaps in the tree cover allowed the moonlight to penetrate. Simon took a long deep breath. *Here goes.*

Putting fears aside, he set forth into the woods. Sweat drenched his face as he walked briskly, passing hurriedly by the initial cluster of shacks, through the gnat and mosquito swarms, and finally arriving in the village center. This world seemed entirely different now under the curtain of night. No children playing in the road. No locals outside waving to him. But Simon continued on.

Eventually, he spotted the small, green guesthouse, and a deep sigh of relief flowed from his lungs as he noticed a glimmer of light flickering through the small window. *Thank God they're home.*

Simon approached the door and gave it a sturdy knock. The muffled sound of television noise seeped through the wooden planks. As the door creaked open, Simon spied the diminutive Nina staring up at him, smiling in the entryway. He couldn't help but smile himself. "Hello, Nina," he said with relief.

"*Hola* Simon," she replied, the kindness in her voice doing much to salve his nerves.

"Are Jack and Alice home right now?" he asked.

Nina looked up at him, processing what he'd said. The squat woman's smiling visage slowly melted into a look of apparent confusion. Simon could sense that something was amiss.

"No, sorry. Jack and Alice, they go today," she replied.

The words, though clear, puzzled Simon.

"They went somewhere? Where are they? Will they be home soon?" he asked.

"Nooooo… They *go* today," she replied once again, and taking Simon's hand, led him inside the musty home. As they entered the front room, a heavy-set man and a pair of children sat resting on the sofa, watching television in the otherwise unlit chamber. The three looked up, their faces impossible to distinguish in the dim twinkling TV light, yet Simon could tell they were staring at him, and it made him anxious. Looking to his feet, he followed Nina slowly to the back of the dwelling.

As they entered Jack and Alice's bedroom, Simon could see the bed was now made, and the couple's backpacks were gone. He understood at once what Nina had meant. Jack and Alice… were truly gone, gone. His head fell forward. *I missed them.*

Simon's despondence filled the room. Nina, sensing his anguish, put her arm around his back and led him through the house back to the front door.

When they got there, Simon stood for a minute, stunned.

"Do you know where they went?" he asked.

"*Samook shampay,*" she replied.

The words were unusual and unfamiliar to Simon. He assumed them to be Garifuna or another local dialect.

"'Where… Jack and Alice… go?" he repeated more slowly.

Nina's confused gaze lingered on him. "*Samook shampay,*" she repeated, smiling one last time before slowly and politely pushing him through the door and closing it gently in his face.

Outside, the village was black and silent. Simon stood motionless in the shadowed doorway, contemplating the situation he now found himself in.

Are they really gone? Why would they just leave without saying anything? And what the HELL do I do now? If I spend one more day alone in the Sunshine Bay Resort, I think I might lose my mind. Was quitting my job a HUGE mistake?!

Nausea permeated his gut in rolling pangs as he trudged back towards the resort. The wide-open future he'd foreseen, so luminous and bright just a few hours ago, now appeared as pallid and colorless as ash or fog. Marching on through the woods, Simon stewed in his devastation, growing furious that he'd never been given a chance to say goodbye.

I can't believe they just left me. I should have fucking seen this coming. If I'd been alone, this never would have happened! At least when you have no one, there's no one to do this *to you!*

The curdling pain of his abandonment began to transform within him. After years of mounting insecurities, Simon's reaction to Jack and Alice's leaving was acute. He felt deserted by them, even though he knew it was irrational. Fire burned below his sweating skin as an anger he hadn't felt in more than twenty years—not since his father had died and Jonathan had left him—began boiling to the surface. And as Simon reached the blue barrels of stagnant water, the resident cloud of gnats and mosquitos swarmed and bit at his flesh.

Something awful finally clicked inside of him. A horrid affliction… a lurking shaitan… an internal demon that had remained dormant for years, instantly filled him with a darkness so unyielding and so powerful that he had no choice but to succumb. Bellowing with rage, the normally docile man grabbed at the blue barrels, throwing and kicking them to the ground and spilling their contents onto the brambled earth with a frothy splash.

"Fuck! Fuck! Fuck! Fuck!" he wailed as he toppled barrel after barrel until the last one had fallen.

Simon crashed to his knees in the mud. He pressed his palms to his eyes and struggled for air, whimpering in the darkness as the last gallons of brown water trickled out onto the soil beside him. He glanced up at the wake of his eruption, and immediately realized what a huge mistake he'd made. In the faint patch of moonlight ahead, dozens of large fish lay flopping in the mire, dying in the hot night air. Simon stared at them, stunned. He'd never considered that anything might live inside the murky water, and now he'd inadvertently doomed them all. His mind scrambled for what to do next, yet his body remaining frozen, paralyzed with indecision.

Just then, a yell echoed from behind him, and Simon swung around to find a hoary old local man emerging from a shack nestled in the nearby trees. Hollering at Simon in Garifuna, the man had clearly been awoken by Simon's outburst. Now, as he neared the fallen barrels, he could see the fish flailing and dying at Simon's knees. Shock filled his ancient eyes as he ran towards the scene, causing Simon to jump back with fright from his path. When the feeble elder reached the barrels, he struggled mightily to right them in the darkness.

I should help him! Simon thought. But he did nothing. He just gazed on, dithering in shocked bewilderment at the old man scrambling feverishly to save what was likely his week's catch. It seemed a losing battle, yet the man continued, gathering the fish, tossing them into the barrels with what little water remained. Now and again he glanced up desperately at the trembling gringo

I should help him! Simon thought.

But he didn't.

Instead, he stood and began to run. Down the sandy road and out through the forest… Onto the beach and back towards the resort… Up the stairs and into the embrace of the fortress walls. And when he reached the grassy lawn in the central courtyard, Simon collapsed to the ground, sucking air into his lungs and wiping sweat away from his tearing face. *Jesus, what did I do?!*

The anger he'd felt towards Jack and Alice just moments earlier, had already redirected itself inward. He was furious at himself for his actions and prayed that the old man had somehow saved his fish. *I should have stayed to help him.*

But he hadn't, and Simon cursed his own loathsome cowardice.

***

A short spell passed. Once Simon had caught his breath, he plodded into the lobby tormented and stopped to speak to the concierge at the front desk. "Excuse me, do you know what *samook shampay* means? Is it something in Garifuna?" he asked.

The concierge smiled. "No, sir," he replied.

Simon sighed and, dejected, turned to walk away.

"I mean no, sir... It doesn't mean something in Garifuna..." the concierge continued. "But, I do know what it is."

A twinkle of hope sparkled in Simon's eyes as he swung around towards the man, eyebrows raised. "You do?! What does it mean?!"

"Well, I don't know what it means, exactly... but I know where it is. It's a place pretty far from here in central Guatemala."

"A *place*!?...well how far is it from here?" Simon asked eagerly.

"Very far, sir. Like I said, it's in central Guatemala. In the middle of nowhere from what I've heard. It's supposed to be very beautiful, though."

Without even a thank you, Simon dashed from the desk and into the business center. He began running a series of web searches, trying every phonetic combination of the strange words he could conceive: *samook shampay, shemoock shimpai* and so on, until eventually he found it. "Semuc Champey!" he yelled, startling a woman sitting at an adjacent terminal.

He shrugged off her miffed glares at his sweat and mud-soaked appearance, emboldened in this brief moment of victory. In the corner of the screen, a small image of something resembling a lake appeared. Simon clicked on the adjoining map and spotted the name of a town in its vicinity. "Lanquin," he whispered.

Vaulting out of the business center, Simon sprinted through the lobby and across the parking lot to his waiting car. He unlocked it, sat down in the driver's seat, grabbed his phone out of the glove box and started to feverishly type the words *Lanquin* and *Guatemala* into his GPS app.

"Calculating route," echoed the electronic voice once again through his car, and deeper yet into his heart.

For the next seven long seconds, Simon listened to the sounds of crickets and crashing waves in the distance, lulling him peacefully through his open door. The starry sky shone bright above, and the moon shadows of several palms danced around the lot in the warm breeze. Simon would never forget those seven seconds and the sense of excitement and hope he felt as they passed.

The numbers flashed onto the screen. *426 KM, 6 hours and 43 minutes.*

That's not far at all!

Simon's mind swirled as he raced back towards his room, hatching a plan. It would be a simple one. First thing in the morning, he would drive down to Semuc Champey and try to find Jack and Alice. If he could track them down, he'd at least have a chance to say goodbye. Otherwise, he would spend the night on the lake and drive back the following day. Easy as pie.

That night, as he lay in bed picturing an imminent reunion with Jack and Alice, he grew almost giddy at the thought. *This must have been some sort of mistake. I KNOW what we had was special. Wasn't it? They told Nina where they were going, that must mean something. I can't wait to see them again.* Yet, the Texan was oblivious to what actually lay ahead. What was to come in the next twenty-four hours would prove to be more dangerous than Simon ever could have envisioned. And it would change his perspective on the world forever.

CHAPTER 31

Jonah had laid out the snares the night before in a wide circle surrounding his campsite. He'd had a fair amount of success in the past few days—always managing to catch something for his supper—and had on several occasions been thankful he'd brought along the steak seasoning. Squirrel and cottontail proving to be rather gamey in and of themselves.

But this morning, something was different. As he began to make his rounds, Jonah arrived at the first trap and was disappointed to find it untouched. A nagging growl in his stomach implored him to have more success going forward as it had been almost twenty-four hours since he'd had a proper meal, and the closest river to fish was still nearly two miles off. Jonah collected the first of the snares and proceeded to roll slowly through the woods.

Yet as he reached the second trap, a chill suddenly coursed through him. The mechanism had been activated, but all that remained now was a single ensnared claw and a scattered pool of blood on the dirt. Jonah's eyes darted around, anxious to find the predator that had left behind the gruesome crime scene. But all he could see were trees, shrubs and a thin column of smoke rising from his campfire in the distance. *What did this?* He wondered. But without any other clues, Jonah continued on.

The third trap was empty as well. The fourth the same. But as Jonah approached the fifth trap, the one he'd set a mere ten feet from his tent, Jonah could already see blood splattered across the tree trunk beside it. He froze.

Tilting up the brim of his Tigers hat, he looked over his shoulder and surveyed the scene. Slowly, he reached back, pulling the pole saw from its quiver and unfolding the blade. He clenched it tight in his hands. Without moving, he waited patiently, quietly, anticipating the snapping of a nearby twig or the sound of rustling leaves.

Nothing.

Jonah placed the saw in his lap and moved slowly forward, following the trail of blood from the mangled snare, as it passed within three feet of the back of his tent and off into the woods. Jonah knew there were predators out here: from bobcats to black bears, there were a dozen animals that could do him harm. He felt prepared, but still, this felt a little too close.

He put away the saw and began to pack up his camp. He'd never find out just what had lurked outside his tent in the forest that night.

CHAPTER 32

The Hummingbird Highway is an alluring stretch of scenic road extending west from the Belizean coast, almost to the Guatemala border. As Simon set out that day, he felt confident that he could reach Semuc Champey with relative ease, and the pleasant two-hour drive through the rolling green hills of the Belizean countryside only bolstered that confidence.

Just as he'd done three days earlier with Jack and Alice, Simon soon arrived at the border station near *Cayo*. He'd noticed his company phone had yet to be disconnected, so he downloaded an offline Spanish dictionary app and hoped it could get him through the border. Aided by this and a military officer who spoke rudimentary English, Simon passed through the border station easily and once again found himself driving through the Guatemalan backroads.

It was another small victory for him in these dawning moments of courage. Courage that was about to be tested to its fullest

Shortly after crossing the border, Simon's GPS squawked a fateful command. "Turn left ahead."

It was a harmless seeming instruction at first. However, it wasn't long before Simon would sorely regret having heeded its command. Barely twenty minutes after turning onto the desolate road headed south, things began to transform. The well-maintained tourist road to Tikal that they'd taken just a few days prior, soon became a distant memory. The route Simon now found himself on was something entirely different. This… was a *real* Guatemalan road.

Massive potholes filled with gravel dotted the treacherous track as it climbed precipitously, winding higher and higher into the towering green mountains. Small villages of scrap metal shacks with garbage fires began to appear, peppering the narrow roadside. Mangy dogs and animals wandered on and off the road ahead with indifference. And yet the higher Simon climbed, the further the route somehow managed to deteriorate. A route he now began to call into question. *Jesus, is this REALLY the right way?*

His GPS insisted it was, though Simon was starting to doubt its competency. Deep ruts began to appear every few hundred yards, forcing Simons car to bottom out and scrape hard against the fractured concrete. The paved road disappearing altogether for lengthy stretches, replaced instead with mud and rock-strewn earth. Simon's compact sedan and his nerves rattled louder and louder with every passing minute.

And then… there were the buses. Simon had grown painfully aware of them shortly after crossing the border. Terrifying machines, growling through the mountains with blitzkrieg ferocity. Refashioned from the remains of classic American, yellow school buses, these behemoths no longer cruised lazily along the smooth lanes and avenues of the U.S. from Athens, Georgia to Wala Wala, Washington. Their cushy lives of taking schoolchildren and their lunchboxes to and from class five days a week were now long gone. They had become something else entirely. They were now… Guatemalan *chicken buses*.

It was a metamorphosis that extended far beyond just a simple reassignment of purpose. The second-hand *Bluebirds* had been transformed radically upon arrival in the Central American isthmus, painted top to bottom in a blistering amalgam of vivid, airbrushed patterns and imagery from devils to the Virgin Mary, half-naked women and more. The graphics, combined with dazzling chrome trim and eye-popping neon lighting, made the roving hell-mobiles a cosmic explosion of color, hurtling at breakneck speeds against an otherwise drab backdrop of green and brown terrain. One couldn't possibly miss a chicken bus in Guatemala. It would be like looking to the eastern horizon at dawn and missing the sunrise.

Yet their audaciousness of appearance was only their second most extreme characteristic.

As Simon struggled to maintain his composure on the frighteningly rugged winding road, the mechanical beasts repeatedly flew up on his bumper, air horns blaring, coming within inches of collision. Invariably, they'd swerve to pass him at the last possible moment, forcing oncoming drivers to slam on their brakes or veer off the road to avoid being hit. All those who ventured this way were at the mercy of the devil-may-care drivers who carelessly inflicted their hazardous wrath upon the road.

Such is the law of the chicken bus. Anything goes.

An hour into Guatemala and Simon was already gripping the steering wheel with both hands, white-knuckled and drenched with sweat. The journey up into the mountains was growing ever more harrowing by the minute. The higher he went, the steeper the cliffs beside the road became, and the faster his pulse quickened. He found himself holding his breath at every blind curve—each one bringing unknown potential dangers.

Breathe.

As the road he was driving on began to skirt the edge of a mountain, a staggeringly steep cliff appeared on his left-hand side, plummeting hundreds of feet down into the rocky abyss below.

Breathe.

Across the deep valley, Simon could see a similar twisting road running parallel to his own on an adjacent mountain. It, too, was edged by a 500-foot cliff dropping straight down from the railing-less pavement. From Simon's vantage point, he could now see the base of the opposite cliff. He quickly glanced over and looked down. What he saw in that second horrified him and nearly stopped his heart.

Dear God, breathe.

There... far below... strewn obliterated across the valley floor.... lay the wreckage of a dozen cars, trucks and even the burnt-out remains of a *chicken bus*.

The discovery that people really did die on these roads only added gut-wrenching realism to the terror already gripping Simon. He leaned in towards the windshield with his eyes wide in vigilance. Simon didn't know what he feared more, the unknown that lay ahead, or whatever might be bearing down on him from the rear. So, on he continued, snaking back and forth on the narrow, fractured road along the cliff's edge. *This is insane*

Soon, and quite abruptly, the forests on the mountainsides above him thinned. Haphazard, cabin-like structures appeared here and there scattered about. Patches of cornfields seemed to grow vertically up the mountainsides with impossibly steep dirt trails winding circuitously upwards to reach them. Simon could see small, wiry farmers and young boys trudging up and down the paths to the gravity-defying crops. *They're growing corn... up HERE!?*

As Simon drove around an especially tight bend, he suddenly swerved, narrowly avoiding impact with a cluster of boys trudging uphill on the edge of his lane.

There were four of them, all about ten years old, he judged, though their weathered faces made it hard to tell precisely. Tattered brown shirts and trousers hung from their thin frames, and they each wore black mud-covered, rubber rain boots that reached up to their knees. Traipsing slowly up the hill, they carried giant bundles of firewood on their backs, cradled in fabric bands that hooked up and over their foreheads. Their small hands gripped the slings beside their ears, but Simon could tell that their heads and necks were supporting the heavy load's weight. The boys were emaciated, and in their dusty young faces he could see excruciating pain. It was nearing noon on a weekday, and it occurred to Simon that these mountain children probably never went to school. This was their life.

"Jesus Christ," he muttered as he rolled past. Simon couldn't imagine a world where parents would ask their children to do such things. Though he resented his mother immensely, his childhood looked blessed in comparison to what these kids were already facing. For a moment, he debated offering them and their burdens a ride up the hill.

They probably wouldn't understand me, though. It's not really my place anyway. There might not be room for all four of them.

He continued to formulate *reasons* why he shouldn't stop until he'd passed the children by and rounded a bend, putting them out of sight. As Simon continued on, his mind dwelled on images of his empty trunk and the pain he'd seen in the young boys' faces. He immediately regretted his decision. *How could you do that, Simon?* Fraught with contempt for his apparent heartlessness, the cold callousness of his inaction permeating his body, his focus drifted inward, towards his own thoughts and superseded the vigilance that the outside world required. He entered a turn, his foot heavy on the accelerator, subconsciously hastening him away from that moment of self-disgust. With his car accelerating to thirty mph, he barreled around the bend—the face of the mountain hiding his view of what was to come.

Suddenly, his eyes grew wide and his skin turned white. His worst nightmare was unfolding right before him.

CHAPTER 33

Suddenly they appeared. Twenty feet ahead of Simon, a chicken bus was in the midst of passing another at full speed. Side by side, the two vehicles blocked the entire road from edge to edge like a raging, grating plow of steel and glass. Deafening horns wailed, getting louder by the microsecond as the two thundering vehicles barreled furiously towards him. Terror gripped Simon as an explosion of thoughts and questions raced through his mind. The most pronounced being *Shiiiiiiiiiiiiiiiit!!!!!!!*

In that moment, Simon knew he had but two choices: maintain his trajectory, crashing head-on into the bus dead ahead… or swerve off the cliff into an arching swan dive to the canyon floor. Instinct took control.

Simon's foot slammed down upon the brake, putting metal to metal as his tires locked and squealed piercingly against the asphalt.

His heart stopped.

The oncoming bus in his lane slammed on its brakes in response and clouds of smoke billowed from below its fenders.

30 feet…

25 feet…

The hulking metal facade grew massive in Simon's windshield…

20 feet…

15 feet…

Simon gritted his teeth and braced for impact. There was no way they'd stop in time...

10 feet…

5 feet…

Then suddenly, with mere inches to spare, the charging mountain of steel ahead cut hard to the right sending it swerving back into the opposite lane behind the other chicken bus. Its front left bumper missing the driver's side corner of Simon's car by less than a yard.

"Holy shiiiiiiiit!!!!" Simon screamed as he screeched to a halt at the edge of the road in a cloud of smoke and gravel. As the car finally came to a rest, Simon swung his head around and gasped as the braking bus swerved and rocked back and forth, the driver fighting desperately to regain control and prevent his vehicle from rolling over the cliff.

He was losing.

The bus pitched hard to the cliffside, and Simon could see the inside wheels lifting up off the ground. *Oh no.*

In that split second, Simon visualized himself inside the bus. One of the numerous terrified passengers—mothers, fathers, children—looking out the side windows as the deep chasm came into view below. He imagined screams of desperation filling the vehicle as those faced with their impending violent demise were overcome by helplessness. Meanwhile, the bus angled harder. It's tilt approaching the point of no return that would take it furiously towards a terminal plunge.

"Jesus Christ!" Simon bellowed and gripped the edge of his seat.

Then—as though the prayers of those inside were somehow answered—the wheels of the staggering vehicle miraculously dropped back down to earth, crashing hard to the patchy pavement. The bus set off again, careening across the lane, smoke still billowing from below, and vanished around the bend out of sight.

Silence filled the car as Simon continued to stare out the rear window for several long seconds, drenched with sweat, trembling and barely capable of breathing.

"Oh my god," he muttered to himself, stupefied at what he'd just witnessed.

Shit, I'm still in the road!

Hurriedly restarting his stalled car, Simon lurched forward and drove ahead until he found a gravel shoulder where he could pull safely off the road. He killed the engine and, for a moment, just sat there, trying to gather himself. All of a sudden, he felt a furious disbelief at what had just transpired. Rage boiled inside him. *I JUST decided to begin my life again, and then that asshole almost kills me!*

"Fuck YOOOOUUUU!" he screamed, slamming his hands hard on the steering wheel and sending a honk echoing through the valley. Though he was unsure if his castigations were directed at the bus driver or himself, he knew both were deserving of scorn. He'd ignored the boys in need, and the universe had quickly responded.

"Fuck! Fuck! Fuck!" he belted, continuing to punch the wheel repeatedly.

The tenuousness of his mortality hit him with the force of a brass-knuckled hook across the face, and Simon looked down to his trembling hands and struggled to control his breathing. His wrists hurt, his chest hurt, his back hurt—all of him hurt. Water welled in the edges of his eyes, and he wiped it away in disgust. *Not now!* He loathed his body's incessant capitulation to cowardice. The faith he'd had in himself a few short hours ago, now seemed dashed by the realities of his own weaknesses. Any semblance of courage obliterated in ten calamitous seconds.

In the grave silence on the mountainside, Simon felt more isolated and cut off from the world than ever. Though he'd buried thoughts of his family for years, now, in this moment of vulnerability, he couldn't control it. *If I had just died, would anyone even care that I was gone? My brother? My mother?* He longed to tell his brother Jonathan how much he truly missed him. *What if I never have another chance.*

Simon grabbed his phone. Scrolling to his brother's number, he stared at Jonathan's name flickering on the back-lit screen. *What would I even say at this point?* Simon froze, desperate for an answer that wouldn't arrive. After a few moments, he switched off the phone and placed it back in the console. *You're a fucking coward.*

Glancing around himself, he began to take stock of his situation. *How have I ended up in such a horrible place? Who am I kidding? I don't belong here...I'm just not fucking cut out for this type of thing...*

Simon knew he wasn't inherently adventurous and certainly wasn't the strongest of men. He spoke no languages and had absolutely no idea how to prepare for the challenges ahead. Yet despite all that, as he sat trying to find one reason to keep going among hundreds steering him the other way, one unusual thought floated unexpectedly into his mind. *How do I KNOW I'm not cut out for this type of thing?*

He realized in that instant that he had no idea exactly *what* he was capable of. He'd never challenged himself to do anything even remotely like this before, and yet had somehow made it all the way to this remote mountain road in the middle of Guatemala. *Maybe I do have it in me. If I don't try... I might never know.*

As Simon sat there pondering this, the four mountain boys trudged up the road past his parked car. Their large bundles of firewood still hanging painfully from their heads. Simon gazed at them through his dusty window glass. Seeing Simon sitting there, two of the boys waved to him and gave him a smile. Simon nearly erupted in tears, but instead managed to wave back. *I have to keep going.* Wiping the muck from his eyes, he started the engine and tried to shift the car into drive. But the shift lever remained stuck in PARK.

Simon wiggled it for a few seconds, but it still wouldn't shift. "Oh, come on!" he yelled and pressed his face into his palms.

He took a deep breath. Then another. Then another. Suddenly, he had a thought. "Hmmm, okay... Late-model Toyota... smart key system... I know this car...I literally wrote the book on this car! Okay, okay... Troubleshooting appendices 5.... Step 1, set the parking brake."

Simon looked down to his side and pulled up the parking brake. *Easy enough.*

"Okay... step two, turn the engine start-stop switch to accessory mode."

Simon looked on the dash and located the switch, he turned it and smiled. *So far, so good.*

"Okay... Let's see...Step 3, depress the brake pedal." Simon stepped on the pedal.

"Haha!... okay, okay, step 4, pry the shift cover up with a flat-head screwdriver or equivalent."

Simon scanned around the car, but besides some old McDonalds bags, it was pretty much empty. He unzipped his duffle bag and rifled through its contents. Suddenly he saw it. "Yes!" Simon pulled out the nail clippers he'd taken from his courtesy kit in his room at the resort. Using the attached nail file, he popped the cover off the shifter.

"Holy shit, that worked! Okay, okay... Step 5, press the shift lock override button," Simon pressed the button, and the shifter easily moved into drive.

"Yes! Yes! Yes!" he shouted, rejoicing as he popped the cover back on and tossed the clippers in the duffel.

Maybe I'm not as helpless as I think!

It was only a minor triumph, but, at that moment, it felt enormous. *Alright, let's do this.*

In the distance, somewhere far ahead… an unseen and nameless force continued to pull Simon towards it. The road ahead beckoned him forward with an urgency and an inspiration that reached deep into his chest and yanked him from his soul. *This is mad* he thought to himself as he pulled back out onto the rugged road. Driving onward once again into the unknown.

CHAPTER 34

Hours passed as Simon advanced undeterred, deeper and deeper into the mountains. The further he pushed on, the more the cracked pavement below him disappeared, until soon the "road" was nothing more than a slipshod sprawl of crumbling earth and rock. It was slow going, to say the least, plodding along at 5-10 mph, the underside of his car sustaining a beating all the while. Simon glared at his GPS with angry eyes and cursed its faulty guidance. The display stated the current speed limit as 60 mph. It didn't take long to deduce it was going to take Simon a whole lot longer than 7 hours to reach Semuc Champey.

In the early afternoon, a group of local villagers halted Simon's vehicle temporarily as they struggled to repair a section of the battered road in the broiling midday sun. Though frustrated by what was clearly going to be a lengthy delay, Simon couldn't help but admire the coordinated effort he observed from his air-conditioned car. Just ahead of his bumper, the men and boys toiled tirelessly, layering load after load of different sized stones into deep grooves with systematic efficiency, until a reasonably flat driving surface was eventually formed. Even the women helped, bringing water, food and wheelbarrows of gravel out to the laboring men. Simon realized there was no government agency out here to tend to such things. It needed to be done, and so the locals were doing it. Together.

As the day wore on, the rattling sedan's gas needle wandered dangerously near E. Simon hadn't seen a gas station since Belize but maintained hope that he was just a single turn away from finding the paved road that would undoubtedly lead him down the mountain to Lanquin. In the back of his mind, however, he knew there was a very real possibility that such a road might not exist. The sky began to darken, and glancing at his GPS, Simon could see he'd been driving for nearly eight hours and wasn't even halfway there. *Fuck. Curse you, you dumb robot.*

Fuel wasn't the only pressing concern. Simon knew that driving on these roads after nightfall would be equivalent to a death sentence. Though the chicken buses were less frequent at this altitude, they still passed him on occasion and nearly ran him off the road each time. Without streetlights, the precipitous cliff beside him presented an even more horrific danger. He wanted to get down the mountain… but not that fast. *I should look for a hotel,* he thought.

But there was one more problem. There was absolutely nothing up at this elevation. Just rock, road and the dimming sky. As the sun drifted behind the mountains, the blue glow of twilight became the sole illuminator of the perilous path ahead, and Simon's growing worry turned towards panic. Soon it would be dark, and he knew that if nothing else, he needed to find a place to pull his car off the road. Preferably, *far* off the road.

Soon his prayers would be answered. Simon rounded a bend, and a small, dilapidated farmhouse suddenly came into view, nestled in the crook of a nearby hillside. Between it and the road was a narrow but flat dirt clearing. Simon pulled onto it without hesitation. As he did, he noticed an old man stood in front of the house, sweeping plant detritus from a wooden box cart. The man wore a wide, flat-brimmed hat and the same mud-covered, black rubber rain boots all the Guatemalan mountain farmers seemed to wear. He looked up at Simon's car as it came to rest in the dirt just a few feet from where he stood and began ambling slowly towards Simon's window.

Oh boy.

Seeing the man approach, Simon hurriedly entered the word "hotel" into his translator app, hit the *translate* button and held the phone out the open window. The elderly farmer stopped in his tracks, staring at the brightly lit screen in the fading twilight. The confusion on his face was easy to read in its radiant white glow. Simon wondered if the man had ever seen a smartphone before. Almost certainly, he hadn't. For several seconds, the man gazed at the screen as Simon waited patiently. Then, raising a finger for Simon to wait, the old man turned and traipsed slowly away and into the house.

Simon's eyes lingered on the front door as the last modicum of twilight dimmed greater still. A few long moments passed before the door finally opened, and the man emerged once again, this time joined by a pudgy, young boy, maybe 9 or 10, who skipped along beside him. The boy wore dark-rimmed glasses, and his face held an unmistakable look of childlike curiosity. As they approached, Simon once again held up the phone for the pair to see—causing the boy to smile excitedly at Simon and the glowing gadget. Several of his front teeth were missing, and the grin on his cherubic, round face made Simon smile in return.

The eager child pointed up at the old man. "*Abuelo* no can read," he said and gave a little chuckle.

Oh, thank god he speaks some English!

The child stepped forward to look closer at the phone. "Why you have on phone? You no can say 'hotel'?" he said with a smile.

Simon turned the phone towards himself to find the Spanish translation of hotel was, in fact, "hotel" and felt like an idiot. "Oh, haha, sorry," he said, putting away the device.

"It's okay," the boy said, laughing. "No hotel near here, though, sorry sir," he continued. "You need go toooo... El Campo."

"El Campo?"

"El Campo."

"How far is that?" Simon hoped for the best.

"Um, I don't know... It's very far. Maybe two... three hours?" he said.

"Two or three hours?!"

"Yeah, but I no think you should drive in mountains in the dark, sir."

You and me both kid.

Simon felt as though a curse had been placed upon him. He dropped his forehead to the steering wheel, unable to conceive of a next move. There wasn't one. The young boy could see the hopelessness mounting on Simon's face and turned to the old man, chatting with him for a few moments in Spanish. After a lengthy back and forth, he turned back to Simon and spoke. "Okay, sir," he said.

Simon looked up.

The boy smiled widely at him through the window and sucked air through his tooth gaps, rocking back and forth on his heels with obvious excitement. "Me...um...me *abuelo* says... uh... you can sleep with us tonight!" he sputtered jubilantly.

Simon looked him up and down and then back up to the old man. The elder gave him a reassuring smile and a nod. Simon didn't know how to react. "Stay here with you?" he asked quietly.

The boy laughed again, "Yeah, with me!" then turned and looked around the clearing beside his home. "Go put you car there," he continued, pointing to a thin patch of dirt beside the house.

Why are these people inviting me to sleep in their home?

"Come on," the boy said with a smile and began walking towards the house. He turned and waved to Simon in a summoning motion like one would do for a pet. "Come...come."

Simon's eyes followed him. But the rest of his body remained motionless as he processed. "Well, I guess I don't have much of a choice," he muttered to himself, and then slowly started the engine and drove over to the clearing. Grabbing his duffel and locking his car doors, Simon followed the pair into the scant dwelling. As was becoming the norm, he ducked under the door frame to enter and nearly hit his head on a sea of corn ears hanging from the ceiling to dry. Though he was only 5'11", Simon had begun to feel like a giant in Central America.

Night had fallen, and inside the small abode, it was mostly dark. Simon could just make out several grass mats lying on the packed dirt floor and weathered wooden walls that flickered orange in the light from a fire burning in the corner. As Simon's eyes began to adjust, he noticed the mother of the house crouching beside the fire, cooking something in a large black pot. When she glanced up and found Simon standing there, the young woman nearly fell over with surprise. Turning quickly, she spoke wildly with the *abuelo* in Spanish. "*¡¿Quién es este hombre y por qué está en nuestra casa?!*"

"*Está perdido en el camino y necesita un lugar para descansar hasta el amanecer.*"

"*¡¿Le dijiste que puede quedarse aquí?!*"

And so on.

After what Simon assumed was an explanation of his presence, the woman eventually gave him a smile and stood, dusting off her dress. "*Hola, buenas noches,*" she said politely.

"*Hola, buenas noches,*" Simon replied, causing the woman to smile at his clumsy accent.

"Me llamo, Mita," she replied, tapping her chest.

"Simon," he said, mimicking the movements.

A small hand grabbed Simon's from below and he looked down, startled, to find the boy pulling him towards the back of the house. "Come on… come on," he insisted.

Simon chuckled and followed him through a small door to a back room. Two thin grass mats, some old toys and some shelves with clothes on them sat on the dirt floor.

"You stay in here with me tonight," the boy said, pointing to one of the mats. "I'll share this bed with my brother Luis."

The boy spoke in such a matter of fact, grown-up way that Simon's heart wrenched with endearment. The Texan was beginning to feel overwhelmed both by the family's hospitality and by the destitution they seemed to be living in. He lamented forcing the boys to share a *bed*, yet the child appeared so thrilled by Simon's presence, he couldn't possibly say no.

"My name is Simon," he said, offering his hand.

The round-faced boy looked on eagerly, wrapping his small hand around Simon's fingers. "My name is Martine," he said.

"Nice to meet you, Martine," Simon replied.

"Nice to meet you, Simon," he repeated.

"You speak very good English, Martine. Where did you learn it?"

"I- uh- learn in school."

"Well, it is very good."

"Thank you, sir," Martine said, blushing.

"I'm glad to hear you go to school. Is it nearby?"

Martine laughed. "No, school is very, very, very far away... Down the... uh... hill... Two-hour walk."

"Two hours?!" Simon said shocked.

Martine looked at him and smiled. "Yes.... two hours... that is the close... uh... the most close school to here."

Simon pondered the idea of walking two hours to school each day, down and up a mountainside, and concluded that Martine was probably in much better shape than he was. "Thank you for letting me stay here, Martine."

"Thank you for letting me stay here, Simon," replied Martine. Quickly realizing what he'd said, he began to laugh. "I mean, you are welcome." He smiled giggling. Clearly proud of his ability to speak English.

Simon was feeling quite fond of him already.

After showing his guest the pit toilet out back and lighting a small metal oil lantern for his use, Martine returned Simon to the fire where the pair sat to chat as Mita cooked. With great enthusiasm, Martine told Simon of a trip the family had taken the year before, to the volcano lake Lago de Atitlán in southern Guatemala. While there, they had visited the local god, Maximon. Martine kept laughing now and repeating "he full of grass!" which Simon didn't understand but laughed along with anyway. When his tale was finished, Martine asked Simon a myriad of questions about life in America and sat wide-eyed and captivated by every answer. Simon was happy to tell story after story, his utterly dull, uneventful life in the States seeming almost magical to Martine. The boy hung on his every word.

After an hour or so, Martine's father, Tian, arrived. The hulking man burst through the door outfitted with the ubiquitous rubber boots and a wide-brimmed hat and carrying a long machete in his grasp. Simon froze at the sight of him, and Tian stared back at Simon, glassy-eyed in the flickering light from the fire.

Uh oh.

Mita spoke softly to her husband for a few seconds and, before Simon knew it, Tian was charging towards him, his scowl turning quickly to a grin, and his hand outstretched ahead of him. "*¡Hola! ¡Bienvenido!*" he hollered as he took Simon's hand and shook it wildly.

Simon laughed, wishing him "*hola*" as well and feeling relieved to see the man's friendly and jovial nature.

Sitting down beside his unexpected guest, Tian at once began to ramble on in Spanish to Simon. The Texan, attempting to be polite, just stared at him blankly, smiling.

Martine snickered to the side. "*¡Papá! Él no habla español*," he shouted and began to laugh uproariously.

Tian's face suddenly soured, and glancing over to Mita, he received an unwelcomed nod of confirmation. "*Demonios*," he muttered to himself.

Simon could see the disappointment in the brawny man's face. He felt it, too. "What did your father say?" he asked Martine.

Tian was preparing to stand and walk away, when unexpectedly his son spoke.

"My papá ask where you are going," said Martine.

Tian looked at his son, bewildered. Though he was well aware that the boy studied English in school, he'd never before heard him speak it. Not a single word.

"Oh! Tell him I am going to Lanquin," replied Simon.

"*Él va a Lanquin*," Martine said.

Tian continued to stare at his boy, stunned. After a few moments, he mustered the gusto to respond. "*Ah, Lanquin. ¿Por qué?*"

And with that, the two men began an engaging conversation, each chatting in their own language at length, with Martine translating as best he could. As they spoke, Simon couldn't stop thinking how the tough and hearty Guatemalan mountain farmer seemed like his diametric opposite, and yet Tian's rough exterior belied a friendly and kind man whom Simon immediately liked. The unlikely duo chatted easily for almost an hour as Simon asked a litany of questions about their life in the mountains, and marveled at how hard it was and how differently things functioned here. Meanwhile, Tian was marveling at his son.

Though Simon was unaware of it, Tian had staunchly opposed Martine and his younger brother, Luis, attending school. He hadn't gone to school, nor had his father or his father's father. As part of a family of rural mountain farmers that went back generations, Tian had expected Martine and Luis to continue the tradition, working in the fields to help support the family. In the village, family was everything. As a boy, he himself had begun working with his father when he was just seven. He hadn't stopped since. Now, he felt blessed to have been given two boys who would eventually work the family's land. But Mita had carried other thoughts.

When she was only 14, Mita's father and half of her village had been killed in a mudslide working the mountain. Later, when she was 20, a passing car had killed her two nephews while they carried firewood up the road. Mita wanted her sons OFF the mountain, and had pressed Tian to send them to school against all his resistance.

Eventually, she wore him down, and several years ago, the boys had begun their education in the valley. As a result, Tian's father, the *abuelo,* had to continue farming at an advanced age. This angered Tian greatly, yet the boys' grandfather had been happy to do it. He had concurred with Mita, and believed there was a better world out there for the boys. It had been at his recommendation that the family had visited Lake Atitlán, to pray to the god Maximon for Martine and Luis to be successful in school. Tian, however, had always resented the decision, continuing to feel strongly that his sons belonged by his side in the fields.

That is until now.

As Simon talked with them by the fire, throughout the night, and the young boy translated for the family, Tian watched his son, captivated by his ability, and felt an unexpected wave of emotion overtaking him. He'd always returned home from the fields long after the boys had finished their homework and was unaware of their burgeoning knowledge. He couldn't believe now how adept Martine was at speaking this foreign language, and a new respect for his eldest son took hold. Here was his son, speaking to an American, in English... and about the world outside of Guatemala and away from the farm. As the night carried on and Martine translated more and more for him and continued to speak with Simon, Tian could see how happy it truly made his son. And he too was happy.

Simon, meanwhile, was having an extraordinary time with the family, finding their hospitality a true testament to the kindness of strangers. Soon, Mita served everyone dinner in the living room, and they all sat by the firelight, resting on the mats on the floor, eating beans, vegetables and rice with tortillas. Together.

Though he couldn't explain it, Simon felt as though he were somehow part of the family that night. It was a feeling he hadn't experienced in a long, long time, and he grew emotional with every kind word, every collective laugh and every shared morsel. His eyes grew teary, but he blamed the smoke from the fire and continued making conversation with Martine to distract himself. He enjoyed talking to all of them so, so very much.

By eight o'clock, everyone was preparing for bed, and Simon took his spot on the mat across from the two brothers. Curled up beside each other, Martine and Luis wrestled and jockeyed for space and the blanket as Simon lay there watching them in the faint glow of the fire still alight in the living room, shining through the open doorway. He remembered how scared and angry he'd felt on the road earlier that afternoon. How he'd regretted ever coming into Guatemala and had cursed his arduous journey. How he'd felt doomed and feared the unfamiliar world outside his car.

Yet now he felt so warm, so soothed, and so strengthened. His experience with the family had given him so much joy that he was grateful for all which had brought him to this point.

As he drifted off towards sleep, rain began to fall on the tin roof above and, again, Simon thought how incredible it was that he was here.

And again, he wished his father could see him now.

CHAPTER 35

Simon awoke just after sunrise. Tian and the *abuelo* were gearing up to head out to the fields as Mita prepared breakfast in the front room. Simon ate a light but filling meal of scrambled eggs, beans and tortillas with the family before heading outside to his car. When he reached it, however, he realized he had a problem. Its tires sat buried entirely in mud from the rain the night before. As he stood there staring at it, Tian stepped outside and saw the focus of his gaze. "*No hay problema*," he said and laid his hand upon Simon's shoulder.

Within minutes, Martine had fetched half a dozen village men, and together with Tian, the group dug methodically around the wheels with their shovels. Simon tried to help at first, but soon realized he was just getting in the way of the more skillful locals.

Fifteen minutes later, the car was free from the mud, and the village men, including Tian, bid Simon farewell and headed up the steep mountain paths to the awaiting cornfields.

Simon found it impossible to articulate how thankful he was. He said his goodbyes to Mita and Martine and realized sadly that he'd have no way of getting in touch with them ever again. They had no phone, no mail and no internet. Simon had a difficult time comprehending that.

Thanking them profusely, he offered them some money, which they politely declined. And as he drove away from the farmhouse, his eyes watered yet again as he watched Martine waving to him in his rearview. *If*

I can ever help someone the way they helped me, I will. He hoped to see them again someday, but he knew he never would. At least in a few days' time, Mita would find the $40 he had left in a jar in the kitchen for them.

***

Simon pressed on through the mountains, and soon the fuel light began to flash on his dashboard. *How on Earth do people get gasoline up here?* As he drove on, he noticed that beside the winding road, every few miles or so, sat people outside, in front of their homes, watching the cars and buses pass by. Beside them, resting on old wooden crates, sat dozens of unmarked 22oz glass beer bottles full of an unidentifiable, pinkish liquid. Simon's earlier suspicion had been that it was some kind of pink lemonade moonshine. But now it dawned on him that maybe, just possibly, it was gasoline. He pulled off the road near a young man pedaling the liquid, and the teenager immediately carried a bottle towards Simon's gas tank.

AHAAAAA!!!!! Thank God.

Simon popped the fuel flap, and the boy emptied the entire bottle into the nearly dry tank. When he'd finished, he walked around to Simon's window for payment, only to find the odd *gringo* pecking away on his translator app. Simon showed him the message he was typing: *Fill it all the way*, and the boy's eyes lit up as if he'd won the lottery.

Off he went! Dashing back and forth between the car and his crate, he eagerly fed bottle after bottle into Simon's waiting vehicle. After a few minutes, all that remained were empty glass bottles, and the young man exuberantly held up a finger, indicating that Simon should wait. Simon nodded with a chuckle, and the boy darted into a small house nearby as fast as he could, leaving Simon alone by the high-octane lemonade stand. *I wonder if I can get some 5-cent psychiatric help while I'm here,* he thought with a smile.

A few moments later, the teen came bursting out of the house chased by a smaller boy, likely his kid brother, who scurried along behind him with equal alacrity. Both of them carried as many bottles they could hold and bore huge smiles on their faces. Simon realized he was probably making their month. Eighty-two bottles and roughly forty-five US dollars later, Simon bid farewell to the grateful duo and drove off as they ran jubilantly into their house. He smiled warmly, feeling delighted that he'd given his business to them.

Soon, Simon really began to make progress. He caught a stretch of newly paved road heading straight down the mountain that allowed him to reach a hitherto unthinkable fifty m.p.h. He took full advantage, and in a moment of elated satisfaction, he held his head out the window, feeling the wind rush across his face and howling loudly into the sky as if he were setting a new land speed record. "To Semuc Champey!"

***

It was 11 a.m. when he entered the remote village of Lanquin, a desolate, two-road mountain town graced with a smattering of local restaurants and little else. Lanquin wasn't much to look at, and Simon's arrival felt about as anticlimactic as could be imagined.

Oooookay? What now?

Asking around town as best he could, Simon eventually met a local man with a 4x4 pickup who spoke a bit of English and who offered to drive him to Semuc Champey for a small fee. "No can go in your car," he repeatedly cautioned, shaking his head with conviction.

Simon eventually conceded and, leaving his car in town, set off with the man on a dirt road into the jungle. Seconds into the journey, Simon realized how right the man had been. Up and down they charged violently over rocky terrain unlike any Simon had ever experienced. Like a shaken coke can about to burst, Simon's stomach roiled and expanded and threatened to let loose its contents with every vigorous rumbling. Yet he was too concerned with holding on for dear life to let that happen.

When they finally arrived at the Semuc Champey trail entrance half an hour later, Simon staggered out of the truck, rattled and quaking. Ahead lay a dense forest, and a heavily armed and camo-clad soldier stood five feet in front of him.

"He's there to protect you," the driver said ominously.

From what!?

After taking a moment to shake off the motion sickness, Simon approached the trailhead and its resident sentry with caution. Without a word, the armed man lifted a hand and pointed at a sign staked in the earth nearby. *El Mirador* was scrawled across the plank, and behind it, a dirt path disappeared into the forest.

This way, I assume?

In Simon traipsed, and soon he found himself alone in the rambling thicket. The trail ahead climbed sharply up the hillside as Simon trudged onward, ever upward, sweating in the brutal midday heat. A daunting and exhausting thirty-minute vertical hike to the top eventually brought him to a flat plateau at the mountain's apex. Huffing, puffing, sweat-drenched and exhausted. Simon was beginning to realize just how out of shape he really was.

I could use a hamburguesa.

Ahead, the path continued, meandering along the tree-lined hilltop. Though weary, Simon pressed on further, and the trail eventually led him to an aged wooden viewing balcony perched high over a cliff. Ambling out onto it, Simon gazed over the edge into the valley below. What he saw in that moment was one of the most spectacular things he'd ever seen in his life. The pain and exhaustion Simon was feeling, all melted away. "Good lord…" he whispered in awe.

There, far below him, at the base of the sprawling green valley, lay a wide turquoise pool of unparalleled vibrancy. Below that lay another, equally as beautiful, and then another, and then another still. Each terraced pool spilled into the next via a dozen or more cascading waterfalls now glistening in the sun. From above, the entire valley floor appeared to be a sinuous stairwell of electric blue lagoons, painting an icy slash through the emerald-green woodland. At the pools' edges, brightly colored wildflowers of violet, marigold and crimson bloomed in clusters making the entire lush scene look like a magical, almost mythical, oasis. If there was ever a Garden of Eden on Earth, this would be it.

"Semuc Champey," he muttered to himself with a grin.

Down the mountainside Simon dashed, and into the valley, hungry to get closer to the shimmering, backcountry paradise. As he burst out of the forest alongside the top pool, the sounds of rushing waterfalls and jungle life enveloped him. A cool and refreshing breeze swept across the valley floor as Simon walked along the pools' edges in a state of wonder and bliss. Nature seemed to have achieved such utter perfection in this isolated locale, something so extraordinary, that Simon paused in solemn reverence, quietly thankful for the chance to walk amidst it.

Just then, as the grandiosity of the scene threatened to overwhelm him, a voice rang out through the valley. "Simon!" it called.

Simon swung his head side to side, wondering if he'd just imagined it.

"Hey, Simon!" he heard yet again.

He definitely wasn't imagining it.

Hurrying quickly over to the edge of the pool below him, Simon glanced down to see Jack and Alice swimming lackadaisically in the blue water just a few feet away. It was one of the most gut-wrenchingly happy moments of his life.

"I can't believe you're here!" Jack bellowed, smiling wide.

Simon, too, couldn't believe he was there.

"Simooooooooon!" Alice hollered, waving from the water.

"Hey, Alice!" Simon shouted jubilantly.

"Welcome to freakin' Xanadu, *amigo*!" Jack belted.

In a flash, Simon considered the situation he now found himself in. He'd just followed the couple, without an invite, hundreds of miles through the Guatemalan countryside. What he said next might determine whether they thought him a friend... or some kind of weird stalker.

"I heard you were headed this way, so I thought I'd check it out!" he called down.

"Awesome! Get the hell in here, man!" Jack responded before ducking underwater.

Nailed it! Simon watched as Jack swam deep through the crystalline liquid, approaching Alice and pulling her underwater by her feet before blasting up to the surface.

"My swim trunks are in my car in Lanquin," Simon responded.

"Dude, there's no one here, just jump in in your skivvies!" Jack replied.

Simon deliberated for a second, how hot and sweaty he was and how nice the water looked. *It would be a shame to have come all this way....*

Off came the clothes. As his pants hit the ground, Simon gave a quick thanks to the stars he'd worn his dark-colored boxer briefs today instead of his tighty-whiteys. *I really need to get rid of those things.* And seconds later, he was airborne, jumping out and down the five feet or so into the blue lagoon with a giant splash. The rush of water over his skin felt cool and instantly refreshing as he burst forth from below to see green jungle cliffs towering above him on all sides and waterfalls plummeting into the lagoon beside him. *This is heaven on earth...*

Simon swam over to Jack and Alice, who hugged him lovingly in the water before pushing his head under. When he popped up again, they all three laughed hysterically.

"So, I take it you got our message?" Alice said.

"What message?" he said, confused.

"The message we left at the hotel sayin' we were coming here," Alice replied.

What? "No, I didn't get any message. I went over and talked to Nina, who said you had come here. So, I looked it up online and drove down."

"Oh shit, really?" Jack said. "We didn't know your last name, and two Simons were staying at your hotel, Simon Hill and Simon Hastings. You looked like a Simon Hastings, so we left the message for him. I take it you're-"

"Simon Hill, yep," Simon said, laughing. *They didn't just leave without saying goodbye...*

"Nice detective work, though, Jessica Jones," Alice chimed in, laughing. "How was the drive down?"

As they swam from pool to pool, Simon told them of his death-defying adventures on the road of terror and about his experience in the mountains with Martine and his family. How he'd felt sure that he would have missed Jack and Alice since it had taken so long for him to get down here.

The couple explained that upon their return from Tikal, a friend of Nina's had offered them a ride to Lanquin, so they had all too hastily jumped at the opportunity. Unfortunately, the driver hadn't mentioned the dozens of stops he needed to make on the way, so it had taken them two grueling days in the back of a truck to get here. The pair had spent the previous day in Lanquin walking around the village, exploring local *tiendas* and buying supplies for their stay in town.

"So, when I got to town, I had this bizarre craving for avocado," Alice began. "I asked all over the village, and people kept tellin' me there was a lady with an avocado tree in her yard. We must have spent three—"

"Four," Jack corrected.

"Four hours goin' house to house lookin' for this elusive Avocado Lady. Everyone in the village kept tellin' me to go to a different house so, when I finally found her, I couldn't believe she actually existed!" Alice laughed. "Speakin' of which, are you hungry?"

"Starving," Simon replied with a grin.

Damn, I missed you.

The three climbed out of the water, grabbed Alice's backpack and situated themselves on top of a sun-soaked flat rock between two of the large sapphire lagoons. Simon had never eaten a meal in such a beautiful place in his life, he thought. And then there was Alice. The sun sparkled on her wet, bikini-clad body, and Simon kept catching himself staring. *Definitely the most beautiful place.*

From her bag, Alice pulled a paper-wrapped stack of fresh, handmade tortillas that they'd purchased in town, several ripe avocados, a lime and a tiny plastic salt and pepper shaker she'd carried with her for ages. Simon watched, hypnotized, as she carved up the green superfruits with her pocketknife and methodically assembled avocado tacos for each of the eagerly waiting men.

He took a bite. *Jesus, this is good!*

"Damn, that's good!" hollered Jack.

"Seriously!" Simon said, laughing in disbelief at how delicious the simple snacks were.

Before they knew it, each of them had devoured five or six tacos, and they all sat rubbing their bellies, satisfied. Simon lay back on the warm rock, soaking up the sunshine, feeling a deep sense of bliss, with a wide grin on his face. *Thank god I'm here right now.*

***

For several more hours, the trio swam from pool to pool, leaping from the tops of waterfalls and sunbathing on the rocks in the afternoon heat. At one point, while exploring a lower lagoon, they stumbled across a small grotto hidden behind a waterfall and swam inside it to explore. The creamy limestone walls of the chamber flickered from the blue glow emanating from the water below. Simon turned to find a mesmerizing view, gazing out through the sheet of tumbling clear liquid and into the rippling green valley beyond. "This is incredible," he whispered, smiling and treading water in their secret world.

"Agreed," replied Alice, the grin on her face stretching from ear to ear.

Everything felt peaceful and perfect.

Suddenly, Jack yelled out wildly. "Kan Bah!" in a bellow that startled Simon so greatly that he hit his head on the cave's low ceiling.

"Sonofa—!" Simon hollered, rubbing his head, puzzled. "What the hell, man?"

"I just remembered these caves I read about not far from here. Called Kan Bah." Jack's eyes grew wide with excitement. "We should go! Right now!"

"But it's so nice he-"

"Right now!" Jack commanded firmly and swam out of the cave through the waterfall.

Simon, at once, felt taken aback by Jack's domineering tone. He continued to tread water in the secret grotto and looked to Alice swimming beside him for support. Her angelic face twinkled in the brilliant azure light as she forced a tepid smile his way as if to comfort him. Every ounce of Simon's soul wanted to stay here with her, but in that moment, he could sense something deeper going on behind her eyes. He could tell that she, too, didn't want to leave. And that maybe, this wasn't the first time Jack had acted this way.

"If you don't want to go, we can stay here," Simon offered gently.

Alice stared at him, emotion visibly rising inside her. She feigned another smile, and then turned, swimming out of the cave without a response.

CHAPTER 36

After quite a bit of coaxing, Simon begrudgingly left Semuc Champey behind and followed Jack and Alice down the trail towards *Kan Bah*. The path they soon found themselves on was extraordinarily beautiful. A wide river flowed beside them on their left, lazy and blue. A fifty-foot waterfall cascaded down the hillside on their right, spawning a stream at its base, which crossed their path ahead. A log bridge traversed it and, as Simon stepped cautiously across the mossy wet wood, the water gushed below his feet to the river beside them. A thought popped into his head yet again. *I should be at work right now.* He couldn't help but smile.

Soon, a diminutive shed appeared nestled amidst a grove of cocoa trees. A few local teenage boys sat on a plank bench out front. "*Hola, ¿qué tal?*" Jack called out as he approached the young men. One of them rose to meet him, and the two spoke in Spanish for a few moments. Simon watched as Jack handed the teen several bills of cash, an act which the Texan found suspicious and possibly dubious.

"This way," called Jack, and the three followed the teenager up and over a hill through the woods. Before long, they arrived at the boulder-strewn mouth of the cave, and the teen stopped, turning and motioning his palms to the ground for the visitors to wait. The young man reached into a bag and pulled out four, foot-long white candles and handed one to each of the *gringos* huddled beside him. Simon's jaw dropped. "Are we seriously going into this cave with just candles?" he asked, horrified.

"Yep," Jack said, smiling.

"Well, what if they go out?"

"That's why we have a guide," Jack chuckled.

The teen pulled a lighter from his bag and ignited the four candles.

"Well, why don't we just bring Alice's headlamp?" Simon continued.

"It's not waterproof," Alice said, smiling, as she and Jack began to follow the boy down into the cave.

"Waterproof?" Simon mumbled, cautiously following after his friends. *Why would it need to be waterproof?*

As he stumbled down the rocky pitch to the edge of the cave's broad entry hole, Simon peered inside. The reflected remains of sunlight illuminated the front chamber just enough for him to make out something quite peculiar. At once, Alice's words made sense, and Simon realized Jack had forgotten to mention one, especially important detail: The cave was almost entirely full of water.

Simon stared at the pool, its far end disappearing into the darkness as Jack and Alice began stripping off their clothes again. *You have GOT to be kidding me.* Simon watched spellbound as their guide, Jack and Alice crawled into the murky water and swam a short distance in. As they moved through the dark chamber, the burning candles held high above their heads sent the cave ceiling and walls aglow in rolling pools of orange candlelight.

"Come on!" Alice called out from deep within, the echo of her voice ringing out from the dim cavern.

A stunned Simon blinked himself back to reality and then hurriedly stripped off his clothes, clambering into the cold, dark cave water.

As he swam up to his friends, joining them in the radiant halo of orange light amidst the darkness, he couldn't help laughing. "This is nuts!" he bellowed. A sentiment that caused Alice and Jack to laugh in agreement.

In they swam, deeper and deeper into the nebulous void. The pitch-black abyss ahead of them seemed to patiently await the approaching glow of their flickering flames. And as they swam, Simon glanced back over his shoulder—to find nothing behind but the same endless darkness. *Please don't go out candle. Please don't go out candle. Please don't go out candle.*

Swimming with one hand was proving much more complicated than expected, and Simon started to worry he might grow too tired for the return journey. The slick cave walls gave them no perch on which to rest either. *This could be bad.* So, when his feet suddenly hit the sandy bottom, he let out a tremendous sigh of relief and scurried up into the shallows to rest.

"You okay?" they asked.

"Yeah, I'm fine," he lied.

As they continued on into the next chamber, the water sloshing at their knees, Simon was thankful to be wading rather than swimming through the black liquid.

Deeper into the caverns they went. Trudging along from chamber to chamber, the faint glow of their candles illuminating only a thin band of rock and water directly ahead. Simon's mind, conjured images of early cave explorers eons ago. *Their oil lanterns wouldn't have been much brighter than this…And they had no way of telling if wild animals or other dangers lurked just ahead of them in the dark!* The thought made him shudder, and he deliberated what could have driven them into such inhospitable places. Science? Shelter? Dreams of hidden treasures? *Definitely hidden treasure.*

And as they pressed on, his mind wandered further back to the Paleolithic age, and a time when Stone Age man first controlled fire. *What if cavemen had come into this very cave with torches a hundred thousand years ago. Would it have looked exactly the same to them?* The idea fascinated him greatly.

Soon, the single chain of caverns evolved into a convoluted system of chambers, intricate in a way only nature could create. Rope ladders took them from hollow to hollow, the four explorers scrambling with great difficulty across wet boulders and through a labyrinth of narrow passages and portals, all the while desperately holding their candles above their heads. And yet, the more difficult and dangerous their situation became, the more Simon felt a rush of adventure penetrating him. His heart raced, and the world outside of the cave disappeared from his mind. *This is incredible.*

And then he saw it. Well, first, he heard it.

Wading through ankle-deep water, the group rounded a bend and soon emerged into a massive dark chamber, larger than any they'd passed through before. At their feet was a large, shapeless pool, stretching out across the cave floor and disappearing into the distant shadows. And there, twenty feet ahead, a roaring, fifteen-foot waterfall gushed down from a cavern above, sending ripples across the water lapping at Simon's toes.

"Holy shit!" Simon, Jack and Alice said in near unison.

In the twinkling glow of their candles, Simon could just make out a knotted rope hanging down amidst the foaming white falls. The guide, meanwhile, proceeded to take the candle from Jack's hand, blow it out, tuck it into Jack's waistband and point to the chamber above the falls. Simon immediately realized the implication of the guide's motions and looked to his companions for unity in refusing such an outlandish idea. But in the darkness, he could see Jack had a huge smile on his face.

"Here goes!" Jack hollered, leaping into the pool ahead.

Goddammit, Jack!

Swimming across the dark water, Jack reached the rushing deluge, grabbed hold of the rope and began to climb. One hand at a time, he slowly pulled himself up through the pounding water as Simon gazed on, still not wanting to think about the fact that he might have to follow soon.

Around the halfway point, Jack let out a loud yelp that echoed through the caves, and Alice laughed in the darkness.

Simon did as well… nervously.

Soon Jack reached the waterfall's summit, and jumping to his feet, he kicked water through the air and howled into the darkness. "AAAAAAoooooooooo!"

Simon stared on, still in disbelief. *Stupid Jack made it look easy.*

Alice went next, and the young woman proceeded up the rope a bit more slowly than Jack had. When she reached the top, she took an exhausted gasp of air into her lungs and rested her hands on her knees.

Simon at once felt he couldn't possibly follow.

"You can do it, Simon, it's no problem!" she yelled down to him while trying to catch her breath.

"Easy for you to say," Simon grumbled to his feet.

It was his turn. Simon blew out his candle and stared at the waterfall in the near blackness. *You can do this.* The faint glow of the guide's solitary candle was the only remaining illumination in the large chamber. *You can do this.* Simon tucked his candle into the waistband of his underwear, hopped into the pool and swam towards the rope. *You can do this.* Within seconds, the thrusting current from the pounding waterfall began to force him away. *Oh crap! You can do this.* Simon swam with all his might, fighting the waves and the spray. *You can do this! Juuuust a little bit further!* Simon reached out as far as he could, and with a hard kick and a lunge, he extended his hand through the mist and snatched the thick wet rope. *You did it!* He pulled himself under the curtain of pummeling water, the roar of it deafening. Suddenly, he began to flip and twist like a fish on a line. *Jesus Christ!* But he held on, finally managing to get his feet onto the rope and brace himself. *That's it.* He reached up and grabbed the next knot, and then the next. One knot at a time. Each time he lifted his feet to stand on the next, he struggled to keep his hands from slipping off the rope in the relentless torrent of water.

Confidence swelled inside him with each move upward toward his goal, and when he finally reached the top, Jack and Alice pulled him to his feet, and they all yelled a resounding "Woohooooo!" that echoed throughout the caves.

I can't believe I made it!

Alice grabbed Simon in an unexpected embrace, and Jack rubbed his wet hair.

As she held him, Simon looked into Alice's eyes, barely visible in the near darkness, and one thought consumed him: *I want to kiss you.*

He wasn't sure, but in that second, he felt as though, maybe, she did too.

Letting go of her quickly, he turned to see the guide, already halfway up the rope. He was climbing up one-handed with his other arm stretched out behind him, holding the last lit candle. *No way!*

On reaching the top, the wiry teen handed the fire up to a stooping Jack who lit the other three candles. A moment later, the four glowing flames flickered to life again atop the great obstacle.

They had made it. *This is incredible,* Simon thought yet again and smiled wearily at his friends—their faces glowing amber as they smiled back at him. Jack put his hand on Simon's shoulder. "Good job, Mr. Hill," he said kindly.

"Thanks."

From the waterfall's apex, the group turned and walked deeper still into the tangled cave system. And it wasn't long before they found themselves entering yet another massive, cathedral-like cavern. The faint light from their candles illuminated only the lower portion of the towering walls. Walls that disappeared high into the blackness above them. Another large pool lay ahead.

"*Esta manera,*" the guide whispered, leading the group to the edge of the pool and up onto a stone outcropping which sloped, like a ramp, up the tall chamber wall. Pressing their backs to the flat edifice, the group stepped inch by inch, slowly up along the rising ledge until they eventually found themselves so far up the cavern wall that they could no longer see the water below and could go no further. The guide stopped and pointed down into the abyss.

"I thiiiiink, we jump from here," suggested Jack.

Simon stared down into the dark chasm below his feet. He had no sense how far below the water now lay. "I'll go first this time," he said, stunned by the words emanating from his mouth. And before he had a chance to reconsider, Simon took a bold step forward, gliding off the ledge and out into the black.

As he descended through the darkness, time seemed to slow down for the enraptured Texan. He recalled a moment as a young boy when his father had encouraged him and his brother Jonathan to take a plunge into a black lake one moonless night long ago. The feeling of leaping off into the darkness was unlike any other sensation he'd ever experienced. The sense of giving in to the universe it invoked, both terrifying and empowering at the same time. And as he now plunged into the dark water, the chill of it encapsulating his body wholly, Simon felt himself graciously succumbing to it, and allowing himself to feel as though he was becoming a part of it. A part of the water… a part of the darkness… a part of the cave… a part of the world.

When he resurfaced a few lingering seconds later, he looked up into the sheet of black above him. Now, enveloped in an orange halo far above, Jack, Alice and the guide stood perched high on the rocky ledge, peering down towards him. He knew they couldn't see him down below.

"I made it!" he called out.

Swimming over to the far side of the cavern, Simon took pause to rest alone for a spell. A wave of euphoria consumed him as he remained hidden under the shroud of darkness. Invisible to the world.

Suddenly, the sound of a splash echoed through the cavern. One of his friends had made the leap. Simon smiled wide. *This is incredible.*

CHAPTER 37

Jonah stared at the obstacle before him. He scratched the prickles of beard on his jaw, formed in his six days in the wilderness, and pondered his next move. *If my measurements are correct, my van should be just on the other side of that thicket.*

Reaching over his shoulder, he grabbed his pole saw from its sheath, telescoping it out in front of him. Then slowly, methodically, he began cutting a path through the dense undergrowth. It was a time consuming and laborious process, but one he'd already become quite adept at from his trials. His sun-scorched arms ached as he gradually made his way through the gash forming before him. When he breached the brush to the other side, Jonah looked through the patchy woodland and located his van a hundred yards ahead—parked exactly where he'd left it.

He let out a sigh of relief and grinned. *Hello beautiful.*

CHAPTER 38

Upon leaving the Kan Bah caves, Simon, Alice and Jack made their way down a dusty road back towards the Semuc Champey entrance. As they walked and talked, they eventually came upon a yellow, steel trestle bridge spanning over a wide river through the forest and began to cross. Jack, always cavalier, hopped up onto the bridge's outer rail and stared down at the rushing water a few dozen feet below him. It looked deep enough, he thought, but the current was moving fast from the heavy rains in the mountains the night before. Turning to his cohorts, Jack smiled, winked and gave them a salute. Then suddenly, he stepped off the rail into the air, free-falling twenty feet down into the river below.

Simon and Alice gasped at once and ran to the bridge's railing, looking down to see Jack splash into the rippling water and then disappear under their feet. They sprinted across to the other side of the bridge, but Jack was already fifteen feet downstream from where they stood… and moving fast. Simon could see his friend swimming full force, struggling to reach the shore. But he was barely gaining any ground, and panic filled his eyes. In his hubris, Jack had vastly underestimated how fast the current was.

"JAAAAACK!" the two yelled at him from the bridge, but it was too late. The sound of the raging river muffled their distant voices. Seconds later, Jack disappeared around a bend in the river.

Simon took off running.

Off the bridge's end he sprinted, and down the side of the riverbank with Alice following closely behind. *The river's bending hard here. If I cut through the woods, maybe I can get ahead of him!*

Simon dashed into the woods, crashing through brambles and branches whipping at his face and legs. Through the forest, he could hear Jack yelling off in the distance and ran harder than he ever had before. *Just… a little… farther…* Bursting back out onto the river's edge, Simon cast his eyes quickly around the scene and sucked air into his lungs.

"Simon!" he heard from below, and looked down to find Jack clinging desperately to a long branch jutting out from the shore. Water pounded him relentlessly, and Simon could see his grip was failing. Simon knew if he could wade a few yards out into the swift-moving water, he might be able to grab Jack and save him. But the sound of the raging river struck fear into his heart and he froze… paralyzed. *What do I do!?* His mind raced with indecision, his heart pounding in his chest as he watched Jack struggle to hold on for dear life.

Alice, however, had no such trepidation. And before Simon could pull himself together to react, she shoved past him and dove headlong into the water, grabbing the branch with one hand and Jack's weary arms with the other, struggling mightily to pull him up towards the shore. Simon stood petrified, shell-shocked at what was transpiring. And as Alice made it closer to where he stood, she looked up from the rushing water and locked eyes with him. He could see the panic forming in her eyes as she too was losing strength.

Jesus, Christ, they need me.

Without another second of hesitation, Simon rushed into the shallows to his waist, reached out as far as he could and grabbed Alice's wet arm. Digging his heels into the rocky riverbed, he grabbed the branch under his other arm and pulled the pair towards shore with all his might. Slowly they moved forward against the relentless torrents. Simon let out a guttural yell and yanked with every last ounce of strength in his body. "Aaaaaaahhhhhhhhh!" Suddenly, Alice's feet hit the ground below her, and Simon could see a glimmer of hope flash into her eyes. *We can do this!* Charging forward with everything they had, Simon and Alice dragged Jack up from the frothy spray until he, too, could touch the rocks below. And when the shaken group finally pulled themselves out onto land, they collapsed onto the muddy riverbank, gasping and straining to breathe.

Simon looked at his hands, covered with mud, scraped and battered, and wiped the sweat and water from his eyes with his sleeve. He was about to ask if everyone was okay, when suddenly, Alice reeled around and punched Jack hard in the arm and screamed, "What the fuck is wrong with you!" she cried, her impassioned voice clearly burdened by a flood of both love and rage. She began to weep, leaning over the bedraggled young man, and pulled his head into her lap, holding him tight and crying over his body.

Simon could see how much she truly cared about Jack. They were the yin to each other's yang. He, meanwhile, sat beside them in silence, feeling more alone than ever and furious with himself for his initial cowardice. He was sure that his "soon to be former friends" would resent him for his hesitation by the river's edge. He'd nearly allowed Jack to be swept away after all. *What kind of a friend am I?*

But just then, Alice reached out, grabbing Simon and pulling him close into a one-arm embrace, Jack's head still resting in her lap. "Thank you for helping us," she whispered to Simon and held him close.

"Thanks, both of you," Jack said in a raspy voice, reaching back and putting his still shaking hands on their legs.

Simon wanted to speak but couldn't. As he gathered his breath beside the river, his mind filled with questions he could not answer. *Why aren't they mad at me? Shouldn't they be angry?* He wondered if, perhaps, they didn't care about his hesitation, just that he'd been there for them in the end, when they truly needed it. Maybe they saw the good in him, and not only the weaknesses. Maybe there were more profound things at work here than the superficialities Simon had become accustomed to in his relationships. Whatever it was, it meant the world to him.

For ten minutes, the three lay there in the mud without another word. There was nothing else to say.

***

That evening, as Jack showered, Alice approached Simon in their room to speak. The expression on her dirt-streaked face was tender, revealing obvious pain and a vulnerability Simon had never seen in the ordinarily confident young woman. "I know he can be controlling, and obviously he's a fool," she said with despondence. "But he's probably the most intelligent, adventurous and insightful person I ever met… and I love him more than anything. He knows more about life and about me than I ever could hope to," she continued.

Simon looked into Alice's eyes and felt he could now see deeper into the young woman. He couldn't recall the last time anyone had opened up to him in this way.

"But, jumpin' off the bridge like that…" she went on, pausing to look down for a moment before continuing. "tryin' to be funny all the time… acting like a joker, without a care as to how it affects other people . . ."

Simon noticed tears forming in her eyes.

"Goddamn, he drives me mad sometimes!" she burst out. And with that, she began to cry, wiping the murky tears from her cheeks.

Simon put his hand on her shoulder, and she stepped forward into his arms. He could feel her arms squeeze tight around him, and he wrapped his arms around her, tighter still. She looked up at him and pressed her forehead to his—their faces just inches apart. Simon could feel her breath on his chin and her tears on his own cheek now. And when their eyes raised to meet each other's yet again, Alice didn't let go, but just lingered there for a beat, staring into Simon's eyes for what felt to Simon like eons. *She really does want me to kiss her.*

Simon leaned in slowly towards Alice's face, anxiously anticipating the realization of all his days of want. It was actually happening. And as his lips neared hers, their eyes locked together in an intimate moment. Simon's eyes saying *YES!*... and Alice's saying, *WHAT ARE YOU DOING?*

But it was too late.

And with just a hair's width to spare between them, Alice lurched backward out of Simon's arms, and narrowly avoided his incoming lips.

Just then, the shower water turned off.

Alice stepped away, shocked, wiping away her tears and lips. "Sorry! Sorry!" she exclaimed.

"No, I'm sorry!" Simon responded, frantically adjusting his clothing.

Alice glanced over her shoulder at the closed bathroom door and spoke quietly. "I hope you don't think that—I mean, you know I love Jack but—but I mean, since we've been on the road, I just haven't had anyone else to talk to about these things," she fretted.

"I'm sooo sorry," Simon responded, embarrassed beyond comprehension.

"Don't be," Alice said, and quickly adjusted his collar and gave him a loving smile.

The door opened, and Jack strolled from the bathroom. "Ooooh boy, Simon, you got a sunburn today. Your face is as red as a lobster!" said Jack.

Simon smiled.

***

Later that evening, the three sat around a table at a local restaurant in the village, weary from their physically and emotionally taxing day. Nobody said much at first, and Simon wondered if Alice was mad at him, or at Jack, or at both of them.

"Have you ever heard of Maximon?" he asked, trying to perk up the conversation.

The two shook their heads. "No, who's that?" asked Alice.

"He's like a god or a deity that they worship down on a lake called Atitlán, down south of here a-ways."

"The volcano lake?" asked Alice.

"Yeah, I think so. That boy in the mountains, Martine, told me about him. Sounds kinda cool...I guess you can pray to him for help if you need it."

"Well, that's cool," Jack mumbled.

"So... I was thinking about maybe going down to see him," Simon continued. "Dooooo you guys wanna go down there with me?" he asked cautiously.

Jack and Alice looked at each other for a few seconds before Jack turned back to Simon. "Don't you have to go back to work this week, man?"

In a flash, Simon realized that amidst the madness of the day, he'd failed to tell his friends his important news. "Oh! Shit, I forgot to tell you! I quit my job a few days ago," he blurted, and gave them a huge smile. "My schedule is wiiiiiide open!" he chuckled.

And with that, Jack and Alice turned from groggy and morose to wide-eyed and joyful as if at the flip of a switch. "Seriously?" Alice shouted, slapping him across the arm.

"Yeah, I hated that job anyway," he replied giggling.

"Well, congratulations, man!" Jack said excitedly. "We need to celebrate!"

"Simon, I'm so happy for you!" Alice exclaimed.

As Jack flagged down a waiter and ordered a round of beers and rum shots, Simon sat aglow, ruminating over the positivity of the couple's reaction. He felt fairly certain that back home, people would have reacted very differently to such news. They'd have told him what a horrible idea it was to quit a good paying job in this economy. They'd have asked him why he would quit without a new job lined up. And they'd have questioned with harsh judgment what his plan was going forward. Basically, they would have acted exactly as Simon had when Jack and Alice told him they had no career plans a week ago.

But not these two. Not in the least bit. They were over the moon for his decision, and he loved them even more for it.

For the rest of the evening and deep into the night, the trio drank and talked about their day of adventures, reveling in life and the simple joys and beauty of living. Throughout their celebration, Simon couldn't stop contemplating all that had happened, and the things Alice had shared with him. He cared for her greatly and was glad he could be there for her. Even as a friend. Now, more than ever, though, he believed that she and Jack belonged together.

But they weren't perfect.

CHAPTER 39

"My mamma said that's the Devil's church," the young boy warned ominously.

Eight-year-old Simon and ten-year-old Jonathan stared wide-eyed out the school bus window, their sweaty hands pressed against the glass. Through the dusty, thick pane, a dilapidated white chapel passed by, resting amidst a brown field at the side of the road. For years, the boys had passed the same church every day on their way to and from school. They'd always thought it abandoned and empty. That is until they started seeing cars parked in the field beside it for the past few months.

"What do you mean, the Devil's church?" the diminutive Simon said, his voice trembling.

Their mischievous classmate just smiled.

"Oh, he's just messin' with you, Simon," Jonathan replied, and rubbed Simon's back in an effort to comfort his kid brother.

But the damage had well been done. From that point forward, every day, Simon and Jonathan stared out the window at the old church. And every day, Simon expected to see the Devil come walking out through its big white doors.

Soon, nightmares formed, and after a month or so, Jonathan had grown weary of being awoken each night by Simon's screams.

Then one Sunday, things changed.

When the boys were younger, Madeline Hill had taken them to church on this day each week, but the family had long since stopped attending or doing much of anything together for that matter. Now, she usually did chores at the house while the boys had adventures in the back yard or built forts out of couch cushions in the living room.

But today was a different kind of Sunday.

"Where we goin'?" Simon asked, his short legs working overtime to keep up with his taller big brother as they jaunted down the street.

"I'm gonna show you once and for all that that church ain't got no Devil in it!" Jonathan said, charging ahead.

Simon stopped in his tracks. "What?!" His young voice cracking with fear.

"Come on now!" Jonathan yelled, making the young Simon jump where he stood. Jonathan continued walking ahead, and after a few seconds, Simon chased after him... as always.

When they reached the dry field, the two boys could see dozens of old cars parked in the dead grass in front of the decrepit church. Music hummed from inside, and they could hear voices whooping and hollering from across the lawn.

THE TRAVELERS WITHIN: INTO THE UNKNOWN

THE TRAVELERS WITHIN: INTO THE UNKNOWN **163**

"Let's go home!" Simon pleaded on the verge of tears.

"Come on!" Jonathan hollered back at him and grabbed his kid brother's small hand, pulling him across the grass towards the church's front door. Simon began to cry, but Jonathan kept dragging the boy closer and closer until they finally made it up onto the front porch. "Shut up!" Jonathan yelled to his sobbing brother and put his ear to the door.

Simon sucked up his tears and bit his lip.

Jonathan grabbed the door handle and slowly pulled it open. The two boys gazed through the widening crack.

Inside, the congregation danced feverishly and screamed, "Hallelujah!" into the sky. The reverend perched up on the front stage held his arms up high to the heavens. In his hands, the boys could now see dozens of writhing snakes.

"AAAAAHHHHHHH!!!!!!" the two boys screamed in unison upon seeing them, turning on their heels, running out and slamming the door shut as hard as they could.

Off they ran, bounding off the porch… Away from the church… Across the field…. Screaming "AAAAAHHHHHH!" the whole way. Down the street… Towards their house… Across their lawn… Screaming "AAAAAHHHHHH!" the whole way. Into their house… Up the stairs… Into their bedroom… Screaming "AAAAAHHHHHH!" the whole damn way.

That night, it was Jonathan who woke Simon up, hollering from a bad dream. Likely of snakes.

The two boys hadn't set foot in a "house of God" since.

CHAPTER 40

Religion can be such a wild thing, Simon thought. Memories of the snake handler flashed through his mind now as he sat quietly on a wooden bench in the broiling house, struggling to breathe in the thick grey smoke that filled it. The stifling room he now found himself in, was alight in a blazing inferno—not with large flames devouring the walls and scorching the ceiling, but with hundreds of lit wax candles covering the floor like an incandescent twinkling carpet of fire. Against the walls sat a dozen or so local worshippers, mostly elderly men and women, barely visible in the thick candle smoke and the hazy orange aurora of the glimmering flames. An old woman, hunched on a bench beside him, mumbled prayers repetitiously and bobbed her head up and down. Her wrinkled face shone amber in the glow from the fire below as she chanted. Throughout the small dwelling, thousands of notes, beads, prayers and other small offerings fluttered on the walls and ceiling. And through the lambent haze, Simon squinted, and could scarcely see the infamous straw figure across the room, staring back at him with glass eyes. A life-sized effigy of the Mayan god *Mam*, it was an ominous scarecrow-like form, made entirely of wood and straw and adorned in a wide-brimmed hat and colorful garlands. It rested motionless in a chair against the wall. A burning cigarette hung precariously from its wooden mouth.

This was *Maximon*.

Throughout the year, the ancient Mayan deity was moved from home to home in the lakeside village. So, Simon, Jack and Alice had spent several days asking around town before eventually finding someone who'd agreed to bring them here. Now they sat in this dark room, watching spellbound as one of the elderly men stood and walked through the billowing fog to the idol, pulled the lit cigarette from its mouth and poured rum from a small flask into its wooden lips. He returned the cigarette and sat back down to resume his prayer once again.

Though the scene was bizarre beyond words, Simon found a quiet respect for the strength of belief in the people who worshipped here. After a few more minutes, though, he'd had enough of the choking air and tapped Alice's knee as he stood to leave the room. The trio stumbled out of the house and onto the street, their eyes squinting as they took a moment to adjust to the blinding daylight. Above them towered two massive green volcanoes.

"Well, that certainly was interesting," Simon said as he struggled to catch his breath, coughing in the noisy Santiago streets.

Alice and Jack chuckled. "Serious understatement there," joked Alice.

"Did you guys pray for anything?" queried Jack, fighting with his clothes to air the smoke from them.

"I did," Alice offered.

"What for?"

"I'm not telling you!" she responded, laughing as the men joined in.

Simon had considered praying. He'd never actually prayed in his life. But on their long drive down to Lake Atitlán a few days before, knowing he was going to encounter an ancient god, he'd deliberated at length over who or what he *could* pray for. Yet nothing seemed important enough. When the time had come, in the dark room with *Maximon*, he had impulsively made the same prayer he had quietly made for years, alone in his apartment. *Please let me meet a good woman.* Yet when he realized how selfish that must have sounded to the powerful Mayan deity, he quickly added: *And please give health and prosperity to everyone I care about.*

A decent save, he thought.

***

Twenty yards from where they stood, the cobalt blue waters of Lake Atitlán lapped against the rocky shore. The volcano lake, as it's often referred to, lies majestically encircled by a crown of three towering green volcanic peaks. An imposing and powerful sight, the dark *lago* has been worshipped as a sacred and mysterious place by indigenous tribes for thousands of years. Among them, the Maya, who greatly feared its power, had therefore established their settlements high abreast the slopes of the forested volcanoes, placing themselves and their homes hundreds of feet above the shadowy surface of the water.

They had been wise to do so. When the Spanish and other later European settlers eventually arrived over subsequent centuries, they, in turn, chose naively to found their own towns near the water's edge. Yet the Mayans had clearly known something powerful that the new migrants were just beginning to learn.

Every hundred years or so, for reasons that have eluded scientists for ages, the dark lake waters of Atitlán, slowly, but surely, begin to rise. Not by a few feet. Not by a few yards. But by as much as a hundred feet. The most recent cycle, begun just two years ago, had already sent businesses, hotels, roads, homes, and anything else constructed too close to the coastline, deep under the silty water. The Mayan communities, up high, could only watch as the new arrivals gradually sank beneath the waters of the sacred lake.

***

As Simon, Jack and Alice walked through Santiago, they clattered precariously across makeshift plank pathways towards the newly constructed dock, a jackleg construction which now lay fifty feet above where the previous dock currently resided, deep underwater.

Cramming themselves aboard an overcapacity *lancha*, the three soon found themselves packed like sardines into the little water taxi, alongside several dozen other people, piles of cargo and numerous live animals. Simon sat looking on, aghast, as the load weighed the boat down so much that small waves lapped over the edges onto the passenger's legs. *This is insane.* The six life jackets for twenty-five people didn't help calm Simon's nerves either.

Since his father's death in the Gulf of Mexico as a boy, Simon had remained terrified of deep or fast-moving water. And as the boat puttered across the vast, dark lake towards their hotel in the distant village of San Pedro, he gripped the side-rail tightly with one hand and a life jacket with the other.

Alice could sense his substantial trepidation. "It's going to be okay, Simon," she whispered with a smile, placing her arm around his shoulders to comfort him.

Simon, in turn, released a deep breath and surveyed the scene around him. A pair of Mayan women in ornately hand-sewn purple dresses huddled near the boat's stern, clutching stacks of blankets set for sale at the local markets. A family sheltering several small goats in their laps sat atop bags of rice up front. Jack, meanwhile, smiled wide, perched high up on the bow. And as Simon sat with his legs pressed against the countless strangers in the teetering boat, he began to imagine his future, and the many other adventures that lay ahead with his new friends. He imagined weeks of audacious Guatemalan expeditions taking them God knows where in the wild world now embracing them. A world he was just beginning to see clearly. And after Guatemala, who knew? As long as they were together, anything was possible.

Later, thinking back on this time, Simon would wonder whether these optimistic thoughts had perhaps been the jinx that had sent everything so horribly awry. He would never truly know.

CHAPTER 41

"Let's go cliff jumpin' in San Marcos today!" Alice exhorted as the three sat eating breakfast on the roof of their hotel the following morning.

Built by a female French expat a decade ago, and dubbed the first modern hotel on the Lake Atitlán waterfront, the grand *Calasa* was a six-story, resort style behemoth, and hardly the type of place one would expect to find the thrifty Jack and Alice. Boasting an expansive patio restaurant and bar, several outdoor Jacuzzi tubs, immaculate lawns and exotic lakeside gardens, it had been *the* chic hang out spot for the better part of a decade. But that was before the rising waters.

These days, those luxurious amenities lay deep underwater, including the lobby, the spa and the entire first floor of hotel rooms. The concrete building now rose from the lake itself like a gargantuan, white water lily. Its reception area now relocated to the second-floor stairwell and accessible only via an improvised wooden bridge. Though the hotel would have to close soon, eventually succumbing to excessive water damage, until that day, its owner Renée, was trying desperately to recoup any money she could before closing its doors. That meant cheap rooms in an elegant hotel with unparalleled lake views. 360-degree lake views.

The idea of cliff jumping appealed to all three travelers, yet a strong gale had set upon the lake that morning and the frothy black water now teemed with curling white caps. From his vantage up in the hotel, Simon could see *lanchas* still plying the rough and dangerous expanse of water, slowly crisscrossing from lakeside town to lakeside town. The thought of getting back in one of those boats terrified him, and he didn't hesitate to tell his companions so.

Not to be deterred, Alice and Jack grabbed an area map from Renée's collection and searched for another option. Of the dozen or so towns that remained on the waterfront, only a handful on the northern shore, such as San Pedro, were even accessible by road. The others, such as San Marcos, were typically reached only by the *lancha* water taxis. Yet as they stared at the map, they noticed a mysterious unlabeled road that went from San Pedro, ducking behind one of the volcanoes, passing through a small inland village and then hooking around to connect to San Marcos. The trio showed it to Renée, and though she'd never driven it, she advised them against taking the unmarked route.

"Keep your doors locked if you go off the lake," the middle-aged French woman cautioned when told of their decision to drive. The words of warning seemed unnecessary— they'd driven safely through the entire country after all, but they thanked her, nonetheless. Going ahead with the choice was a moment of bull-headed impetuousness that Simon would always regret.

Shortly after breakfast, they departed on their excursion to San Marcos. The dirt road proved to be coarse and uneven but relatively well-maintained in comparison to the mountain roads near Lanquin. As they proceeded, the route felt desolate and forgotten, the only other vehicles along the way a few pick-up trucks loaded with rough trodden locals packed in the rear. Simon couldn't help but notice the stares they received as they drove by, and he began to get the strong impression that outsiders like them didn't travel away from the lake too often.

As they rolled through the isolated village behind the volcano, Simon grew even more anxious. The whole town seemed to stop and watch them as they passed through, the late model sedan standing out like a sore thumb amidst the worn 4x4s and pick-up trucks on the dusty road.

"Speed up a little," Jack whispered with a crack in his voice.

Simon was all too pleased to gas it out of town, and soon the road curved wide through a deep forest, eventually emerging into the village of San Marcos. *That was a little nerve-racking.*

Parking the car and setting off on foot, the threesome ultimately arrived at the thirty-foot cliff-jumping walls in the exact location the guidebook said they'd be. Yet they quickly deduced the error they'd made. The clifftops were now only five feet above the risen lake surface! "What do you think, Simon? Do you have the *cojones* to jump?" Alice joked.

"Hey, at least I have *cojones*," Simon replied, forcing Jack into a spit take.

Electing to make the best of it, the three enjoyed a lackadaisical afternoon, swimming in the cool water and sunning themselves on the warm rocks. The day was hot, and after a while Simon dozed off, lying on his towel in the tranquilizing rays.

When he awoke some time later, Simon immediately realized that the sun had already fallen behind the ridgeline. Glancing over, he found Jack and Alice cuddled up on a towel nearby, lost in each other's presence, not having noticed the sun's setting.

"Let's head back, guys," Simon called out to them with a sense of urgency, rousing them to gather their things hastily. A few moments later, they were headed back into town.

By the time they reached the car, it was virtually dark. Simon's anxiety was running high. *Keep your doors locked once you get off the lake.* Simon remembered Renée's words and hit the power lock button as they shut the doors and drove out of town, once again on the unmarked dirt road leading back to San Pedro.

Soon they were back in the forest. The view ahead now pitch black, save for where the Corolla's headlights met the trees and the earthen track before them. Simon gripped the steering wheel tightly.

Several draining minutes passed, and as they rounded a wide curve in the road, Simon noticed something peculiar in the distance. Fifty yards in front of their vehicle, a man stepped from the forest into their path, his hands waving above his head in an attempt to flag them down. And as they grew nearer, Simon saw that the stranger bore a handkerchief tied around the front of his face.

"Oh shit!" he called out, abruptly becoming aware of what was happening.

But before Simon could react, another man stepped from behind an adjacent tree, pulled a revolver from his hip and pointed it directly at Simon's windshield.

"Oh shit! Oh shit! What do I do?" Simon looked over to find Jack equally wide-eyed and petrified with fear.

"I think you have to stop, or he'll shoot us through the windshield!" Jack hollered. "Alice, get down back there!" he yelled to Alice in the back seat.

Terrified, she ducked down into the footwell and hid as best she could.

With muscles clenched and his stomach in his throat, Simon reluctantly slowed the car and came to a stop beside the man pointing the gun. He pulled the little cash he carried from his pocket and pressed it to the glass. Meanwhile, the second man circled the vehicle and approached the passenger side. Pulling a gun from his waist, he pointed it at Jack through his side window. "Fuck," Jack muttered, slouching into his seat.

Simon rolled down his glass a crack and pushed his money through, "Here! Take it! Take it!"

But the man just grabbed the cash and began yelling at him furiously "*¡Abre las puertas*! *¡Abre las puertas*!" he shouted, shaking the gun wildly through the window. Simon shuddered and held his hands up. "What is he saying?" Simon yelled to Jack, panicked.

"They want us to open the doors or they'll shoot us!" Jack yelled back.

Louder and louder the men yelled. "*¡Abre las puertas*! *¡Abre las puertas*!*" The man on Simon's side repeatedly hit the nose of his gun barrel against the glass just inches from Simon's face. Simon winced and closed his eyes as the two men began hammering on the top of the car with their fists.

"I think you need to open it!" Jack hollered, his hands pressed tight over his ears.

"Fuck!" Simon yelled before clicking the unlock button and putting his hands on top of his head.

In a savage instant, the two men threw the doors open, yanked the two Americans out and threw them violently onto the hard ground next to each other. Simon gasped, trying to get air back into his hammered chest and barely managed a breath before one of the men stomped his boot down on his back with crushing force. "Take whatever you want!" he yelled in desperation. But the two men ignored him, digging feverishly through Simon and Jack's pockets before one of them headed to the car. He grabbed Jack's backpack from the front seat and threw it on the ground. Then he headed towards the back doors.

"*No mas! No mas!*" Jack pleaded.

Alice! Simon thought in terror.

The gunman glanced back to Jack but then continued to the rear door and peered through the window. When he saw Alice curled up in the footwell, he again began yelling wildly, pointing his gun at her through the glass.

"*No mas! No mas!*" Jack continued to yell in desperation.

But the gunman paid him no attention. Yanking open the door, he grabbed Alice by her hair and pulled her out of the car, screaming onto the dirt road. He threw her to the ground, and her face slammed hard against the earth.

Alice's eyes locked with Jack's a few yards away. He could see the horror and fear deep inside of them.

The man sat down on Alice's back and ran his hands over her body looking for money. Then he began running his hands over her body, not looking for anything. She began to shriek and struggle, but he was twice her size, and she could barely move under his weight. Jack raised his head and yelled at the man to stop, but the other gunman just kicked him back down with his boot.

Jack could do nothing but watch as the man felt her breasts and then ran his hand between her legs, up her dress and into her bathing suit. Alice screamed.

Simon, too, watched helplessly. A fury began to overwhelm him, and he clenched his fists, dreaming of ripping the head off the man in the bandana. Every ounce of his soul wanted to hurt him. Hurt him badly. His blood boiled and his heart threatened to burst from his chest. He began to hear a ringing in his ear that drowned out the sound of Alice's cries and Jack's yelling.

The man on top of Alice yanked her bikini bottom down to her thighs and began undoing his pants.

Jack couldn't take it anymore. Struggling free with all his strength, he attempted to stand and charge at the man. But as he reached his knees, the gunman standing above them fired a shot into the dirt just inches from Jack's head. The loud blast rang out through the dark forest with a crack and dropped Jack back down onto his chest, holding his ears.

The man molesting Alice leapt up on hearing the shot, and the two gunmen began yelling at each other, arguing loudly as Alice pulled up her bathing suit and curled into a defensive position. Seconds later, the man rebuckled his belt, picked up Jack's backpack and took off running into the woods.

"¡*Nunca nos viste!*" the gunman above Jack yelled and then kicked him once again before running off into the night.

Jack immediately sprung to his feet and dashed over to Alice, who was weeping and screaming in the direction of the thieves. "Motherfuckers! Motherfuckers!!!" she yelled at the darkness around them. She tried to stand as if to chase after the men, but Jack held her tight and tried desperately to console her.

But she was inconsolable.

Simon, too, tried to conjure words of comfort, but it was useless. "Let's get out of here," he said, glancing around at the dark woods.

As they drove through the backcountry town, Simon looked for a police station, but there was none, so he continued on to San Pedro.

***

That night Simon booked a second room in the hotel, so Jack and Alice could be alone. Alice hadn't spoken a word since the incident and wouldn't even leave her room to talk with the police officers when they arrived. Simon told them the story, and the police officer explained that *banditos* sometimes robbed tourists on the back roads as the police only patrolled the major thoroughfares into San Pedro and Panajachel. The gunmen had probably seen them driving through the remote village earlier in the day and had staked out in the forest to ambush them upon their return. As the officer enumerated his hypothesis, Simon knew it to be true. It made him sick. All of it. His stomach wrenched with pain, his bones ached, and his skin slickened with sweat. He blamed himself entirely. It was at his insistence that they hadn't taken the boat. His chicken shit fear of open water was the root of all their anguish and had nearly cost them their lives. They never should have been on that road. *Why didn't we just wait a day!*

That night, as Simon tried to sleep, visions of Alice's dirt-soiled face pressed against the ground, frozen and wide-eyed with shocked terror, burned like fire in his eyes. He couldn't even imagine how she felt and wished he could somehow go back in time to make it all go away. But he couldn't. So, he pulled a pillow over his face and screamed.

Things won't be the same now.

As the first light of dawn trickled in through his window, Simon lay there still awake and wondered what would happen next.

He wouldn't have to wait long to find out.

"We're goin' home today," Jack said solemnly, sitting down to join Simon at breakfast.

"What?!"

"We fly out of Pana in two hours and connect through Guatemala City and Houston on our way to Nashville tonight."

Simon sat frozen, staring at Jack, devastated.

"Alice and I talked about it last night. I asked her to sleep on it, which was stupid since she couldn't sleep anyway... This mornin' she was still firm about it, so we bought the tickets online."

"Shit," Simon said, dropping his head in disbelief. The news shattered him, and he still felt to blame for it all. *I wonder if Alice hates me for putting them in that situation.*

Just then, two hands grabbed his shoulders, causing him to flinch. Turning around quickly, he found Alice standing behind him, her eyes red and swollen from crying and a subtle smile on her lips. She leaned down and wrapped her arms around his neck in a soft embrace. He reached back and held her tight. *I can't believe you're leaving.*

Throughout the somber breakfast, Jack and Alice tried to express to Simon how meaningful their time together had been and how special it was to have met him. Simon tried in vain to articulate his feelings as well, but only managed to muddle through it. He was at a loss for words but hoped Jack and Alice would grasp his meaning.

An hour later, Simon walked them to the dock to catch a *lancha* over to the airport in Panajachel. When they arrived at the gangway, Alice turned and hugged him tight. "You keep explorin' now Simon. I want to hear about all your new adventures next time I see you," she said, maintaining her embrace for a good long while. When she eventually let him go and walked onto the boat, Simon wanted so badly to hold onto her shirt and pull her back as she'd done to him on the dancefloor, way back in Brasilito.

Jack walked forward, and Simon reached out to shake his hand, but, as he might have expected, Jack growled and pulled him in for a hearty bear hug. Simon laughed, patted his friend on the back and wiped his eyes while Jack couldn't see his face.

"Be strong out here, man, and do some livin' for all three of us," Jack said with a laugh. "You have to keep goin', *amigo*."

"I don't know where to go . . ." Simon said, having never considered where to go next. Together they had been an adventure team. And yet alone, he felt lost.

Jack stared at him. "Do ya really *need* a place to go, Simon?"

Simon considered Jack's words, but they seemed more a rhetorical riddle than the answer he needed. Yet before he had a chance to respond, Jack drifted off into one of his classic romanticized orations. "Life is an odyssey, man…" he began with gusto.

Here we go.

"…and there's always gonna be new experiences to have, new places to go, and more life to live… You never know where this wild world will take you, but figuring it out as ya go is half the fun. That's a big part of the journey. You know what I mean?"

"I guess so."

"This here…" Jack continued, pointing to the ground, and then the lake and the volcanoes around them. "The sea… the earth…. the stars… the sun… they're always gonna be here man…. I think that maybe WE should be the erratic ones… the unpredictable, aimless ones…. the wanderers… the explorers… the roamers… the crazy ones. Hell, let the earth stand still for a while and we can do the turnin'," he said with a big grin.

Simon chuckled. Jack's theatrical proclamations never ceased to entertain, and yet his words often found a surprising resonance within Simon. Perhaps it was because Jack truly believed what he said. He didn't want anything from Simon and didn't care how the Texan perceived him. He spoke his mind with conviction, and that, to Simon, felt like a revelation.

As Jack stepped onto the bow of the *lancha* and the small craft started to putter away from the dock, Simon stood lost in thought, considering what Jack had just said. Suddenly, Jack yelled out to him one last time. "Remember, there are travelers within all of us, Simon!... But… if ya need a place to go… just keep heading south like the birds, man... winter's just around the corner!" he hollered with a final smile and a wave.

Simon laughed and held his hand up, waving in return.

For ten minutes, he stood there, watching as the boat and his friends disappeared slowly across the lake. The further they went, the more a sense of loneliness began to creep up inside him, until he truly was... alone.

What do I do now?

CHAPTER 42

The tendrils of weeping willows drooped low towards the edges of the tree-lined lane as Jonah glanced at the address scribbled on a piece of paper in his hand. "This must be it. Number forty-four," he mumbled, pulling the nose of the van up to a "44" hand-painted on a plank and nailed to a post by the country road turnoff.

Jonah stared at the dirt drive disappearing into the forest beside him. He knew that what lay further up that way was capable of killing him a thousand times over, but that was precisely why he'd come to this remote corner of Louisiana. Putting the van in drive, he turned onto the desolate lane and pressed on into the woods.

A few minutes later, he arrived at a large gate at the end of the road. Jonah stared at a weathered wooden sign hanging from the massive chain-link fence encircling the largely forested property. Menacing skull and crossbones stared at him above the words "Danger—Keep Out!" in flaking red paint. The words and imagery completed the not-so-welcoming impression that the fence had begun to convey.

Jonah rolled down his window and pressed the intercom buzzer on a panel beside the van. As he awaited a reply, he gazed through the fencing at a large, rustic, cabin-like structure sitting beyond it, amidst the trees. An equally large glass greenhouse sat beside it, attached via a ten-foot wooden tunnel. Several trees on the property bore spray-painted red X's on their trunks.

"Hello?" an old voice crackled through the speaker. "Who is it?"

"It's Jonah Shaughnessy, Dr. Perrimen. We've been chatting over email the past year. You invited me to come visit?"

A lengthy pause endured.

Then suddenly, the gate began to open.

"Come park at the front of the house, Jonah, and while you are outside, for GOD'S SAKE, don't touch anything!" Perrimen warned.

Jonah pulled up to the building, parked and made his way to the front door. As he reached it, the door slowly creaked open, and an eccentric looking man in his sixties, with frazzled, brown hair glanced over and past Jonah towards the driveway.

"Hello, Dr. Perrimen," Jonah said, startling the man, who looked down quickly to find Jonah staring up at him with a smile.

"Oh, good heavens, you never mentioned you were in a wheelchair! Sorry, I was expecting someone rather taller, I suppose!" he said with a jovial snort. "Come in, come in. And for GOD'S SAKE, don't touch anything!" he demanded yet again.

As Jonah followed the ambling doctor through the doorway and into the house, he was at once stunned by what lay ahead. His jaw fell.

What appeared as a two-story house from the outside, was actually a vast, barn-like structure, almost entirely open in its layout. Inside the cavernous space sat row after row of towering shelving units covered with cages, aquariums and glass cases filled with snakes, spiders, frogs, fish and more—slithering, crawling and swimming all around them. As Jonah made his way through the central aisle taking it all in, Dr. Perrimen began to speak again.

"So, Jonah, you never fully explained to me your fascination with Toxinology. You mentioned you wanted to learn about the geographic distribution of toxic species and the viability and availability of self-administered anti-toxins in your emails. Still, I'm not quite clear exactly what for. Is this for a research paper or something of the like?"

"Something of the like," Jonah mumbled from behind him.

Dr. Perrimen turned to find Jonah in a trance staring at dozens of small blue octopi floating in an illuminated glass tank. "They're blue ring octopi," the doctor said with a chuckle.

"They're gorgeous," Jonah replied in awe.

"Yes, yes, but each one carries enough poison to kill you and thirty of your closest friends in an hour. You'd never even see it coming either. Their bite is entirely painless... but a few minutes later, you'd go completely blind. Then your body would go numb... and finally, the muscles needed to breathe would cease to function. Not a very nice way to go, I don't think!" he concluded with yet another snort.

Jonah looked up at the doctor with a smile. *A bit mad, isn't he?*

"Well, doc, I'm mostly interested in tropical species, actually."

"Well, that's 95% of the world's deadly species, Jonah. I'm afraid you'll need to be a little more specific. Any aquatic animalia? Octopi, pufferfish, cone snails and the like?"

"No, primarily jungle based," Jonah replied.

"Ah! Jungle based! My favorite!" exclaimed Dr. Perrimen. "Yet quite diverse. Well then... let's begin with the snakes, then shall we? Families *Viperidae* and *Elapidae*!"

"Okay . . ."

"Then we'll move on to the Arthropods. The Brazilian Wandering Spider, the Deathstalker Scorpion, and so on and so forth...but for GOD'S SAKE don't touch anything!"

"You have all of those species here?" asked Jonah nervously.

"Jonah, my boy, I have over five hundred species of venomous and poisonous animals and plants living right here alongside us."

Jesus, where am I right now?

"That reminds me, what's with the red X's on some of the trees outside? Are those ones you plan to cut down or something?" asked Jonah.

"Haha," Dr. Perrimen laughed. "Those are Manchineel trees..." he replied. "Or, in Spanish, *Manzanilla de la Muerte*."

"Little apples of death?" Jonah said softly.

"Ah! You speak Spanish! *Bueno*! Yes, they do, in fact, bear a deadly, apple-shaped fruit. But the X's are a warning that goes well beyond that. The entire tree is toxic. Stand beneath one when it rains, and your skin will begin to burn and blister!"

Lovely

"Alright now, follow me to the snake enclosures so we can begin. And for GOD'S SAKE—"

CHAPTER 43

For several long days after Jack and Alice left, Simon felt adrift. His brain struggled to process the loss, and with every passing moment, he questioned what he should do next. *Should I go home? Should I stay in Guatemala? Should I go back to Belize? Or somewhere else? But where?*

On occasion, he would wander aimlessly around San Pedro in a desultory search for answers, but mostly he spent his hours at the hotel, chatting with its benevolent owner, Renée. One afternoon as they sat eating an early lunch, she mentioned a bookstore in Panajachel or "Pana" as the locals called it, which sold English language books and other imported knick-knacks.

"They sell books in English? Why here of all places?" asked Simon, finding it peculiar that such a store existed in this remote corner of Guatemala. Renée's eyes immediately lit up, her face bearing an unmistakable expression that loudly exclaimed: Have I got a story for you!

And that she did.

As Simon sat listening intently, Renée spun a bizarre tale of a mass migration of American "spirit seekers," a.k.a. *hippies*, to the mystical lake in the 1960s. Searching for cosmic energy vortexes and ancient Mayan enlightenment, these flower children and lotus-eaters had settled in the town of Pana on the shores of Atitlán seeking a simpler life and a far-flung refuge from Western conformism.

Simon recalled seeing numerous Pyramid-shaped buildings around the lakeshore and had heard rumblings of the area's New Age reputation—but he didn't know the half of it.

"The lake has mystical powers, they say!" Renée quipped satirically, clearly finding the whole thing a bit preposterous. And yet as she went on speaking of her quirky expat neighbors, her voice revealed a sense of endearment and fondness for their eccentricities. Especially when it came to the English bookstore's character of an owner, Green Gene, as they called him.

"Gene's quite the guru and a local legend in the area," she added. "If you're looking to be amused in a most peculiar way… Green Gene's your man!" Renée laughed, taking another sip of her glass of wine.

It was 11 a.m.

Oh, the French.

Simon grew thrilled at the prospect of acquiring some low-tech, evening entertainment, since having to think himself to sleep each night had become quite painful since the loss of his friends. So, that afternoon he hopped on a *lancha* to Pana and soon arrived in Atitlán's largest and most diverse lakeside settlement.

***

Ambling off the dock onto the bustling cobblestone streets of Pana, Simon immediately found himself engulfed in a melee of hawkers, touts and market stalls crammed along the main road and spilling into adjacent alleyways. As he made his way through the flurry, Simon noticed rather quickly a surprising number of westerners mixed in amongst the Guatemalan locals. Their near uniform height advantage made them easy to spot as countless white heads bobbed above a sea of brown and black hair.

Looking around for some of the *spacier* of the lot, Simon eventually crossed paths with a fellow who certainly looked the part. Adorned in a tie-dyed shirt stretched over his round belly, green suspenders and short trousers, the jolly old soul seemed happy to just be living as he waddled through the marketplace, smiling wide. Long grey tufts of frizzy hair protruded outward from beneath his brown apple cap, complementing his fluffy white mustache perfectly.

This guy has GOT to know Gene.

"Excuse me, do you know where Green Gene's bookstore is?" Simon asked the old, heavy-set son of the Sixties.

"Well, good afternoon to you, too, my friend!" he said with a hearty chortle and patted Simon on the shoulder.

Simon couldn't help but chuckle. "Sorry… Good afternoon. Do you happen to know of a place called Green Gene's around here?"

"Hmmmmm," The man looked to the sky, deep in thought, taking time to rub his pondering stache. "You mean Gene's place?" he eventually replied.

"Yyyyyyeah-" *Didn't I just say that?* "Do they sell English books?" Simon replied.

"Oh, ole Gene sells lots of things," he guffawed with a wink, and then pressed a couple of fingers together in front of his lips, pretending to take a toke off an invisible doobie.

Oh, man.

Simon chuckled awkwardly.

"Yeah, I can help you out there, *amigo*," the gent continued.

And as Simon patiently listened, the hearty old timer proceeded to ramble off directions, guiding Simon through the town and back again, around the village *and* through it, past landmarks and backtracking a number of times before eventually concluding that Simon could just walk forward, and he'd eventually find it.

"So, it's literally just on this road, up there on the left?" Simon asked in disbelief.

"Right."

"So, it's on the right?" Simon joked.

The quip confounded the old timer for a few seconds before, at once, he seemed to get it and bellowed with laughter. "Riiiiiiiight!" he guffawed. "Catch ya' on the flipside!" he said with a turn, and waddled off down the road through the crowd.

As Simon watched the eccentric old expat disappear into the hustle and bustle of the local Guatemalans going about their daily lives, the juxtaposition of cultures seemed bizarre—and yet somehow it apparently worked. Simon couldn't imagine picking up everything and leaving the US to go live in a third-world country like this. Yet he recognized that the old man had emigrated during a different time. He wondered if the man had fled America to avoid the Vietnam War, or if there was a more cosmic reason for him heading to Pana.

This rambling train of thought was quickly interrupted by Simon's sudden arrival at Green Gene's Place… and the remarkable display in the shop window. *You gotta be kidding me,* he thought.

Beneath a seven-foot-wide, cardboard rainbow, sat an eclectic hodgepodge of giant purple geodes, wood and brass incense burners, new age books on crystals and pyramid power, used books of poetry, and several manifestos and political books on communism, socialism, anarchism, and any other *ism* that might strike one's fancy. Simon looked around to be sure he hadn't passed through a wormhole into 1964 Haight-Ashbury. *This oughta be groovy.*

A bell dinged as Simon entered into the far-out shop. The man at the counter glanced up from his book, removed his reading glasses and gave Simon a kindly smile. Simon felt at once that this must be Gene.

"Welcome, my friend. What can I help you with today?" the jovial Gene said, his voice deep, raspy and calming. Gene's dark, weathered skin and flowing silver locks gave him a surprisingly distinguished and handsome aura.

"Just browsing," replied Simon, offering a casual smile before turning his attention to the rows of store racks. Yet upon entering the daunting catacombs of Gene's store, he quickly called back. "Aaaactually, can you tell me where the travel books are?"

"Well, that depends, my friend. Are you looking for travel guides or travel literature?"

Simon had never considered there was a difference.

Noticing his customer's hesitation, Gene continued with a chuckle, "Awe, hell, they're both over on the left there. Got a whole Latin America section, too... Anywhere in particular?"

Simon searched his mind but knew very little of the region. "No, I actually don't know where I'm going yet," he said.

Gene cracked a grin at Simon from behind the counter. "Hell, none of us KNOW where we're going in life, my friend," he said with a deep guffaw. "You might think you have it all planned out, but the next thing you know, you're in a bookstore in a small town in Guatemala!" And with that, he burst into laughter.

Simon laughed along courteously and wondered which one of them Gene was referring to. He eventually deduced Gene probably meant both. Or maybe neither.

"Ah yes, so you've got a bit of the wanderlust, eh? Well, you should find plenty to inspire your soul over there," Gene said, waving a finger towards the back of the shop.

"Something like that," Simon muttered, continuing deeper into the store until he eventually stumbled onto the travel section.

As he flipped through the eclectic collection of books, he was ecstatic to discover an extensive guidebook spanning all of Latin America, and a pocket English-to-Spanish dictionary, as well. Placing these treasured finds under his arm, he decided to give the travel literature section a once over, and proceeded to peruse the intriguing titles. *The Great Railway Bazaar, The Innocents, Into the Wild, In Patagonia, The Alchemist, Chasing the Monsoon.*

"I've read every one of them books if you want a recommendation, my friend," Gene hollered from the counter.

"Thanks, my friend!" Simon shouted over his shoulder. *My friend?*

Simon lingered for some time, skimming through the various fascinating yet unfamiliar titles one at a time – until one item, in particular, jumped out at him. The book, an old, used copy of *The Lighthouse at the End of the World* by Jules Verne, bore a cover photo of a tall red and white lighthouse perched high on a rocky outcropping by the sea. Flipping it over, Simon read the extract on the back of its well-worn binding and discovered it to be a tale of adventure and intrigue at the southernmost tip of Argentina.

"Tierra del Fuego," Simon whispered to himself, reading a description of the far-flung cluster of islands deep in the frozen south. It was a location so remote and spectacular in its isolation that Simon found himself instantly beguiled. And, as he continued to read, a peculiar sensation of yearning glinted inside of him that was as alien to him as it was unexpected. He opened the Latin America guidebook to its map and found the dense archipelago, just north of Antarctica. *Tierra del Fuego... The bottom of the world.*

Simon shook off the bizarre feeling and carried his assortment of books up to the waiting Gene. "I see you found some good fodder," the eccentric old man said with a smile, fumbling through them curiously. Yet before Simon had a chance to respond, Gene suddenly directed his gaze up to Simon's eyes and began to speak in a peaceful and entrancing voice. "The sea is everything," he began. "It covers seven tenths of the terrestrial globe..."

Ooooookay...

"Its breath is pure and healthy. It is an immense desert, where man is never lonely, for he feels life stirring on all sides. The sea is only the embodiment of a supernatural and wonderful existence. It is nothing but love and emotion. It is... the living infinite..."

When he'd finished, Gene continued to stare at Simon, smiling.

Simon smiled back at him, baffled.

"20,000 Leagues under the Sea," Gene said.

Simon still wasn't sure what was happening.

"Jules Verne," Gene continued, holding up the Verne book Simon was buying.

"Oh, yeah. Looking forward to reading that," Simon said, finally getting it.

"Thought you were a fellow Verne-head... Sorry about that," Gene said, rolling his eyes and ringing up the purchases.

Gene fascinated Simon. And as the man took his time wrapping Simon's books in brown paper and tying them into a bundle with twine, Simon felt as though Pana might be an ideal place for someone of his particular ilk. A naturally beautiful area where one could easily escape the rat race of Western society, open up a small shop such as this, and while away the days reading Jules Verne. *Maybe in another lifetime, this could even have been me?* Simon wondered.

Just then, a waft of Gene's signature scent, sweat and no deodorant, gusted past Simon's nostrils.

Meh— maybe not.

***

For the remainder of the afternoon, Simon read with unwavering delight. Burying himself in his Latin America guidebook, he found himself engrossed wholly in Guatemala's tumultuous past, Belize's colonization by the British, the arrival of the Garifuna, and so much more. He read enlightening passages on the rise of the Mayan people, their near decimation by foreign conquerors and disease, and their miraculous survival and cultural preservation to this day. He read of the turbulent political and economic struggles Guatemala had faced in recent decades, rife with violence, revolution and civil war. And with every engaging page shedding new light on the places he'd been and the people he'd met along the way, one remarkable thing stood out to him among all others. The descriptions in the guidebook, no matter how fanciful and detailed, couldn't even come close to capturing what it felt like to actually be here. The people, the culture, the scenery—even the unique sounds and smells— none of it could be conveyed with any sincerity through the written word.

At once stunned by this realization, Simon began to question how different other countries might be from his previous perceptions. *What would it be like to actually* be *in Africa... or the Amazon Jungle... or to walk on the Great Wall?* The little knowledge of Belize and Guatemala that he'd gleaned from social studies textbooks, or the odd television program, clearly hadn't come close to telling the whole story here. *Where were mentions of the kindness of Guatemalan mountain farmers? Or the thrill of Garifuna music and the taste of stewed chicken? Or the feeling of swimming through caves by candlelight?*

It occurred to Simon that he'd never have even known these wonderful things existed had he not come here. *What else am I missing out on in the world?*

The inexplicable yearning he'd felt at Gene's bookstore was somehow growing, gnawing at him greater with every turned page. A sense of urgency began to consume him. An urgency to continue his journey forward, and to continue to see what life was really like *out there*. He began to feel as though he didn't just want to...he *needed* to.

South for the winter, he recalled Jack saying to him on the dock.

The bottom of the world, he remembered thinking in Green Gene's bookstore.

And as Simon lay in bed later that night, beginning to read the Verne tale, set on a lonesome island at the bottom of the world, he began to dream of a mysterious land, far away, past mountains and seas and ice and rock. A bone-chillingly cold place that inexplicably began to spark a fire inside him.

The bottom of the world.

CHAPTER 44

The next morning Simon awoke newly invigorated. After a quick breakfast, he wandered out onto a wooden dock beside the hotel to relax in the sunshine, read through his guidebook and maybe even pick his next destination. He was just getting comfortable on his towel and had barley cracked open his book when his simple plan took a most unusual twist.

Blump!

The sound was faint. And glancing up over the pages, Simon surveyed the lake and his surroundings in search of its source. Nothing. He looked back down to the book.

Blump!

Simon's eyes darted up, yet again. This time, however, something caught his eye—a mysterious round object emerging from the murky water ten feet off the end of the dock. The guidebook dropped into his lap. *What the hell?* Simon stared at the spherical black entity, baffled as to what he was looking at. Slowly it rotated towards him. A loud *PFFFFFT!* could be heard as the scuba diver removed the regulator from his mouth, the apparatus hissing air for a moment before falling underwater. Simon gawked into the goggles of the mysterious man in the water.

"Oh, hallo there!" the boisterous man bellowed on finding Simon perched on the dock. His voice was oddly chipper, and his thick accent hinted at British. As he peeled off his mask and hood, Simon caught a glimpse of a rather handsome fellow in his mid-thirties with a dark mocha complexion. He smiled at Simon through his well-groomed beard, clearly awaiting a reply from the slack-jawed Texan. Simon stared on, dumbfounded by the bizarre situation and struggling to articulate a response.

"Um, hello," he eventually squeezed out, offering a quarter smile and an awkward wave.

"You wouldn't bloody believe what I've found down here!" the man continued with gleeful enthusiasm.

His blithe disposition intrigued Simon greatly. "What is it? What did you find?" Simon asked eagerly.

"Well, I can't just tell you, now can I?" he teased with a light laugh. "I'll have to show you!"

"Haha, riiiight," Simon chuckled, staring at the unusual fellow and patiently awaiting the punchline. Yet the man just continued to stare at Simon, grinning. *He's messing with me, isn't he... Isn't he?* "Seriously though, what did you find?"

"Seriously mate, I'll have to show you, come on then," he replied earnestly, still maintaining his wide, toothy smile.

Seriously?

"Um, I don't have any scuba gear," Simon called out, attempting to put an end to the preposterous line of dialogue.

"That's okay, I have extra," said the man. And raising an arm from the water, he pointed to a spot beside the dock. "That's my boat right next to you."

Simon squinted with trepidation, then slowly crouched down on his knees and leaned over the edge of the planks. A small motorboat sat tied off just beside him.

"Do you see the equipment bag in there?" the man continued.

Simon stared into the boat. The equipment bag was the only thing inside.

"In there are a mask and some fins... Grab them and come on in. You can use my secondary air source," the diver said, and pointed at a duplicate yellow mouthpiece hanging from his chest.

Simon froze, flabbergasted by the proposal as he knelt on all fours in dismay.

"Well come on then," the man hollered jovially, beckoning Simon to join him with a friendly chuckle.

Simon recalled enjoying his time "snorkeling" in Belize, but that had been in crystal clear, two-foot deep water. This, on the other hand, was a massive and foreboding lake. A lake of unknown depth—which more than vaguely terrified Simon.

The man in the water could see the apprehension in Simon's face. "Don't be afraid!" he called out. "It's only ten meters down and trust me… You'll be gobsmacked!" he said with a laugh.

Gob-what now?

As the curious stranger floated in the water awaiting a response, the Texan remained motionless, puzzling over the myriad reservations he had about such a potentially dangerous endeavor. *This is just insanity* he reasoned, searching for an excuse, a simple yet polite one, that would enable him to distance himself from the absurd conversation. Suddenly, he had an idea.

"So, whatcha got there?" he began. "That a single-hose, two-stage, open circuit demand regulator?"

The man in the water smiled. "It sure is."

"Nice, nice… Has it received its manufacturer's suggested service in the last 12 to 24 months?"

"Haha, that's a good point…" the man responded.

Ahaaaaa!

"Of course, it has."

Dammit!

Simon racked his brain. "And the O-rings are good?"

"Yep," replied the diver.

"Diaphragm in good shape?"

"Yep."

"Any hoses cracked?"

"Nope."

Dammit!

"I take it you're a big diver then?" the man asked.

"Never been diving in my life," replied Simon. "Wrote an owner's manual for the Prodive RX9 last year, though."

The man in the water burst into riotous laughter. "Hey, don't get your balls in a bunch mate, if you don't want to come, it's alright," he said, generously offering the clearly anxious Simon an easy exit strategy.

Perfect, Simon thought. And yet, as he prepared to dismiss the idea altogether and get back to his book, an unexpected thought popped into his mind: *Maybe I actually* do *want to do this. I mean, this is why I'm here, right? To try new things and see where the world takes me? Maybe I should just go for it?*

Simon looked back to the man in the water. "You sure it's safe?" he asked one last time.

"Absolutely," the man replied, still grinning.

Simon took pause. The sound of the water gently lapped against the dock below him as a litany of concerns and fears bombarded his brain. *Stop it!* He demanded.

Then, ignoring the cautious voice inside him that was begging him not to go through with it, Simon placed his book beside the towel, grabbed the mask and fins from the boat and plunged into the water.

When his head reemerged, he swiveled round to find the man swimming alongside him.

"You made it!" the man laughed.

"Yeah, I guess I did, "Simon replied, extending his hand. "Simon."

The amused diver shook his hand. "Davis... Nice to meet you."

"Nice to meet you too, Davis. So, I know how a regulator works, but I have no idea how to scuba dive," Simon elucidated, trying to keep his head above water as he wrestled clumsily to get his fins on below the surface.

Davis handed him the second mouthpiece and uncoiled its three-foot hose. "This is going to be real easy," he said. "Here, take this... Now when we go under, just breathe normally. I'm going to hang on to you and lead you down slowly. Your ears will pop on the way down, but that's normal. I won't let go of you, trust me. If somehow you lose your air source just swim up to the top. We're not going deep enough that you have to decompress or anything. If you can't tell which way is up, follow the bubbles!"

Simon felt reassured by how confident and experienced Davis seemed. "I take it you've been doing this for a while," he said.

"More than 20 years," Davis grinned. "Now, let's go."

Simon put the regulator in his mouth. A few seconds later, the two slowly submerged. *Oh, man.*

Ducking under the rippling surface, Simon found it much darker than he had expected. Disoriented by the unfamiliar sensation of breathing underwater, his arms began to flail amidst the bubbles, and he sucked air rapidly, trying desperately to keep from panicking. Davis could see Simon spiraling and pulled him close to his chest, the two locking eyes as Davis began to move the palm of his hand slowly back and forth in front of his mouth. At first, his gesturing confused Simon, but after a moment he realized that Davis was setting a pace for his breathing. Simon followed the rhythm of Davis' hand until he'd regained his composure. *Jesus, I'm really breathing underwater!* Simon started to breathe normally, the sunshine glinting through the rippling water a mere foot above his head. Davis gave Simon the OK hand signal, and Simon offered it back.

Deeper they sank into the chilly grey water.

The sensation was extraordinary, gliding downwards through the ether as Davis pulled Simon along in a diagonal trajectory towards the lake's bottom. The muscular man was a strong swimmer, and the pair advanced swiftly down through the frigid liquid growing pitcher black the deeper they went. After a few seconds, Davis switched on a dive light that flashed into a conical white beam that cut through the darkness, illuminating the murky depths below.

It grew hazier down near the lake's floor, but Simon soon began to see outlines of something unrecognizable appearing below them. *What the hell is that?* He could tell that it wasn't natural, but rather cohesively flat, and yet hopeless to distinguish in the silty fog. As they grew closer, however, everything gradually came into clearer focus. And then it hit him. *The flood!* And Simon immediately realized just what it was he was looking at. The ground below them wasn't the sand and rock floor of the lake at all. It was a paved road.

Oh...my...God.

Simon's heart skipped a beat. And as they arrived at street level, Davis angled their bodies horizontally, allowing them to skim over the lane just a few feet above the concrete. Simon's eyes gradually adjusted to the dark as they made their way down the avenue, and he gawked in amazement as shop windows and storefronts began to appear through the hazy water along the road beside them. He could barely breathe, awestruck by how surreal the scene surrounding him now was. This town, these homes, these businesses, these lives—lost to the cold and lightless depths.

A few more seconds passed before the pair rounded a corner, and something ahead caught Simon's eye. In the milky grey beam of Davis' light, a building lay before them with its door visibly open. Davis seemed to be leading them straight towards it. *Where is he taking me now?*

Simon's heart raced as they reached the door and Davis paddled the two men through the entranceway and into a cavernous room. *What are we doing!*

Entering the room, a thick cloud of silt churned up through the water, temporarily blinding Simon and sending his heart and breathing into full panic mode. *Why are we in here!* Fear gripped him as he questioned how he could possibly resurface now if he needed to, the roof and walls now blocking his escape.

Davis, meanwhile, maneuvered to the center of the room and then brought them to a stop. The silt slowly began to settle around them. And though Simon could barely see in the murky soup, he could just make out Davis placing his flashlight on what appeared to be a table and pointing it upward into the ceiling. *What is this guy doing?*

The man continued to fiddle with the light's position as Simon averted his eyes towards the cloudy room, trying to gather exactly where they were. *What have I gotten myself into?*

Simon was preparing to tug on Davis's shirt to indicate his need to surface, when suddenly, something rather remarkable happened. Something that Simon would never, ever forget.

In an instant, the powerful beam emanating from the dive light in Davis' hands, connected with a crystal chandelier hanging from the ceiling above. And in a spectacularly brilliant flash, its rays exploded into a radiant sunburst, sending shimmering points of light dancing around the room like a swarm of iridescent fireflies.

If the nerve-wracked Simon hadn't been gripping his mouthpiece like a pit bull, his jaw almost certainly would have dropped. The room around him, previously black and lifeless, was at once transformed into a constellation of luminescent stars now twinkling around Simon's hovering body in what felt like his own sunken galaxy. His space odyssey.

Davis was right… I DID have to see it. As the pair floated weightless amidst the underwater cosmos, the silt settled further, and the room slowly grew clearer around him. What Simon had previously taken for a shop of some sort, was in fact a lounge-style restaurant—and a chic one at that. Or at least it had been a long time ago, in its terranean days. Staring, mesmerized at the dreamlike vision around him, Simon struggled to wrap his head around the remarkable under-lake town that was now lost to the surface world. It was simultaneously depressing… and utterly bewitching.

After a few moments of shared awe, Davis towed Simon across the room to the bar and sat him down on a stool beside him. Fetching a couple of abandoned beer bottles from behind the countertop, he handed one to Simon before holding his own up in a toast.

"Here! Here!" Simon gurgled through his mouthpiece as the two smirking men cheersed and pretended to drink from the bottles. At this, Simon laughed so hard that he began to choke, coughing saliva through his regulator and surrounding his face with bubbles.

For five minutes they just sat there, milking their drinks at the bar before eventually skipping out on the tab and heading back out onto the road. Gradually, they made their way to the surface.

***

Emerging into the warm sunshine near the dock, Simon spit out his regulator immediately and tossed it into the water. "That was freakin' incredible!" he shouted to Davis, who burst into laughter.

"Haha, I *told* you it was the dog's bollocks!" he said.

Dog's what?

The two men climbed up onto the dock, and Simon collapsed in the sun on the hot planks. "So… I take it you're from England?" he said, trying to catch his breath after all the "swimming" he'd done.

"Not even close, mate," Davis replied, chuckling. "From Mozambique… but I did learn English at a British school though—hence the accent."

Mozambique? Simon searched his memories, pondering whether he'd ever met someone from Africa before. He quickly determined that he hadn't. "Mozambique, huh? A lot of scuba diving there?"

"Oh yeah. I've been scuba diving there since I was a kid," Davis replied unexpectedly.

"Really?"

"Indeed," Davis said with a chuckle. And as he began to remove his scuba equipment methodically, he began to spin a tale that soon had Simon entranced. "When I was fourteen, I began working as a clean-up lad in an English owned dive shop. It was a tedious job, for sure, but after a while I hustled my way up onto the boats, cleaning and helping load and offload the gear. Then, after a year or so, one of the owners, a proper nice fella, agreed to take me diving with him one day. And, let me tell you… I immediately fell in love with it."

Davis paused, smiling as he reminisced for a brief moment.

"At first, I started diving every month… then every week… then every day. I helped along with the tours and began to shoot videos of the rich people that hired us. It was hard work, but I was in the blue every day and I loved it. All was tickety-boo in my world."

Davis gave Simon another hearty grin as he continued to take apart his gear. Simon couldn't help but giggle to himself at Davis's odd slang.

"Then we had a group of documentary filmmakers there maybe… ten years ago or so... and I took them out to some of the most beautiful places in the area to film. I brought my camera along as well, and at the end of the week they ended up liking my footage better than their bloody own!" Davis laughed deeply. "Next thing I know, they invited me to come film with them throughout southern Africa. I'd never left Mozambique before, mind you, so when we went to Cape Town and swam with Great White sharks off the coast of South Africa, I was a little ...you know… Holy shit!"

Davis roared with laughter again, and Simon couldn't help but join in.

"When we were done in South Africa, I thought they were going to ship me home... but after that, I heard them talking about the Great Barrier Reef and the coast of Australia... Then, one month to the day I'd taken them on that first dive, I landed in Sydney, Australia as a professional underwater cinematographer."

"Holy shit!" said Simon.

"Holy shit is right!" yelled Davis, and the two burst into laughter yet again. "Been doing it ten years now and it neeeeever gets boring!"

Davis stared up towards the sky, letting the sun soak his face. The look of genuine happiness in his eyes as he spoke of his life was something Simon had only ever dreamt of. Davis was passionate about what he was doing, and Simon hoped that one day, something in his own life would give him that kind of satisfaction.

"Do you believe in destiny?" Davis continued.

"I don't know... I think so," Simon said. As he replied, however, Simon realized he'd never truly considered the concept or the real existence of destiny.

"Well mate, I believe it was destiny that I first got that shite job hosing off equipment at the scuba shop," Davis continued. "You know what? I got offered another job the same day, for more money, too, at a local restaurant. But I'd already told the bastards at the scuba shop I'd work for them."

"Really?"

"Just imagine. If I'd taken that gig at the restaurant instead, I might still be cleaning dishes today in Mozambique. Instead, I've been to over thirty countries in the world and swam in four oceans and ten seas."

"And a volcano lake," Simon added.

"Haha! Yeah, I've never seen anything right like this before!" Davis roared, sending Simon into fits.

"So, are you working on a documentary now then?" Simon asked.

"Naw... I'm between projects now, just traveling a bit, shooting stock footage. I can sell good footage to all these smaller nature shows and cable channels, and it pays good money. Bonus, I get to go to places I really want to! Nice being my own boss, too!" he beamed.

Simon was smitten with Davis's jolly personality and gazed out at the lake in reverence as his new companion finished putting away his gear and then sat down beside him.

"So, who are *you,* Simon?" he asked.

It was a tough question for Simon and one that he'd just begun trying to figure out. And as the pair sat drying off in the sunshine, Simon rattled off an abbreviated version of how he'd arrived in Atitlán from San Antonio, all the while making sure he left out any mention of the thirty-eight years before that. Davis visibly hung on his every word as Simon related his journey south and his wild adventures with Jack and Alice. The Texan swelled with pride that he had such an interesting story to tell—for once in his life. When he wrapped up his tale, he felt an unusual kind of gratification—something resembling self-respect.

"Quit your job, eh? That takes a lot of bollocks!"

"Yeah, I suppose it did," Simon replied with a smile. "So how long are you in town here?"

"Well... I'ma film this underwater neighborhood this afternoon and then leave tomorrow. What about you, mate?"

"No plans at this point. Was just trying to figure out where to go next when you popped up actually. Where are you headed after this?"

"Ah… off to the Bay Islands of Honduras," Davis replied.

"The Bay Islands? Are those on the Pacific side or the Caribbean?" Simon asked. He'd seen in his guidebook that Guatemala's southern neighbor was bi-coastal and was thrilled to use this tidbit to now sound *worldly*.

"Caribbean side," Davis replied.

"Ah, I love the Caribbean. The water there is magical, right?" Simon mused. He stared out at the lake, awash in recollections of the Caribbean back in Belize and thoughts of what it might be like down in Honduras.

Davis grinned when he saw him. He could sense from Simon's face what he was thinking. "Yeah, it really is," Davis added.

The pair sat dreaming for a spell before Davis finally broke the silence. "So, you wanna join me in Honduras, mate?"

CHAPTER 45

Several hours had passed since Simon had made the brash decision to join Davis on his journey south to Honduras. After inexplicably agreeing, he'd quickly set about learning what he could of the mysterious country, diving headlong into the Honduras section of his guidebook. The first words he read, however, sent a shiver running through his body. *"Honduras is known grimly as the murder capital of the Western Hemisphere…"*

Wait. What was that? Simon reread it to be sure he'd understood it correctly.

"Honduras is known grimly as the murder capital of the Western Hemisphere…"

Shit, I read that right.

Immediately he began to second-guess his hasty decision, flipping through the pages in a desperate search to find something more encouraging about the deadly destination. Yet political corruption, poverty and widespread violence were the inescapable running themes.

Then he reached the section on the Bay Islands. *"Three laid back island paradises surrounded by picture perfect Caribbean blue water and the second largest coral reef system in the world, the Bay Islands couldn't be more different to the Honduran mainland..."*

Whew! As Simon continued to read, the book resounded with praise for the tropical islands and Simon's mounting dread rapidly transformed back to excitement. *Back to the beach!*

That afternoon, Simon decided once again to check his social network, logging in on the Calasa's public computer. Though the post he'd uploaded from Guatemala had received several comments, all of them appeared to be some variation of: *Is this a joke?* Or *Where are you really?*

At first glance, Simon found the widespread doubt about his whereabouts a bit insulting. But on further contemplation, he realized just how much it made sense. A month ago, he wouldn't have believed himself either.

Then, as he prepared to log out, Simon noticed a pair of private messages in his inbox. The first one was, surprisingly, from his brother Jonathan. He paused for a moment, hesitant to open it. Finally, he clicked.

What's going on Simon? What is this weird message about you being in Guatemala? I called your office in San Antonio after I saw this, and they said you just didn't show up to work one day and hadn't been back since. Are you having a nervous breakdown or something? Should I be worried? This isn't like you Simon. Tell me where you really are, and I'll come get you and we can get you help if you need it.

Simon stared at the words in disbelief. *Does he really think I've lost my marbles and am lying about being in Central America? I mean, I haven't spoken to him in a long time, but he knows me better than that. Doesn't he?*

Jonathan's words bit Simon deep as he realized just how disconnected they'd become. In the 26 years since their father's death, they'd grown further and further apart with each passing year. But it sickened him now to think that Jonathan could ever think of him that way. They were still the *Hill Brothers,* after all.

Aren't we?

Simon closed the message quickly and clicked on the next one. He stared at the sender's name with disbelief.

Madeline Hill.

Mom?

Simon hadn't heard from, nor spoken to, the woman in more than ten years. He hadn't even known if she was still alive. Nor did he care. He clicked on the message and read the five words patiently. *Are you really in Guatemala?*

Simon found a bitter familiarity in his mother's lack of feeling and the brevity of her message. *Spoken like a true ghost.*

He pressed it from his mind and rather than respond, opted instead to write a new public post:

To those of you who didn't believe from my last post that I was in Central America two weeks ago, I assure you that I was. In fact, I still am. Right now, I'm in Guatemala on the shore of Lake Atitlan, a beautiful lake surrounded on all sides by giant green volcanoes.

After last I wrote, I departed Belize and headed deeper into Guatemala. My first day, I almost was driven off a cliff by a speeding bus in the mountains. Then I spent an evening with an incredibly gracious local family of farmers in their home, sleeping on a grass mat on their dirt floor. They were some of the kindest people I've ever met, and their hospitality was inspiring. From there, I headed south to the jungle paradise of Semuc Champey. I spent hours swimming in its blue pools and dozens of waterfalls with my friends Jack and Alice. Best avocados I've ever eaten! That same day we swam through the Kan Bah caves by candlelight. An unbelievable experience.

Further south I went to visit the straw god Maximon in a house in Santiago and almost choked on the thick smoke of a thousand candles lit in the room. Then, this morning, I went scuba diving through an underwater village, deep beneath the lake! My friend Davis and I pretended to drink beers in an underwater bar, which was as hilarious and bizarre as it sounds. Tomorrow I head to Honduras and who knows what. The unknown before me is so different from anything I've ever experienced, terrifying at times, and yet I've possibly never been happier.

Simon paused for a moment, pondering how to conclude his entry. Then it came to him.

If I never really knew before what life and friendship were, I'm definitely learning it now. I'm only sorry I didn't understand that sooner. So glad it wasn't too late.

He hit send and sat back, smiling. He wondered what kind of reaction it would receive this time. As he left the computer to plan the next leg of his journey, Simon once again felt proud of himself. *I can't believe I'm actually going to do this.*

***

That night, over dinner, Simon and Davis formulated a plan to head across Central America. It would take them roughly ten hours to reach the Honduran coastline, and catching the last ferry to the islands at 4 p.m. was imperative. Missing the final boat would leave them stranded in the dangerous port city of *La Ceiba* for the night. Simon had read about the seedy beach town in his book and knew he didn't want to end up there after dark.

At 3:59 a.m. the following morning, they bid farewell to Lake Atitlán and set off across the Guatemalan countryside. Simon, in his sedan, followed closely behind Davis's pickup truck as they headed east through the green forested corridors of the southern flatlands. The sun rose, and hours passed by as they made their way along a cracked and muddy stretch of road in what felt like the middle of nowhere. A light rain began to fall outside, and Simon began to question if they were heading in the right direction.

Soon, the rain grew heavier, and Simon struggled to see through the sheeting water over his windshield. As they pushed further on down the backcountry road, he started to notice blurred shapes nestled in the trees beside them. He rolled his window down to get a better look.

What the hell?

Beyond the gravel shoulder, squads of army soldiers and military vehicles sat tucked into the trees every 50 feet or so. Water dripped down their olive rain ponchos as they watched Simon drive by. Simon's already building anxiety was ticking up several more notches, and he quickly rolled his window back up.

Time went on, and through the haze of the pouring rain, Simon suddenly spied a cluster of red orbs glowing ahead off in the distance. He leaned forward, clutching the wheel ever tighter. As his car approached, Simon soon recognized them to be the taillights of numerous vehicles stopped at a blockade. Moments later, he'd reluctantly joined them in line.

The rain began to ease, and Simon lowered his window to peek outside. Ahead, he could see the caravan now sat surrounded by military watchtowers and an intimidating contingent of jeeps and heavily armed soldiers. Bolstered concrete barricades covered with razor wire coils sliced across the road, and the steel arm of a barrier gate blocked their path.

The rain continued, and through his actuating wipers, Simon watched as Davis spoke to the armed men before being waved through the military border checkpoint easily. Then it was Simon's turn. The guard beckoned him forward, and Simon pulled ahead cautiously until he'd come to a stop at the blockade. He rolled down his window, and the expressions on the soldier's faces changed the second they laid eyes on him. In an instant, the men gathered together and began jawing loudly amongst themselves as Simon watched bewildered, unsure of what exactly was happening.

After a few moments, several of the soldiers broke off from the group and approached his window. A stern-faced man stepped from the pack and spoke loudly at Simon in broken English. "One hundred dollars," the hardened soldier demanded.

What?

Simon stared blankly at the soldiers.

Clearly frustrating the impatient guard. The soldier spat on the ground below Simon's car door and whistled for reinforcements. Several other troops approached, pressing closer in a blatant attempt to intimidate the helpless gringo. It was working. Simon was rattled.

"One hundred dollars go through," the soldier howled again in Simon's face, thrusting his open palm through the window. Simon's heart raced and his eyes darted around quickly to survey the scene. Davis' truck was parked fifty feet or so up the dirt road ahead, but the barrier gate and numerous armed guards stood between him and his friend. A dozen soldiers surrounded his car now.

Suddenly, a rusted old pickup truck in line behind Simon's car honked loudly, nearly giving Simon a heart attack. One of the soldiers turned and began to yell furiously at its elderly driver. Simon looked over his shoulder and watched as the soldier kicked the side of the man's truck, continuing to berate the poor old man in Spanish. *Okay, these guys aren't messing around.*

Simon pulled the wallet from his pocket and grabbed the cash from inside. He held a combination of U.S. dollars and Guatemalan Quetzals totaling roughly eighty dollars. He handed the wad of bills to the disgruntled soldier who snatched it from his grasp and turned to give it a count. Other soldiers gathered quickly around the man to catch a glimpse of the payoff. When the guard finished counting, he glared back up at Simon with piercing eyes. "More tax!" he bellowed.

Simon held up his hands and showed him his empty wallet. "I don't have any more money!" He pointed to Davis' truck up ahead, trying desperately to indicate his need to pass through. But the soldiers weren't having it.

"More tax!" the lead soldier yelled once again and stepped closer to the car.

Simon frantically dug deep in his pockets, searching for loose change. He knew he was going to disappoint the guard again and braced for the unknown consequences. Whatever it would be, it wouldn't be pretty. Just then, a deep and familiar voice cut through the sound of the falling rain. "What the hell is going on?" Davis yelled to Simon.

Simon looked up to find his cohort now standing on the opposite side of the border gate, a mere five feet in front of his car's bumper on the

Honduran side. Simon leaned his head out the window cautiously. "They want more money," he yelled. "I gave them all I have. Do you have twenty more dollars?"

Davis looked at Simon as though he were crazy. The soldiers, meanwhile, turned their gaze to the strong Mozambican. Davis glared back at the motley crew angrily. As he ran his gaze over them, seemingly taking stock, Simon's eyes swung back and forth. The mounting tension in the triangle of characters growing unbearable.

Then… slowly… Davis walked casually up to the border gate, lifted the blockade bar, and began to wave Simon through.

Simon looked at Davis with a distinct *what the hell are you doing!* look in his eyes.

The soldiers meanwhile stood staring at Davis, stunned by his audacity. Everybody was frozen as the soldiers glanced back and forth between the pair of anomalous strangers.

After a few seconds, Simon knew what he needed to do. *Jesus here goes something.* He put his car into drive and rumbled forward towards Davis, keeping his eyes directed forward, ignoring the bewildered guards as he drove past. A few breathless seconds later, he was in Honduras.

As soon he'd passed through the gates, Simon gassed it up the road to where Davis' truck was sitting. He pulled over and stepped out.

Looking back, he watched as Davis closed the gate and began walking back towards him. He had a massive smile on his face.

"What the hell was that?!" Simon whisper yelled to Davis as he approached. Over Davis' shoulder, Simon could still see the soldiers back at the border gate staring at them dumbfounded.

"The dodgy bastards were trying to intimidate you into paying them a bribe," Davis said casually.

"He said it was a tax!"

Davis chuckled. "That's dog shit. Trust me. The bloke was trying to pull a fast one. Happens every bloody half mile or so on the road back in Mozambique. Arseholes saw a white man way out here, and you looked like a paycheck to em'. You really think they'd lock up or hurt an American like you for not having money for a bribe?" Davis exclaimed, laughing even harder now.

Simon strained to smile.

"The biggest load of bollocks is that they didn't try to swindle me cause I'm black!" Davis turned and hollered "Racists!" pumping his hand in the direction of the checkpoint and chuckling.

Simon was flabbergasted by the humor Davis was finding in the situation. Though he pretended to laugh along, Simon was scared shitless from the horrid affair.

"Hey, truly though," Davis said, growing serious. "If you have the dosh, it's usually better just to pay it. You never bloody know after all!" And with that, he slapped his hand on the roof of Simon's car and headed back to his truck, laughing.

Simon simply stood, still trembling. *Thank god, I'm alive.*

***

Five more hours passed as the two men gunned it across the Honduran countryside, stopping as little as possible in the daunting country. When 3 o'clock arrived and they still hadn't reached the ocean, Simon began to worry. But a few minutes later, they rounded a bend near the town of *Tela*, and through a thin grove of tropical palms, Simon caught a quick glimpse of the Caribbean Sea running alongside them. *There you are.*

It was 3:15 p.m. They hit the gas and down the coast they flew—until eventually, they arrived in the bleak port town of *La Ceiba*. It was 3:30 p.m.

Davis had prearranged for them to leave their cars at a hotel for the week, and after a couple of wrong turns, they finally located the building and pulled into its gated parking area. It was 3:41 p.m.

Constructed like a citadel, the structure's walls were lined with broken glass and razor wire, and Simon noticed the attendant carrying a machete. *I can't imagine there's any forest to clear or corn to harvest around here.*

But Simon knew he had no time to fear for his life. *We've got to GO! GO! GO!*

And with that, the two men furiously set about unloading Davis's camera equipment, cases and scuba gear onto a pair of rolling carts he'd brought with him. When they'd finished, it was 3:52 p.m.

Off they went, sprinting through the city streets, pushing the overloaded trollies as fast as they could on the uneven, cracked roads. The unwieldy carts wobbled and pulled them from side to side, and the two men began to giggle wildly as they raced each other down the street. Ahead, a gaggle of hookers on the sidewalk stared at the passing pair as if they were mad men. "Well, if we miss the boat, at least we know where to find a good time tonight!" Davis hollered, and Simon nearly buckled over with laughter, sucking wind hard as he ran.

Finally, they saw the dock.

Dashing across the planks of the gangway and up to the boat, they arrived just as the last passengers were boarding. They pushed their weighty carts on, barely getting them aboard before the ferry gates creaked closed behind them. "I can't believe we made it!" Simon yelled, leaning against his cart and trying desperately to breathe.

The much fitter Davis just laughed. "Thanks for legging it with me, mate. Glad we're not stuck in that town for the night. This gear costs a bomb!"

The two glanced back at the run-down city behind them, its barred windows and walled structures looking more akin to a military compound than a Caribbean beach town. "No shit," Simon replied.

The boat's engines roared to life, and the large vessel began heading out to sea. Simon watched as the land moved slowly away from them. He turned forward to see the open ocean disappearing into the horizon ahead. Simon had never been on an ocean vessel nor an island before in his life. Though he tried to keep it from Davis, as he sat there looking out at the vast blue expanse before them, he grew utterly petrified.

CHAPTER 46

After securing their carts, Simon and Davis made their way into the congested ferry cabin. Finding a few seats amongst the hundred or so passengers bound for the islands, Simon noticed that most were local Hondurans, but a smattering of foreigners also sat about. A group of middle-aged white men in clean, collared shirts sat across from the pair, and Simon noticed one of the men kept giving him and Davis troubled glances.

Soon, they reached the open sea, and as the boat rolled up and down in the large swell, Simon's stomach rose and fell along with it. Ferry attendants roamed the aisles, handing out plastic bags to passengers on the verge of vomiting. Simon took one immediately when it was offered.

"Not very good on the ocean, eh mate?" Davis jested.

"I've actually never been this far out on the ocean before," Simon replied, leaning his elbows to his knees and closing his eyes. "Actually, I've never been on an island either... To be honest, the ocean terrifies me."

Davis glared at him, astonished by the revelation. Seeing Simon's wet skin turning a greenish-grey color now though, he knew it wasn't a lie. "What's so scary about the ocean?" he asked.

Simon opened his eyes and looked up at his smiling friend. "My father died in the ocean when I was twelve," he said, closing his eyes again.

"Oh bollocks...sorry to hear that mate...Well, I guess there's gotta be a first time for everything," Davis said, patting the ailing man on the back. "Hold tight. I'll be back in a tad."

Davis exited the ferry cabin, disappearing out onto the deck. A few minutes passed before he returned and handed Simon a thick sliver of some sort of root.

"What is it?" Simon asked, rolling it in his fingertips.

"Smell it."

The Texan held it to his nose and took a whiff, flinching from the pungent odor. "Ginger?" he asked.

"Yeah, got it from a farmer on the deck bringing food to the island. Chew it a couple times, then press it between your gums and your cheek. It's an old remedy for seasickness that my mum taught me. I used to give it to sick divers on our boats in Mozambique all the time."

Simon did as suggested, and after a few minutes, the queasiness miraculously began to dissipate. "Wow… that actually works," he said, shocked. "I mean, if I tried to stand up right now, I'd probably fall flat on my face, but my stomach feels much better, thanks."

Davis laughed heartily and patted Simon on the back once again. As he did so, the staring man sitting across from them suddenly rose to his feet and walked briskly towards them.

"Is this man bothering you?" he growled to Simon, unexpectedly.

Simon swung his head up with a start and found the stranger glaring down at them with ireful eyes. Goosebumps froze on Simon's increasingly lizard-like green skin. *Who the hell is this guy? And who is he talking about?*

The man's eyes darted towards Davis, and suddenly Simon understood. "Who, him? No, of course not, he's my friend," Simon replied.

The incredulous stranger scanned his eyes over Davis with visible contempt. The Mozambican instantly recognized the malevolent look on the man's face—it was one he'd seen far too many times in his lifetime. Without hesitation, he rose to his feet and stood chest to chest with the stranger, their searing eyes simultaneously trying to bore a hole through the other. Simon fell back into his seat, shocked and puzzled by the sudden engagement. *What the hell is going on here?*

The two men stepped closer together, squaring off in an escalating moment and drawing the attention of many in the packed cabin. Simon, clueless as to what was happening, valiantly attempted to stand up and separate the men. But quickly fell from his wobbling legs back into his chair. The look in Davis's eyes was unflinching, Simon could see it. The passengers could see it. The stranger could see it, too. After several tense seconds, the older man turned and retreated back towards his seat, Davis maintaining his cold glare all the while. Simon finally took a breath as Davis sat back down. "What the hell was that about?" he squawked.

"He's Afrikaans," Davis replied. "From South Africa... some of the older Afrikaners are still quite racist these days."

"Seriously?" *Why did you ask that, of course, he's serious.*

"Yeah, unfortunately."

"Well...how do you know?"

"Orange and blue patch on his bag over there. That's the apartheid era flag of South Africa, from the time when the whites ruled."

Simon glanced over and could see the patch on the bag resting beside the old stranger. He admittedly knew nothing of the dynamics or history of the country a million miles from Odessa. How could he, he thought. Simon recalled the African history section of his high school textbooks beginning and ending with ancient Egypt.

"Jesus, have you had run-ins with them before?"

"Racist Afrikaners? Only in South Africa... but there are racist bastards everywhere, of course."

Simon was from Texas and knew Davis spoke the truth. "Do you ever deal with racism in your travels?" Simon asked, his curiosity piqued.

"More often than I bloody should, that's for sure," Davis continued. And as he did so, his voice turned graver and more severe than Simon had ever heard from the typically jovial man. "You know it's much harder than you think being a successful African man working in a wealthy person's sport," Davis began. "These days, I typically charter my own boats, but I used to go out with international dive groups all the time. And don't get me wrong, I enjoy diving with other people, discovering new things together, talking about what we saw afterwards.... but I would *always* be the only black man on the boat—without fail. Almost every time we began suiting up on the boat and prepping our gear, some American or European who had recently learned to scuba dive in their country club swimming pool would come up to me and try to explain what everything was and how all the little tidbits worked. Like they assumed I didn't already know. I've been scuba diving for twenty years!" Davis threw his hands in the air at the absurdity of it all.

"And then I'd take out my bloody camera equipment. And all these wealthy Europeans on holiday would ask me to get some good shots of them with the fish so they could buy my DVD after. Like I worked for the charter company or some shite?"

Though Davis laughed at this, Simon could sense how infuriated the man truly was by it.

"And you know I've been arrested for possession of stolen property in three bleeding countries for carrying all this equipment with me! You think that would happen to an American or a Canadian or a Brit? No bloody way! They see Mozambique on my passport and twenty grand in camera equipment, and they assume I must have stolen it. Now I always carry multiple copies of my receipts and my carnets everywhere I go. It's bloody infuriating. You know what I mean?"

Simon had, of course, hardly considered these things before. He knew he'd felt like an outsider in Guatemala, a white man in a Latino country, but he was certain that what Davis had faced was vastly different. In Guatemala, Simon felt as though people had viewed him as *different*... but not necessarily as *lesser* or a *criminal*. He began to ponder whether there was anywhere on earth he could go and feel the way Davis did. A place where he would be looked down upon solely for the color of his skin. He didn't know of such a place.

Growing up in Texas, racism had been such a prevalent part of daily life that Simon had gradually become numb to the matter, often pretending not to notice in the naive hope that it would just go away. He disliked speaking or even thinking about the volatile subject, and as such, had blocked it out and ignored it for decades. *Maybe now it's time for me to start forming some stronger opinions about it.* He knew that it was.

CHAPTER 47

It was nearing sunset when Simon and Davis reached the smallest of the three Honduran islands, Utila, and Simon stumbled off the boat feeling like death and looking equally as such. Taking pity on him, Davis hired a pair of local boys at the dock to shuttle their luggage to their hotel and even inquired about throwing Simon into one of their wooden pushcarts.

"I can walk, thank you very much," Simon interjected with an eye roll and a laugh.

Wobbling and listing heavily as he trudged down the narrow road, Simon did his best to avoid the throngs of pedestrians, scooters, bicycles and ATV's now plying the single route that encircled the minuscule island. It seemed an excessive number of people for such a small island, yet there was something else noticeably different about the place. In jarring contrast to other areas Simon had visited previously, he was surprised that the oval speck of land contained far more foreigners than locals. Dive shops peppered the waterfront bearing signs in English. Restaurants and bars blared reggae music and advertised two-for-one shot specials.

"I thought we were going to Honduras?" Simon jested.

Davis chuckled. "Hey, I know there's a lot of bloody foreigners here, but that's because the diving is some of the best on earth…And once you get in that ocean, it doesn't matter where you are or where you're from. It's a whole different world on the reef, mate."

Simon smiled at the thought.

In those few moments that they'd spent underwater on Lake Atitlán, it had unarguably felt like an alien world to him. He wondered if he'd ever get back there someday.

Part of him hoped he would.

***

As was to be expected, the following morning, Davis departed bright and early to dive and film out on the reef. Simon meandered around the island, now desolate and strangely devoid of people, perusing the few open stores, restaurants and bars that he could find. Eventually, he located the island's one small sandy beach, but was disappointed to find it crawling with sand fleas, and again…completely bereft of people. *Where is everybody?*

Around lunchtime, Simon wandered into a lonesome, but open, dive shop slash restaurant and took a seat on its stilted patio over the Caribbean Sea. A lanky beanpole of an Aussie waiter, Ben, took his order, and before long, the only two folks in the place were sitting together chatting easily.

"Sooooo, I kind of feel like you and I are the only people on the island right now," Simon teased. "When I got in last night, this place was crawling with people. Where is everyone?"

Ben laughed, as it wasn't the first time he'd been asked this. "Ah yes, you're a newbie, ahn'tcha. Everyone on the ahland leaves after brekkie to go dive during the day here, mate. There's really not much else to do here in the day, honestly! Reckon everyone'll be back along this evening to wash up and get pissed, though!" He laughed.

Simon laughed as well. Mostly at Ben's accent.

"Come to think of it, mate, why ahn'tcha out diving?" Ben asked.

"Me? Oh pshhh, I don't really scuba dive... Well, I did once, but that didn't really count. It was in a lake," he said.

"Well, did you like it?"

"I loved it!" Simon replied emphatically. "Truthfully though, I'm horribly afraid of the ocean."

Ben squinted at him with a confused half-smile. "You know you're on a bloody island, right?"

"Yeah, don't remind me," Simon quipped. He really didn't want to be reminded.

"Well, if you've come this far, mate, you might as well get over it and enjoy yourself. Don't be a bludger. Honestly, once you're down there, mate, it's no worries. So calm, ya cahn't be afraid."

Simon grinned and politely nodded.

Clearly, Ben underestimates what a coward I am.

And yet Simon took the advice to heart. He'd loved those moments in the lake, and imagined how much different—*better?* it might be in the turquoise sea beside them now.

"Well... if you wanna try it again, we have a class starting tomorrow, mate... If you're keen, we could get you certified in four days. Start you off in shallow water and let you suss it out. If you don't like it, you can piss off before we go out in the tinny."

The what now?

Simon took a spell to mull the proposal. *Davis IS going to be diving all week, and there isn't really anything else to do here. Ben's right, too, I HAVE come this far, I'm already on an island in the middle of the ocean. And that WAS amazing diving with Davis in the lake. I mean, I could always quit if I don't like it... Jesus, am I really thinking about doing this?! Is this crazy?!*

"Okay, I'm in," Simon blurted to Ben.

"Beauty!" Ben bellowed, slapping his hand on the bar. "I'll get you the sign-up paperwork. Hope you brought your bathers!"

My what?!

As Simon walked back towards the hotel, he resolved to keep his diving lessons a secret from Davis. Diving was Davis's passion, and if Simon tried to quit, he knew his new friend would have more than a few things to say about it. *Better just to keep him in the dark... for now.*

***

The next day Simon went back to school for the first time in decades. Beginning the day with bookwork and tests, he quickly concluded that in the eighteen years since he'd graduated college, bookwork and tests had not gotten any more fun. Especially not with views of the Caribbean Sea outside his classroom window. *What am I doing in here!* So, when the time came for doing basic drills in the water, Simon's heart hopped. *This is where I shine!*

But Jacques Cousteau he was not.

From the get-go, Simon felt utterly lost and disoriented in the training pool. Just maintaining balance with the awkward equipment on seemed discouragingly difficult, and Simon toppled over more than a few times. Much to the amusement of the other students, all of whom were ten to twenty years his junior. But Simon kept at it. And by the end of day one, he was exhausted, a little humiliated and theoretically, a whole lot better at underwater survival.

The next day they'd visit the shallow reef.

The boat rocked hard in the waves as they motored through the spray out to the first dive site. The water turned deeper and darker the further they went from shore, and, in turn, Simon's anxiety grew deeper and darker as well. He was scared to death, having expected nothing less. And as they arrived at their location, his pulse was racing and sweat filled his wetsuit. The boat anchored. The first group of divers entered the water. Then, gathering every ounce of courage he could muster, Simon jumped into the open ocean for the first time in his life.

***

Simon's masked face burst to the surface as he found himself bobbing up and down in the waves and sucking air rapidly through his regulator. Unable to see what was below him, he flapped his arms wildly, struggling to maintain his buoyancy as the loud sound of the boat sloshing next to him added to the franticness of the moment. Simon glared over to the boat ladder and wanted nothing more than to climb up it to safety. He was about to swim to it, when his instructor grabbed his vest and turned him around, towards him. Seizing Simon's BCD inflator hose, the instructor pressed the deflate button, and as the air hissed out by his ear, Simon slowly began to descend under the water. *What have I gotten myself intooooooo!"*

Five seconds later, everything changed.

The trepidation and distress, so tangible on the loud, rocking surface, felt instantly washed away in the serene underwater universe. Everything was calm and silent. The water was still, the sound of the sea a hushed hum. Fish swam around him in 360-degree vistas that stunned Simon at every turn of his head. The undulating coral reef below him teamed with life, and everywhere, everywhere the colors of the sea swirled and danced around him.

Simon would experience many things that day. Massive undulating white sea anemones. A rainbow-painted school of parrotfish. The long, spiderlike legs of an arrow crab, and the vibrant green body of a moray eel. But, above all else, he would experience the beauty, tranquility and bounty of something that had terrified him for the better part of his life. The sea.

Breaking through his fear that day, and finding something so awe-inspiring and wondrous on the other side, was the greatest discovery Simon could possibly have hoped for. And later that night, as Davis relayed tales of his daily dive to Simon, taking special care to describe the moray eel he'd been fortunate enough to see earlier, Simon had to grit his teeth to keep from telling him that he'd seen one too.

"Yeah, well I spent the day at the beach bar, playing checkers with the bartender," he fibbed.

"Sounds very eventful," replied Davis sarcastically.

Yet behind his expressionless face, Simon was inwardly laughing to himself to tears.

***

For two more days, Simon dove at various parts of the reef, practicing his craft and observing a menagerie of colorful fish, eels, rays and even a few barracuda. Each time they set out in the boat, his heart would race furiously, and he would undoubtedly get nauseous out on the choppy sea. But once he splashed into the cool water, and submerged himself in the quiet, azure depths, he would become entirely at ease, floating effortlessly through the spellbinding world below the surface. *It's so peaceful down below.*

He soon discovered that when he surfaced, the above-water world seemed comparatively loud, harsh and violent—filled with a cacophony of deafening noises and constant worries about life and the future. Down below, however, none of that seemed to exist. *Fish don't know how good they have it.* He laughed at the crazy thought, but honestly felt a tad jealous.

In four days' time, Simon successfully completed the course and received his diving certification card. With his hand in his pocket, he pressed it tightly to his thigh the entire walk back to his hotel.

That night at dinner, Davis rambled on about his final dive the following morning and how upset he was to be leaving Honduras soon. "So, can I come dive with you tomorrow?" Simon asked coyly.

Davis gave him a subtle grin. But the disheartened look in his eyes said everything. "Really wish I could, mate, but I can't share air with you tomorrow, sorry. I'll be out filming for a while and need to get a good bit done. Can't hang on to you AND the camera, now can I?"

Simon could tell that Davis deeply regretted having to say no.

It was time.

"Well then, it's a good thing you don't need to share air with me, now isn't it?" Simon replied, pulling out his dive certification card and holding it up in Davis' sightline.

Davis' eyes lit up, and a huge smile burst onto his face. "Bollocks! Where did you get that?" he yelled, stunned.

Simon laughed hysterically. "I've been in dive school all week. Just passed the class today. Surprise!" he hollered, buckling over with satisfaction.

Davis began to laugh riotously as well. "Bloody hell! Would you look at that! I can't believe it. Of course, you can come with me tomorrow… and the next round's on me!" he shouted, giving Simon a shockingly firm slap on the back.

As Davis left to grab them drinks from the bar, Simon just sat there giddily. He was overwhelmed with pride, not only for having completed the course and conquering one of his greatest fears, but for having withheld a secret from his friend for so long. After thirty-eight years of having virtually nothing exciting to talk about, keeping such a secret had proved inconceivably challenging. But he'd done it.

That evening they drank beers in a thatch-roofed bar by the sea, and Simon told Davis of his many adventures in dive school and on the reef. As they shared in the moment and talked into the night, Simon couldn't help but pause on occasion to take in where he was, who he was with and what he had just accomplished. There were glimmering moments where it didn't even feel real, like he was living life through another person, or about to wake from a dream. But it felt *so* unmistakably good.

CHAPTER 48

The next morning, they arose at the crack of dawn and were on the boat by 6:30 a.m. As the boat's captain steered them out to see, Simon began to grow anxious. Davis planned to take them towards a broad channel where "large marine life" reportedly came to feed, but had been noticeably vague as to what *kind* of large marine life.

By 7:15, the pair were in the water, swimming along a towering reef wall amidst legions of extraordinary things. *This is* very *different than the shallow reef!*

The sheer depth and magnitude of the area intimidated Simon immensely, but having the highly skilled Davis nearby placated his worries to a small degree. His friend also had an incredible knack for spotting wildlife amidst the fields of undulating coral, continually pointing out strange creatures that Simon would never have noticed otherwise. Lionfish, sea slugs, christmas tree worms and more.

As they continued to swim along the reef, they spied several large stingrays gliding by and a pair of small nurse sharks, which caused Simon's heart to skip a beat. Davis filmed a bit here and there, but by midday they had yet to encounter any larger animals, and Davis grew disheartened. After several air tanks, they took a break to have lunch on the boat. Davis tossed his gear to the ground in frustration.

"You okay amigo?" Simon asked gingerly.

"I'm getting nothing here, mate. Bloody nothing!" he yelled, throwing his mask across the boat. "I think I'll have to dive on the ocean side of the reef," he continued, staring out across the water.

"Okay, let's do it then," Simon replied naively.

Davis turned to him and smiled. "I like your moxie mate, but it's deep water out there, Simon. The inner reef is great for how many small creatures there are everywhere… but the open ocean is where all the bigger things are."

Um…what kind of things?

"Well, if that's what you need, let's do it," Simon said with a nervous swallow.

Davis laughed and stared at Simon to be sure he was serious. When Simon grinned back, he knew he was. "Well, off we pop then. Let's do it!" he cried and cued the pilot to fire up the engines.

Simon had no idea what he was in for. As they made their way further out to sea, nothing could have prepared him for what was to come.

***

"This is going to be unlike anywhere you've ever dived before," Davis began in a stoic and ominous tone that made Simon's legs tremble. Simon listened to his friend carefully as he struggled to pull on his cumbersome gear, the boat rocking back and forth wildly on the churning swell. "There's strong current in the water here. Currents that can take you all the way to bloody Mexico if you let them, so keep one eye on the reef wall, and one eye on me at all times, alright?"

The way Davis was speaking made Simon's stomach clench up. A stomach already in shambles from the roiling sea.

"If you get lost, and we get separated away from the reef wall, you probably won't be able to see the seafloor or the surface—just blue everywhere. It can be really disorienting. Remember, blow out some air bubbles, and they'll show you which way is up. Follow them. If you go a different way, I probably won't get to see your handsome face ever again," Davis chuckled.

Simon forced a smile.

"Hopefully, we can find something worth filming in the top eighteen meters. That's as deep as you can go… If not, I might have to leave you on the wall and dive deeper to see what I can find."

Simon didn't like the idea of being left alone in deep water… or anything Davis was saying for that matter. He hadn't the slightest idea what they might encounter down there, but he desperately needed to get off the undulating boat as soon as possible—*the SS Queesemaker.*

It was half-past one when they jumped in the water and began to descend. Simon soon realized just what Davis meant by "deep." The coral-covered reef wall looked similar to others he'd experienced, yet this one took the form of a sheer cliff, falling down as far as he could see into a hazy, dark abyss below. Away from the wall was an endless blue void: above, below, *everywhere.*

For the initial twenty minutes, they swam along the wall at a reasonable depth, Davis' eyes keeping a mindful watch on the open ocean beside them. Though Simon tried desperately to appreciate the beauty of the vast reef, he couldn't shake an overwhelming fear of whatever lived out in the blue nothingness behind him. Every few seconds, he'd glance over his shoulder to be sure they were still alone. *This isn't so fun anymore.*

After a spell, Davis stopped and signaled to Simon that he was going to descend further. Simon was to hold steady at this point on the wall and wait for him. *Oh, Jesus.*

Simon forced his hand up to give him the "OK" signal, and then watched as Davis swam down the reef wall, gradually, slowly, getting hazier and hazier until he disappeared completely into the murky, blue depths below.

Simon hovered motionless for a few minutes.

The reef wall, teeming with colorful fish beside him, gave him a modicum of comfort, and he turned his back to it for reassurance. The strategy, unfortunately, left him staring straight out into the vast blue ocean. It seemed beyond immense and unnerving in its thick, cobalt opacity. Simon strained to breathe calmly.

Sssssshhhhhhhh Hwoooooooooo Sssssshhhhhhhh Hwoooooooooo.

As he stared out into the blue, Simon slowly began to notice something changing in the otherwise even-toned seascape. In the infinite distance, an amorphous shadow slowly emerged, darkening a patch of blue like a thundercloud rolling in across a clear sky. Distance and space felt warped by the billions of gallons of water between him and the shadow, and Simon struggled to tell if what he was seeing was actually anything at all. He squinted and looked around in the blue. Then back in the direction of the shadow. It was dark, increasingly so, and had one characteristic that Simon was finding particularly alarming.

It was moving towards him.

What… what is that?

Simon's heart raced faster, and he sucked oxygen rapidly to feed his bloodstream.

Ssshhh Hwooo Ssshhh Hwooo Ssshhh Hwooo Ssshhh Hwooo.

Looking frantically down the wall below his feet, Simon desperately hoped to find Davis heading back up to him.

But there was no one. Just a slow trickle of bubbles rising from the void.

When Simon glanced back up, the slaloming anomaly was even closer. Though it was moving slowly, Simon could tell that whatever it was, it was massive. He stared wide-eyed at the large entity bearing down on him.

Sshh Hwoo Sshh Hwoo Sshh Hwoo Sshh Hwoo Sshh Hwoo.

Simon froze, mortified beyond comprehension and subconsciously inching backward closer to the reef wall in the hopes that the animal would lose him against it. A dorsal fin on the creature's back emerged from the haze. *Dear god, that's the biggest shark on earth… and it's coming this way!*

The word *terror* couldn't do justice to what Simon felt in that moment. His muscles began to seize, his pulse spiked to twice its normal rate, and his breathing all but stopped. And just when Simon felt sure that death was fast approaching, he felt a hard thump on his shoulder.

BAAAAAAAAAA!

Shuddering and screaming through his regulator, he turned sharply in horror, to find Davis's face right alongside him. Simon clutched his chest, and Davis could see the panic in his friend's eyes. Davis gestured for him to calm down, and began making his slow breathing hand motions once again.

Are you kidding me right now? Simon pointed wildly out at the creature headed straight for them.

Davis again gestured for him to calm down and motioned for him to breathe slowly. Then, calmly reaching down to his hip, Davis retrieved a mini whiteboard and took out a marker. He began to write something on the board as Simon stared at the massive lumbering beast coming closer… and closer… and closer.

Oh my god! It's Megalodon!

Davis tapped on his shoulder again and Simon swung back to see the whiteboard being held up in front of his face.

It's a WHALESHARK. NOT dangerous! Eats plankton.

Simon read the words, and then looked back at the slow-moving creature… Then back to Davis…. Then back to the creature… Then back to Davis, who was giving him a thumbs up… Then back to the creature.

Slowly, Simon's heart began to slow.

His breathing eventually followed.

His pride, however, would take a bit longer to recover.

Simon pulled on his collar to let some cool water rush through his wet suit and evacuate the warm liquid in his nether regions.

Once again, Davis tapped him on the shoulder and signaled Simon to follow. The Texan, now feeling like a fish out of water in the water, didn't want to go anywhere but up. But he had no interest in letting Davis out of his sight again. So out they swam, away from the reef, slowly paddling into the vast blue towards the massive animal.

As they got near to the colossal creature, it slowly came into clearer focus. It was swimming shallow, only twenty feet below the surface, and rays of sunshine shone down through the water, causing beams of light to dance across its huge body. It was magnificent, shark-like in shape, smooth and grey with white spots, and nearly the length and girth of a school bus. Yet somehow the massive creature glided gracefully, arching and sliding through the water with astonishing ease.

Simon and Davis moved up alongside it, and the three swam lazily together for several breathtaking minutes. Simon laughing into his air regulator with joy. *This is incredible.*

Easing down below the animal, he glanced up and could see the whale shark's enormous black silhouette against the rippling sunbeams far above. The rays of light twinkled around the creature as Simon floated in awe of its tremendous size and gentle demeanor.

Davis pulled out his camera and began filming. The large animal playfully swam past them, coming to within just a few feet of where they floated. Simon laughed again into his regulator—overwhelmed by the moment and in disbelief of how astounding nature could be.

The pair spent ten more minutes swimming with their new friend before heading back to the boat. When they climbed aboard and dropped their gear, Simon let out a deep sigh and stared out at the open ocean with a huge, satisfied grin on his face. A grin strikingly akin to Davis's, back on the dock of Lake Atitlán that first day.

"Bloody amazing right?" Davis said, seeing Simon's blissful air.

"That, my friend, is an understatement," he replied.

Simon had never experienced anything like it before. And as he laid back on the dive boat's deck, he let the sun start to warm him, and began to contemplate just how many things he'd done or seen for the first time on this journey. This dive would undoubtedly be yet another new highlight in his life—one of a dozen of them that had begun just a few weeks ago. That first day when he took a chance and went to dinner with Jack and Alice in Brasilito. *So, so much has happened since then.*

Davis put a CD into the boat's stereo, and some joyous, rhythmic African music began to play. The Mozambican cracked a beer and began singing and bobbing along to the lively music, Simon smiling wide as he watched his jaunty friend.

"Oh, Happy Thanksgiving by the way!" Davis called out between choruses.

Today is Thanksgiving?!

"Shit, I didn't even realize that was today! Thanks!" Simon was astounded that he hadn't realized it earlier, and he suddenly recalled his plans of several months ago: to spend Thanksgiving at the Sunshine Bay Resort, eating their special Thanksgiving buffet feast. The thought of it now made him laugh, and he gave thanks that he wasn't there.

The music continued to play, and Davis's singing and dancing fell into tempo with the lapping waves for a few moments. The sun hit hot on Simon's grinning face as he lay there, brimming with a euphoric contentment about where he was, who he was with and most extraordinarily, in the man he felt he was becoming.

CHAPTER 49

The morning ferry would depart for the mainland at 8 a.m. Davis would be on it. Simon debated staying on the island for a few more days but eventually decided it was time to move on. Where to, he had no idea.

The two men took the morning boat back to La Ceiba and then caravanned southeast towards Tegucigalpa, the sprawling capital city of Honduras. That evening, Davis had a 36-hour series of flights back to Mozambique, taking him through San Salvador, Washington DC and Addis Ababa. He was less than thrilled about the journey ahead.

When they arrived at the airport, Simon helped Davis get his cases checked in, and then walked him to the security gate. "Have a safe flight back, man, I wish you could stick around longer," he said, giving Davis a comradely hug. He was sorry to see his new friend leave so soon. Though they'd been traveling together for a mere eight days, it had been quite the extraordinary week. Each day of Simon's life seemed so much more special, more meaningful and unique to him now.

"Yeah, mate, well I have to be getting along home now. But remember, I'm just over in Mozambique!"

"*Just* in Mozambique?" Simon scoffed.

"Hey, the world isn't really that big these days," Davis laughed. He pulled out a card and handed it to Simon. "Drop me a line anytime. You should come dive with me in Africa someday. It would take your bloody breath away."

The idea enchanted Simon greatly. Before last month, Africa had seemed like a wild and unreachable land a million miles away from anything he'd ever know. A distant place that six weeks ago, he never could have even imagined visiting in his lifetime. Yet now, anything was beginning to feel possible.

"I will," he said.

***

After bidding his friend farewell, Simon drove away from the airport and made his way deep into the dense urban fray of Tegucigalpa. Though he needed to find a hotel for the night, as he arrived in downtown, Simon cringed at what he saw before him. The narrow, almost tunnel-like, congested city roads sat cloudy with smoke and packed with honking cars and pedaling touts. Everywhere, a palpable lawlessness seemed to fill the lanes, from police clashes on nearby sidewalks, to hookers approaching his window glass at every red light. Simon felt a pounding urge to speed to the city limits and escape the mare's nest. *But where would I go?*

He had no answers. So, on he went.

The sky drifted into darkness as Simon himself drifted, lost, through the city streets. His doors were locked. His windows wound up tight. It would be a white-knuckled hour before he'd finally stumble onto a promising place to stay. A recently built single-story, concrete motel sardonically named La Hotel Bonita sat nestled in a comparatively quiet off-highway neighborhood. Simon pulled into the parking lot mentally exhausted, begging the gods above for a vacancy.

"*Yo.... yo quiero....um...yo quiero el roomo...*"

The plump lady at reception, stared quietly at Simon as he floundered mightily to formulate a sentence with the few words of Spanish he *knew*.

"Oh, to hell with it," he conceded, pulling out his Spanish phrasebook and pointing to its translation of *Do you have a room?*

"*Ah, si, si,*" she said, relieved to finally understand the jabbering *gringo*.

Tottering around the counter, she led him out of the reception office and through the parking lot towards the rooms. Adjoining the motel sat a small bar, Cantina Marigold, and Simon peeked inside to check if they served food. Ten hours had passed since he'd eaten breakfast on Utila, and a gnawing swelled in his empty stomach. All he could see in the cantina though were little foil bags of plantain chips. *Shit.*

Settling into his dingy but passable room to rest, Simon sat on the hard, flat bed, pondering how his standards for accommodation had transformed over the past three weeks. *All I need is just a place to rest my weary head.*

He tossed his books onto the nightstand and unrolled a map of Central America that Davis had given him. He spread it out on the bed and looked over it closely now, tracing with his finger the circuitous route of his journey so far. He couldn't believe how far from Belize he'd already come.

From Tegucigalpa, his finger then wandered south. Down through Honduras… Nicaragua… Costa Rica . . . eventually reaching Panama near the map's southern edge.

Wow, that's really far.

Simon glanced over to the Jules Verne book sitting by the bed and thought again about Tierra Del Fuego. *That…is impossibly far,* he thought, and quickly put the ridiculous notion out of his head.

One thing, however, was certain. Simon needed to leave Honduras as soon as possible. Examining the map, he found the nearest borders to his current location—West into El Salvador, or south into Nicaragua. Both countries summoned dubious images in his mind, and the mere thought of traveling to either one of them by himself felt daunting. *But maybe I have it in me?*

***

Though the sun had set, the gnawing in Simon's stomach was unrelenting. Dismissing the idea of a plantain chip dinner, he decided to venture from the hotel on foot and hopefully locate some food nearby. He'd barely made it two blocks when he began to sense what a significant mistake he'd made.

All around him, the entire *barrio* sat closed and boarded up for the night. The few orange streetlamps that functioned at all flickered intermittently, leaving only occasional pools of pulsing light in the urban blackness. The buildings that lined the sidewalk bore heavy metal gates and concrete walls crowned with broken glass shards—a cold reminder of the dangers of this city. He began to imagine numerous eyes lurking in the darkness, watching him. The silence racked his nerves. Only the sound of puttering footsteps and distant sirens reached his ears.

I don't care if this is just paranoia. I shouldn't be out here right now.

Simon turned to head back to the hotel. But as he did, the calm in the streets was suddenly pierced by the sound of barking street dogs nearby. Simon swung his head over his shoulder just in time to witness the frenzied pack barreling around the corner in a ragged stampede and charging straight towards him.

The dozen or so feral animals galloped through the shadows as one.

Simon froze in fear, certain that the pair of grizzled mastiffs leading the great swarm were preparing to attack. *Here comes death.*

20 feet…

15 feet…

Wild fury seemed to burn in the dog's eyes, sending a shudder through Simon's spine.

10 feet…

5 feet…

The dogs were closing in fast on the quaking man, and a grueling death, torn to shreds by a pack of Honduran street dogs seemed all too imminent. Simon threw his arms over his head and dropped to his knees.

He closed his eyes.

In the darkness, the sound of the charging dogs whisked by both ears, and the breeze from the passing pack blew against Simon's cheeks.

In a few seconds … it was over.

Simon opened his eyes. His body remained paralyzed as he turned his gaze to find the dozen hellhounds hurtling on down the darksome road. The mad barking eventually tailed off into the night as silence once again filled the air. *I really* need *to get back to the hotel!*

Springing to his feet, Simon hastened in the direction of his hotel once again. But as he walked briskly onward, he soon began to hear footsteps approaching him from the blackness. *Where is that coming from?*

Seemingly out of nowhere, a disheveled man suddenly appeared beside him, exclaiming frantically in Spanish, "¡*Usted no debería estar aquí! ¡Déjeme caminar a casa con usted, para que regrese a salvo!*" the man yelled repeatedly.

Simon leapt back, horrified by the stranger's surprise appearance, and darted off faster and faster towards the hotel. Yet as he did, the man followed close behind him, continuing his hectic banter all the while. Simon didn't know what he was saying, but he didn't care. He just needed to get away.

When at last Simon arrived back at the hotel, he burst through the door into the reception office, slamming the door shut behind him and turning to look out the window. Outside, the strange man came to a stop in the parking lot under the florescent glow of the *La Hotel Bonita* sign, and stared at Simon through the glass. Then oddly, he waved to the trembling Texan before walking away into the night.

Simon turned around, exasperated, and suddenly locked eyes with the chubby receptionist who was staring at him curiously from behind her counter. Latin gospel music crackled on an old radio behind the desk as the two remained locked in a staring contest for what felt like an eternity. Simon wouldn't dare leave the hotel again, but his stomach continued to growl below his shirt. He decided to take a chance. "*Comida?*" he asked politely, holding his fingers up to his mouth as if to eat from them.

Perhaps it was the fear the woman had seen in his eyes just moments earlier, or possibly sympathy for the seemingly helpless man, or maybe, it was just plain old kindness, but after a brief awkward moment, she held up her index finger, and then disappeared through a beaded curtain behind the desk.

As the strings rustled back and forth, Simon could see through to an attached apartment tucked away in the back. In it sat another heavyset woman and a child on a couch, glowing in the faint white flicker of a television. Simon began to pace around the office anxiously as the Latin gospel music slowly began to soothe his frazzled nerves. He noticed Christmas decorations and tinsel hanging in the windows and homemade snowflakes cut from coffee filters strung about. *I can't believe it's nearly December. I guess Christmas begins early in Central America.*

When eventually the hearty woman returned, she carried with her a steaming plate of beans, rice and tortillas. She handed it to Simon, and the thankful Texan took it appreciatively.

Simon reached for his wallet, but the woman waved her hand in a gesture of refusal. So, instead he offered her a warm smile and a *"muchas gracias,"* with an accent that was improving by the day.

"De nada," she replied, smiling and nodded in return.

Latin American hospitality was something Simon was growing rather fond of.

Before exiting the office, Simon glanced again out the window to make sure the coast was clear, and then scuffled hastily back to his room.

Once the door was locked, he plopped down on his bed and scarfed down the hot, homemade meal ravenously.

When he'd finished, Simon continued to pore over his map and guidebook, now feeling shaken from the night's encounters and very much alone. A quiet hour passed, and slowly Simon dozed off in bed, his guidebook in his hand as it lay resting gently on his chest.

Suddenly, a loud banging sound ricocheted through the night, jarring him awake.

Simon didn't know it at the time, but his life was about to change forever.

CHAPTER 50

What was that? Simon launched up quickly in bed, catapulting the guidebook from his chest onto the motel room floor. His head darted side-to-side, searching for the source of the noise. But all he found was his empty room still aglow from the light of his bedside lamp.

He glanced at the clock. It was 9:15 p.m.

Did I just dream that?

Holding still, his ears perked to attention and patiently awaited any further commotion. Silence filled the air. So, after a few moments, he laid back down in bed and reached to turn off the lamp.

Just then...BANG!

The booming sound cracked yet again, sending Simon's head swinging towards the door, his eyes locking onto it with spooked expansion.

It's coming from right outside.

The directional origin of the sound was unmistakable. Simon's car... and something else... now lurked just beyond the wall.

Shit.... What should I do?

Pausing for a beat to gather his rattled thoughts, Simon eventually slid out of bed and crept quietly to the window, pillow shield in hand, and gently pulled back the curtain to peek outside. Through the thick pane, he could see his car, still parked right where he'd left it under the florescent glow of the hotel sign.

The previously empty parking space beside it, however, now contained a towering, jacked-up, brown cargo van adorned with unusual metal fittings.

Its tail end was pulled up to the room next door to his and was racked out with a giant spare wheel and half a dozen rectangular, metal fuel cans.

From Simon's angle, he noticed an empty wheelchair resting on the concrete beside the van's driver's side door. He stared at it, perplexed, its shadowy presence seeming ghostly in a way. Then, suddenly, a head emerged from the front seat of the van, and a thin man followed, lowering his body down dexterously and swinging it into the rolling transport.

What the hell?

Simon was stunned to see another caucasian at the hotel, especially a disabled one, and he squinted to try and distinguish the man's face in the dimly lit parking lot. But it was impossible.

As the stranger rolled through the scattered patches of light towards the back of the van, Simon could see a tattered Detroit Tigers baseball cap on his head. Below it, greasy brown hair hung down to his chin, his thin face remaining dim in its umbra.

The man opened the hulking van's rear doors, and as he did so, its innards fell partially into Simon's view.

What is all that?

Intricate cargo shelving lined the interior walls, loaded with countless cases and satchels. A large, cylindrical plastic tank towered near the van's rear. On the passenger side, steel brackets retained a mélange of electrical apparatus with numerous cables running up and into the ceiling. Simon had never seen anything like it and stood transfixed, staring through the window with mounting fascination.

As he watched, the stranger reached up to one of the lower shelves near his eye level and pulled from it a green duffle, placing it on his lap. Behind it on the shelf sat a grey plastic bin, and Simon's eyes lingered while the man tried to retrieve that as well. Yet it appeared to be stuck—snagged on something hidden from view—and the man struggled mightily to free it from its position. After several seconds, he gave up on the fruitless endeavor.

Poor guy...

Without a second thought, Simon unlatched his door and stepped out into the night. "Let me help you with that," he called out, emerging from his room.

"I don't need your help!" barked the irritated man without so much as a glance.

Though the tone in his voice rang sharp and brusque, beneath it lay a youthful softness that gave Simon a shiver and stopped him in his tracks. "I know you don't NEED my help, but I'm just offering," Simon continued tactfully. But the man chose not to acknowledge him, and just sat there silently staring into his van.

Feeling vaguely slighted, Simon was preparing to head back inside, when suddenly the wiry man launched into a flurry of action.

In a flash, the man's muscular arms thrust up and latched onto a series of metal bars bolted ladder-like onto the inside of the van's rear door. Then using nothing but his tremendous upper body strength, he began to climb, hand over hand, pulling his entire body effortlessly up and out of the chair.

Simon stood there, slack-jawed. *Holy shit!*

Swinging his lower half into a seated position on the van's tail end, the man quickly found what was restraining the grey bin, freed it and then lowered himself back down to the chair, all in a matter of seconds.

Simon was dazzled by the display of strength and dexterity.

With the bin in his lap, the stranger picked up the duffel again, slammed shut and locked the doors, and then turned to face the bewildered Texan. As the two sets of eyes met, Simon was once again left stunned.

Jesus, he's just a kid...

The young man's eyes were a deep blue, and his face was clean shaven. He couldn't be a day over twenty-five, Simon thought. His face, cold and emotionless, harbored a furrowed brow, which seemed to harden his looks beyond their years. He paused for a second and looked Simon over with a distinct *Who the hell is this guy?* cast on his face, before wheeling himself past the dumbfounded *gringo* towards his room.

Simon stood dismayed by the young man's presence in urban Honduras, and equally so by his petulant attitude. Curiosity and loneliness, however, were getting the best of him—and before he could control it, his emotions suddenly hijacked his vocal cords.

"Well, hey man, at least let me buy ya' a beer at the bar next door... I mean, you're the only other person that speaks English around here, after all."

The kid stopped rolling in front of his room door and paused for a moment.

He turned back to Simon and looked at him with what appeared to be pity for the pudgy old man. A free beer after a long day's drive sounded pretty damn good, he thought. He considered Simon's intentions for a moment before determining him harmless. "Fine... gotta shower first though, meet ya out here at ten," he replied, again offering no emotion.

"Great! My name's Simon!" Simon sputtered with a huge *shit-eating* grin on his face.

"Jonah," replied the stranger with an eye roll before disappearing into his room.

For many years after, Simon would wonder what his life would have been like had he just gone back to bed that night.

CHAPTER 51

When ten o'clock came along, Jonah rolled outside to find Simon waiting for him. As the two made their way towards the cantina, Simon quickly noticed that Jonah's wheelchair was markedly different from others he'd seen before. The young man pushed levers on the sides forward and backward to move, rather than grabbing onto traditional handrims. Simon asked Jonah about this, and he explained the origin of the remarkable device and its function for traversing rough terrain.

"I've added a lot of my own enhancements, as well," he added. "This baby is one of a kind."

Simon was growing more and more fascinated by the kid with each passing second.

As they entered the bar, Simon was relieved to find the space more or less empty—his experience on the streets having left a sour taste in his mouth for Tegucigalpa locals. Jonah, on the other hand, seemed indifferent to the matter, and wheeled straight to the bar to flag down the bartender.

"*Dos cervesas, por favor*," he said softly with a well-practiced accent.

As the bartender and Jonah exchanged a few words in Spanish, Simon realized Jonah actually knew the language…and knew it well.

"So, where you from, Simon?" asked Jonah as they came to rest at a table.

In his voice, Simon could sense a detached indifference—like he was just going through the motions to get his free beer. Simon, however, elected to ignore it.

"Texas. You?" he replied.

"Michigan. Ann Arbor area."

The beers arrived, and they each took a pull. Jonah knocked down half his bottle in one swig. "So, what brings you here, man?" Jonah continued.

"To Tegucigalpa?"

"To not-in-Texas-anymore," Jonah smirked.

Clearly, he wasn't taking Simon seriously.

"Long version or short?" Simon asked.

"Well, I just started drinking, and I got a strange feeling we're not gonna have much to talk about. Better make it the long version," he said brusquely with a half-smile.

Simon forced a phony grin in response, and then began to chronicle his tale once again.

He told Jonah of his drive down through Mexico and his time in Belize… about meeting Jack and Alice and sunrise in Tikal… about Martine and the family in the mountains, the blue pools of Semuc Champey, candlelight caves in Kanbah and the god Maximon in Lake Atitlán…and about his journey to Utila off the coast of Honduras.

And as Simon spouted on of his adventures through northern Central America, Jonah's outward demeanor towards him slowly began to change. Something in the way Simon spoke—with his distinct sense of wonder for the world—started to disarm the young man.

When Simon told his story of the secret scuba lessons and his big reveal to Davis, Jonah actually laughed, which Simon viewed as a small breakthrough with the tough kid. It was the closest thing to emotion he'd yet seen in the now grinning young man. Simon continued, recounting his experience swimming in the ocean with the whale shark.

"It was possibly the most incredible thing I've ever seen!" he beamed, bouncing in his seat as he remembered it.

Yet as he did so, something suddenly changed in Jonah. A look of anger and frustration filled his eyes again, and the young man turned away sharply to drink his beer.

"You okay?" Simon asked.

Jonah felt his usual urge to tell this Texan to fuck off, and turned back to Simon to say just that. But when he saw Simon's face and the look of genuine concern it now held, he paused, trying to wrap his mind around it.

"Yeah, well…. I… I just won't ever be able to go scuba dive now that I can't swim, but you know… it sounds amazing," he said and forced a smile. "Finish your story."

A regretful Simon stared at him, thinking about what he'd said. *Of course, he can't swim…*

"Oh, I'm sorry Jonah… there's not much more to it, really," Simon said.

Jonah grinned. "That's quite a story, man... I have to admit that it was much, much more interesting than I was expecting."

Simon chuckled. "Oh yeah, what were you expecting?"

"I felt for sure you were going to say you're here for a few days on business attending some sort of nerd convention and that the HOJO was full, so you ended up staying here," said Jonah as he began to laugh under his breath.

Simon joined in, looking down at his slacks and button-up shirt.

Man, I REALLY need to get some different clothes.

Simon had never met anyone as guarded as Jonah, and especially not at such a young age. He sensed a deep sadness in the kid that betrayed his tough exterior. Simon was hesitant to ask Jonah for his story because of this, but then decided it was the proper thing to do, regardless.

"So, what's your story, if you don't mind me asking?" he asked lightly.

The young man just sat there staring at him, debating how much he felt comfortable saying. He took a few pulls off his beer as he deliberated. Simon seemed like a good guy, he reasoned. Besides, it had been a while since he'd talked to anyone about himself. It had been a while since anyone had asked. A long while.

"Well... as you can see, I'm in a wheelchair..." Jonah began.

Pausing, he turned and called across the room to the bartender for another couple of beers and swigged down the remainder of the one in his hand.

"So, I wasn't always in a wheelchair... In fact, most of my life, I wasn't."

Jonah gave a sad, reminiscing smile as he remembered that time, years ago.

Simon smiled back, politely.

"I was a pretty big outdoorsman as a kid, actually... loved to mountain bike, fish and hike. Had plans to backpack the Appalachian Trail for the summer after my junior year in high school with some friends. I was soooo excited for it, and we had the whole thing mapped out…. But then, that spring, I went on a mountaineering trip up to the U.P."

Simon gave him a confused look.

"The Upper Peninsula in Michigan."

"Oh, okay."

"Well, I went with some friends… and one afternoon we were hiking along a—what was a pretty easy rock face actually. Easier than most of the faces we'd climbed. But I guess… maybe that was the problem. Well, somehow, I stopped paying attention to what I was doing for just a few seconds… I lost my footing on some loose rocks… and fell sideways down the mountain face and… well… into this chair."

He paused and looked down, shaking his head. "Stupid shit," he mumbled to himself under his breath.

"Jesus," Simon muttered.

"Anyway, I fell about twenty feet down onto a rock bed, landed on my back, and the next thing I knew, I was in a hospital and couldn't move my legs."

As Simon sat in silence, listening to the story, he noticed how much older Jonah seemed when he spoke than his youthful exterior conveyed. It was also apparent how hard Jonah labored to maintain his tough facade and restrain his emotions at times. But Simon was beginning to sense that deep down the kid was more than that. That maybe he'd just been hurting for an awfully long time.

"The outdoors were my life," Jonah continued. "And then, all of a sudden that was gone… and it started to feel like, well, like my life was over."

Jonah paused and stared at his beer deep in thought. He looked up at Simon and saw how well the Texan was listening—how genuinely interested in Jonah's life he appeared to be. It felt good to talk to someone about it after so long, but it felt a little odd that it was to this stranger. He took a deep breath. It was difficult to let Simon into his personal life, but he decided he might as well keep going.

"So anyway, I lost my shit… My life sucked for a really… really long time. Just all kinds of screwed up... It was tough on my family, too, and, well, eventually I started to notice my dad was acting almost like . . . like he didn't want to have to take care of me anymore."

Jonah paused, lost in a memory.

"My mom, on the other hand, kept trying to pretend like nothing had changed. Which was almost just as bad."

Jonah looked as though if he weren't so hardened, he'd be on the verge of tears. Simon wanted to say something, but he had no words.

"I really felt like… like I had nothing to live for anymore. And I actually started to accept my own death, to be honest… So, I thought, shit, if I'm okay with dying— not afraid of it anymore—why stick around?"

Jonah's bloodshot eyes told Simon what he meant. Before discovering pharmaceutical relief, Simon himself had gone through similar bouts of depression back in university. What Jonah had endured, however, seemed exponentially greater.

"But then, the more I thought about it, the more I wanted to live again," Jonah continued. "And I mean *really* live again."

He took another pull off his beer.

"But like I said, I felt like I didn't have anything to live for... You know what I mean?"

Simon nodded, trying to understand what it must have been like. There was no way he could fully relate, though.

"Then, one day, I decided that what I needed was to challenge myself again. And in a bigger way than I ever had before. I had to find something *so* difficult, something no one else could do or had done, and I needed to devote myself to it entirely. If I could do something like that, shit, maybe I wouldn't feel so meaningless all the time."

He stopped and stared at Simon. Then he continued. "Now, the four-minute mile had already been accomplished and, let's be honest—" Jonah's eyes darted down to his legs, and he chuckled. Simon began laughing as well.

But as he finished laughing, Jonah's face grew stolid once again. "Have you ever heard of the Darien Gap, Simon?" he asked.

Simon pondered it, but soon accepted that he hadn't. "No. I don't think so."

"Well, you see... it's this dangerous stretch of jungle between Panama and Colombia, wild and thick with deadly animals. Jaguars, poisonous snakes and every nasty critter in between."

Lovely.

"But more dangerous than those even, are the drug smugglers and the arms traffickers, the kidnappers, the Colombian FARC guerillas . . . They all live in the Darien and call it their home. Armed to the teeth, they've got secret camps hidden all over deep in the jungle there. Between the lot of em', they usually kill or kidnap anyone that tries to make it through the area. It's gotten so bad over the years that people often call the Darien the most dangerous place on earth. It's the only gap in the Panamericana Highway that stretches from Alaska to Argentina, because it's just too damn dangerous to build a road there."

"Sounds charming," Simon quipped.

"Well, that's where I'm headed," Jonah continued. "If I can make it through the Darien, Simon, shit, I can do anything with my life."

He finished his sentence and pounded the rest of his beer before ordering another round.

Simon just sat there, stumped and waiting for the punchline.

He has *to be kidding.*

Having already seen some craziness in Jonah's eyes as he spoke, Simon knew that what Jonah was suggesting was ludicrous. He was a confident kid, but he didn't seem that foolish.

"So, you're just going to drive through?" Simon mocked with a chuckle.

"You can't just drive through Simon," he said. "Only two people have ever made it all the way through in a four-wheeled vehicle overland: Loren

Upton and his wife Patty Mercier in 1985. You know how long it took them to go the 124 miles through to Colombia?" Jonah asked, clearly knowing the answer.

Simon thought he'd guess high. "A month," he said, feeling confident about his guess.

"Nope....741 days," Jonah responded.

"What!?" belted Simon in disbelief.

Jonah maintained his straight face, and Simon soon realized he wasn't joking.

"Shit! Are you serious?!"

"Yep."

"Two years?!" Simon exclaimed, still refusing to accept it.

Jonah smiled a deadpan smile. "I shit you not. Look it up if you don't believe me."

Simon *did* believe him, however, and he was beginning to question whether the kid was right in the head. He also started to wonder if he should try to convince Jonah what a foolhardy plan it was. Then, without thinking it through, he began to speak his mind.

"So, I hate to state the obvious here, Jonah... but there were two of them in 1985...and my assumption is they both had functioning legs. I think you're crazy if you think you're going to make it through there alone!"

Almost immediately, Simon regretted his words.

The look that came over Jonah's face showed Simon was right for such feelings.

The young man just stared at him for what felt like an eternity, until Simon had to say something. "I'm sorry I said that, Jonah," he muttered with sincerity.

Jonah continued to stare at him, and Simon grew increasingly uncomfortable until eventually, Jonah spoke.

"I've been planning and preparing for this journey for four years, Simon. It's been what's carried me through life and kept me getting out of bed in the morning. Every fucking day for four years, I've thought about how to make this happen and what it would feel like if I come out on the other side alive. Shit, *when* I come out the other side alive. I'm going to get through there, Simon... or I'll die trying," he said with unwavering confidence.

Jonah's fervor, courage and focus were unlike anything Simon had ever witnessed. The Texan felt like a fool for having questioned it. He wanted a chance at redemption, and even though Jonah seemed sad, angry and slightly self-destructive, Simon had already grown quite fond of him.

He didn't know it yet, but Jonah liked him too.

"Well, can I come with you?" Simon asked, breaking the silence with a startling proposition.

Jonah stared at him blankly.

"Not through the Darien, of course, but down to Panama? I'm headed south anyways," Simon continued. "I've got my own car, of course."

Jonah's gaze into Simon's eyes was unflinching. He looked deep into Simon's soul to seek out any ulterior motives for the odd Texan's bizarre request. But none seemed to exist.

As Jonah considered the proposition, the wait seemed interminable to Simon.

Finally, Jonah spoke. "I'm going to Granada tomorrow... You're welcome to follow me down there." Jonah muttered. "After that, we'll see. Thanks for the beers, Simon."

Jonah turned and rolled out of the bar, leaving Simon sitting alone and bewildered by the events of the evening.

He's mad, isn't he?

Once back in his hotel room, Simon unrolled the large map and laid it out flat on his bed yet again. He scanned it with his finger, looking everywhere for a town called Granada. Eventually, he found it.

"Nicaragua?" he whispered to himself.

Down, down, down I go. Where I'll stop, nobody knows.

CHAPTER 52

The sun sat low in the sky as the two men drove south across Honduran cowboy country. The terrain, flat and arid, was a stark departure from the lush green jungles of Guatemala. Scattered across these barren plains sat the occasional corn farm, cattle ranch or ramshackle village—but little else. Simon was fascinated to find the majority of locals passing by on horses rather than in cars.

Having stayed up the night before practicing some basic Spanish from his phrasebook, Simon managed his way through the border easily and was thrilled by his growing abilities. As he drove on, it occurred to him that before this trip, he hadn't learned anything new in years. Maybe decades. *I guess you* can *teach an old dog new tricks...*

Arriving in the Spanish colonial town of Granada around dinnertime, Simon found the jarring contrast between it and Tegucigalpa worthy of rejoice. It's cobblestone streets, plazas and ornate churches, instantly bewitched the smitten Texan. The city seemed like a vision from his imaginations of old Europe. *Is this the same Central America?* He wondered.

The two men checked into a quaint guesthouse and headed to their respective rooms to relax after a long drive. Within ten minutes, however, there came a loud knocking on Jonah's door.

"What do you want?!" he yelled, having just maneuvered from his chair to the more comfortable bed.

"There's a McDonalds in town here!" yelled Simon, his voice carrying with it a childlike enthusiasm.

Jonah smiled wider now, knowing Simon couldn't see him. "So?!" he hollered.

"I'm gonna walk over there, do you wanna come?"

"No man! Just wanna rest for a bit," Jonah replied, waiting to hear Simon walk away.

But the sound never came.

After thirty seconds, Simon's voice came booming through the door, yet again. "You want me to bring anything back for ya'?"

If Jonah didn't know any better, he'd have thought it was an eager ten-year-old outside his room. He couldn't believe how excited Simon was for McDonald's, but he found it quite entertaining. Giggling to himself, he let Simon wait a second before responding.

"Double quarter pounder, fries and an orange soda!" he hollered back.

"Okay!... What if they don't have orange soda?" Simon replied.

"This is Central America, Simon. They might *only* have orange soda!" Jonah laughed.

***

Forty minutes later, the pair sat on Jonah's bed, eating burgers and drinking orange soda as Simon debriefed Jonah on his wanders through Granada. "This is easily the nicest and safest feeling city I've been to in Central America, so far," he declared giddily. "I kinda love it!"

Jonah just smiled.

"So how long we stayin' in town here?" Simon asked.

"Well, *I'm* leaving the day after tomorrow," replied Jonah.

Simon recognized the clarity and stress in the "I'm" part of Jonah's statement and hung his head. "Okay then, where are *you* headed?"

"I'm going on my final test run," Jonah replied.

Simon looked at him, confused. "What kind of a test run?"

"My last wilderness test run before the Darien... In two days, I'm gonna head from here, across Nicaragua to the town of Bluefields on the Mosquito Coast," Jonah continued.

Simon glared at him with wide-eyed curiosity. "Mosquito Coast, huh?"

Jonah had started to notice this curious and yet confused look Simon kept showing. It was oddly endearing and made him chuckle a bit inside each time.

"So, most of this country is still jungle..." Jonah went on. "A large piece of it is called La Moskita, which stretches from southern Nicaragua, all the way up into Honduras. It's named after the Miskito people, an indigenous tribe that still lives there in the jungle."

A tribe? Thought Simon.

Jonah went on. "The trek across the country from here to Bluefields on the coast is just about as unfriendly as they come. Dirt roads without signs that cross dangerous jungles filled with wild animals, drug dealers and guerillas."

"Well, that sounds familiar," Simon quipped, unwrapping his third burger.

"That's the whole point," Jonah replied, his mouth full of fries. "This is the closest thing to a Darien-style testing ground that I'm going to get. I'm gonna use it as a trial run for my van and for the survival skills I've been working on for the past several years. It's dangerous and tough, but not nearly as rough as the Darien. There are a few roads and trails, so I should get through in just a few days, instead of months, hopefully."

Simon couldn't believe that Jonah planned to embark on a different dangerous journey right before the real one. That being said, the idea of training for the Darien in Nicaragua sounded understandable. Simon knew there was no way Jonah could have recreated something like the Darien in Michigan. *Detroit's gotten bad, but not THAT bad.*

Simon also hoped that maybe a few days in a sweltering, treacherous jungle might be enough to dissuade Jonah from attempting the more perilous Darien journey. He had begun to sense a kinship growing between them, and with each shared smile, he wanted more and more for Jonah to change his mind and relinquish his audacious goal. "Sounds like it could be a valuable experience," Simon said, attempting to act as encouragingly as he could.

Jonah nodded and continued to eat, drifting off deep into thought. After a few minutes, he spoke again—his earnest words surprising Simon wholly.

"You wanna come through the jungle to Bluefields with me?" he asked. "Not in your car, of course, but with me in my van? I could bring you back here after, of course... if we're still alive."

Simon couldn't tell if the last part was a joke, but the hairs on the back of his neck stood on end, regardless. He was thunderstruck by the offer. The road to Bluefields sounded like an arduous and terrifying journey. A journey Simon felt ill-prepared for.

What an absurd idea.

Simon had never been on, nor considered going on an adventure of this magnitude. Yet for some reason, in the moment, the new, emboldened incarnation of Simon thought it sounded like quite the opportunity. Regular Simon was scared shitless just imagining it.

"Lemme think about it, alright?" he eventually responded.

"Of course," said Jonah.

The pair quietly finished eating, and Simon returned to his room to retire. The choice weighed heavily on him, and that night he lay in bed for hours, staring at the ceiling fan and mulling the proposal. Simon liked Jonah a good deal. The young man impressed him beyond words, and the thought of traveling with him through the jungle sounded extraordinary and wild. Yet there was so much to it that also terrified him.

As he lay there, he thought back to when he'd traveled into Guatemala on his own in search of Jack and Alice. How that decision had terrified him as well, but it had turned out to be an overwhelmingly positive and life-changing experience. Then he considered his decision to learn scuba diving in Honduras. How that, also, had terrified him. But again, it had transformed his life for the better. *Maybe Davis was right about destiny. Maybe Jonah came into my life for a reason.*

Simon wondered where he would be now if he hadn't woken up when Jonah arrived at the hotel in Tegucigalpa. Or what if he'd been out eating somewhere at the time? Or what if one of them had stopped at a different hotel? Their lives, very likely, would never have even crossed.

Simon questioned whether this could all be part of something much bigger and more meaningful for him. He couldn't shake the penetrating feeling that it was.

Twenty minutes later, Jonah woke to a loud knocking on his door. "Simon, I know that's you. What the hell do you want?!"

A second later, a response came. "I want to come to Bluefields with you!" Simon yelled through the wall.

"Okay, great, glad you woke me up to tell me that now, idiot. You know I don't leave for two days, right?"

"Yeah, but I wanted to tell you before I changed my mind."

Jonah rolled his eyes and smiled in the darkness. "Okay, go back to bed and we'll talk in the morning, dude," he hollered, throwing a pillow at the door with a thump.

Simon smiled in the hallway. "Goodnight!" he yelled and returned to his room.

Jonah lay there in the dark, listening to Simon walk away and pondering the odd Texan. A big grin came over his face. *I like this guy. Tomorrow I'll show him "The Van."*

CHAPTER 53

After eating breakfast together, Jonah invited Simon outside to see... *The Van*. An imposing vehicle at first glance, Simon had no idea just what he was in for.

"The Van is built for jungle adventure," began Jonah in classic sales pitch form.

Simon snickered.

"A stripped-down, highly modified '99 Ford E350 diesel 4X4 Club Wagon, this baby has 350 horsepower and more than 500 pounds of torque under the hood. Raised 16" on top of 35" Mud Monster all-terrain tires, an off-road suspension, dual tower shocks and heavy-duty axles... this thing has everything, man. Crash panels underneath keep the custom 4WD conversion safe, and a cow plow over the front end can clear small trees, brush and almost anything else that gets in my way."

Mercenaries? Zombies? Thought Simon. *What, no flame throwers?!*

"On the front and rear are a pair of 12,000-pound cable winches that can pull the whole van up the side of a building if I needed them to... and the whole cabin and the electrical are all water sealed. With the engine snorkel, I can drive through water up to four feet deep... actually tested that in Lake Eerie!" Jonah said, chuckling.

Simon just stood there, grinning at the way the young man was describing the vehicle like a proud parent. Simon could already tell it was Jonah's baby.

Then Jonah opened the back doors.

"Holy shit!" Simon exclaimed in awe.

Inside the bowels of the beast lay an efficiently constructed mobile bunker that immediately reminded Simon of several cold war holocaust shelters he'd seen back in Texas as a child. At once, his brain conjured memories of visits with his father to some of their more eccentric neighbors, and speeches about *preparations* and *getting ready for the end times*. Yet there was something markedly different about those calamity havens.

They were ten feet below the ground.

This one was built into a van. A van about to be intentionally driven into its own hell on earth. Simon suddenly got the heebie-jeebies.

"So, this 40-gallon tank is for drinking water," said Jonah, patting the large plastic tank towering at the back of the vehicle. He reached below it and retrieved the end of a coiled hose. Then connected it to a levered device at its base. "I can run this hose 20' out to a river, or a large puddle and pump water into it through a purification system to make it potable."

"Is it a reverse osmosis filter or a ceramic filter system?" chimed Simon

Jonah looked to him, surprised. "Hey, you know your filtration systems."

"Well, you don't write technical manuals for living and not learn a little about how things work."

Jonah smiled and laughed. "It's a ceramic filter system."

"Nice," Simon approved.

Moving across the aisle to the unique electrical system, Jonah went on. "This is the power station here, four deep cell marine batteries with a 600w inverter that can run the radios, GPS and LED lights at night. They're trickle charged by solar panels on the roof... but under here is a 1000w backup generator I can use to charge the system if I need to. I'd prefer not to fire that up though since it makes a lot of noise, and there are murderers in the jungle out there."

Simon found it interesting how nonchalantly Jonah kept saying things like that.

"Well, hey, do you know about the water bucket trick?"

Jonah turned to Simon, intrigued. "No, I don't think so, what's that?"

"So, I read you can run a hose from the exhaust nozzle of the generator into a bucket of water. Most of the sound comes from the exhaust, so the water acts pretty much like a silencer."

"Holy shit, that works?"

"From what I've read, yes, but every generator manual I've ever written recommends against it!"

Jonah laughed, "Why?"

"I guess if the water source is higher than the generator, then water can run up the hose and flood the generator engine. But put the generator above whatever you're using for water, a bucket, a puddle, or anything, and you should be all good."

Jonah stared at Simon for a moment. "You said you knew a little bit about how things work, Simon, but you seem to know way more than you give yourself credit for."

Simon smiled. "Thanks, Jonah."

I guess maybe I do, don't I?

Jonah pulled himself up the ladder bars and into the van again, as Simon had seen him do once before. His strength and nimbleness astounded the out-of-shape Texan, and Simon began to wonder if he could do even a single pull up. *Doubtful.*

Jonah slid a compact folding wheelchair out from behind the water tank, popped it open and pulled himself up and into it comfortably. His "in-the-van" chair was narrow enough to move up and down the center aisle and even up to the driver's seat. Simon stepped up into the vehicle and found the entire, elaborately outfitted interior to be racked out with lightweight metal shelving packed efficiently and meticulously into the space.

"This cot down here is where I'll sleep," Jonah said, identifying a nearby shelf with a foam mat on it. The front half appeared tall enough for the young man to sit up and read, yet the lower half was just tall enough for his legs to slide under. "You'll sleep up top in the pop-up camper," he continued, pointing up to the roof above the aisle.

Simon looked up and winced at the thought of the small space, but his blood had already begun to race with the spirit of adventure now surrounding him. He hadn't been camping in nearly twenty years, not since that final trip with his father and brother.... But this would certainly be very, very different.

Jonah carried on with his tour, pointing to a dozen or so plastic bins neatly organized on a rack of shelves lining one side of the vehicle. "These containers have enough food and supplies for six months... if I stay in the van that long... but I'll probably have to switch to the kayak for the last leg." Jonah glanced upward, and Simon's eyes followed. Above them, a rack along the ceiling supported an orange kayak running the length of the aisle and extending forward up to the windshield. Simon had to crouch beneath the watercraft as they continued moving forwards into the van.

The attention to detail and efficiency of design in the interior layout was extraordinary. A small desk behind the driver's seat held a laptop and various cartography tools. Above it were shelves of marked maps, old books and a pair of large radios. Jonah flipped a switch, and small LED's throughout the vehicle illuminated the windowless space in a soft, even glow. *Brilliant.*

"These steel lockers hold other supplies. Rope, carabineers, tarps, a small stove, first aid kits, extra filters, flares, sunblock, repellent. ... Pretty much anything I could need OUT THERE is IN HERE," Jonah said, wrapping up his tour.

Simon was awestruck by the level of planning Jonah had put into this. As he continued to explore the vehicle's interior, he noticed several cans of olive-green spray paint in a crate on top of the lockers. "What's the paint for?" he asked, curiously.

"Oh, that's to camouflage the van before I head into the Darien... so the bad guys don't see me," Jonah responded.

Simon's stomach sank at the thought.

***

For the rest of the day, the two men drove around town, collecting last-minute supplies and discussing the plan. At dinner, Jonah brought out a weathered old map of *La Moskita* and pointed out the dotted line route he had plotted. "This last section is all dirt roads and swamps," he said, running his finger along the brown paper.

"Where did you get this map?" asked Simon intrigued.

"eBay," laughed Jonah.

The tattered document looked remarkably like a treasure map to Simon, and his mind drifted to visions of his favorite movie treasure hunters. Indiana Jones, Jack T. Colton and more. Guys he had idolized as a child but had long since been forgotten.

Until now, that is.

As they ate, Jonah shared with Simon his accumulated knowledge of *La Moskita*, from its sordid history as a pirate enclave, to the many indigenous tribes that still lived there today. Enraptured by the tales, Simon imagined seeing "tribespeople" out in the jungle. The mere concept of which was wondrous to him.

Jonah's descriptions and warnings went on, cautioning Simon of the numerous dangerous animals that dwelt in the *Moskita* jungle; jaguars, pumas, fire ants and the lethal fer-de-lance pit viper—the deadliest snake in Central America. "Don't worry, though… if you get bit by a viper, I have an I.V. bag and a mechanical suction to pull the venom out. Should keep you alive for a while, at least."

Simon had begun to find Jonah's bedside manner less than comforting. Though the journey sounded like the adventure of a lifetime, as Jonah continued to rattle off a mounting list of dangers, Simon couldn't help but feel as if the whole endeavor was foolhardy.

That night, as he lay in bed brooding over their impending departure, Simon questioned his decision to join the mission. As he pounded through the various scenarios the pair might face in the jungle, something abruptly occurred to him. Something that convinced him that he was making the right choice. *Surely, there will be a situation where my legs will be needed to help Jonah get through. When that happens, he'll see once and for all that it's ridiculous for him to think that a person without use of their legs can get through the Darien alone.*

It's the right thing to do, he concluded—*the charitable decision.*

In that moment, Simon resolved to accompany Jonah, looking after and protecting the young man from the wild world outside the van. *When Jonah needs me, I'll be there for him.*

Simon felt proud to fill that role.

He never could have imagined how wrong he'd be.

CHAPTER 54

Only a few years had passed since the long, winding track to El Rama had been paved. Prior to that, it would have taken Jonah and Simon an arduous backcountry week to reach the distant, central Nicaraguan jungle town. As a result of this new road, however, they'd already made significant progress in the first four hours of their cross-country expedition.

It was noon, and Simon looked at the GPS to find they'd already traveled more than halfway across the country. *Perhaps Jonah is wrong about how hard this is gonna be*, he thought. "So, is this what you expected? Doesn't seem that bad," he suggested, naively.

"Yeah… this is what I expected," Jonah replied. "But this nice road we're on here only goes to El Rama. It's the last sixty miles to Bluefields that'll be the hard part."

The young man's face was eerily calm, and Simon sensed that his mind was hard at work, chewing over plans and scenarios for what was to come. Jonah hadn't smiled in hours, and it began to make Simon anxious.

By two o'clock, they entered El Rama, and Simon immediately knew why Jonah wasn't in a smiling mood. Situated deep in the jungle on the edge of the Nicaraguan wild, El Rama, or just "Rama," as the locals call it, was a seedy, riverside port city at the convergence of three rivers. Ragged concrete and corrugated steel structures packed around dirt alleyways as men gathered on stools in the shadows of wooden awnings.

"Rama is a town of jungle traders and smugglers," muttered Jonah. "We're well beyond the reach of the Nicaraguan government out here... "

Jonah's words sank in Simon's gut.

"That river over there is the biggest in the area, the Rio Escondido... it runs through town here and connects this village to the Caribbean Sea. Traders from the mountains, deep in the jungle and out on the coast, all gather here to sell their products."

Simon gazed out at the brown river running beside them. His eyes widened in amazement as several cattlemen puttered along in small wooden boats, their cows tethered to the sides with ropes, swimming along in the river beside them. He had never seen anything like it. *Swimming cows?*

As his eyes continued to wander around the rambling scene, he spotted a large rotted wooden sign beside one of the river docks: *FERRY A BLUEFIELDS* it read. A hulking boat, the *Captain D*, sat at its end, and several vehicles drove aboard. A cadre of men loaded cargo onto its decks.

"Look, you can take a ferry to Bluefields," Simon exulted, pointing at the sign.

Jonah smirked. "I know you can take a ferry... but we're going *that* way," he replied.

Simon's gaze followed Jonah's pointing finger through the crumbling village to a wall of dense jungle on its far side.

But... there's a ferry?

After grabbing a few final supplies, the two men made their way through the town to a gushing river running along the jungle's edge. A rickety crossing ferry made of wooden planks sat before them, perched on the muddy riverbank.

"We'll cross the river into the jungle here," said Jonah

You've got to be kidding me thought Simon.

The "ferry," if one could call it that, consisted of numerous odd slats of wood lashed to two large, rusted pontoons to form a tottering, floating platform. At the near and far ends of the structure, steel cables extended up to a pair of pulleys which ran along a third steel cable, stretching from riverbank to riverbank between two 10' wooden posts buried into the mud. The swift-flowing water beneath the pontoons seemed to keep the cable apparatus pulled taught, and Simon quickly came to the morbid conclusion that if any one of the three thin wires were to snap, the entire ferry, and anything atop it, would promptly roll over into the deep, rushing river.

Simon sat mortified as Jonah exchanged a few words with one of the ferrymen, and then, putting the van into drive, slowly eased the heavy vehicle off the land and precariously out onto the aged wooden raft. Simon gripped his seat tightly. *This is fucking crazy! This thing can't possibly hold us!* He thought.

But it did. And for several agonizing minutes, they bobbed up and down in the current as local men loaded crates and bags of wet sand onto the platform beside them. With each additional load, the ferry sank lower and lower until the rough water splashed over the edges and onto the deck.

Dear God, no mas!

Finally, it was time to cross.

Standing on the edge of the raft, one of the ferrymen turned a large steel rudder hanging from the platform into the river. At once, the strong current began to push them towards the far side.

Simon glanced up at the creaking pulleys above, rolling slowly along the cable and guiding them gradually along. The whole structure teetered precariously as it progressed, atypically top-heavy from the giant van. And though Simon sat frozen, terrified to his core, he couldn't help but appreciate the simple ingenuity of the river-powered transporter.

Four o'clock arrived as they finally reached the opposite riverbank. The sun had begun to dip below the tops of the surrounding trees. "We need to get into the jungle immediately and find a safe place to camp for the night," said Jonah.

Simon could sense the urgency in his voice.

Numerous men around them unloaded sandbags onto animal drawn carts and repeatedly glanced at the pair with quizzical looks. Simon knew that a flashy van and two white men appeared rather out of place in this remote corner of the world. And he quickly grew uneasy as the target of so many staring eyes.

Seconds later, their tires met the earth.

Jonah gassed it away promptly, steering them onto a well-trodden horse path that cut deep into the jungle. The narrow clearing was barely wide enough to accommodate the hulking vehicle and branches and shrubs banged and scraped along its outside walls as they went. A thin lane of packed dirt rested in the middle of the path for horses and carts to make their way, but the vans wide wheelbase forced its tires into deep mud gullies on the lane's outer edges. It wasn't long before Simon realized *this* was the road marked on Jonah's map. And he comprehended at once why their journey would be so difficult.

Deeper into the wood they advanced, Jonah forcing them through the mud and bramble as fast as he dared in such abhorrent conditions. The low, tunnel-like jungle route grew darker and darker as the sun lowered further into obscurity. Simon held on tight as they lumbered up and down, flinching at every branch that smacked the mud-spattered windshield in front of his face. *This is absolutely crazy.*

Seeing a more sparsely wooded patch of forest ahead, Jonah made a quick decision. "I'm going in here," he called out suddenly. And before Simon knew what was happening, the young man pulled the accelerator lever, cut the wheel hard and launched the van off the dirt path and into the jungle.

Holy shiiiiiiit!

Simon catapulted clear out of his seat and onto the floor with a thud, fighting desperately to pull himself upright in the lurching and rumbling machine. When he finally climbed back up into his seat, he glared through the windshield in horror. The van, tearing through the woods ahead, was leveling and pushing aside any small trees or vines that crossed their path. Jonah, meanwhile, steered them with the focus of a downhill slalom skier, weaving them back and forth past heartier obstacles and leaving Simon holding on for dear life in the deafening turmoil.

*Holy M****@$%^%&^%!*

Ahead of them, the jungle was growing dense again. And making another snap decision, Jonah accelerated further, faster into the thick vegetation, crashing hard into the dense bramble with a crack.

Simon shut his eyes tight.

Jonah slammed on the brakes.

The massive vehicle entered a chaotic slide into the serried thicket, until suddenly, the forest's countless organic tentacles snagged them in its grasp like a great catcher's mitt.

With a growling boom, the van was stopped in its tracks.

Jonah killed the engine, and the vehicle slowly sank a few inches into the wet earth below. At once, everything was silent.

"Well, that was exciting!" Jonah mused and glanced over to find Simon curled in a fetal position on the passenger seat, his seatbelt twisted and wrapped around him like a nylon anaconda. The young man chuckled at his dazed compatriot. "Hahaha, it's okay Simon, we're alive."

Simon opened his eyes slowly, half expecting to be in heaven or hell, but instead finding himself in the dark van with Jonah staring down at him smiling. *The tumble cycle has ended... now get me out of this infernal machine!* Discombobulated, Simon freed himself from the serpentine tangle and began to push open his door.

"Whoa, whoa, whoa!" Jonah hollered at him to stop. "Go out the back if you need to. Always out the back. There could be a viper at your feet right there... Out the back, the van has already cleared the way for you."

A tingle of terror pulsed through Simon as he darted a glance down through the cracked door at the jungle floor. He quickly yanked his door shut. Jonah's reasoning made sense, he thought, and wondered why he hadn't thought of that himself. Likely, it was because his brain currently felt like pudding.

Making their way to the back of the vehicle, Jonah instructed the shaken Texan on how to open the camper pop-top, and still trembling, Simon released the latches and a small lofted bedroom sprung open in the roof of the van. With the A/C off and the windows rolled up, it was stiflingly hot in the vehicle, and Simon found himself sweating profusely.

"Go up there and see if you can see the road from the window. If you can, we'll have to close the top," Jonah said. His matter of fact tone was all business, and Simon took his orders seriously.

Climbing up top, Simon peered out the windows and found that they were fully concealed in the dense vegetation. Night had fallen, and he couldn't imagine anyone would notice them in the darkness. "We're all good," he called down. *Who would be out here anyway?*

Jonah flipped a switch on the inverter, activating the LEDs and illuminating the interior in a gentle white glow. Two small fans in the corners of the chamber hummed to life as well. Simon hadn't even noticed them previously, but now he was thankful for their existence.

"Can we open the door or the windows?" he asked hopefully.

"You can open the windows up there in the loft since they have screens, but anything down here will let animals and insects in. We'll just have to live with the fans," Jonah replied.

Simon opened the pop-top windows and pressed his face to the screen, taking in a long breath of hot fresh air.

Suddenly, a crackle of music began echoing from below.

What the hell?

Poking his head down from the loft, Simon found Jonah sitting at his desk and adjusting the tuning on one of his radios. The reception was poor, and the signal full of static, but the Caribbean sounding music was lively, and Simon was happy to hear it.

"Probably Radio Bluefields," Jonah said, smiling up at him. "It's the only city within a hundred miles of here, and this is a local signal."

Simon grinned. The rhythmic tropical beat of the Soca music instantly harkened memories of Tulu's place back in Brasilito and brought a little much needed sunshine to an otherwise bleak and claustrophobic space.

"Well, it sounds great," Simon replied and climbed back down into the aisle. He took a seat in the cot across from Jonah and scanned his eyes around the chamber. Though it was tight in the narrow vehicle, its interior was laid out so effectively that there seemed just enough space to live in with relative comfort. When Simon imagined spending months in the cramped hotbox, however, the idea seemed torturous. *A month in the "hole."*

Jonah, meanwhile, was rooting around in one of the lockers. When his hand eventually emerged, Simon's eyes lit up.

"Want a taste?" Jonah asked, cracking open a large bottle of Nicaraguan dark rum and taking a long pull.

"Damn straight," Simon replied, giddily taking it from Jonah's outstretched hand. Typically, the Texan would have asked for a glass, being *civilized* and all… but there was nothing *typical* about where he was right now. Simon took a long swig off the bottle with reverence. "So… do we need to worry about bad guys or wild jungle creatures tonight?" he asked.

"Naw, we're close enough to town that we should be fine… but just in case, we should keep the doors locked," Jonah added half-jokingly. The young man reached down and grabbed the cuffs of his pants, lifting his legs up to rest on the desk.

Simon had already begun to notice a subtle change coming over Jonah in these first few minutes in the jungle together. The young man seemed much more comfortable and more relaxed out here in the wilderness. *Maybe this feels more like home to him,* Simon wondered.

"So… tell me about yourself, Simon," Jonah asked, taking another long pull from the rum bottle.

Simon pondered the vague question and was at a loss. "Well… there's not a whole lot to say, really. I already told you about how I got here."

"So, tell me about your family and friends... or your harem of women back in Texas!" Jonah chuckled.

"My harem? Riiiiight." Simon rolled his eyes. "Well, like I said, there isn't a whole lot to say, I guess. I grew up in Odessa, and I've lived in Texas my whole life."

"Your whole life, huh? Anywhere else you've gone before?"

"Nope, nowhere."

"Really, you've never left Texas before?!" Jonah's eyes widened.

"Well, I went camping in Utah once, but that's it."

"Wow... and now you're here in Nicaragua."

Simon laughed. "Yes, wow, and now I'm here in Nicaragua."

"Hmm," Jonah mumbled. "Well, what do your parents do? Do you have any brothers or sisters?"

"Yeah, I have a brother, he does something with an insurance company in Houston, but I'm not sure what. We don't talk much anymore. I haven't seen him in years, actually."

As Simon spoke of his brother, his voice softened noticeably, and Jonah could sense regret in his words.

"Years, huh. Were you two ever close?"

"Yeah." Simon smiled, remembering back. "We were best friends when we were kids... used to do everything together... and with our dad when he was around, too. It was great."

Jonah could sense that Simon longed for this time in his life.

The Texan went on. "But then our dad died when I was twelve... and everything changed," he said.

"Oh man, I'm sorry to hear that. Sorry I didn't know."

"Oh, it's okay, it was a long time ago," Simon said, solemnly. "After my father died, my brother Jonathan and my mom fought every day, and I sort of became an afterthought. When he turned seventeen, Jonathan left Odessa for Houston and never looked back. We talked often for the first few years, but for the last ten, we've only occasionally spoken on Christmas."

Simon paused for a moment, debating how much more he should say. He recalled how open Jonah had been with him back in Tegucigalpa and could see the young man was there to listen. So, he went on.

"When Jonathan left… I ended up trapped in Odessa alone with my mother. I soon started to feel like… well… like she resented me… us… for taking away the prime of her life. She and I never talked about it, or about much of anything, actually, so for my last two years of high school, I just kept my head down and worked all the time. Partly to save money for college… and partly to avoid going home. After I graduated high school, I left Odessa, and she moved to St. Louis, and we've barely spoken since. I don't really even know what she does these days."

"Jesus, man, that's tough. I couldn't imagine not having any family to lean on. Do you have some good friends back home?"

Simon looked at Jonah, and a deep sadness grew on his face. "Naw, I don't really have any friends anymore. I used to, back in college… but then I- I guess I focused a little too much on my work in the last ten years and kinda lost track of everyone."

Simon was growing emotional just mentioning it. Jonah could tell he was upset.

"Damn, you are one lonely sonofabitch!" Jonah said to break the tension.

Simon laughed and sniffled, trying to gather himself.

"But hey, you got me, *amigo*," Jonah continued and slapped his hand on Simon's shoulder. Simon looked up at him and smiled.

"Thanks. I'm glad we met."

"Me too."

That night the two men sipped lazily on dark rum and chatted about life and purpose, listening to music while tucked in the back of the van in the middle of the Nicaraguan jungle.

It was a moment Simon would never forget.

After several hours, he eventually climbed up into the loft and lay there with the music still playing quietly below him. He could hear Jonah working his way into bed and smiled wide. A few seconds later, the lights and music turned off, leaving the van quiet and pitch black. A few sounds emanated from the jungle surrounding them. The chirping of insects. The rustling of leaves. The mesh windows were just a foot or so from Simon's face, and he wondered what was just on the other side. He hadn't slept in nature in twenty years, he recalled.

"Goodnight, Simon," Jonah said from below.

Hearing his friend's voice instantly calmed him.

"Goodnight, Jonah," he responded and closed his eyes.

CHAPTER 55

Simon awoke, drenched with sweat as the roasting sun shone down on the top of the camper. His muscles were cramped from dehydration, and he was startled to find he could barely move. Pushing through the pain, he crawled down from the loft and into the aisle below.

"Good morning!" Jonah greeted him with a smile. The young man looked surprisingly clean, oddly chipper and as though he'd been awake for hours.

Simon could see the van's back doors were resting open to the green jungle, and a pot of water was boiling on a small camping stove at its rear. Jonah tossed him a Nalgene bottle of water, which the bedraggled Simon promptly chugged in its entirety. When he'd finished, he glanced back to Jonah with a grave look on his face. "Shit, did I just drink too much water?" he asked.

Jonah laughed. "Not at all, that's a 40-gallon tank and it's full. Help yourself."

Simon didn't need any more convincing, refilling the bottle three times before he was through.

"Do you wanna take a shower?" Jonah queried casually.

The sweat-soaked Texan regarded the dubious question as some sort of sick joke. Yet as he stared dazed at his compatriot, he soon realized that perhaps Jonah was serious. He gave the young man a simple, stone-faced nod, causing Jonah to break into laughter. "Well, alright then..." Jonah snickered.

Wheeling himself to a position beside the water tank, Jonah bent down and switched a flow control lever at its base. From a nearby bin, he retrieved a small threaded showerhead and screwed it onto the end of the water system's intake hose. Feeding the head and hose up through a loop of rope hanging on the inside of the open van door, the apparatus was left arching downward just outside the back of the vehicle.

Simon was, as always, captivated by the young man's orderly and systematic movements.

Jonah reached over and pumped the tank system's large handle a few times. As he did so, a burst of water flowed up through the hose and out through the showerhead, splashing down onto the leaf-strewn earth behind the van.

Genius!

Without a second thought, Simon hopped out the back of the van and stripped off his clothes, feeling strangely little shame in his weary condition. As he pumped several bursts of refreshing cool water over himself, he couldn't help but glance around to see if anyone was spying on his exposed naked self. But the lush, verdant jungle was the only thing staring back at him.

It was one of the best showers of his life.

After the cooling rinse, Simon threw on his underwear and climbed back up into the vehicle. Jonah had since made coffee with the boiling water, and the two sat drinking a cup of Joe and eating granola bars on the back of the van. A refreshing wind breezed through the bright green forest around them, and birds chirped from the canopy above. *This is an excellent way to start the day.*

"Today is going to be a tough one," warned Jonah. "The trail will get worse from here on out. Also, we'll be heading into a drug trafficking area tonight, so no music and no chatting after dark." His voice carried a sobering earnestness that gave Simon pause. Jonah seemed to be bracing himself for the day.

He definitely needed to.

***

After breakfast, the van's 4WD muscled them out of the deep mud and carried them back onto the dirt horse path. Slowly but steadily, they pushed on further and further into the unrelenting wilderness. The route was lonely and predominantly devoid of life, yet on rare occasions, they came upon local traders headed in the opposite direction. Each person who passed seemed utterly baffled as to why these *gringos* were driving into the jungle here. The ferry was back in the other direction, after all. Simon could do nothing but watch as Jonah spoke with several of the men, each of whom pointed emphatically back towards El Rama.

But Jonah kept going forward.

Do they know something we don't?

Staring out the window, Simon noticed several dilapidated farmhouses tucked deep into the forest. *What kind of people live way out here?* He wondered. Small dirt trails splintered off from the road, disappearing towards unknown realms of the dark jungle. Simon was utterly fascinated by them, imagining where they might lead and the types of people who might use them. *Maybe one of the "tribes" Jonah mentioned? Maybe the drug smugglers?*

It wasn't long before the terrain began to grow significantly craggier and more mountainous. The van staggered up and down wildly on the broken trail as Simon's stomach grew nauseous from the constant roiling movement. He closed his eyes to gather himself. *Maybe this was a bad idea.*

Suddenly the van skidded to a stop.

Simon's eyes opened with a jolt.

"What's happening?" he gasped.

"Look," said Jonah.

Simon leaned forward, glancing down through the dirtied window glass. A few feet ahead, a deep ravine was now obstructing their path, stretching out wide in each direction. A small stream coursed through its nadir. "Jesus…" he mumbled.

The chasm was far too deep and precipitous for the van to cross, and the impenetrable jungle surrounding it made circumnavigation an impossibility. Ahead, the locals had laid several wooden planks side by side across the ditch, producing a broad platform for horses and carts to cross. But Simon noticed the boards were only an inch thick and ten feet long or so.

Yet Jonah was inching closer to the edge.

"There's no way those boards can hold us!" Simon belted, sensing Jonah might be on the verge of something foolhardy.

"Maybe," Jonah replied, easing the van ever nearer.

Oh, God, no.

But as they reached a point just a few feet from the bridge, Jonah slowly brought the vehicle to a standstill. He killed the engine and threw open his door.

In a flash, the young man sprang into action.

Reaching behind his seat, he snatched his all-terrain wheelchair, opened it and lowered it to the ground. Then, holding bars on the inside of the door, he swung himself gracefully out of the vehicle into his awaiting chariot.

Simon watched perplexed as Jonah rolled across the earth towards the planks. *What is he doing?*

Simon hopped from the van and took a long, deep breath. The jungle air was hot and musty and smelled of wet earth and rain. After being in the cramped vehicle for several taxing hours, it was perfection.

Joining Jonah by the front of the van, he found the young man closely examining the wood boards and feeling them with his hand. "This is mahogany," Jonah said, looking up to Simon.

Simon stared back, blankly.

Jonah rolled his eyes. "It's a hardwood," he added, seemingly stating the obvious.

Ah yes, a hardwood.... Huh?

Leaning over further, Jonah reached down and grabbed one of the planks by its end with both hands and rolled it over onto the board next to it. Then straightening them into a stack, he did the same to another. Then another. Until Simon finally realized what was happening.

"Do you want some help with that?" he asked.

Jonah flipped over the final plank and adjusted the two stacks of boards. "No, I think I have this one," he chuckled—eying the alignment of the pieces of wood before making his way back towards the van.

Simon crouched down and stared at the boards' positions. Pressed together in even piles, they were each four inches thick now, yet Simon still questioned whether they could support the weight of the heavy vehicle. The van's engine roared to life behind him. *Man, that guy is quick!*

Back in the cab, Simon buckled up and watched anxiously as Jonah began inching forward onto the edge of the planks. The young man revved the engine, and the front wheels lurched up and onto the wooden spans. Simon glanced down through his side window but couldn't see the boards underneath them at all. Just the fifteen-foot deep crevasse below. The creaking of the boards was agonizing, and he looked over to see sweat on Jonah's brow. *That can't be good.* But the boards seemed to be holding, and slowly, slowly, they inched forward.

He held his breath.

Jonah strained to keep the wheels straight—both men well aware that the slightest deviation would mean certain disaster. It was a dangerous task, and one that Simon was reasonably sure he'd be incapable of. *Thank God I'm not driving.*

Forty-five gut-wrenching seconds later, the front wheels of the van dropped suddenly off the stacks and onto the dirt, temporarily stopping Simon's heart. Jonah adjusted his side mirror downward, maintaining the rear wheels' alignment as he rolled the vehicle forward slowly…slowly… until… *Thump!* The back wheels fell to the ground.

"Woohoo!" Simon hollered joyously. "Let's roll!" he bellowed, pointing into the jungle ahead.

But Jonah pulled the van forward just a few feet and stopped. "Hold on. I have to go put the boards back the way we found them for the next people," he replied.

Simon laughed, thinking the young man was kidding. But as Jonah unclasped his seatbelt and opened his door, Simon realized just how serious he was. *I guess he's right. Of course, we should put it back the way we found it.*

Simon saw this as his chance. "Wait, I can do it faster!" he yelled, leaping from the van and dashing back to the gully. Two minutes later, when he hopped back in and buckled up, he turned with a smile to Jonah, proud of his contribution. But the young man scowled at him, seething.

"I could have done it, you know!" he barked; his piercing eyes focused squarely on Simon, who now sank into his chair beneath the weight of Jonah's glare. *Jesus, what did I do?*

"I know," Simon offered. But Jonah gave little to his utterance, starting the van and driving forward into the woods without another word.

***

For nearly an hour, Jonah's stern gaze was fixed forward in silence. Simon struggled to comprehend why Jonah was so upset at him. He was petrified to ask.

Around noon, they stopped for lunch and ate quietly on the back of the van. Finally, Jonah broke the silence, his voice quiet and sincere. "I'm sorry I snapped at you back there, Simon... I know you didn't mean anything by it."

"It's okay. But what did I do wrong?" he asked.

Jonah could sense he honestly didn't know.

"Simon, I really need you to understand something, man. The whole reason I'm doing this test run is because I need to test myself and my abilities. So when you jump out of the van and go do something in thirty seconds that it would take me ten minutes to do…. Well, that… that just kind of makes me feel *less* capable… not more capable if you know what I mean."

Jonah's words struck Simon like a sock to the belly. He tried for a few seconds to muster an apology, preparing to beg forgiveness and hoping Jonah's anger could somehow be quelled.

But then Jonah continued.

"And I know you didn't mean anything by it, Simon… but honestly… I'm scared as shit to go into the Darien. And so, if I don't know with absolute certainty that I can handle this little adventure… how will I have the confidence to survive something so, *so* much bigger… and so, so, *so* much more dangerous?"

Simon was taken aback by the tough as nails kid admitting he was scared. "I'm so sorry, Jonah, I didn't even think about it," he replied softly. "I won't help again unless you ask for it. I promise."

Jonah's frown turned to a half-smile. "I can do this Simon. You might not think I can, but I can."

"I know you can," Simon said, smiling in return and placing a hand on Jonah's shoulder.

***

After finishing lunch, they pressed on further up the trail. The pair joked as they rambled on about the ravine crossing and how they'd both nearly wet themselves. And as they laughed in the bouncing vehicle, Simon couldn't help but feel a growing kinship with Jonah. *Everyone's human,* Simon had begun to feel, and the young "badass" Jonah was no exception. Maybe the fear Jonah felt was a good thing, he thought. Perhaps it would keep him cautious and allow him to accomplish his extraordinary goal. A goal Simon was beginning to believe the young man could actually achieve.

Yet, as Simon pondered this, suddenly, the van came to an abrupt halt. The Texan now looked on in amazement at what sat in the path ahead of them. He shuddered. "Jesus, Mary and Joseph...," he whispered, slack-jawed.

"Fuck," muttered Jonah.

CHAPTER 56

"Daddy, look!" Jonathan hollered, staring out the passenger side window at the peculiar sight drifting across the valley in the distance.

Kyle Hill wanted to heed his boys call, but was already straining to see past his fast-moving wipers as thick sheets of heavy rain poured across his windshield. The road ahead was dark and clouded. A sign for Midland, Texas passed by as Kyle gunned his old pickup down the slick highway. Almost home to Odessa... and almost out of the storm.

"Whatcha see, son?" he asked.

"I don't know!" Jonathan belted louder.

"I see it too daddy!" Simon yelled out from the back seat.

"Jesus!" Kyle exclaimed, frustrated. "Sorry, Merle," he harrumphed, and turned the volume down on the cassette deck.

But the moment the radio turned off... he knew exactly what his boys were looking at.

The rev of the truck engine continued to grind.

The rain whipping across the glass continued to pound.

Yet beyond that, sounding like a slow rolling thunder coming across the plains, there was something else. You didn't grow up in this part of the world without knowing that sound.

Kyle's eyes went wide. He darted them out the side window.

Through the glass and the streaking raindrops, he could still make it out distinctly. Though only a category F-2, he guessed, the seething tornado was cutting diagonally across the field right beside them. "Boys, sit back and put on your seatbelts!" Kyle yelled, the force and fear in his voice startling the two youngsters. Reaching over with one hand, he pushed his eleven-year-old boy Jonathan down into his seat.

Simon immediately began to cry in the back. He was already nine years old, but he'd always been a crier.

"Simon, it's going to be okay," Jonathan said softly to his kid brother. He leaned over the seatback to try and comfort him, but Kyle yanked him back down.

"Put your damn seatbelt on!" he yelled once again.

Cotton shrubs and corn stalks began to fly across the highway ahead of them. Kyle could sense the funnel was gaining on them—the rain beating down on his truck in increasingly torrential waves. He struggled to keep one eye on the road and one eye on the storm—speeding faster yet and trying desperately to stay ahead of the churning tempest. He laid on the gas, accelerating his truck down the wide, empty highway at nearly sixty miles per hour.

He glanced over to spot the tornado once again…

It was a critical error, but one whose consequences never could have been avoided.

Where the grey sky met the grey road ahead, an invisible lagoon of water had flooded a dip in the pavement below an approaching overpass. The moment the pickup truck hit the pool, the entire vehicle went from 58mph to zero, slamming to a back-breaking halt as a massive wave of water arched up over the truck with the sound of a freight train. The Hill family's limbs flew forward in the thunderous chaos as their seatbelts dug hard into their skin, and the air in their lungs was suddenly crushed from their bodies.

Then, just as suddenly, it was quiet.

It took Kyle a few moments to regain his senses. A searing pain coursed through his body, and water clouded his eyes. He tried unlatching his seatbelt but discovered that his left arm, which had been on the steering wheel, was now shattered and limp. Looking up, he found water pouring over his truck's hood. "Oh shit," And glancing to his right, he saw Jonathan buckled over, coughing and wheezing for air. "Are… are you boys, alright?" he asked. Turning over his shoulder, he discovered Simon in the back seat with a look of terrified shock on his face. When the young boy saw his dad and the two locked eyes, Simon instantly started bawling.

Kyle quickly took stock of where they were and the situation. Water was flooding in through the door jams and trickling into the footwells. Outside, the water was rising faster, and he looked behind him to see a shredded sorghum field gushing water out onto the pavement. Probably, he figured, from a felled water tower or a busted irrigation main. The rain was still coming down heavily around them as well, but at least they were shielded by the overpass above.

"Daddy, I don't feel so good," Jonathan muttered.

Kyle looked over to see vomit on his son's chest.

"Can you help your brother now?" Kyle asked.

Jonathan nodded.

Kyle prayed another vehicle wouldn't come barreling down the road towards them. But as he turned back to check, he noticed something else that gave him pause. The rising water suddenly breached the top of their pickup truck bed and quickly began to fill its interior. In the cab, the water was already up to Kyle's knees, and the whole vehicle was sinking with the added weight.

"We have to get out of here," he muttered to himself. "Get your brother, we have to get out of here!" he commanded Jonathan.

Jonathan, still stunned, stared at him for a second before unlatching his seatbelt and crawling into the back seat. Simon was still crying but immediately stopped when Jonathan reached him. The nine-year-old wrapped his arms tight around his older brother.

Up front, Kyle rolled down his window and spied the water already up to the door handles. "We're heading up onto the roof," he said, and reaching back with his good arm, he lifted Simon over his shoulder and up onto his lap. The diminutive boy crawled out the window and climbed onto the steel roof, causing it to depress above Kyle's head. Jonathan followed after him.

When the boys were clear, Kyle managed to free himself from his seatbelt and pull himself up to sit on the window frame. With only enough room for the boys on the roof, Kyle sat in the open window, his legs dangling into the water filling the truck cab.

In the distance, he watched as the tornado cut across another field and wound its way across the Permian Basin towards Andrews. He'd seen more than his fair share of twisters... but never this size... and never this close. After a few minutes, the rain and wind slowly began to subside, and the water around them stopped rising.

Jonathan held Simon tight, keeping his brother calm.

"You boys okay?" asked Kyle.

"Yeah, we're fine," replied Jonathan smiling.

"I'm okay, daddy," added Simon.

Kyle picked up a handful of water from the lagoon surrounding them and splashed it on Jonathan's chest, trying to wipe away the vomit. Jonathan, not understanding what his dad was doing, leaned over and splashed his dad back in retaliation. He and Simon burst out laughing.

"Hey!" Kyle yelled and smiled before throwing a handful of water at his two boys.

Ten seconds later, the three were splashing each other wildly and laughing from the top of the submerged red Dodge.

Pickup Truck Island as they began to call it.

After a while, Kyle managed to flag down an oncoming car to help them. The truck was towed out of the water, and Kyle was taken to the hospital. But the Three Musketeers would always laugh about that crazy day.

At least for the few years they still had left together.

CHAPTER 57

"*Pickup Truck Island,*" Simon muttered to himself with a reminiscing smirk.

"What?" asked Jonah.

"Oh, nothing," said Simon, knowing now wasn't the time for stories.

Ahead, a flooded swamp the size of a football field stood between them and the next leg of the trail. Dark water coursed through countless half-submerged trees from right to left. Where the road rolled off into the murky black morass, boards and felled trees had been cobbled together by locals to build what was once a zigzagging cart path across the watery expanse.

Carts... not cars.

But now the makeshift bridge disappeared into the water only a quarter of the way to the far side, swallowed up by the slow-flowing marsh.

"Do you think we can drive across it?" Simon asked.

"Maybe... but this is giant, and the water is moving," Jonah said, scanning the surroundings diligently. After a few seconds, he slid into his in-van wheelchair and rolled back to his desk. Checking the GPS and his map of the *Moskita*, he let out a sigh as he placed their location. "This is a swollen river," he said exasperated. "If that's the case, it could get very deep in the middle."

Wheeling himself back up front, Jonah stared long and hard at the water again, taking his time to process the situation. Simon didn't say anything, though he very much wanted to.

Eventually, Jonah turned and made his way into the back of the van once again. Simon looked over his shoulder as Jonah pulled himself up on the rack and released the latches on the vehicle's pop-up top. He climbed up into the loft, and though Simon could hear him doing something up there, he couldn't ascertain what. After a few seconds, Jonah climbed back down and returned to the driver's seat.

"Okay, so the windows in the pop-top are completely open. The screens are off. If it gets deep too fast or the van rolls onto its side in the water, those windows could be your best chance at escaping. Don't try to open the doors, you probably won't be able to anyway, and it'll flood the van. We need to keep these windows down here closed, too."

Jonah spoke with confidence, but his words only increased Simon's anxiety.

"And take your seatbelt off. We're definitely not going to hit anything at high speed, and you should be ready to get out of here fast if you need to."

Simon unlatched his seatbelt and stared at Jonah, sweating.

"You got all that?" Jonah asked, raising his usually soft voice to a commanding tone.

"Yeah," Simon said. His heart felt like bursting from his chest.

Slowly, and without another word, Jonah gave the van some gas.

Simon clutched the dashboard and instinctively took a deep breath as the vehicle descended rapidly into the darksome water. Questions swirled through his mind. He wondered how deep the bog must be, and more chillingly, what strange creatures might be lurking within. Though he tried desperately to control his outward demeanor, inside, he was wholly terrified.

But Jonah continued forward undaunted, steering them on a meandering course as they lumbered over rocks, branches and anything else that stood in the van's way. And with every bump and sink into the water, Simon's heart bumped, and his stomach sank. *This is crazy!* He thought. Yet the water was proving to be shallower than expected… at least for the first fifty feet or so. But then, rather quickly, it grew deeper… and then deeper… And it wasn't long before the murky brown water was sloshing halfway up the doors.

Simon stared nervously out the side window at the shadowy surface of the vast flowing wetland, just a foot below the glass. His eyes scanned the scene, spying the water creeping higher and higher until, eventually, the van was submerged up to its door handles. The opening of the engine snorkel was still a foot or two above the water's surface, sucking air into the straining engine and giving it life. Simon could only watch in agony as the black tube sank inch by inch deeper into the marsh.

Deeper…

Deeper…

Deeper they went…

Though the water wasn't fast, it was plentiful, and the weight of the current pushed the van to the left as they moved along slowly through the mud and silt. Jonah gave it more gas, accelerating to keep them from sinking into the soft riverbed.

This is crazy! Simon thought once again as Jonah powered them faster, forward through the wide river.

Then, in a flash, chaos struck.

As though the starting bell at a bull ride had just rung out, the hood of the van suddenly launched upwards out of the water, tossing Simon back into his seat with a crash. "What the hell!" he cried out. And as his words of despair ricocheted around the cabin, the whole vehicle then pitched forward hard into a nosedive, plunging into the frothy water and sending liquid exploding over the windshield. "Oh shiiiiiit!" the pair hollered in unison, bracing themselves as the swamp threatened to engulf them in one giant swallow.

"Dammit, it must be the riverbed!" Jonah shouted as water obscured the windows and thrust the two men into darkness. "I can't get traction!"

Jonah yelled, laying on the gas, the wheels whinnying loudly, as the van staggered wildly to the side. The thick current pushing them violently along whatever muck covered surface they'd run upon. The vehicle listed hard to the left, and Simon stood over his seat preparing to evacuate. *We're gonna roll!* Jonah laid on the gas harder in desperation. The engine roaring loudly as they slid further… and further…and further.

"Get ready to jump out!" Jonah yelled.

"What about you?" screamed Simon.

"Going down with the ship!" he replied.

"Fuck tha—"

Simon had barely started to articulate this thought, when in an instant, five feet below the surface, the van's all-terrain tires suddenly gnawed hard into the rocks and locked on, thrusting the entire vehicle forward and up with a tremendous jerk. Simon's teeth smashed together as the front end of the van launched wildly out of the water like a great acrobatic Orca.

Jesus Chriiiiiiiiiiiiist!

Time seemed to move in slow motion as Simon turned towards Jonah, his eyes wide with shock and terror. The pair locked eyes. And Simon could see the sweat-soaked young man staring back at him with an equally shocked look of alarm… and yet there was something peculiar about him. For some reason, as the van soared through the air over the flooded river in the middle of the jungle, a small grin appeared at the side of Jonah's mouth.

You've gotta be ki—

With a thunderous splash, the massive vehicle crashed back into the water, plunging its hood deep into the river yet again and tossing Simon forward like a rag doll into the dashboard. They slammed to a halt, the vehicle coming to rest atop something unseen below, its front end submerged deep beneath the broad river. The windows, however, were still thankfully above the surface. Jonah pulled hard on the accelerator, smoke and water spewing upwards from the rear exhaust like an exploding depth charge. But in the mud below, the wheels just spun freely.

Eventually, Jonah surrendered. "Shit!" he yelled out, taking his hand off the gas lever.

The water was high, but the snorkel's mouth could still grasp air, and the engine kept on chugging. Simon, dazed from the impact, pressed his hands against the side window, now half underwater. *Holy shit, we're done for...*

As he turned back to Jonah, he fully expected to find the young man in a similar state of abject panic. Yet what he found was a cucumber, cooler than Miles Davis, quietly surveying their predicament and ruminating on a plan of attack.

*Who the f*** is this guy?*

In typical Jonah cyborgian fashion, the young man methodically set to work.

"Don't turn the engine off," he instructed Simon, reaching up to unclasp several latches on the hinged front windshield. Releasing it from its brackets, he pushed it forward to fold flat onto the hood.

Simon stared at the eerie jungle water as it moved across the bow of the van from right to left, only a few inches from entering through this newly opened front portal. It was just two feet from his face, and he envisioned again what menacing river monsters might lurk in its foggy depths. He slid back a few more inches into his seat.

The tree line at the far shore was still at least fifty yards off. *Jesus, I hope he doesn't want me to swim us to safety.* Simon's mind quickly turned to how best to talk his way out of taking a dip.

Jonah, meanwhile, paid him no mind. Instead, he reached above his head and unfastened the Velcro strap securing the front nose of the kayak to the inside of the roof. Then, yanking hard on the craft, he pulled it forward over his right shoulder, and slid the narrow vessel easily over its u-shaped rack bars and out through the front windshield. It splashed onto the water just beyond the dashboard.

Simon looked on in awe.

Attaching the kayak's tether to the hood's radio antenna, Jonah left the floating craft dangling in the current just a foot outside the vehicle. Simon then watched in sheer astonishment as the young man, in a series of swift, calculated moves, grabbed a paddle off the rack above them, maneuvered himself dexterously out of the front of the van, lifted his legs up and into the kayak and then strapped himself inside.

As he secured the kayak's spray skirt around his waist, Simon sat slack-jawed once more. *He's unbelievable!*

"I'll be back," Jonah said with a wink.

I knew *you weren't human!*

Detaching himself from the antenna, Jonah paddled out a foot in front of the van and stopped. As he turned the kayak around in a 180, he faced Simon and gave the bewildered Texan a confident smile. Then, without warning, the kayak flipped, rolling completely over with a splash and placing Jonah entirely underwater.

Simon jumped up frantically, leaning forward out the front window. The scratched orange bottom of the kayak stared up at him. *What the hell?!*

Bobbing up and down in the rippling river, it sat quietly on the surface of the water just four feet away. *Did Jonah just fall out and sink to the bottom?! I know he can't swim!*

Simon stared at the capsized boat, sweating like mad and wondering when or if Jonah would ever resurface. Aching seconds passed by as the only sounds to be heard were the quiet murmur of the jungle and the trickle of slow-moving water around him. Simon knew that a time would soon come when he'd have to jump into the mire to save his friend.

Five more gut-wrenching seconds passed... then ten.

He gazed at the orange bottom of the kayak.

I'll wait ten more seconds and then dive in.

He counted down. Ten... nine... eight...

Still nothing.... just the orange hull, the gentle murmurs of nature and the timpani roll of Simons beating heart. Seven.... six.... five...

Sweat gushed down his face, and he wiped it away with the back of his sleeve. Four...three...

Simon climbed onto the dashboard, preparing to make the leap. *I froze when Jack needed me back in Guatemala, but not this time.* Two...

He took a long deep breath. One...

Bshshhhh! Suddenly, in a flash, the kayak twirled back over, and Jonah burst from the water in a blinding cloud of spray.

"Jesus Christ!" cried Simon as he fell backwards into his seat with a look of sheer terror on his face.

As Jonah gasped air into his lungs and came to rest upright, the two men's eyes connected, and Jonah offered a smile.

"What the fuck, man!" Simon yelled.

Jonah raised his thumb to his stunned compadre, before leaning over and hooking something in his other hand to his kayak. Simon bent forward to get a better look. *It's the damn winch hook!*

Jonah was off. Paddling towards the far shore as Simon gazed on dumbstruck. Seconds later, the young man slung the hook and cable around a large tree like a rodeo wrangler, latching it back onto itself and pulling the whole thing taught. He paddled back towards the van.

"Goddamn this kid's a badass," Simon muttered to himself quietly.

Crawling back up onto the hood, Jonah pulled the kayak in behind him and then pushed it up onto its rack. As the drenched young man slithered into his seat at the steering wheel and dried off his hair with a towel, Simon's mind burned with one pounding thought.

I can't believe I thought he would need me! I'd be dead out here without him!

Jonah activated the winch, pulling the cable tight ahead of them with a twang. The van jolted forward violently, yanking the vehicle's nose up and out of the water.

"Whoa!" hollered Simon as he fell back into his seat.

Jonah eased on the gas again, and though the front wheels were now far off the bottom, the back wheels and the cable winch pulled the van forward over the underwater rocks in a steep wheelie formation. "Yeeeeehaw!" Jonah yelled and turned to Simon, who burst out laughing. "That's what y'all cow folk say, right?" Jonah continued in the worst imitation of a southern drawl that Simon had ever heard.

"Yeah, something like that!" Simon guffawed, still holding on for dear life. The vehicle plowed ahead, nearly vertical, bouncing up and down over whatever lay at the floor of the thick swamp.

When finally they reached the far side, Jonah climbed out with his chair into the shallow water, detached the cable and returned to the van to secure everything. Simon just sat watching, speechless. The admiration in his eyes having paralyzed his tongue.

As they rolled back onto the continuation of the horse path, Simon released a deep sigh, causing Jonah to turn his way. Though the Texan smiled and tried to act cool, the sweat on his brow told a different story.

"You okay?" asked Jonah.

"Yep, I'm fine," Simon replied, lying through his teeth.

Jonah snickered and steered them back into the jungle, down the dirt road as if nothing had happened. He didn't say a word.

Simon sat in quiet amazement. A few minutes passed before he dared to speak. "That was completely fucking amazing, by the way," was all he could think to say.

Jonah chuckled. "Thanks," he said, and continued driving.

***

Several hours went by, and as the sun began to set, they searched and eventually found a place to pull off the road for the night. They ate a quiet dinner, keeping the lights off, and then crawled into bed quietly for the evening. As Simon drifted off to sleep, he couldn't stop thinking of all that had happened earlier that day. No matter what obstacle had been thrown their way, Jonah always seemed to have a solution. Maybe he *could* make it through the Darien after all.

***

It was after 2 a.m. when Simon awoke abruptly to the sound of people moving through the jungle nearby. Pressing his face to the mesh window, he stared out into the darkness, unable to see who or what it was. Suddenly, the flicker of flashlight beams cut through the forest. He rose from his perch and quietly crawled down from the camper top into the center aisle. Looking down, he found Jonah staring up at him, wide-eyed and silent with a finger over his mouth. His other hand signaled Simon feverishly to get down. Fear gripped the Texan as he realized this could be bad. Very bad.

Carefully he lay down on the floor beside Jonah's cot, trembling in the darkness. The light of the flashlights danced past the windows again, and voices could be heard a short way off.

Jonah leaned over and whispered to Simon. *"Narcotraficantes."*

Simon looked at him, terrified but confused. Jonah whispered again. "Drug smugglers."

At once, Simon comprehended the magnitude of the situation. His body seized with fear at the prospect of being discovered. He prayed the petrification of his muscles wouldn't soon transform into rigor mortis.

With the fans off now, it was broiling hot in the vehicle, and Simon's sweat formed a puddle on the floor around him. Several mosquitos landed on his face, and he swiped at them quietly. Carefully.

As he lay there, Simon's mind began wandering through memories of the last few months. From San Antonio… to Belize… to Guatemala… to Honduras and now here. He questioned the collection of decisions that had brought him to this godforsaken place. Yet surprisingly, amidst all the swirling emotions he now felt, regret wasn't one of them.

The two men laid there, frozen in the silence for what felt like hours. After twenty minutes or so, the voices outside faded away into the distance.

Ten minutes later, Jonah whispered quietly. "Okay, you can go back to bed now."

Simon crawled delicately back into the loft and lay there the rest of the night listening.

Listening to Jonah breathing.

Listening to the jungle.

Listening to his own heartbeat.

Listening for more voices.

CHAPTER 58

The next morning, they rose early and wasted no time preparing to leave. Both men were eager to depart this swathe of the jungle as soon as possible after the previous night's dark encounter. Making their way hastily back to the path, they pushed on further towards the sea.

"We should make it to Bluefields by this afternoon," said Jonah. His words carrying with them a breath of relief to Simon. Having barely set foot outside of the sweltering van in the last forty-eight hours, he felt a stir-crazy madness growing inside him. He couldn't imagine Jonah spending months in the oppressive vehicle.

As they continued on their journey towards the coast, Simon and Jonah soon noticed some odd movement further ahead on the trail. Jonah slowed the van, cautiously rolling them forward. The undulating patch of road ahead grew nearer. And the pair grew curiouser and curiouser. *Is that some sort of animal?*

They soon realized that it was, and many animals at that.

"Peccaries," elucidated Jonah casually, the van pulling to a halt a short distance from the pack of twenty or so hairy, pig-like animals milling about on the dirt path.

"Wild pigs, huh?" said Simon, leaning forward and grinning at the furry little buggers in front of them.

"More or less," replied Jonah, himself leaning closer to observe the twee creatures.

For several minutes, the two men sat watching and laughing at the frolicking furry animals, making up names as they did for some of the more unusual looking specimens. Spot. Ebenezer. Pinocchio. They even found a Jonah, looking morose with a scruff of black hair atop his head, and a chubby Simon sniffing around aimlessly. After the trials of the previous twenty-four hours, it felt good to laugh again, and Simon could feel his muscles finally relaxing.

Then, suddenly, the adorable scene was dashed into madness.

Out of their periphery, something large and spotted launched from the jungle beside them and onto one of the pigs. "Whaaaaaa!" the two guys yelled in unison as they reeled back from the windshield and crashed into their seats. The remaining heard of pigs scattered into the jungle as Simon and Jonah looked on in horror. The pouncing jaguar dug its teeth deep into its now bloody prey, crushing the last ounce of life from the quivering swine.

"Holy shit!" Simon squawked. His booming voice causing the large cat, only a few feet from the front bumper, to turn its head quickly and glare up at the scared spectator. Simon slouched deeper yet into his seat and mashed his open palm down on the door lock. The large cat's facial fur dripped with blood, and the neck of the peccary oozed the crimson liquid from its speckled jaws.

"Is that a freakin' tiger?!" Simon warbled, terror filling his voice.

Jonah's face—focused in wild fascination on the nature documentary unfolding before him—quickly turned to an exasperated eye roll. "Oh my god! A tiger? Seriously?" Jonah threw up his hands and glanced over to Simon. "A tiger has stripes, idiot. That's a jaguar," he said with a *harrumph*.

Who am I, Siegfried and Roy over here?

"A jaguar? Holy crap," mumbled Simon, his jaw agape in wonder.

"A jaguar holy crap is right. This is amazing," Jonah agreed, his voice filled with reverence for the rarely seen predator.

For several minutes, the two men sat and watched spellbound as the jaguar dragged its lunch into the dense thicket and then finally disappeared into the jungle. The only things remaining were a small pool of blood in the center of the dirt path and the men's shared disbelief at what they'd just witnessed. After taking a few moments to process and absorb, the pair finally exhaled and pressed on.

On towards a remote Caribbean pirate town nestled far off on the *Moskito Coast*.

On towards Bluefields.

CHAPTER 59

Of all the numerous locations in the world that seem so utterly out of place amidst their surroundings—Ayers Rock, the Taj Mahal, Ski Dubai—few compare to the desolate tumbledown eyesore that is Bluefields, Nicaragua. Like a smoking impact crater sandwiched between the vibrant green forests of *La Moskita* and the crystalline turquoise waters of the Caribbean, the rugged, ramshackle blight of a city has an apropos history pulled straight from a Robert Luis Stevenson novel.

Drawing its name from the 17th-century Dutch pirate Abraham Blauvelt, the sordid, backcountry port town was born more than 300 years ago atop the blood-soaked tides of Spanish plunder reaching its shores. Straddling the border of Nicaragua and Honduras, Blauvelt initially used the secluded bay as a clandestine nesting ground for his attack ship the *La Garse*. Yet he soon found it to be the ideal launching point for the raiding of Spanish galleons departing the New World loaded with gold, silver and other precious "exports."

Shortly after its inception, Blauvelt's far-flung colony of scallywags began to flourish, growing over several centuries into the central hideaway for pirates and marauders from across the Caribbean. Its international reputation as a buccaneer's safe haven attracted all sorts, as pirates from throughout Europe made their way to the rich hunting grounds.

Then, in 1641, the town's population of pirates and indigenous *Miskito* tribespeople was suddenly bolstered by the shipwreck of a Portuguese slave ship just off its shores. Several hundred surviving African slaves swam ashore, settled in the community and made the demographics of the town an amalgam unlike any other. To this day, Bluefield's rowdy character remains unchanged: a seedy, rough and tumble town, a smugglers depot and a lawless land of scoundrels and rogues.

Nevertheless, when the van finally emerged from the dense jungle onto the muddy streets of the backwater town, Simon couldn't help but let out a tremendous sigh of relief. He was just thankful to be somewhere. Anywhere.

"Can we stay in town here a night before turnin' back?... Pleeeeeease?" Simon begged Jonah, desperate for a shower and a reprieve from the jungle heat.

"Why the hell would you want to stay here?" Jonah dismissed. "Sorry, partna, we're getting lunch, and then we leave in half an hour."

Simon's face lengthened in dejection at the prospect of heading straight back into the jungle. His stomach turned ill.

After a few minutes of rolling through town, they came across a small local cafeteria, and Jonah pulled the van over in search of some much-needed nourishment. It would quickly prove to be a mistake. Within moments of exiting the vehicle, more than a dozen touts rushed to surround the two white men, hollering at them in English, Spanish and Creole.

"Don't say anything," Jonah whispered to Simon.

Simon didn't have time to question the directive and pretended to ignore the generally unsavory lot gathering around them. The crowd yelled louder in broken English, offering rooms, drugs, women and more. The unruly men's voices grew to a boom as they pushed and shoved each other, jockeying for prime positions around the out-of-place *gringos*. Simon and Jonah ignored the barrage as long as they could until a physical altercation seemed inevitable. Looking to defuse the tense situation, Jonah turned towards the tempestuous gathering and held up his hands, speaking loudly to the group. "Nishonigo keshmish bahosho doo ninanahee?" he yelled.

Almost at once, the men stopped yelling and stared at him, dumbfounded.

"Sir, I have good room for you tonight, very good price!" One of the men called out.

"No… English…" Jonah yelled in an odd accent. "Nishonigo keshmish bahosho doo ninanahee?" he continued.

Simon could tell from the strange looks on the men's faces that Jonah definitely wasn't speaking Spanish.

"Ninanahee?" Jonah yelled loudly again to the stunned men.

The group stood frozen, staring at Jonah, baffled, until, to Simon's surprise, the frustrated pack slowly disbanded and walked off into town.

When at last they'd all left, Simon glanced across to Jonah. "What the hell did you say to them?"

"When surrounded by people who want something, always pretend you don't speak their language… or English."

"Was that just gibberish?"

"Of course not," said Jonah, deadpan. "I wished them a Merry Christmas and a Happy New year in a language I knew none of them would know."

Simon chuckled and shook his head. "What language?"

"Navajo," Jonah replied with a wink, and turned to order his food.

I think I love this guy….

After scarfing down their lunch quickly, and despite Simon's reluctance, the pair climbed back into the van to continue their journey. Simon felt a profound dread as they drove across town towards the jungle in the searing hot machine.

Yet as they rolled along, it soon became apparent that Jonah was leading them in a slightly different direction. When they reached the edge of the wild town, Simon was shocked but elated to find them pulling to a stop at a small inlet with a large dock and a ferry moored beside it.

"Thank god! We're taking the ferry back to El Rama!" Simon blurted with relief.

"Nope," Jonah replied softly, before mysteriously ducking his head out of the window and yelling in Spanish to a nearby ferry worker. The man approached, and Simon watched as Jonah and he chatted.

Five minutes later, Jonah pulled the van onto the ferry, joining several cars and cargo trucks.

"Well, if we're not going to El Rama, where the hell are we going!?"

Jonah turned to Simon and offered one of his mellow half-smiles. "The Islas de Maize," he replied cryptically.

"Islas de Maize," Simon repeated under his breath, pondering its meaning. "Corn Islands?" he asked.

"Hey! Your Spanish is getting better!" Jonah said, chuckling and elbowing Simon hard in the arm.

Simon grinned, exultant at his small accomplishment. As he stared out the window at the vast ocean, all he could see was an endless sheet of blue disappearing into the horizon. *I don't see any islands out there, but anything is better than going back into that jungle.*

An hour later, as the ferry made port at a dilapidated stretch of rubble-strewn concrete on the northwest shore of Big Corn Island, Simon wished he had some salt to season the words he was now eating.

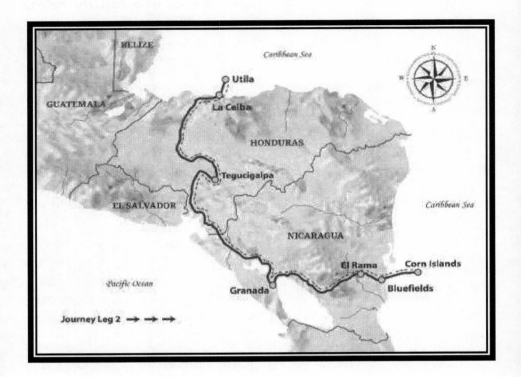

CHAPTER 60

Not what I was hoping for but STILL, better than the jungle.

Jonah pulled the van off the ferry, navigating through the tin-roofed buildings clustered around the pier and onto the dusty streets of Big Corn. Making his way to a hotel a block over, the young man parked the van, grabbed his duffel and headed into the reception office. Simon followed suit, looking forward to the shower he'd been dreaming of for days. *Here I come!*

As he entered the minuscule entryway, Jonah was handing the lady behind the counter a stack of *cordoba*s.

"How much do I owe you for the room?" asked Simon.

"Oh, we're not staying here," Jonah replied nonchalantly before turning, rolling outside again and heading back up the road towards the docks.

Sonofa! Simon chased after him, duffel in hand, and was stunned when Jonah boarded a slight wooden skiff moored beside the pier. "Where are we going now!?" he called out.

"Hermanito!" yelled Jonah without looking back.

The boat's driver started the engine, and Simon hopped in and sat down alongside his compatriot. "Hermanito?" Simon mumbled.

Please don't be in the jungle. Please don't be in the jungle. Please don't be in the jungle.

***

Thirty minutes later, as the small vessel approached Big Corn's diminutive brother, Little Corn, Simon's eyes nearly burst from their sockets. *This… is more like it.*

Ringed with pearlescent white sand, verdant coconut palms, and some of the bluest water Simon had ever seen, Little Corn Island sat like a paradisiacal jewel amidst the Caribbean. The moment the boat came into contact with the dock, Simon dashed from its bow, and before even reaching the end of the pier, dove headlong and fully clothed into the sparkling azure water.

The normally straight-faced Jonah couldn't resist bursting into rollicking laughter. "There you go!" he yelled to the swimming Texan.

Clean at last!

***

For the next several days, the two lounged on the snow-white beaches of the sparsely inhabited Little Corn, relaxing, drinking *pina coladas* and enjoying the warm sea breeze. Similar to Belize, but without the roads, tourists or large hotels, Nicaragua's Little Corn was possibly a *better* Belize, Simon thought now. And the cool Caribbean water was even more refreshing than he'd remembered.

Several lazy days eased by, one after another, until one afternoon, Simon approached Jonah lying in a beachside hammock. "Come with me," he said simply.

Jonah grunted, and lifted the brim of his hat off his resting eyes. "Where to?"

"You'll see," said Simon, offering nothing more than a mischievous grin.

Jonah stared at him a few seconds, amazed that Simon was actually trying to surprise him. "Ug, let's get this over with," he said and climbed into his chair to follow.

As they made their way down the sandy beachfront sidewalk, the usually stolid Jonah secretly grew eager with anticipation. For years, he'd asked his parents on birthdays and Christmases to give him money towards his van rather than presents. They'd been happy to oblige, but deep down, Jonah missed the universal thrill of anticipating an unknown gift.

That is, until he and Simon reached their destination.

As Simon led them onto the dock, Jonah looked on with simmering acrimony as a heavyset Nicaraguan man methodically loaded scuba gear onto a wooden motorboat.

"What the hell is this?" Jonah said, stopping in his tracks. "I can't swim, you idiot!"

His glare was piercing as he eyeballed the boat—and Simon.

"Don't worry about that," smirked Simon.

"Don't worry about it?!" Jonah fumed. "Are you kidding! Maybe you shouldn't worry about being a jackass!" he bellowed and turned to leave.

"Relax!" yelled Simon, nearing his wit's end with Jonah's bouts of indignation. "Dammit, Jonah, just wait a second!"

Hearing the dispute, the boat's captain, Jorge, quickly spoke up, attempting to diffuse the situation. "Good afternoon!" he bellowed in a deep, jovial voice. "Is this the guy you been talking about, Simon?" he asked with a smile.

Simon tidied his sour face and turned back to Jorge, "This is the guy, Jorge," Simon replied. "Jorge, this is Jonah. Jonah, Jorge."

Jorge chuckled. "Nice to meet you, Jonah! It's a beautiful day!" he said.

Jonah turned and offered a strained grin to the amiable boat pilot.

"Just come out with me today," Simon insisted. "I'll explain everything when we're on the water.... Please," he implored once more.

Jonah stewed for a lengthy spell, unsure what the Texan was up to. But he couldn't help but lean towards giving him the benefit of the doubt. Eventually, he conceded and boarded the boat in silence.

A few minutes later, the vessel launched out to sea. And as they drifted away from the dock, Simon pulled a crate of gear onto the deck and began to explain the various pieces of scuba equipment to Jonah. As he attempted to give the young man a crash course in each item's purpose, Jonah just stared at him blankly—years of tribulation, furor and torment swelling inside of him until, finally, in a moment of overwhelming despair, he belted out angrily.

"None of this matters since I can't swim, idiot!" His voice echoed across the water, and even Jorge turned with a start. The pain in Jonah's voice was penetrating. Simon immediately fell silent and laid down the gear in his hands. When he glanced up to Jonah again, however, a broad smile was stretched across Simon's face, catching the young man off guard.

"That you can't swim is actually what doesn't matter," Simon said slyly.

Baffled by the reaction, Jonah gazed on in silence as Simon reached beneath his seat and pulled out a large black vest. "This is a BCD," Simon began. "Think of it as a life jacket that can float or sink to exactly where you want to be. Press this button and air comes out, sinking you down into the water. Press this button over here, and air from the tank refills it, lifting you back up. Just give the buttons a little burst one way or the other until you hover." Simon smiled. "No need to tread water."

Jonah gazed on, processing Simon's words. "So, I can just go up and down? Do I use my arms to move forward? Sounds exhausting."

Simon's grin grew more devilish. He rose and walked to the boat's helm, returning a few seconds later, holding what appeared to be a giant fan with handles and fins on its sides. Simon pressed a button on the handle, and the blades whirred to life. "This... is a Scuba Scooter. All you need to do is hold onto it and point it where you want to go. Up, down, any direction you want. Do you think you can handle that... idiot?" Simon said with a wink.

Jonah sat quietly. He gazed at the device for a few seconds before taking it from Simon's hands, gripping its two handles and pressing the button. The blades spun with a hum, and he glanced up and locked eyes with Simon, emotions swelling inside from the extraordinary gesture. Such kindness had become unfamiliar to him, and he felt terrible for having barked at the well-meaning Texan. But the walls he'd spent years building around himself weren't ready to fall, and he wasn't quite capable of expressing just how much it meant to him. Without realizing it, though, he slowly smiled.

Simon understood.

When the boat reached the drop point Jorge had chosen, he and Simon helped Jonah get suited up and then lowered him down into the sea. The young man hadn't been in the water in years, and clutched to the ladder tightly as he waited for Simon to enter. Simon plunged in and swam up beside him, passing him the scuba scooter. "Now, you can't go very deep with no training and all, so stay close to me, okay?" he said.

"No... problem," responded Jonah with an atypical warble in his voice.

"Are you sure you want to do this?" Simon asked with growing concern.

"More than you know," replied Jonah, putting the air regulator in his mouth and giving Simon a thumbs-up.

"Okay, then, let's do this..."

The sun was high as the two men slowly descended below the rippling surface. Jonah positioned himself alongside and slightly behind Simon as the propeller of the scuba scooter buzzed to life and pulled him along effortlessly towards a nearby reef. Beams of sunlight twinkled around them like great luminous columns as he glanced around in wonder at the bizarre universe he now found himself in.

Suddenly, an unexpected sensation swept through him. A sensation that flooded the young man with an overwhelming emotion, unlike any he recognized. Jonah's mind grasped to understand what it was, and then, at once, it hit him. *There's no gravity here.*

Since that fateful day five years ago, gravity had become an unyielding, soul-crushing force in his life, pulling him down tirelessly against all his efforts to rise up. Jonah struggled daily to pull himself up into bed, up into his chair, up to the sink, up into the van, up to everywhere. The malevolent force of nature fighting him tooth and nail at every turn.

But now, this tormenting burden— his nemesis for so long—had somehow been vanquished. Jonah yelled victoriously through his regulator, a cloud of bubbles billowing around his face.

Simon heard and saw none of this happening behind him. Yet to Jonah, it was one of the singular greatest moments of his life.

Soon they reached the reef, and as they passed over the undulating kaleidoscope of colors, a vast, swarming school of hundreds of radiant Blue Tangs engulfed them in a glittering, cobalt swirl. Simon glanced over his shoulder to find Jonah's eyes and cheeks growing wide with delight.

It was only the beginning.

For the next thirty minutes, they waltzed, drifting and sliding past the abundant reef, which teemed with fascinating sea creatures of every size and shape. Jonah, having long been denied entry to this wondrous blue world, suddenly had the freedom to explore the aquatic realm with abandon. When he spotted a small, green sea turtle cruising playfully along the reef, he grabbed Simon eagerly, and the two men pursued their chelonian friend around a massive red fan coral. Suddenly, the two divers stopped, hovering in awe at what lay on the other side.

"Oh man," Simon gurgled through his mouthpiece.

Soaring past them just a few yards ahead was a group of several spotted eagle rays. The eight-foot-wide, majestic creatures gracefully flapped their sprawling wing-like appendages, propelling them past the reef, past their awestruck spectators and off into the open blue. Simon looked back to Jonah, smiling wide. He couldn't tell for sure, but it appeared as though Jonah's eyes were watering up inside his goggles. Jonah would later deny it, explaining it away as "condensation," but Simon never believed him. "Condensation happens on glass," he would say. "Not on eyeballs!"

When they got back to the boat and Jorge helped the two men inside, Simon began removing his tanks and gear while Jonah sat silently on the bench. Simon finished, and as he leaned in to help Jonah remove his tanks, Jonah suddenly reached out and grabbed him, pulling him in for a strong embrace. Stunned by the surprising display of affection, Simon froze, unsure of what was happening. But when he realized that the hardened kid was really trying to hug him, he put his arms around Jonah and held him back.

"Thanks, so much, man," Jonah said softly to Simon, his tough guy exterior disintegrating momentarily into warm vulnerability.

"Of course, man," Simon responded.

"Aw, you two are soooo sweeeeeet!" Jorge belted in his deep voice and began laughing his hearty Santa Claus laugh.

The two men immediately released each other and composed themselves.

Yeah, that looked weird.

***

The next morning, they returned to El Rama on the ferry from Bluefields via Big Corn Island. Simon was thankful they weren't returning through the jungle again, and after a night in a tawdry hotel in El Rama, they drove back towards Granada.

As they made their way across the country that afternoon, the two men chatted about life and the Darien, and joked about the "tiger" they'd seen in the jungle. Jonah told Simon of his plans to resupply and head straight to Panama the next day, and they brainstormed places Simon might venture to next. But as they pulled into the hotel parking lot, they immediately noticed something missing.

"Where the hell is my car?!" Simon yelled. The space in which he'd parked just over a week ago was now empty. Simon dashed quickly up to the front desk, where the receptionist gave Simon a look that said everything. "*Su coche fue robado hace tres días,*" she said, looking despondent and apologetic.

Simon turned to Jonah. "It was stolen three days ago," he said.

"What! Did she call the police?"

Jonah and the woman spoke for a moment while Simon tried to wrap his head around it. Despair hit him, and anger coursed through his blood. *What the hell am I going to do now?*

"She called the police when she noticed it was missing but hasn't heard anything. She thinks the US license plate made it a target for thieves," Jonah said sympathetically. "I'm really sorry, man." His words of empathy meant little in the moment.

Simon hung his head, stunned with disbelief, and stared blankly into the wall. Fire burned below his skin. After a pensive moment of silence, he unclenched his fists, accepted a key from the woman, turned and exited the reception office, ambling in a catatonic state towards his room. Jonah rolled quietly along behind him in his wheelchair, trying to think of something he could say. Then, something struck him, and he looked up at Simon. "Hey, think of all the gas money we'll save taking only one car down to Panama," he blurted in an un-Jonah like, upbeat tone. "It's a blessing in disguise, man, it really is."

Simon came to a stop and stood there, his head remaining down and his duffle bag dangling in his hand.

Jonah hoped for something, anything. "I mean, if you want to come with me, that is," he continued.

The pause was interminable.

Then slowly, Simon turned around to Jonah, revealing a grin on his face. "Well, we'll have to share stereo privileges then. I'm not listening to that crap you like the whole way down," Simon said, beginning to snicker.

Jonah laughed. "Deal, you idiot... No easy listening, though," he joked.

The two exchanged a smile before Simon turned to unlock his door and entered the room. As he closed his door, he called out a few last words for Jonah. "Kenny G is a genius, you cultureless moron," and with that slammed the door shut behind him.

Jonah sat there a few minutes, grinning.

It had been a long time since he'd had a friend.

CHAPTER 61

The smooth sounds of alto saxophone filled the van as Jonah and Simon cruised southeast towards the Panamanian border. For ten hours, they'd been driving down the Panamericana Highway, through Nicaragua and Costa Rica, and Jonah was heartily regretting allowing Simon to share music control. He hadn't realized Simon was actually in possession of a smartphone containing a plethora of what Jonah considered absolutely terrible music. Still, he was happy to have the company.

As they eased down the road, Simon finished reading *The Lighthouse at the End of the World* and dropped the book into his lap with a sigh. "Hey, have you ever heard of Tierra del Fuego," he asked.

"That's the southern tip of Argentina, right?"

"Yeah! How did you know?" Simon replied, stunned.

Jonah laughed. "Before I chose the Darien as my ultimate mission, sailing across Drake's Passage from Tierra del Fuego to Antarctica was on my shortlist," Jonah replied.

Of course, it was.

Well, I think I might actually try goin' down there," continued Simon, staring at the book in his hands.

"You definitely should. It's supposed to be beautiful. When I was researching that trip, I spoke to some people at a place called the Lighthouse Inn in the town of Ushuaia. If you end up going down there, tell 'em I said hi!" Jonah chuckled.

Simon smiled. *The Lighthouse Inn?* He looked down at the image of a lighthouse on the cover of his book.

Destiny?

"Maybe I will," he replied.

***

After crossing the border into Panama, the pair pulled off for the night in David, a surprisingly modern city in western Panama. In stark contrast to the Spanish colonial gems of Guatemala and Nicaragua, David was clean and contemporary, and Simon was thrilled to find an actual shopping mall across the street from their hotel. Once again, Jonah took great pleasure in witnessing his friend's feverish, childlike excitement. It reminded him of the day Simon had discovered the McDonalds back in Granada.

Dashing from the hotel to the mall straight away, Simon entered through the double doors into an air-conditioned central atrium in a moment of evanescent bliss. It was a refreshing, cool reprieve from the sweltering heat, so for an hour, he wandered around the comforting and familiar American chain stores, feeling somehow temporarily transported back to the US. Tommy Hilfiger. Pandora. The Vitamin Shoppe. There was an almost surreal quality about seeing them now. Though Simon had only been gone for six weeks, San Antonio and its modern conveniences felt like a world away and a lifetime ago. A sense of nostalgia began to wash over him. Yet as he meandered through the galleria, he was surprised to find that, rather than longing to have these things in his life again, he felt somehow alienated by them now. *I need to get out of here.*

Before departing, Simon stopped in an American bookstore chain and purchased a book on the Darien region of southern Panama. That night in the hotel, he read at great length about the infamous swath of land, about its staggering biodiversity, its treacherous and impenetrable landscape and the sinister groups that called it home. He read horror stories of the many failed attempts to pass through the deadly region, and wild tales of the few who had succeeded. Simon noticed three things that seemed to be a common thread in all the accounts:

1. All had been led by previously accomplished adventurers. 2. Each of them had huge budgets and support teams. 3. Everyone who dared to attempt the arduous journey would go on to say they would never, ever do it again.

Simon's concern for his friend mushroomed as the reality of the expedition came to appear more and more perilous. So, the next morning, as they ate breakfast, Simon decided to broach a question that had been weighing on him throughout the night. "So, what is your plan for getting through the Gap?" he asked casually.

He knew Jonah needed a serious plan for something so treacherous, and he prayed that the young man wouldn't say something as foolhardy as *you can't plan for these kinds of things.*

Without speaking, Jonah took a long swig of his coffee and reached over his shoulder into a thin storage pouch on the back of his wheelchair. Pulling out a waterproof pocket folder, he retrieved a large, creased item and began to unfold it. Simon moved their plates and mugs aside to make a clearing in the center of the table as Jonah spread out what appeared to be a patchwork map between them. It took Simon a few moments to realize what it was.

"That's the Darien, isn't it?" he said.

"Yep," replied Jonah. "No one makes a map of the whole Darien region, so I had to take a topo map of Panama and splice it together with a different map of Colombia. Looks pretty good, though, right?"

Simon could see the line of tape, but, besides that, it looked seamless. "It's perfect," he replied. As he continued to stare at Jonah's one-of-a-kind

"Darien Map," Simon noticed hand-drawn lines, symbols and numbers marked in various colors and places throughout.

Jesus, it looks like a military battle plan.

Simon wasn't too far off. As Jonah began to explain his detailed markings and notes, the intrigued Texan just stared on at attention.

"So, the various lines on the map represent routes taken by previous Darien expeditions from the '50s to the 2000s," Jonah said. "This line represents the Trans-Darien expedition of 1960." He slid his fingertip along a winding black line that ended roughly halfway down through the Darien. "The Land Rover that made it through was known as *La Cucaracha Cariñosa*, or the affectionate cockroach," He chuckled. "Their journey started on land, but when they reached the huge Atrato River, they loaded the vehicle onto pontoons for the rest of the trip. Their team averaged 220 yards per hour over 136 days."

Jonah took another sip of coffee while Simon's eyes remained locked like lasers to the map in front of them. Jonah continued. "This line here is Chevrolet's attempt in 1961 with three Chevy Corvairs. They eventually had to abandon one of their cars but managed to get the others through in 109 days, but again, by boating them most of the way as well."

He took a bite of toast. "This one is the British Trans-America Expedition of '72. Two Range Rovers with a massive support team, including helicopters and a military escort. But, again, most of the trip was by boat…Here's Mark Smith's Jeep team in '78 through '79. And once again…" Jonah rolled his eyes, "they finished it by boat. Now this one here, this is the only complete overland crossing. The Upton crossing in '87. The one that took two years remember?"

"Of course, I remember," said Simon.

"This is the one I hope to follow at least the first half of the way. It's been decades since then, but I'm hoping I can retrace the key sections of their route. The problem is this." Jonah pointed at a large cluster of red X's around the southern half of the route and a red line cutting north to south. "These red X's are where either the Panamanian or Colombian governments have reported spotting drug compounds or guerilla camps."

"All of these?!" Simon gestured frantically at the fifty or so X's on the map.

"Yes, all of those. And this red line here, from the FARC controlled village of Bijao on the Cacarica River in Colombia to Yaviza in Panama, that's where the *coyotes* roam."

"Coyotes?"

"Yeah, human traffickers. This is where those with no other option in the world, usually Somalis, Cubans, Bangladeshis, or Syrians, try to get from South America to Panama in an attempt to reach America the hard way. They're desperate for asylum as refugees but have no idea what lies ahead. Many don't make it at all, succumbing to the perils of the jungle. Others are robbed of their last possessions by jungle bandits or the *coyotes* themselves and left for dead."

"Jesus."

"Yeah, though this would be the fastest way through, things have changed a lot since '87 when their team made it through. Most, if not all of those X's didn't exist before. That's why I have all these other routes marked, even though many might no longer exist or be impassible. I'm going to have to avoid this whole region and stick to this area between their path and the cartel-controlled coastline between Turbo and Capurgana. Regardless, this swampland here…. this is where I'll probably have to ditch the van and switch to the kayak."

"Ditch the van?!" Simon sputtered. "You can't take it all the way through?"

"Naw, man. A big van like that near all these red X's?! That would be much too loud and dangerous. I'll go as far as I can in the van, but I'm sure I'll have to leave it at some point."

Simon couldn't believe that he would leave his baby behind in the jungle. *What kind of a parent are you?!*

Jonah continued. "These numbers on the map in black are high elevation points I gathered off of topo maps. I can use them as viewpoints to gain perspective if I need to. The ones in blue are estimated seasonal water depths for rivers and swamps I'll be crossing."

Simon was astonished by the level of detail on the map.

"I've been training for the last several years in cartography and orienteering as well, so I'll use my GPS to draw new paths and features on the map as I go."

"Jesus, you really have been planning this a long time," said Simon.

"Every day for four years," Jonah responded.

Simon gazed at the map, still in disbelief that Jonah was actually going to go through with his plan. Though he felt a modicum of relief that Jonah was so well prepared, the sheer quantity and uniform dispersion of those red X's was distressing. *These are just the camps they know about.* Simon imagined Jonah stumbling into a group of guerillas deep in the jungle. He had to ask. "So, what'll you do if you run into bad guys in the jungle?" he posited cautiously.

Jonah just stared at him for a bit and then started eating again. "Let's just hope that doesn't happen," he mumbled under his breath.

***

The rest of the day was spent driving across the country to Panama City. The two men barely spoke. With Jonah's impending departure into the jungle just two days away, a heaviness had filled the van. As they drove, Simon repeatedly glanced at his young friend, who seemed increasingly focused and deep in thought. He wondered if the fun the two of them had been sharing the previous two weeks was making Jonah reconsider his death-wish-of-a-goal. Simon hoped it had. Every minute he grew more worried about what lay ahead for him.

That night, as he lay in his hotel room, reading his book on the Darien, Simon heard a knocking on his door. As he opened it, he found a morose Jonah sitting in his wheelchair just outside.

"Can I come in?" he whispered.

"Of course."

Taking a seat on the edge of the bed, Simon locked eyes with the young man sitting across from him. For a moment, the air between them thickened with melancholy, and Simon struggled to keep his composure.

Jonah appeared somber and was holding a few envelopes in his lap. He began handing them one by one to Simon, speaking softly as he did. "This is a letter to my parents. After I go into the jungle, I'd like you to mail it for me."

"Absolutely," replied Simon. The gravitas of the situation was now really sinking in.

"This is a copy of my Darien map. It also has on it my expected timeframe, though it's mostly just guesswork. Should be able to put someone within a hundred square kilometers of me though if need be."

Simon took the envelope.

"This is a letter for you. Once I head into the jungle you can open it, but not until then."

Simon looked down at the envelope with his name on it and wondered what it could say.

"And this is a letter for me when you see me next time," Jonah said with a smile. "It also has my house keys in it, which I don't want to lose in the jungle." Jonah laughed awkwardly to try and lighten the mood. Simon laughed too, but in his heart, he just wanted to cry.

He could hardly sleep that whole night.

The next morning the pair visited the Panama Canal together, a longtime dream of Jonah's. From high on the viewing platform, the two men stood in silence as massive freighter ships moved through the giant locks below them. Both were fully aware that this was likely one of the last times they would ever spend together. The next morning Jonah would head into the Darien.

Simon stood beside his friend, staring out at the Canal, filling with emotion. Finally, he had to say what he'd wanted to for days. "Don't go."

Neither of them moved, continuing to stare out at the passing ships.

"I have to," Jonah replied.

Simon could tell there was something different in the young man's voice these last few days. Pain and sadness, but also resolve. He knew there would be no deterring him, and he didn't speak another word of it for the rest of the morning.

Around noon, they left the Canal Zone and drove south towards the Darien. An hour outside of Panama City, they came upon their first military checkpoints. The *Servicio Nacional de Fronteras* or simply *Senafront*, are the militarized border police who strictly monitor all those who come and go from the Darien Province. Because of its decades-long attraction to smugglers, the lone road into the Darien stood heavily guarded, and every thirty minutes or so, the pair were stopped for document checks and re-checks.

For three hours, they continued down the increasingly small and rugged road towards Yaviza—the town at the southern end of this piece of the *Panamericana*.

In the late afternoon, they arrived in the small village and managed to get settled in at a riverside guesthouse. After dropping off their bags, Simon and Jonah took a twilight stroll down the riverbank to the literal 'end of the road.' Just twenty feet from their guesthouse, the uninterrupted chain of highways and roads that run south from Alaska all the way through the US and Central America, dramatically came to an end more than 6,000 miles later in this pile of cracked pavement at the edge of town. From that point on, the only way further south was a hanging footbridge over a wide river into the dark Darien jungle. Jonah and Simon rambled out onto the bridge and stopped to watch the sun setting orange over the trees. The wild sounds of the Darien wilderness came echoing from the dense thicket across the river. Simon stared at the shadowy woods in the failing light, intensely aware of the countless dangers that lurked in its shadows. *I still can't believe he's going in there.*

***

The next morning, they awoke at sunrise and ate breakfast in silence. Jonah's departure loomed like a black cloud over their meal, and Simon wondered if a priest should be there, giving the young man his last rights. As they climbed in the van and drove out along the riverbank, Simon stared out his side window at the Darian jungle looming ominously across the brown water. Though he'd never stepped foot in it, Simon hated those woods, envisioning them as a great amorphous beast preparing to consume his truest friend.

A short distance outside of town, they came upon a rickety platform ferry intended to shuttle jeeps and supplies to the last remaining Panamanian military outposts in the Darien jungle. Jonah bribed the haggard boat operator $200 US to take his van across the river, an act that would likely land them both in prison for the rest of their lives if they were discovered.

"Why would he risk his life for $200?" asked Simon.

"That's probably more than he makes in 6 months," replied Jonah.

Arriving on the far side, they pulled off the ferry onto a narrow military jeep path that disappeared off into the jungle. The second their wheels touched the soft Darien earth, the emotions swirling through the van reached palpable levels.

But there was no time to dwell on it.

Jonah accelerated slowly and cautiously down the dirt trail, fully aware that detection here would bring a very harsh end to his four-year, personal journey. They had to disappear, and fast.

After three excruciating minutes on the exposed path, Jonah finally veered off into the jungle, the van's steel cow plow clearing a route through the trees as he went. Once concealed from the road, the vehicle lumbered to a stop, and Jonah killed the engine. "This is where you get off," he said.

Simon hopped from the vehicle and stood watching as Jonah exited the van and began to clear an area ahead with a machete. It was swelteringly hot and humid here, and a cloud of mosquitoes had already descended on them. Simon remembered reading how, on the British Expedition into the Darien, the clothes had actually rotted off the team's bodies due to the extreme humidity. He also recalled how everyone had gotten horribly ill from various insect bites along the way. "This is crazy," he mumbled to himself as he watched Jonah hacking away and clearing the jungle slowly. Very slowly.

After ten minutes, Jonah climbed into the back of the van and returned holding the crate of spray paint and some tools. "Here, you can start painting the van," he said, tossing the cans to Simon. "There are different shades of green there, so try to make the pattern organic and uneven like camouflage," he said.

Simon took the cans and reluctantly set about the task. The heat had already begun to affect him, and though he craved water, he didn't dare take any of Jonah's. It was too late for that.

As Simon continued to paint, Jonah suddenly crawled from his wheelchair and dragged himself underneath the vehicle with his set of tools. The sounds of ratcheting and clanking came from below, and Simon paused, perplexed as to what the young man was up to. When, eventually, Jonah slid back out, Simon could see he was holding several objects wrapped in a black cloth on his chest. He pulled himself back into his wheelchair and unwrapped the items.

Simon now saw a 9mm pistol, a disassembled AR-7 rifle, a sawed-off shotgun and several boxes of ammunition. "Oh, thank god!" he rejoiced, an exuberant sigh bursting from his lips as he dropped his hands to his knees.

"What?" Jonah said alarmed.

"I thought you were about to go in there unarmed!" Simon replied. He turned back to continue spray-painting the van. "I guess you're not the idiot I thought you were, Jonah," he continued mockingly.

Jonah smiled and stared at Simon. "You're the idiot," he countered.

"Agree to disagree," Simon said, smiling wider.

"Everyone knows Simon is the idiot here, Simon. Stop trying to fight it," retorted Jonah.

"Says the guy about to walk into a snake-infested war zone for no good reason," laughed Simon.

Jonah's face quickly soured. "I'm not *walking* anywhere.... and I have my reasons," he barked sternly.

Simon knew he'd chosen his words poorly but remained silent as Jonah turned and tucked the guns under the driver's seat. The young man was fickle and capricious, but Simon understood why—and now certainly wasn't the time to get into it.

After finishing his olive-hued masterpiece, Simon sat down for a spell in the shade.

"It's time for me to go," Jonah said eventually.

"I know," replied a somber Simon.

The two hugged one last time before the young man climbed back into the driver's seat to depart. He leaned out the window one last time. "Just walk back up the road. I already paid the ferry driver to take you back over the river."

"Thanks," Simon said, his heart welling with emotion. "Just remember something, will you?"

"What's that?"

"You're not invincible," Simon smiled.

"Believe me, I know," Jonah chuckled and glanced down at his legs.

Suddenly, he reached back into the van and returned holding something out to Simon.

"What is it?" asked Simon.

"Duct tape, *amigo*," said Jonah, placing the tiny roll of silver tape into the Texan's hand. "Never leave home without it. Trust me. You'll need this on the road someday and be glad it's there." He gave Simon a wink.

"Thanks," Simon laughed, pocketing the pill-bottle sized roll.

"See you on the other side," Jonah said with a smile.

An aching sadness clamored inside of Simon, but he fought it back as best he could. "Be safe out there," he replied.

Jonah grinned, gave him a half wave and began driving slowly into the jungle. Simon just stood there watching the van disappear into the green forest until he could no longer see it.

He knew he'd probably never see Jonah again.

Likely no one would.

CHAPTER 62

Simon traipsed out of the jungle and back onto the desolate military road. As he made his way towards the ferry, his mind swirled with visions of Jonah's journey deep into the unknown. Simon felt like he, too, was now heading into the unknown. Though he wasn't marching into the Darien jungle, the world before him seemed equally vast, challenging and unexplored. He had no car, no idea where he was going, and now he was all alone. Yet, for the first time on his journey, being alone didn't frighten him. It was a tremendous revelation, and he questioned why he felt as he did.

Perhaps the sensation was just *relative,* he wondered. That, no matter where he went in the wild world, it couldn't possibly be as dangerous and difficult as the path Jonah had chosen.

Or perhaps it was something *evolutionary.* Maybe he'd grown so much in the past month on the road that he now possessed the confidence and resiliency to press on by himself.

Or maybe it was merely *perceptive.* The Earth was changing, not he, and what Simon once viewed as a menacing, impregnable *beyond*—the world outside of Odessa—he now saw as a wide-open realm filled with wondrous places, gracious people and unique experiences to be had.

Perhaps it was a little bit of all three.

After returning over the river, Simon wandered along the riverbank back towards Yaviza. As he trudged on, he recalled the one final request Jonah had made of him. "Wait a day before you leave, could you?" he'd asked. "*Senafront* keeps tabs on any foreigners coming this close to the Colombia border. The moment you attempt to leave the Darien on foot without me, they'll know something isn't right. It'll only be a matter of time before they put two and two together and come looking for me...,"

Jonah needed a head start, and Simon intended to give him one.

That afternoon, the Texan settled into his sparse room at the rustic but clean Sousa Guesthouse. A mere block from the 'end of the road,' the old two-story, wooden home belonged to the genial Maria De Sousa and her mountain of a son, Alfonso. Perched above the riverside road, Simon's second-floor room looked out on the flowing brown water and the foreboding Darien jungle beyond it. He pulled his chair up to the window and sat there gazing out across the river at the vast wilderness, wondering where Jonah was and how far he'd made it in the past few hours. He feared for his friend, but at the same time, he tried desperately to believe that Jonah could do it.

A few yards down river from Simon's roost sat the modest wooden docks of Yaviza. As Simon rested there all afternoon staring out his window, his gaze would often fall upon the long dugout canoes arriving periodically along its banks, overflowing with fish, plantains, coconuts and other fruits and vegetables. *Where are they coming from?* He wondered. *And where are they going?*

As the narrow vessels came to berth, Simon watched as the local townspeople worked together, loading and offloading cargo from the traditional wooden crafts. Yaviza, which seemed to be the lone trading center for the jungle farmers and fishermen throughout this sweltering and remote region, beguiled Simon as he watched. The people, their lives, and the river culture unfolding before him.

Gradually, his mind began to wander back to 24 hours prior. Just one day ago, he'd stood watching thousand-foot-long mega freighters moving through the computer-controlled locks of the Panama Canal. Now, here he was in what felt like a different epoch and a different world, watching the primitive, fifteen-foot dugout canoes bringing life and commerce to this far-flung part of the jungle. These boats had likely been the primary mode of transport in this region for hundreds of years. And somehow still remained so.

With every new encounter, Simon's perspective on the rural communities he came into contact with was evolving. He no longer viewed them as entirely separate or less civilized than his world back in America. Rather, he'd begun to see the roots of the modern world still alive in each of them. *I bet America a few hundred years ago would have looked a lot like this.*

And yet it wasn't just the lack of technology that stood out. Equally alluring to him was witnessing the small-scale organization of community that seemed to come with such isolated places: the Guatemalan mountain farmers laboring in the precipitous cornfields together, the hamlet of villagers repairing the patchwork mountain roads together and now these jungle farmers and river traders working on the docks together. There still was such a thing as *the common good* here, he thought.

People don't work together in America anymore.

When Simon was a child, his family had known every person in their neighborhood. They would have block-wide barbecues, help each other repair homes after a storm and collect each other's mail when they were away on vacation. He was a son and a neighbor, and that had been plenty good enough. But, by the time Simon was in high school, he'd felt an increasing pressure to think of himself as a Texan more than an Odessan. He went along with the newfound state pride instilled in him without questioning its significance. *Don't Mess with Texas!* They always said.

Then 9/11 happened. And Simon at once was told that he was an American, first and foremost. American patriotism became the word of the decade, and he allowed it to define him as well. *We will never forget.*

Soon after, social networks, a 24-hour news cycle, expanding international economic interconnectivity and global issues like terrorism and the environment transformed Simon into a "citizen of the world." And while the far-reaching designation certainly sounded inclusive at the time, Simon noticed that he'd somehow grown more and more detached from the world around him. *Je Suis Charlie.*

Considering these things now, it occurred to Simon that he couldn't name a single person on his street back in San Antonio. A neighborhood he'd lived in for nearly three years.

How diluted have our lives become? Have we completely lost the value of local community?

Simon's mind became flooded with thoughts of the world, and an odd longing for the simpler times of his childhood. As his gaze remained on the river docks and the people who worked them—the inspiring dynamic between the townspeople and the river traders, laughing, toiling and working together—a scene unlike any he'd ever been a part of before, a strange sensation began to find a foothold within him. An unexplainable desire to experience what these people had and to somehow be a part of it. To be a part of something tangible. Something "real."

And as the remains of the day dwindled towards dusk, this yearning swelled greater inside him. Simon recalled how absurd the concept had seemed to him back in Belize. How he'd thought Alice was mad for wanting to know more about the local people's daily lives. But now it struck him like a bolt. *I actually do want to know about these people and how they live their days.* It was a remarkable epiphany, and one that made Simon realize just how much he was changing.

Heading downstairs at once, Simon inquired with Maria De Sousa about staying a few more nights in the guesthouse. The soft-spoken but tough-skinned woman could see a light in Simon's eyes as he spoke, and somehow recognized there was something different in him from her previous visitors. She was happy to oblige. "*Sí, absolutamente.*"

That night Maria and her son Alfonso invited Simon to join them for dinner in the kitchen. The three sat around a wooden table eating fried fish from the river, rice and fresh plantains recently harvested from the jungle. It was a simple yet delicious meal, hearty and flavorful, and Simon savored every homemade morsel of it.

As they ate, the Texan communicated sporadically with the family using his limited Spanish, his translation dictionary and a whole lot of patience from Maria and Alfonso. He'd begun to notice how much people appreciated his attempts at speaking their language. This family was no different. They greatly respected Simon's efforts and helped him along as best they could. He, in turn, was thankful for their patience and repeatedly told them as much.

Simon was quick to learn that Maria De Sousa was not only kind and motherly, but also smart as a whip and seemingly omniscient of all activity in the village. With a reputation as one of the finest cooks in town, Maria often prepared meals for those who had fallen on hard times and would graciously deliver them to the needy out of the public eye. Her son, the towering Alfonso, typically served as her mule.

Himself in his early thirties, Alfonso bore a thick black mustache, a gargantuan barrel of a chest and arms the size of tree trunks. Nevertheless, he had the same kind and soft-spoken demeanor as his mother, and Simon perceived him as a gentle giant. Simon could also sense how deeply the man loved his mother. Clearly, he'd always been the man of the house.

Earlier that day, Simon had seen Alfonso down on the docks, assisting in the loading and unloading of the canoes and trucks by the riverside. When Simon asked him about it at dinner, Alfonso explained how he typically received a small portion of the cargo as payment for his labor. That morning, for instance, he'd helped a fisherman get his fish to market, and now they were eating fish for dinner. Likewise, for the plantains.

Alfonso went on to explain that the only real money the family possessed was from Maria's guesthouse rentals to outsiders. In the village, they typically bartered labor and home cooking for the things they needed. Simon was again captivated by this simple, traditional system.

Suddenly, he had an idea. "*Es possible... yo ayudar...* tomorrow?" he blurted out awkwardly.

Alfonso and Maria stared at him, confused.

"Can I work at the docks with you tomorrow?" Simon timidly reiterated.

"¡Ah! *Comprendo... pero ¿por que?*" asked Alfonso, clearly bewildered by the odd request.

Why? Simon thought.

The Texan struggled mightily to articulate his reasoning, and eventually managed to convey that he just wanted to be a part of the experience, and to help. Above all, he took pains to stress that he didn't want to be paid. Anything that he received for the day, he would gladly contribute to the family and the daily meal.

Maria and Alfonso were flabbergasted as to why Simon would want to do this. No visiting foreigner had ever made such a proposition before. Yet, by the great effort Simon had put forth to ask, they could sense how important it was to him.

"*Sí, nos encontramos aquí a las seis de la mañana,*" Alfonso agreed with a smile.

Simon stared at him, blankly.

"You – me – here – six – tomorrow," Alfonso reiterated, pointing at the table.

"*Ah! Muchas gracias! Muchas gracias!*" Simon exclaimed – jubilantly thanking his hosts who chuckled at his exuberant response.

***

Returning to his room that night, Simon was brimming with excitement about what the next day would bring. But as he came through the door, he pitched a glance at the small nightstand resting beside his bed, and spied the thin stack of envelopes from Jonah. His smile evaporated as he remembered where the young man now was. Gazing across the room, he peered out through the window. Beyond the glass was just the moon and darkness. Somewhere in that darkness was his friend.

As Simon sat down on the edge of his bed, he picked up the letter labeled *Simon* and ran his fingers over it. Tearing the top off, he removed its contents and began to read Jonah's words with a heavy heart.

Simon,

I know we've only known each other for a short time, but it has been an unforgettable experience getting to know you. Under different circumstances I would have loved to continue traveling with you. You have an adventurous spirit and a kind heart. It has been a long time since I've had a friend like you and I'm so happy we ran into each other that night in Tegucigalpa. I think we were meant to meet each other. Honestly, you've made it that much more difficult for me to risk my life in the Darien. But knowing I'll have a friend like you when I get out the other side will make me fight that much harder to succeed. If, for some reason I don't make it... at least we had our tiger in Moskita!

As for you.... Go to Tierra del Fuego. Do whatever it takes to get there, but accomplish that. I know you don't think you can, but I know *you can. We all have courage inside us, and sometimes we just need a reason to dig deep and find it. Remember to be safe, but also remember to take chances. That's what life's all about, right? I can't wait to hear all about your adventures when we meet again,* amigo. *Until the next time,*

Your friend,

Jonah

Simon stared at the letter smiling and fighting off tears. He knew in his heart that their friendship was special, and he, too, was hugely grateful they had met. In the deep recesses of his soul, he still harbored a belief that somehow, somewhere, he would meet his friend again. It had only been a day, but he missed him greatly.

Simon walked back to the window and stared out at the Darien Jungle across the river. The treetops glowed faintly in the moonlight, and he imagined Jonah sleeping in the van alone out in the woods. He slid open the glass, releasing the choral chatter of millions of animals and insects into his room. Listening closely, he hoped beyond reason to hear the Soca music of radio Bluefields echoing from the night.

CHAPTER 63

Rising just after sunrise, Simon washed his face and joined Alfonso at the kitchen table for a hearty breakfast of tortillas, beans and scrambled eggs. The eggs, from Maria's coops behind the house, were the freshest tasting Simon had ever eaten. *Seriously, why does everything taste so much better here?*

With their bellies full, the two men strolled down to the docks to join half a dozen other men from the town already hard at work on the dusty riverside. In the quiet stillness of the blue morning, Simon could see that a pair of canoes had arrived from far off in the wild, piled high with stalks of plantains, green and jagged. As the local men toiled to shuffle the produce into an awaiting stake bed truck, the group suddenly caught a glimpse of the foreign stranger and took a momentary pause to observe him.

Simon froze in his approach. *Maybe this was a huge mistake*

"¡*Buenos días*!" Alfonso hollered to the gang. "*Él está conmigo, su nombre es* Simon."

Simon stared back at the men, something suddenly dawning on him. Perhaps they wouldn't want his help. *Will these guys think I'm trying to take a piece of their livelihood away?*

As Simon stood contemplating what to do next, the rugged men's curious faces abruptly metamorphosed into squinting smiles, and a chorus of "¡*Hola Simon!*" rose from the group.

"*Hola,*" Simon mumbled with a wave. *Well, I guess that answers that question.*

Wasting no time, Alfonso leapt up onto the tail of the truck and hastily set about heaping bunches of plantains into its bed. Simon, meanwhile, remained motionless, watching as the bucket brigade of fruit marched by, unsure of where, or if, he could possibly fit into this assembly line. Everyone seemed to know their place in the swift-moving system.

Everyone except Simon.

Noticing the dazed Texan's puzzlement, Alfonso hollered a few words to one of the local men, Victor, who stood on a second canoe preparing to unload. Whistling a piercing whistle at the dumbstruck *gringo*, Victor beckoned for Simon to join him on his craft.

All right! Here we go!

Without so much as an ounce of thought, Simon dashed over and jumped headlong onto the bow of the thin boat, clearly unaware of the old Chinese proverb, *with great narrowness comes great instability.*

The second his feet hit the wood, the entire vessel rocked spasmodically side-to-side – dropping Victor to his knees and almost tossing the top-heavy Simon straight out into the river. *Oh shit. Oh shit. Oh shit!* Simon had never stood in a canoe before, a fact that was riotously obvious to everyone around, and the gang burst into laughter at the sight of the flailing man.

Flapping his arms wildly, Simon gathered his balance and slowly, the boat stopped rocking. *Well, that was embarrassing.* But there was no time to blush. Before Simon knew what was happening, Victor handed him a massive cluster of plantains, and the awkward American teetered from side to side, struggling to grapple the amorphous mass as it shifted and undulated in his arms. Once again, the heavy load tipped Simon's scales of balance, sending him wobbling and wavering on trembling legs. *Oh shit. Oh shit. Oh shit!*

Suddenly, Simon heard Victor whistle once more. Throwing a hurried glance at him, he spied the man grasping a stalk in one hand and cradling the rest of the fruit with his other. Simon shifted his hands to adopt the technique, and immediately the jumble stopped quivering in his arms. "Aha!" he squawked, giving a pie-eyed smile to the hearty man.

Victor erupted into laughter.

Simon inched his way to the end of the canoe, handed the bunch to the men loading the truck, and then dashed back to the boat for another load. All the while grinning ear to ear.

For forty-five minutes, the crew of men labored in the hot sun, transferring the cargo from the canoes to the rusted old truck bound for distant markets. By the time they'd finished, Simon was running back and forth easily on the watercraft and delivering bunches to the shore with rhythmic efficiency. The team worked well together, and when the job was complete, the group sat on the dock to rest. It was mid-morning, but it was already sweltering, and several of the men leaned over the side of the dock to splash river water on their faces and heads. Simon followed suit, finding the water crisp and refreshing.

Soon, Maria appeared with a bucket of iced bottles of drinking water. And as the men quaffed them down in single chugs, Alfonso grabbed two clusters of plantains he'd put to the side and carried them back towards the house. Simon knew he'd earned one of those bunches for the family, and took incredible newfound pride in it.

Before long, more canoes arrived. And for several more hours, the crew unloaded them in the swampy heat. Most of the men had their shirts off, and eventually Simon had to do the same, peeling the sweat-soaked shirt from his body. At first, he noticed a few eyes on his ghostly pale skin, but after a few seconds, no one seemed to care.

When they'd finished unloading the boats around midday, the gargantuan Alfonso turned and sprinted to the end of the dock, leaping off into the river with a thunderous splash. "Holy crap!" Simon laughed, as several of the other men plunged into the river as well.

For a few moments, he stood pondering the scene before reasoning, *Ah, what the hell!* and dashed to the end of the dock and dove in. When

Simon's giant white head eventually breached the surface like a beluga whale, Victor bellowed *"Bienvenido a Yaviza!"* to a roar of laughter from the swimming men.

For ten minutes, the group cooled off in the brisk river water on the jungle's edge as passing wooden canoes swerved around their bobbing torsos. Speaking in Spanish as they laughed and splashed, Simon only understood bits and pieces of what they were saying, but he was reveling in being here, swimming alongside them. He'd worked hard all day, easily the hardest of his life, and yet working to put food on Maria's table felt rewarding beyond words. Suddenly, Alfonso turned to Simon and beamed, *"Almuerzo!"* which Simon knew by his point meant "lunch."

Oh, thank God! He grinned, hungrier than he'd been in as long as he could remember.

Back at the house, Simon and Alfonso were greeted with a nourishing lunch of chicken, beans and vegetables. They sat in the kitchen sipping on cold cans of Balboa beer as they ate, and Simon recognized this as one of the most satisfying meals of his life. His thoughts drifted to the incredible meal he'd eaten with Jack and Alice way back at Tulu's place in Brasilito. Though it now seemed like an eternity ago, Simon realized it had only been six weeks, and he contemplated just how far he had come since then. Both physically and as a person.

***

After lunch, the men returned to the docks, where Simon was greeted with smiles and slaps on the back from his fellow workers. The warm welcome affected Simon in a striking way, and he smiled back graciously.

For the remainder of the day, Simon and the gang loaded and unloaded at the docks in the scorching heat. Produce, beans and lumber came flowing in from the forest, and manufactured goods like rope, propane, nails and beer flowed out into the wild. As each canoe drifted away, Simon imagined the uncharted corners of the jungle they were headed to, and fantasized about what their homes and villages might be like.

He also wondered if any of the canoe drivers might ever see Jonah out there… somewhere.

Finishing at the docks for the evening, Simon made a decision. He had no desire to leave Yaviza the next day. Working with Alfonso and the other men had given him a surprising level of gratification, and it occurred to him just how fast he'd been moving through Central America. And yet he wasn't really in any hurry. It was December, and in the recesses of his mind, Simon still felt a growing pull towards Tierra del Fuego. *But even if I do end up going to Argentina, wouldn't it be better if I waited until the winter is over? April perhaps?* He decided that this was a sound and logical idea.

Simon never *was* good at geography.

CHAPTER 64

A few days in Yaviza quickly turned into a week and then more, as Simon immersed himself in village life and settled into his new home. Each day passed in much the same way, working the docks with Alfonso, Victor and the others, swimming in the river, practicing his Spanish and most importantly, eating Maria's delicious home cooking. At night, the family would discuss the day and talk at length about the De Sousa's life in Yaviza, and Simon's former existence back in America. Simon enjoyed their conversations immensely, and was proud of his rapidly improving ability to communicate.

By the second week, he found he could have short conversations with Victor, Felix, Javier and the other men who worked at the docks with him. On occasion, a few of them even invited Simon over for beers at their homes, and he enjoyed spending time with them and meeting their families. He often found himself reminded of Alice and her desire to talk to the locals back in Brasilito. Now he truly understood it. He was learning so much from the Yaviza community— a culture so immensely different from what he was familiar with. And though he'd glimpsed it a month earlier, that night spent with Martine, Tian and Mita in the mountains, nothing, he realized now, could have prepared him for the growth and understanding that came from living with this family, day in and day out.

***

Nearly two weeks passed, and the homes of Yaviza were soon adorned with twinkle lights and decorations for the approaching holiday. Simon helped Maria hang a large *"Feliz Navidad"* sign in their front window. Though he'd begun to feel as though Maria and Alfonso were like a family to him, as Christmas Day grew near, Simon couldn't help but think about his mother and Jonathan. So, one afternoon, he asked Alfonso if there was internet in the village. *"Si,"* Alfonso replied, before leading him through the town to a small shop at the edge of the community. The word "Internet" and the logos of various electronics manufactures had been hand-painted on its front wall with varying levels of accuracy.

As the two men entered, they were greeted straight away by a waifish elderly man at the desk smiling a kind, toothless smile. Simon found something instantly endearing about this caricature of a man, his thin frame and large spectacles giving him the appearance of a gangly seahorse or a posturing meerkat. Alfonso spoke with him for a few minutes, and then, with a wave of his tiny hand and a broad smile, the old man beckoned Simon to follow.

Past shelves of old computer parts and bins of doodads, they made their way to a lone console on a small desk at the back of the shop. As the old-timer plugged it in and booted it up, Simon recognized the familiar tone and crackle of a dial-up modem logging in— a sound he hadn't heard in fifteen years at least.

Simon took a seat and logged into his social network.

After several agonizing minutes, the page eventually loaded.

A dozen new comments appeared on his most recent status update. And Simon read through them with a smile on his face.

Oh my god Simon, this sounds incredible!

Way to go, man. Can't wait to hear more updates!

We're so jealous! Have fun out there for us!

Give me a call when you get back!

And several more just like them.

Clearly, people believe me now, thought Simon.

Checking his private messages, he opened the first, and was shocked to find yet another short reply from his mother. With great trepidation, he began to read.

Wow. Be careful out there son. I always dreamed of going to Central America someday. It sounds like an incredible place. Are you going to Nicaragua? I've heard that the Corn Islands are beautiful. Call when you can. I'd love to hear from you. Mom

Simon sat in stunned disbelief at the bizarre message. *Mom always wanted to go to Central America?! What?! She's heard of the Corn Islands?! She wants me to call her?!*

For several moments he gazed at the screen, double-checking that he'd read the message correctly. The tone of genuine caring in her words was difficult to comprehend. *This from a woman who gave me practically nothing for twenty years. And how on earth does she know about the Corn Islands anyway?*

The forty-five words went against everything he knew about his mother.

Then something painful occurred to Simon. *I guess I really don't know anything about her? We've barely spoken in two decades.*

Struggling to find the words for a response, he eventually began.

Good to hear from you Mom. Yes, I am being careful. Thank you for being concerned. I had no idea you wanted to go to Central America. Since when? Yes, I went to Nicaragua and I did go to the Corn Islands. It was so beautiful it would be impossible to describe. I hope you get a chance to go there someday. Where did you read about them? I'll call if I can, but I don't have phone service. Have a Merry Christmas.

Simon

Simon mulled over the message for some time before finally hitting send. The thought of what she would say next churned like a whirlwind in his mind.

The next message was from Jonathan.

Did you get my last message? I'm worried about you Simon. This isn't like you. From your last post it sounds like you really are in Central America. Are you still planning on going back to your job in San Antonio? Do you want me to call them and see if I can get you your job back? I would really like to talk to you. I hope you can call me on Christmas like you usually do. Really concerned about you and what your plan is. I think it's urgent that we talk.

Simon stared at the message, livid. *What the hell is Jonathan talking about? Get my job back?*

Simon's blood boiled. He took a deep breath and re-read the message once more. Clearly, Jonathan was worried for his wellbeing. But clearly, he believed that having a steady job back in America was the only way to achieve that. *Why does this feel so familiar?*

Simon knew why. Two months ago, he remembered saying something strikingly similar to Jack and Alice back in Brasilito. He couldn't believe the rapid evolution of his own personal priorities. He ruminated on it for some time before writing back to his brother.

Yes, I received your last message, Jonathan. I haven't lost my mind. I just decided to live my life differently. No, I don't want my job back. I will try to call you at Christmas if I can. Did you know Mom always wanted to go to Central America?

Simon.

He hit send and posted a new status update.

Hello Everyone. Since I last wrote, so much has happened. I learned to scuba dive in the Bay Islands of Honduras, conquering a fear of the ocean that I've had since I was a child. While there, I swam with a magnificent whale shark. A massive and majestic creature that initially put the fear of God in me when I thought it was a Megalodon. Possibly the most afraid I've ever been in my life! Once my terror was put aside, I realized what a peaceful and graceful creature it was. I've certainly been learning that looks can be deceiving in this world. With people, places and now animals.

After that I made my way to Tegucigalpa, Honduras. It was there that I met my friend Jonah. A strong and unique young man unlike any I've ever encountered before. Jonah would be considered 'disabled' by most as he has been relegated to a wheelchair for years, but I have never met a more 'able' person in all my life. He showed me that courage and will can overcome nearly any obstacle. Together we traveled for several days through the jungle to the Mosquito Coast of Nicaragua. While sleeping one night, we were almost spotted (or worse) by drug smugglers moving through the jungle. Remember when I said the whale shark made me the most terrified I had ever been? Well, this set a new fear record. We hid in the dark, silent and terrified for what felt like ages. Obviously, since you're reading this, we survived.

From there, we went to the beautiful Corn Islands to relax and enjoy the Caribbean once again. What a remarkable place. After that, I returned to Granada to find out my car had been stolen! Which reminds me, I probably should stop paying my car insurance.

From Granada I headed south to Panama City. Together with Jonah, I watched massive cargo ships the size of rural towns move through the Panama Canal locks with ease. I've never seen anything like it.

Which brings me to now. I've been living on the edge of the Darien jungle in Yaviza, Panama for the past few weeks. Loading and unloading canoes on a river in the middle of nowhere to help support my local family, Maria and Alfonso. It is a simple life, but I am learning to cherish it. I find myself contemplating why the more traditional the culture I encounter on this adventure, the more everything just seems to make sense? Life doesn't have to be as complicated as we make it, I guess.

Everywhere I go, I keep making new friends and learning more and more about what I can do and who I am. I have no idea where I'll be next week, but I know it won't be on my way back to Texas. Thank you for all of your well wishes. I really appreciate it.

Simon hit send and smiled at the screen. *Man, I hope somebody reads that.*

***

Christmas day finally arrived. Simon had bought small presents for Maria and Alfonso and a six-pack of beer for each of his new local friends. That morning Maria made a huge feast, and all of her siblings and cousins came over to join them in the festivities. It was a special day for her family, and Simon felt honored to be seated at the table with the gregarious bunch. But as the celebrations carried on, the jovial family somehow evoked lost memories of better times long, long ago. A time when he was very young, and the Hill family would eat and laugh together all Christmas morning. *I can't believe I forgot about that.*

Throughout the meal, a gathering of unfamiliar emotions stirred inside Simon, until eventually, he could bear them no longer. Leaning over, he asked a tipsy Alfonso if it was possible to make an international phone call in town. The gentle giant explained that the only place was the internet shop, but it would undoubtedly be closed for Christmas. At this, Simon hung his head, continuing to eat in silence. Alfonso, however, could sense his disappointment.

Abruptly standing and grabbing a plate, the stout man piled it high with ham, potatoes and other fare from the feast. Then, with his own mouth stuffed, he tapped Simon on the shoulder, mumbled something unintelligible and gestured for the Texan to follow him. Simon stood, excused himself from the group, and followed Alfonso out the door and up the road.

As the two men walked through the village, the crackle of firecrackers and the whirr of rockets echoed through the air. Simon had become all too familiar with the *cohetes,* a children's Christmas tradition in Latin America. The explosions began at 5 a.m. each morning and had become more reliable than the alarm clock on his cell phone—or the neighborhood roosters.

After a few minutes, the pair arrived at a dwarfish wooden shack near the edge of the town, and Alfonso gave the door a sturdy knock. The two men stood waiting until, suddenly, the frail outline of the man from the internet shop appeared in the doorway. Simon was pleasantly surprised to see him, and it was clear the old man felt the same. When Alfonso handed the elderly man the heavy plate of food, his small wrinkled eyes lit up with delight, and a huge smile stretched across his weathered face. *Clearly, he knows Maria's cooking!*

Simon and Alphonso chuckled. But as the old man turned to set the food down, Simon glanced inside his meager home and was disheartened to see that the man had no company on this joyous day—only a dimly lit quiet room and a few odd pieces of furniture. No family or friends. No twinkling lights. No Christmas tree.

A deep sense of melancholy rose in Simon. And yet when the man returned to the door, he seemed to beam with glee, eagerly shaking Alphonso's giant hand, and then Simon's as well. The pair laughed again, and started to inquire about the phone—but before they'd even finished, the old-timer held up a finger, dashed back into his house, and returned holding a small ring of keys out towards them.

Simon and Alfonso thanked him profusely. "¡*Muchas gracias! ¡Feliz Navidad!... ¡Muchas gracias! ¡Feliz Navidad*!"

The old man just laughed and gestured toward the plate of food. "*De nada, ¡muchas gracias a ti! ¡Feliz Navidad para ti!"*

Simon's heart nearly burst.

***

Upon arriving at the internet shop, Alfonso unlocked the door, turned on the lights and led Simon to the phone. When he handed Simon the keys and asked him to return them to the owner when he was done, Simon stared in disbelief. *This would never happen in a million years back "home." They're just giving me the keys to what is essentially the Best Buy of Yaviza!*

Simon thanked Alfonso effusively, yet the hulking man was having none of it, repeatedly exclaiming "*De Nada!*" and "*Feliz Navidad!*" and smiling wide as he exited. With each passing moment, Simon felt an even deeper connection with and love for his new Yaviza family and community.

Simon lifted the handset and dialed Jonathan's number.

As the phone rang, he felt a nervousness building in his stomach. Though he was prepared for Jonathan to give him a healthy dose of shit for leaving his job, he dreaded the thought of having to defend himself. *We haven't spoken in so long, is this how we're going to reconnect?*

Jonathan answered, his voice crackling over the line. "Hello?"

Simon heard his voice and couldn't speak. He couldn't even breathe.

Then, without uttering a word, he hung up the phone. Simon couldn't wait to get back to the De Sousa's and enjoy the rest of Christmas with them.

CHAPTER 65

Christmas and the New Year came and went, and Simon eventually decided it was time to move on. His time in Yaviza had been well spent, he thought. An experience unlike any other in his life. Yet for several days, he'd been feeling a gnawing itch to get back on the road.

For the past few days, things had started to change, and not for the better. Jonah had been in the jungle over three weeks already, and every day Simon stared across the river into the dense tree line, hoping he was safe but fearing the worst. Simon had begun to experience frightening daydreams, waking imaginations of Jonah's body being dragged from the forest by the Panamanian military. On more than one occasion, he swore he'd seen Jonah staring at him from across the river.

He'd also begun to have nightmares—hearing Jonah screaming out for him and crying for help from far out in the jungle. Each time, he'd woken drenched with sweat with only the darkness of his room and the sound of crickets there to greet him.

It was time to go.

Saying goodbye to Maria and Alfonso proved more difficult than Simon could have imagined. As he stood in the kitchen saying his final farewells, Maria wrapped her arms around him, holding him tight for several long seconds in a loving embrace. It was a tender act, and the closest thing to a mother's love that Simon had felt in decades. It moved him deeply.

Wiping his eyes, he promised to return one day.

After a lengthy and heartfelt farewell to Victor and the crew, Simon hopped on a local bus headed towards Panama City. Staring out the back window, he watched as the 'end of the road,' Jonah, the Darien jungle and his Yaviza life disappeared slowly into the distance.

But at the first military checkpoint, he was made.

When the *Senafront* officers found him alone on the bus, they began to ask questions. "*¿Dónde está tu amigo* Jonah Shaughnessy? *¿Dónde está la camioneta en la que llegaste? ¿Por qué has estado en el Darién por tanto tiempo?*"

At first, Simon pleaded ignorance to Jonah's whereabouts, hoping they'd simply believe him and allow his passage. But when the officers pulled him from the bus and escorted him into their tent, he knew it wasn't going to be so easy. They were clearly detaining him while they sent a soldier to town to search for Jonah. Thirty minutes later, the scout returned with the truth. Jonah and the van were gone.

For a grueling hour, the head officer interrogated Simon in the sweltering heat. "*¡¿Dónde está?! ¡¿Dónde está?!*" he barked repeatedly as Simon feigned ignorance, pretending he didn't understand Spanish, or even what was happening. But the officer's patience soon wore thin, and Simon could sense he was growing furious. Simon, in turn, grew nervous.

After a while, the out of place Texan was loaded into a jeep and brought to a regional *Senafront* office in a neighboring town. Once there, he was again given the third degree by several other officers. And, again, he denied any knowledge of Jonah's whereabouts.

By midday, Simon was exhausted and on his way to Panama City— only now he was in the back of a *Senafront* police car. The vehicle was air-conditioned, and Simon noticed it was decidedly more comfortable than the public bus he'd been on previously. *Silver lining?* Yet as they traveled north away from the Darien, Simon's mind concocted a myriad of possible nightmarish destinations he might be headed towards. *Maybe they're taking me to an "off the map" Guantanamo-esque military black site where the Geneva Code doesn't apply? Or perhaps I'll be confined to a military prison for the rest of my life? A Panamanian Gulag where I'll never again see the light of day! Or maybe the firing squad is still in fashion down here? Or something worse I've never even heard of!*

When they arrived at the U.S. Consulate later that afternoon, Simon let out an enormous sigh of relief.

Entering the building, Simon was begrudgingly handed over to a U.S. soldier who escorted him through the security checkpoint and then directed him to a case officer's desk. As he made his way across the room, the young woman assigned to his case, April Silva, gave him a smile as he sat down across from her. "May I please see your passport, Mr. Hill?" she asked courteously.

It was a simple request, and one that Simon typically would have fulfilled easily. But at this moment, he found himself somehow stricken, and incapable of a response. Staring captively at Ms. Silva, Simon continued to smile as her words drifted past his ears and dissipated into the room.

Wearing little in the way of makeup and clothed in a rather drab brown pantsuit, most people at first glance would have thought April had given up on trying to appear attractive long ago. She was thirty-five years young with a healthy build, and her skin was the color of milk caramel. Simon couldn't determine with any certainty if she was Caucasian, Latino or something else entirely. Her straight, almost mousy, brown hair hung over her shoulders, framing her naturally kind face and petite, pert lips. She had what most would view as just average good looks, but Simon saw something beyond that. Her radiant blue eyes shone like sapphires in his vision, and her mesmerizing smile instantly had him hooked. He sank into a trance and resisted the urge to blink. His eyes continued to linger.

"Excuse me, sir, can I please see your passport?" she asked yet again.

Having grown up in Virginia to a Cuban father and a fourth-generation Virginian mother, April had worked tirelessly in the D.C. area for eight years trying to make a career for herself in politics. It was an endeavor she had consistently sabotaged by sticking too hard to her diametrically opposed convictions. Deemed an iconoclast by some, her rare combination of far left and far right leaning beliefs (her father jokingly called her the world's only "liberal-tarian") had left her isolated and without a side to fall in line with.

But falling in line wasn't really April's forte. Ever the individual, the young woman believed what she believed and would seldom back down when faced with a challenge. As a result, she'd bounced around D.C. more times than she could remember.

She had been on the verge of leaving politics altogether, when a few years ago, a former colleague offered her a job at the U.S. Consulate in Panama. April jumped at the opportunity for a change. But for the three years since, she'd been working a bureaucratic desk job which gave her little to no personal fulfillment. For months now, she'd been desperately trying to figure out what she could do next to give her life more meaning. Lacking any close friends in Panama City, and with little to inspire her, her average life seemed to be consuming her prime, day by day.

That is, until Simon Hill walked through the door.

"Hello! Mr. Hill?" she asked louder. Abruptly breaking Simon's spell.

"What? What's that now?" he replied, confused.

"Your passport?"

"Oh yes, of course!" Simon replied, fumbling through his bag and handing April his sacred blue book. "Sorry about that."

But as April took it from his hand, their fingers grazed ever so slightly, and the simple touch made the hairs on Simons arms prickle. He shivered, shifted in his seat, and pulled out his shirt collar an inch.

April began to flip through his passport. "Mr. Hill, where exactly have you been for the last—" April paused, staring long and hard at the photograph in the booklet. It looked almost nothing like the man sitting across from her now. She glanced up to Simon. "Mr. Hill," she said softly. "Is this… is this an old picture?"

"No… not really. Why do you ask?" he replied.

April gave him a lengthy look over, then leaned forward to stare at the passport once more. "No reason."

Simon, however, didn't notice any of this. His focus was instead dwelling contently on the young woman as her hair fell forward to cover half of her face. She slowly pushed it back up over her ear with her fingers, a simple movement that bewitched Simon. She mouthed words and numbers as she read the passport's contents, each syllable plucking harder on Simon's heartstrings. When April glanced back up at him, Simon was still gawking and darted his eyes away instinctively. *Did she just see me staring?*

April had, but smiled it off. "Mr. Hill…I just… I just need to know two things from you right now," she began. "Do you think you can help me understand some things here?" she continued, struggling.

"I can certainly try," Simon replied.

"Well, Mr. Hill… The first thing I need to know, really, is… how on earth did you end up way down here at the Colombian border in the first place? This is a long way from Texas," she finished with a sigh.

Simon smirked, knowing how true her words were. "It is, now isn't it," he replied.

April took a sip of water from a glass on her desk, pausing visibly before formulating her next sentence. Then she went on. "Also, Mr. Hill …and more importantly…. Can you please tell me anything about a missing young man from the U.S. named Jonah Shaughnessy? From what I gather, you were the last known person seen traveling with him…That was nearly a month ago."

Simon glanced up at April and smiled. For the past several minutes, he'd been desperately trying to avoid staring at her, averting his eyes and forcing them to look anywhere, everywhere but in her direction. In so doing, however, he'd inadvertently seen her name on a placard on the desk. Now he spoke with the newly discovered word still on his mind.

"Well, April, do you want the long version or the short?"

Shit, I just used her first name, didn't I? Did I?

April smiled back at Simon. *Did he just call me April?*

***

Simon leaned back in his chair, getting comfortable, and began his tale at the Redding & Company office back in San Antonio, where a hearty woman named Carly and some photographs had subsequently changed his life. Spinning his wild tale with the utmost of detail, if Simon thought he could have gotten away with putting his feet up on April's desk while talking, he almost certainly would have. And as he carried on, April listened to his story intently, growing increasingly enraptured by the bizarre adventures of the odd guy who'd somehow arrived at her desk from the Darien jungle.

At points, she laughed. *You thought you could magically speak Spanish?!* At others, she asked questions. "How big was the whale shark compared to this room?!" But at all times she was absorbed and beguiled by every word from the unusual man's mouth. It wasn't just his fantastical story that captured her. It was him. The way he described things in such detail and with such fascination. His sense of humor which made her laugh. The many insights he'd gained from his travels that moved and touched her. And above all, she couldn't believe how happy Simon seemed to be sharing his story with her now.

By the time he was finished, April was staring at Simon in much the same way he'd been staring at her just thirty minutes earlier. She hadn't been interested in a man in almost five years, and the unfamiliar feelings made her nervous.

"So that's how I got to this point, April," he said, breaking the gaze between them.

"Well, that's quite the story, Simon," she replied, composing herself.

She called me Simon!

"So, what's the plan now?" April continued. "Since you say you didn't aid Jonah in crossing the border illegally, and there's no evidence to suggest otherwise, the police can't deport you. And we can't keep you here any longer."

"Well, that's good to hear," Simon said with a sigh.

"So, are you gonna stay in Panama City for a few days, do you think? Check out all that we have to offer?"

Simon was surprised when April finished her question with a long, coy smile. He was terrible with women and especially at reading them, but he sensed—hoped—prayed—that she was subtly hinting at something. "Actually, yeah, I think I'll stay in town here for a bit until I figure out what to do next. It seems like a nice city, and it's been a while since I had a really good meal. Are there any great restaurants in town you could recommend?" *Very smooth.*

April hoped she knew where he was going with this. Without being aware of it, she pushed her hair behind her ears again and sat upright in her seat to try and look her best. "In Panama City? Yeah, of course. My personal favorite is Havana's. It's a Cuban restaurant with great food and atmosphere." April smiled, but tried not to smile too much. "Do you like Cuban food?"

"I *love* Cuban food," Simon said, also smiling. *What's Cuban food?!*

The Texan could sense a connection growing between them. And yet he was overwhelmed and at a loss for words. *What would Jack and Jonah do?* He thought, struggling, however feebly, to summon the courage of his new friends.

Then, in decidedly un-Simon fashion, he swung for the fences. *What do I have to lose?* "I'm sure you must get this a lot," he began. "But...would you like to join me for dinner tonight?"

April exhaled softly through her teeth. It was a question she had hoped Simon would ask. "Yeah, that would be great," she replied eagerly.

Did she just say "yes"? Simon paused for a moment in contemplative disbelief. As he did so, he continued to sit there smiling at April.

Actually, they both just sat there smiling at each other.

Eventually, Simon worked up the nerve to speak again. "Well I don't have a phone, so what time and where can I meet you?" he asked.

"Oh yeah, ummm, eight o'clock at Havana's?"

"Eight o'clock at Havana's it is," he replied, a goofy grin still etched on his face.

April handed him back his passport and escorted him to the exit. As they walked, she pushed her hair behind her ear with her fingers yet again, and Simon nearly lost it. He wanted so badly to kiss her right then and there.

After wishing her a fond goodbye, Simon exited, and a guard helped him hail a taxi out past the gate. Simon didn't notice April watching him from the window.

As he rode towards downtown in the back seat of the cab, Simon couldn't stop thinking about her. He was in disbelief as to the circumstances of their chance meeting. He was also in disbelief as to his own courage in asking her out. *And she said yes!*

In all his days, Simon had never met a girl he'd felt so instantly attracted to, and so connected to, in one breath. He recollected fondly Davis's talk on the shores of Lake Atitlán about destiny. Simon was vaguely starting to believe him now. And as he stared out the window at the vast city passing him by, memories of all that had transpired leading to this exact moment coursed through him like electricity, and Simon's face bore a smile as wide as the horizon.

CHAPTER 66

A bustling and cosmopolitan metropolis, Panama City starkly resembled an American city more than any other place Simon had encountered on his journey thus far. Having options for the first time in months, and a hot date to boot, Simon elected to splurge for the night, checking himself into a 20th floor room at the Hilton, with sweeping views of the ocean. After paying a paltry ten dollars a night at guesthouses for the past few months, $120 US dollars a night for this room seemed exorbitant, yet it was still a far cry from the $350 he had been paying back in Belize. Just thinking about that now made him cringe.

After checking in at the front desk, Simon visited the hotel's adjoining shopping complex and bought himself a new outfit for dinner. Something casual and stylish, but most importantly, not filthy and ragged like the rest of his clothes had become. XXL didn't fit him anymore, and he had to go all the way down to a Large to find something that stayed on. *Panamanian sizes must be different?* he reasoned.

Once in his room, Simon took a much overdue long, hot shower, put on his new boxers, and then looked at himself in the first full-length mirror he'd seen in the several months since Belize.

The man staring back at him was a complete stranger. Simon was astonished by how much his body had changed. He'd lost close to thirty pounds working the docks in Yaviza, and his once bulbous belly had been whittled down flat. His arms were toned, muscular and strong. His skin was deeply tanned from countless shirtless days in the sunshine, and his hair was considerably longer after two months without a trim. A scruff of a beard had formed on his usually clean-shaven face, and his double chin had vanished altogether. He didn't even recognize himself.

Holy shit.

Simon's confidence had been building for some time now, and his shocking new appearance only fueled the fire. For a split second, he wondered if he might genuinely deserve to be going out with a woman as beautiful as April. The thought evoked powerful feelings, unlike any he'd experienced before, and he stared at himself in the mirror for ages trying to take it all in. Simon didn't know where the night was going to lead, but he sure as hell planned on trying this time. *I'm all in.*

As he made his way through the lobby to the taxi stand, Simon dropped Jonah's letter to his parents in the hotel's outgoing mailbox. Releasing it from his fingers, he imagined what it might say. *How do you say goodbye to your family? Maybe forever.*

***

Arriving at Havana's a few minutes before eight, Simon didn't know whether to enter and get a table or wait outside for April to arrive. It had been such a long time since he'd dated and even longer since he'd actually cared how it went. In and out through the door he went, the host greeting him each time he entered.

Seriously Simon?

He finally resigned himself to waiting outside, and a few minutes later April arrived in the back of a taxi. When she stepped out of the cab, her long green dress hugging her sultry body and her pinned back hair revealing her entire, angelic face and ethereal eyes, Simon gazed on hypnotized. Every ounce of breath immediately pulled from his lungs into the night air. *Dear God, she looks beautiful.* April smiled when she saw him, and Simon's heart skipped more than a couple of beats.

When April first caught sight of Simon standing there, she trembled with a nearly matching sensation. *Jesus, he's the most handsome man in Panama City.* In the recesses of her mind, April already hoped she would get a chance to kiss him and feel those arms around her. Then she would tell him what she really thought of his story.

In they went.

Harkening back to a bygone era, the incomparable Havana's exists as a venerable institution in Panama City. A classic, dimly lit Latin dance hall, the unique brasserie stands complete with a sprawling, well-tread wooden dancefloor, a red curtained stage, and walls lined with candlelit booths. The air carries the aged smell of leather, perfume and Cuban cigars. One might expect Machito or Tito Puente to take the stage at any second, and Simon felt instantly transported back in time to a world he'd only read about.

To April, though, the place reminded her of home. Not Washington D.C., but rather the Silva family living room, where as a child, her Cuban father would play his Latin Jazz records in the evening, and the family would dip and dance to the rhythm until holes were worn in the thin brown carpet. Then they'd dance on the floorboards.

After being shown to their table, Simon and April's dinner began just as expected—at least for two people who were strongly attracted to each other and hadn't dated in quite a while.

Awkwardness? Check. Long pauses in conversation? Check. Overthinking leading to overdrinking? Check and mate.

As the alcohol began to warm their veins and the music began to play, the two slowly slipped into a relaxed conversation, growing more and more comfortable with every passing minute. The pulsing samba added a rhythm to their chatting, and April engaged Simon with stories of growing up in Virginia and her childhood dream of being in politics. She told him of her years studying Poly Sci at UVA, of her decade spent bouncing around DC, taking jobs in whichever camp would have her, and how, after years of treading water, she'd finally accepted the position in Panama. At the time, she'd believed that working in a foreign country might boost her international credentials. But on arrival, she almost immediately realized the error of her decision. Her work at the consulate felt more like a job at the DMV than anything else, and she absolutely abhorred it. Yet she remained, afraid to accept defeat and quit, even though she'd wanted to for years. "Instead, I decided just to stay while I planned my next move," she said casually, taking another sip of her cocktail.

"When did you decide that?" Simon asked.

"Two years ago," she smiled embarrassed.

"So, what's the plan?"

"I don't know yet!" she gasped, thrusting her hands over her face and burying them in the tablecloth.

Simon was positively smitten. "You should just quit and see the world," he said, smiling.

April could tell Simon was only half-joking. "That's easy for you to say. I don't have much money saved, and once you leave politics, Simon, it's tough to get back into it. The last thing I want is to end up broke and jobless at thirty-five."

Simon smiled at her.

She smiled back.

She knew he understood what she meant.

She also knew he disagreed with her.

"There are worse places to be in the world," Simon said, extending his hand and resting it softly on her small knuckles. April glanced down and arched a single demure finger over his.

She didn't pull away.

The pair stared at their two hands linked there together, relishing the touch, each of them contemplating how to touch each other more.

"So, I have a suggestion for you!" April blurted, changing the subject and breaking the spell. "I know where you should go next!"

Simon chuckled. "Where to?"

"Cartagena, Colombia!" she exclaimed. "You can sail to Cartagena from near here, actually. Five days on a sailboat, stopping at beautiful white sand beaches and Kuna villages on the San Blas islands, and then you end up in what I've heard is a beautiful and lively city on the Caribbean. The boats leave from Portobello every day, just a few hours from here. I hear it's not that expensive either."

Simon could see her eyes twinkling as she pictured it.

"Sounds perfect," he said, imagining the two of them going together.

As they continued to talk, a ten-piece Cuban salsa band made their way onto the stage, dressed head to toe in white-on-white suits and burgundy bow ties. Suddenly, the band sprung to life in a melodic barrage of horns, drums, upright bass and maracas. Simon and April's attention was at once captured by the frenetic group's blistering rendition of "Hong Kong Mambo."

"Wow, they're incredible!" Simon yelled.

"Yeah they are!" April laughed.

With the pair's knees tapping under the table, they gawked on with eager smiles as several local couples hustled out onto the parquet floor and began to shuffle and dance. The thumping room was electric, and Simon felt a sudden, uncontrollable need to seize the moment.

At once, he stood—grabbing April's hand and pulling her up to her feet. Surprised by the bold move, April happily went along and followed as Simon led her out onto the dance floor. When they reached the center of the room, they faced each other and stared into each other's eyes, preparing for the dance to take them.

It was at this point that Simon realized something critical... possibly dire. He had absolutely no idea how to salsa dance. *What have I done?!*

April watched Simon intently as his eyes darted side to side, spying other dancers for helpful tips. He began to bob up and down, trying to find the rhythm and hoping beyond hope that at any second it might just come to him.

But it didn't.

And April could tell.

When Simon's attention returned to April, she was smiling and half laughing. "Need some help?" she asked, giggling.

"Um, yeah, I think I do," he replied, turning redder than the stage curtains.

"Look at my feet and follow my lead." She grabbed his hand with her right hand and his shoulder with her left. "You ready?"

"As I'll ever be."

Ten minutes later, they were dancing—sort of—and laughing riotously on the dance hall floor. Though countless spectators may have thought them the worst dancers in the joint, it didn't matter one bit. No one else existed in their swirling universe. The trumpets wailed, the bass rumbled, and the bongos thumped as the duo dipped and coiled—their hands pressed against each other's bodies, growing closer and closer like binary stars swirling towards an imminent fiery convergence. They both sensed that at any second, they could burn up in each other's atmosphere, but there was no stopping it. Their hips and chests pressed hot together, and their eyes locked. Their lips moving closer... closer... until just as the two were about to become one, the song ended in a blazing crescendo of brass.

Neither of them dared to breathe. For several seconds, they lingered on the quiet dance floor, still holding each other tight. Their faces, painfully close to achieving what they had both longed for all day. "Let's go outside," Simon whispered.

April acknowledged with a grin and a nod.

The pair walked out onto the city street and into the cool night air. As April turned towards Simon, neither could resist any longer. Leaning in to kiss each other, their lips met with force. Simon put his arms around April and pulled her close. Her sensuous body, soft and natural in his hands.

She smelled like lilac.

For several minutes they kissed, pausing only to smile at each other occasionally before continuing.

"Would you like to come back to my hotel with me?" he asked. It was a brazen move for Simon as he didn't want to overstep too quickly. "I have a stocked mini bar and great views of the city."

April lingered, deep in thought. She wasn't a one-night stand kind of girl, but there was something else happening here that felt impossible to stop. Also, she hadn't been with a man in too long and had an itch that really needed to be scratched. "Yeah, I'll come over for a drink," she said coyly.

They were in the hotel room for less than three minutes before attacking each other ravenously. Their lips thrust passionately together as their arms yanked each other's bodies closer, cocktails falling to the floor and spilling on the carpet. Simon unzipped April's dress, and it fell to the floor in a pile around her ankles, exposing her sultry curves and smooth caramel skin. He pressed his hands against her trembling, bare body, first sliding them down her soft mid back, and then down lower where the dampness of sweat from her boiling skin had already formed by her waist. Then he slid them lower still.

It had been a long, long time since he'd touched a woman's body, and he had never felt one quite so perfect as this before. Her velvety flesh in his hands and on his lips was delicious as he kissed and licked her down her neck towards her breasts. She unclasped her bra and dropped it to the floor, allowing Simon's mouth to replace it. Down he went, her body spasming with lust as his lips and hands slid across her sweat kissed body. He slid his thumbs into her panties and slid them down to her ankles as she gasped with pleasure. *I've never wanted anyone so bad.*

April fell back onto the bed and gazed at him lasciviously. Simon frantically removed his clothes and joined her, her hand pulling him inside her as their naked bodies writhed together rhythmically. As time disappeared, they eviscerated each other's shame and pent up lust in a whirlwind of passion and sensuous depravity.

When they'd finished, their hearts continued to race as they collapsed, exhausted, on the sweaty bedsheets, still in each other's arms. Simon tried to catch his breath.

"Holy shit," April said with a sigh.

Simon laughed. "Seriously."

April giggled and leaned over to kiss him, burying her tongue in his mouth once again.

***

That night the two spent a good many hours talking, laughing and sharing an intimacy neither of them had experienced in years. Though they'd both been with other partners in the past, this was incomparable to any other experience that had preceded it. There was something exceptional there. Something extraordinary, they thought. A fire they brought out in each other: not just in lust, but also in life.

As Simon fell asleep with April's naked body cradled in his arms, he stared out the window at the lights of the city and the ocean beyond. The moment felt good, and somehow more right than all that had come before it.

CHAPTER 67

The next morning, when Simon awoke, he peeled open his groggy eyes to find April well on her way to being dressed. She seemed in a hurry to leave, which left him addled and concerned. "Leaving so soon?" he grumbled, rising from bed.

April turned to him abruptly. *Shit, he's awake.* "Yes, some of us have to go to work, Simon," she responded curtly.

Simon gave her a confused look. Though he didn't know it, April had been lying in bed for hours contemplating what had happened and what their future might hold. She had already begun to worry that this had been a mistake—Simon was just passing through town after all—and though things had gone extremely well, he was, in all likelihood, leaving soon. It had been too intense and too passionate too soon, she believed. Since sunrise, she'd been devising a litany of logical reasons to end it. But deep down, she was just terrified of getting hurt. April liked Simon way, way too much.

"Well, can I see you again tonight?" he asked.

April smiled. "Here is my number. Give me a call if you'd like," she said, jotting her number on a slip of paper.

"Did I do something wrong?" he asked.

April could see the alarm in his eyes, so she grinned at him and walked over to give him a kiss. "No, I just need to get my head together about this," she said, finishing getting dressed.

Get your head together about what?

Simon didn't understand. He'd fallen for her and felt fairly sure that she'd felt the same. He didn't want her to leave. "So, I think I like your idea about going to the San Blas islands on the way to Cartagena," he said, walking across the room towards her. "I think you should come with me."

April chuckled at him. "Oh, I should, should I?"

"I mean, I *want* you to come with me," he rephrased.

April just kept smiling at him, a cyclone of thoughts whirling in her mind. "I have to go, Simon," she said quietly, and gave him a kiss on the lips and a long hug.

Simon didn't want to let her go. As soon as he did, she was out the door, and Simon found himself all alone. *What the hell just happened?*

For several minutes, the Texan sat on the edge of the bed, stunned and gazing out the window. He was at a loss for what to do next, and he paced around the room for an hour, mulling over things in his head.

That night he tried calling April, but after several tries, he left her a voicemail message.

She didn't call him back.

The next day Simon tried calling her again, but still, there was no answer. The following day brought more of the same. Simon grew heartbroken, furious at himself for reasons he couldn't decipher. *I must have done something to make her leave, but WHAT?* He contemplated going to the consulate but knew it would be wildly inappropriate. And besides, she clearly didn't want to see him. *But why?!*

Simon roamed the streets of Panama City for several more days, hoping to chance upon April. But in a city of over a million people, it was like trying to find a needle in a haystack. A needle that didn't want to be found.

A few days soon became a week, and Simon's angst-riddled longing for her grew all-consuming. He couldn't eat. He couldn't sleep. So, he decided that he had to leave.

Having noticed a tourist office near his hotel, he entered one afternoon and booked a sailboat trip to Cartagena. That night he left April another voice message:

"Hello, it's me again. Simon. So, I made a reservation to go to Cartagena on a sailboat like you suggested. I'm really excited about it and wish you could come with me. I'm leaving on Friday from Portobello on a boat called the Santa Maria. I made the reservation for two, but I understand if you can't make it. Maybe we can see each other before I leave?... I miss you... I really hope to see you again." Simon paused to consider what else he could say to convince her. But there was nothing. "Give me a call at the hotel... Room 2103... Goodbye April."

Simon hung up and stared at the phone. April wouldn't call.

***

When Friday arrived, Simon boarded the historic Panama Canal Railway train for the short journey across the narrow country to the Caribbean. The vintage, glass-domed railcar felt stately in its grandeur, with polished mahogany, brass and leather throughout. Gilt-framed, colorful paintings of tropical birds adorned the walls as Simon sat in a booth, staring through the glass at the canal running along beside him. In one hour, he would cross the continent from west to east. A miraculous proposition.

During the California Gold Rush of the 1800s, it was commonplace for affluent dream seekers to use this very railroad train. Sailing down from the East coast of America to Portobello on the Caribbean shore, those with the means would then ride this train for an hour across the country to Panama City, before sailing up the Pacific Ocean to California. It was unquestionably the long way around, but it was a popular route to avoid attack by Native Americans and bandits on the dangerous wagon trails through the central United States.

Usually, a story like that would have Simon's imagination running wild, picturing the sharp-dressed passengers on the train back then, and the lives they hoped for in the Wild West. But today, Simon could think only of April.

An hour later, he arrived at the rail station and hopped on a bus down to the Portobello docks. As he walked past the various boats loading for departure, he eventually came upon the moored *Santa Maria*. A well-worn, old vessel, it sat covered with barnacles and looked nothing like the picture at the tourist office. Yet when Simon looked down the dock at the scene, something quickly caught his eye, and made him smile and blink a few times to affirm he wasn't dreaming.

April was sitting on her suitcase beside the boat.

Simon would never be able to articulate how he felt at that moment. Surprised. Thankful. Overwhelmed. None of those words, nor any other, could ever do it justice. She was the most beautiful thing he'd ever seen. And when April saw him approaching, her eyes lit up as well. She jumped to her feet, walking quickly towards him. They embraced, kissing long and passionately.

"I can't believe you're here," Simon said, emotions boiling inside him.

"Me neither," April responded. "But I had to come. I couldn't leave it like that."

"I'm really glad you did," he said, beaming.

"Me too."

April and Simon stared at each other for several interminable minutes—people passing them on the docks as the invisible world carried on around them. Then, suddenly, April remembered she had a speech prepared. "So, I didn't quit my job for you," she began. "I just took eight days off, and I fly back from Cartagena on Saturday. So, we'll have to be there by then," she explained.

The well-rehearsed speech was thoughtfully articulated and clearly intended to make sure Simon didn't read too much into her presence. Nevertheless, he found it achingly charming.

"Sounds great," he replied and kissed her once again.

In Simon's mind, he hoped that the romantic sailboat jaunt through the Caribbean would be enough to convince her to stay with him. *How could it not?*

As they climbed aboard the boat, grinning ear to ear and anticipating a relaxing five-day romantic voyage to Colombia, neither of them, nor any of the other passengers boarding the ship, noticed the growing cluster of dark storm clouds brewing far out to sea.

What was to come would be something so unbelievable, that for years after Simon would have to defend its actually having happened.

CHAPTER 68

Captain Ricardo was a cocksure man, as many a sea captain is. Rotund, with a bulbous face covered in grey scruff, the Captain spoke kindly but curtly to his passengers as he welcomed them aboard the *Santa Maria*. As the boat set sail from the Portobello marina, Simon noticed the Captain was already well into a bottle of beer. It was only 11 a.m.

Five other passengers had joined them on the boat: Lars and Almeta, a Danish couple in their mid to late twenties. Avi and Ron, a couple of nineteen-year-old Israeli boys, roaming the Americas after finishing their mandatory military service. And finally, there was Helena, a German retiree in her late fifties.

The existing conditions were perfect for sailing as they drifted out to sea under blue skies and sunshine. But by 3 p.m., a hastening gust had risen, and sheets of rain began to soak the deck.

An hour later, a howling storm was upon them, and everyone but the Captain moved downstairs into the cramped main cabin. Consisting of a small eating table surrounded by a semicircle of seats, a few benches with old tattered cushions and a small kitchen area, the suffocating chamber could barely accommodate the seven passengers. It was hot and stifling with them all crowded into the small space, but a few electric fans made it reasonably tolerable.

Captain Ricardo lowered the sails in the torrential rain and fired up the boat's outboard motor to keep them moving forward. But shortly after doing so, fumes from the engine began to drift into the cabin, making everyone woozy.

In the choppy water, seasickness was also becoming a problem. Simon had brought a ginger root from Panama City, just in case, and was grateful that he had. Helena and Lars appeared to be reaching their breaking points, and Simon cut each of them slices of the home remedy. When it helped, they thanked Simon repeatedly, but the relief was short-lived. Soon, the waves grew ever more violent, and the boat reeled side to side in the churning sea. Six hours had passed since they'd set sail, and already a general sense of unease was permeating the cabin.

Time went on, and the conditions continued to deteriorate. The narrow kitchen area was passable, but the rolling waves made cooking out of the question. The group ate a cold dinner of sandwiches and chips as Simon struggled to keep his stomach in check. The night of romance he'd envisioned was quickly evaporating, replaced by nausea and growing claustrophobia in the sweltering, fume-filled chamber. *If only we could go on the deck for air!*

Just after 8 p.m., the motor shut off without warning, and with it went the internal lights and the cooling whir of the fans. Suddenly, it was pitch black in the cabin, and all they could hear was the sound of lashing rain and the creaking of the wooden hull. *What the hell is going on?*

"I'll see what's happening," Simon said to the frightened group.

"Thanks," a few voices whispered back from the darkness.

Stumbling through the void, the floor rising and falling below his trembling legs, Simon cautiously felt his way to the staircase and pulled himself, grey-faced, up to the deck. The scene he discovered up top was grim and sent shudders through his body.

Through the torrents of soaking rain, he could see Captain Ricardo at the helm, slumped awkwardly against a post beside the wheel. The hood of his rain-slicker was covering his face, so Simon couldn't tell if the man was awake, asleep or dead. Several empty beer bottles rolled back and forth across the wood planks in the undulating waves. Simon slowly made his way across the watery deck to the Captain.

"Captain!" he shouted over the howling wind.

Ricardo's eyes shot open, surprised. "What you want?" he slurred.

"Captain, the motor's out and there's no electricity in the boat. We need the fans and the lights on!" Simon yelled, faking confidence.

The Captain stared at him, confused, and then looked back over his shoulder at the motor. When he turned back to Simon, his face bore a scowl that said everything. "Water in it. Fix it in the morning," he grumbled, pulling his hood back down over his eyes.

Simon's gaze lingered on the man. His temperament waning as he fought to keep his cool. "But Captain we really need—"

"In the morning!" Ricardo yelled, cutting Simon off mid-sentence with a belligerent howl. He lifted his hood an inch, and the two men locked eyes.

Simon felt an ounce of fear and a gallon of fury boiling inside him. He clenched his fists and squared his shoulders, desperate to throw a punch at the brutish lout. *If you weren't the captain, I'd throw you off the boat right now,* he thought. Simon's emotions began to consume him, threatening to finally seize control after countless years of resistance. He took a deep breath and averted his eyes from the contemptible man, considering his next move. *We've got a long trip ahead. Best to let this one go,* he reasoned. And in the dark, tumbling rain, he closed his eyes and stifled his anger once more.

Simon staggered back down to the lower cabin to find April and the group sweating in the oppressive heat. They'd managed to get a few small lanterns going, and looked at him through the orange glow with desperate, hopeful eyes. "Is he going to get the power back on?" April asked.

"He's drunk. He said he would do it in the morning," Simon replied.

"In the morning?! It's so hot in here, though. Let me go talk to him!" she said, rising to her feet with conviction.

"No, don't!" Simon snapped.

April froze, startled, and looked at him in the flickering lantern light. She could tell he was succumbing to the heat and sickness. But there was something else in his eyes as well.

"Well, we're going to our room," muttered Lars, breaking the tension as he and Almeta made their way into one of the four adjoining sleeping cabins. "Goodnight."

Ron, Avi and Helena followed suit, leaving Simon and April alone in the small common area. Simon took a seat on the edge of a bench. "I'm so sorry. There's just nothing else we can do tonight," he exhaled. "I'm really sorry about this April," he continued, placing his face in his hands.

"It's okay," she replied, sitting down beside him and stroking his wet hair. She could sense how bad Simon felt about their situation. "Tomorrow is a new day," she continued and kissed the side of his forehead.

Simon looked up to find April offering him an understanding smile. He smiled in return and slowly unclenched his fists. He was so glad she was there.

That night they slept miserably in the stifling, swaying vessel.

***

The next morning, Simon climbed up to the deck to find it still under assault by the relentless deluge. He tried speaking again with the indignant Captain, but the man dubiously claimed the engine was beyond repair and the electrical on the fritz. "We'll just ride out the storm for a few days till we can put the sails back up," he announced dismissively, taking another long pull from his beer.

"But Captain, we could really use—"

"Just a few days!" he roared in reply.

Simon stood aghast. He began to wonder if the man was just too lazy to fix the engine, or if, perhaps, there was something dodgier going on. *What if it functions properly, but he's just trying to save money on fuel?*

Simon's distrust was only heightened when he begged the Captain to radio for help, and the surly man flatly refused. *Something isn't right here.*

Adrift in the storm, by mid-morning things were deteriorating further. Lars and Helena were both terribly sick, and stir craziness had spread throughout the group trapped below. As the day progressed, the heat swelled in the airless, confined cabins, forcing the passengers to take short spells on the top deck to cool off in the pounding rain. Simon climbed up around lunchtime and was surprised to find the Israeli boys sitting in the rain drinking with Captain Ricardo. They'd apparently been drinking all morning. *This can't be good.*

As day turned towards night, Simon and April made their way up top once more for some desperately needed air. Yet when they reached the deck and tried to find a sheltered area to sit down, they suddenly spied the Captain and the now drunk Israelis staring at them from across the boat. Through the sheeting rain and in the failing light, Simon distinguished the faces staring at them weren't kind ones. A chill of warning slid across his wet skin. "Let's go back down," he whispered to April after a few moments, and once again, the pair retreated into the belly of the ship.

It wasn't long before the Israeli boys stumbled down into the cabin with a raucous. Upon seeing them, the Danish couple immediately rose and retreated to their room, latching the door behind them. Helena, unbearably seasick, had long since passed out by the small kitchen table with a bucket beside her. Simon and April, meanwhile, sat on a long bench seat on the far side of the cabin. Ron and Avi immediately locked in on them with a devilishness in their glassy eyes.

Staggering over, Avi took a seat on the bench beside April as Ron sat down beside Simon. "Hello beautiful," Avi blurted, pressing his shoulder against April's and placing his face far too close to hers. The reek of cheap beer on his breath sent April lurching back—a reaction that visibly angered the young man. "What's wrong!?" Avi demanded.

"Hey guys, why don't you just go back upstairs," Simon interjected, trying quickly to defuse the situation.

"I'm not talking to you, man," bellowed Avi with a piercing glare.

Simon's stomach sank, and his hands clenched yet again.

"Relax, man," said Ron, putting his arm around Simon. But the furious Texan batted it off and turned abruptly to face April.

Simon could see her eyes glinting with dread.

But April could see something else in Simon's eyes. Something she'd only begun to see that first night on the boat.

April sensed a sudden urgency to end things now before they got out of hand. "Seriously guys, just go back upstairs," she asserted with resolve.

But the two young men brushed off her request, unfazed. Avi reached out his arm and draped it around the young woman. April leaned back abruptly and swatted it away, causing the Israeli man to burst with a huff of anger.

Simon flinched his arm but then froze, remembering Ron was just over his shoulder. His muscles grew taught, his pulse quickened, and his heart began wildly thumping. *April is with me... How can these assholes just ignore that?*

Simon strained to process the scenario that was unfolding. He knew Avi and Ron were both younger and fitter than him and, as Israelis, likely had military training as well. Simon, on the other hand, had resisted fighting his entire life. There was no way he wanted it to come to that.

Yet something inside him, something deep inside him... wanted it to.

Simon struggled to rationalize the primitive desire trying to claw its way out. *But I have to defend April,* he reasoned. It sounded good in his mind, but in his heart, he knew there was something else lurking in his subconscious. A dark urge that he'd felt before. He'd seen a glimpse of it that night in Brasilito when he'd trashed the fish barrels in the moonlight—an episode he regretted sorely and had tried to put from his mind.

Simon decided on one last attempt at diplomacy. "Hey, do you mind leaving us alone? We were having an important talk when you walked up," he said.

But Avi and Ron just ignored him, as expected. "So, do you like younger men?" Avi asked, starting to put his hand on April's hair.

In a flash, she jumped to her feet.

Simon leapt up as well, standing next to her.

Avi and Ron rose quickly and faced them.

"Gentlemen, I think we're going to say goodnight," April said, beginning to inch towards their cabin.

She'd barely taken a step before Avi tried to step between her and the door.

That's fucking it.

At that moment, something primordial emerged from deep within Simon. Without another millisecond of hesitation, the Texan suddenly thrust his arms into Avi's chest, lifting him off his feet, moving him five feet across the cabin and slamming him with force into the wall. Ron reeled backwards, and April gasped as Simon yelled at the top of his lungs, directly into Avi's face. "ENOUGH!!!!" The thunderous voice roaring from deep in his chest. Pressing his forearm into Avi's neck, he crushed it harder against the wall.

The look in the young man's eyes was one of sheer terror.

The look in Simon's eyes was unmistakable. *I should kill you right now.* Something burned in his blood like acid, and his muscles were ready for whatever might happen next. He didn't know if this was the courage Jonah claimed was inside everyone… or maybe it was something else. *Whatever it is… it feels good.*

Avi clutched at Simon's arm, straining to breathe. April and Ron may have been screaming at Simon to stop, but he couldn't hear them. In his own ears, the only sound was his pounding heartbeat pumping blood through his body and giving him strength. He prepared to attack further.

Just then, April grabbed his arm from behind, trying desperately to wrest him away from the struggling young man. Simon shrugged her away at first, but then, catching sight of her small hands on his arm, he suddenly snapped out of his crimson hued trance.

As he glanced into Avi's bloodshot, bulging eyes, he could see a terrifying mortal fear. Simon glanced back down to find his own arm choking the boy out. *What the fuck am I doing!*

Shocked and horrified by his actions, Simon's rage immediately transformed from fury to fear. Fear of whatever within had just taken control of him. He released the whimpering Avi, and the young man fell to the floor—scrambling with Ron into their cabin and locking the door.

Simon stared at his quaking hands for a moment, and then up at a tearful April. Her hands were cupped over her mouth in shock.

"I- I'm so sorry," he muttered.

Reaching out, April grabbed his hand and pulled him slowly into their room.

Once inside, Simon latched the door, and putting his back against it, slid down onto his butt with his hands on his knees.

April stood watching him as he stared ahead, lost in a catatonic gaze. She wanted so much to say something comforting, but the words didn't exist.

At last, Simon spoke. "I- I'm sorry I lost my temper in there," he said solemnly. "I'm just gonna sleep here on the floor tonight, okay?" Simon gave April a halfhearted smile in an attempt to make things *normal*. But it was far too late for that.

"Okay," she said, staring at the distraught man, tears filling her eyes.

"We'll figure something out in the morning, I promise," Simon said.

"Okay," she whispered back. "Thank you for helping me in there," she said, still stunned by what had just transpired.

"You're welcome," he replied quietly.

That night, April lay in bed thinking about Simon and all he must be going through. She knew that he felt incomprehensible guilt for the events of the past forty-eight hours. And she wished she could somehow explain to him that she didn't blame him for what had happened. But she couldn't find the words.

For several hours, she glanced up every few minutes to check on the still dazed man sitting on the floor and staring into oblivion. Around 3 a.m., she looked up one last time and found Simon buckled over and asleep against the door.

April released a long overdue sigh. *Sleep well, Simon.*

CHAPTER 69

The next morning, Simon rose with the sun. Everyone else, including the Captain, still slept as the boat rocked gently in the waning storm. Simon slipped quietly from his cabin, moving cautiously through the ship, and slithered, unnoticed, up to the top deck. Rain drizzled lightly from clearing skies, and the air felt refreshingly cool. Simon squinted, scanning the scene, and realized they were still adrift, alone on the vast sea. There was no land in sight.

Continuing his investigation, Simon made his way through the vessel and eventually discovered a latched room off the main cabin. Unsure if the Captain lay on the other side, he opened the door slowly. Inside sat a small desk, and on top of that, the boat's VHF radio.

Bingo.

Simon crept over and switched it on, the amber light of the dial flickering to life. Simon was thankful but furious. *Electrical on the fritz, my ass.* Though Simon had never used a radio like this before, he'd written numerous operating manuals for similar models and, after a few minutes of examination, managed to switch on the system's speakers. A loud crackling static abruptly echoed through the chamber. *Shit!* Simon spun the volume knob down quickly and darted his eyes side to side, scanning every inch of the cabin's interior for movement.

There was none. He exhaled.

Pressing a trembling thumb onto the handset button, Simon spoke quietly into the microphone. "Hello, is anyone out there?"

The crackle of the radio, dead air, whispered, hissing through the cabin.

Simon switched to a different frequency and tried again. "Hello, is anyone out there?"

Again, only static.

One after another, Simon turned the wheel, each new frequency offering renewed hope of contact. "Hello, is anyone out there?" Nothing. "Hello, is anyone out there?" Nothing.

After ten or fifteen tries, Simon suddenly received a response. *"¿Qué es esto y por qué estás en esta frecuencia?"* came an emphatic voice over the small speaker.

"Hola, tú hablas inglés?" Simon responded, knowing there was far too much to explain with his moderate Spanish. He waited for a response, but none came.

The radio crackled. Then suddenly, *"¿Qué es esto y por qué estás en esta frecuencia?"* came again. This time with clear anger.

Simon immediately switched channels. *Shit.*

He carried on searching through the frequencies.

"Hello, is anyone out there?" Over and over again.

"Hello, is anyone out there?" Channel after channel after channel.

After twenty minutes, Simon was on the verge of giving up.

Then, suddenly, a miracle happened.

"Yes, I'm here, who is this?" came back over the speaker.

Simon gasped and nearly jumped out of his shoes. He looked around the silent cabin quickly and knew his time was short. The Captain could awaken at any moment, so he spoke quickly, loudly and efficiently.

"Hello, my name is Simon Hill. I'm on the boat the Santa Maria headed from Portobello, Panama, to Cartagena, Colombia. We departed Portobello three days ago, at which point our engines died, leaving us stranded at sea. Our Captain is a drunk, and I fear for the safety of myself, my girlfriend and the other passengers on this boat. Please help us if you can!"

With that, Simon set down the handset and rushed to check the doors and windows. Outside the radio room, the main cabin remained empty, and no one seemed to be stirring anywhere on the lower deck. With the coast clear, Simon shuffled back to the terminal and waited for a response. There was a long pause. The crackle of the radio was grating, and the heat of the cabin and the intensity of the situation drenched him with sweat.

It was a painfully long pause. *Too long*

Simon picked up the handset and spoke quietly once again.

"Hello?" he whispered, hoping the person was still out there.

Then, at last, came a response. The manner in which the person spoke was bizarrely casual. But after a few seconds, Simon understood why.

"Well, it could be worse, Simon... You could be stuck here with me in the Darien with my van stuck in a trench. I mean, I've been trying to get it out for TWO DAYS! Oh, and when the hell did you get a girlfriend? I left you like a month ago. Man, you work fast!"

Simon nearly dropped the mic and fell to his knees in disbelief. His heart raced, and his mind exploded. "Jonah, is that you?!" he yelled exuberantly into the microphone.

Catching himself, he threw his hand over his mouth and quickly looked around the cabin.

"Who else do you think is out here, idiot?" Jonah responded.

Simon gave up standing, falling to the ground on his ass and breaking down with emotion. *I can't believe it's really him.* His voice cracked as he spoke. "I can't tell you how good it is to hear your voice, Jonah." He shut his eyes to keep the tears in. *Destiny?*

"It's really good to hear yours, too," Jonah responded, clearing his throat. "I'm glad I remembered how to talk—not much call for it out here," he laughed.

Simon chuckled quietly and wiped his eyes.

The two friends chatted for twenty minutes or so, each helping the other brainstorm remedies for their individual predicaments. Jonah gave Simon the frequency channel for SENAFRONT, just in case, and the two came up with a plan for Captain Ricardo.

"You know right now we're probably less than a hundred miles from each other as the crow flies," said an emotional Jonah.

"If I could swing by to help you out partna', you know I would," Simon responded, his eyes welling.

"Naw, I'm good," Jonah said.

The response was predictable, and Simon smiled warmly at hearing it.

After a short while, they said goodbye once again with great sorrow.

"Goodbye, my friend."

"Goodbye, buddy."

In that moment, the sense that they might one day reunite felt somehow restored.

Simon put down the hand mic, walked calmly to the kitchen and picked up a cooking pot and a large spoon. He strolled back to the radio closet and set about hammering on the pot loudly with the spoon as he went.

Clank! Clank! Clank! Clank!

"Everybody up!" Simon bellowed repeatedly, and within twenty seconds, the commotion had brought the entire ship to the radio room's door—weary, angry and looking for answers. Captain Ricardo seemed the angriest of the lot.

"What the hell are you doing!?" the Captain yelled.

Simon stood tall and confident. He wasn't backing down this time.

"So, I just used this radio to notify some people as to what is going on here, Captain. If you don't get us to an island *today,* the authorities will be contacted... and, trust me, you do *not* want that to happen!" Simon glared at the Captain through bloodshot eyes that said *I'm in charge now.*

Yet the arrogant Ricardo rejected such a notion. "Bullshit!" he blasted back at Simon.

Without hesitation, Simon picked up the hand mic. "Jonah, you still there?"

He turned up the volume allowing the crackle of the radio to fill the room. Everyone stared at him. Then at the hand mic. Then the radio. Waiting, hoping to hear a response. But none came. Ricardo was starting to smile when—

"Copy that Simple Simon, this is Bearclaw, how do you read?" came loud and clear over the speaker. Simon nearly did a spit take. *Simple Simon? Bearclaw?*

"Um, howdy, Bearclaw. Please tell the Captain here what will happen if he doesn't get us to safety today," Simon replied into the mic. A mischievous smirk grew across his face, his eyes still locked dead to rights on Captain Ricardo's.

"Oh, sure thing partna'," Jonah responded giddily. "Well, first of all, I'm gonna call the Panamanian Coast Guard this afternoon and report a kidnapping aboard the Santa Maria. I'll be sure to give 'em your position. I have it now... Then, after they come pick you up, and they arrest Captain Ricardo, I'll find out where they tow his boat to and go burn it to ashes, Viking funeral style."

The radio clicked.

Simon glared at Ricardo, straining to keep a straight face.

Ricardo stared at Simon, dumbfounded.

Nice touch there at the end, Jonah. "Copy that, thank you kindly, Bearclaw," Simon responded into the mic.

"No problemo *amigo*," Jonah responded. "Bearclaw over and out."

Within ten minutes, the engine was "fixed," and the boat was chugging swiftly towards the islands. With the room fans back on, April and Simon retreated to their cabin in haste and locked the door, kissing wildly. It was still swelteringly hot, and though they were drenched with sweat, they managed to peel each other's clothes off and fall onto the bed, their wet, naked bodies sliding smoothly against each other in the swaying ship. April's skin was moist and salty in Simon's mouth, but she tasted like heaven, and the moment tasted of victory.

CHAPTER 70

Upon arrival at the first of the San Blas Islands, the disheveled passengers disembarked and relished the feeling of solid land beneath their feet. The rain had faded, and Simon immediately began walking through the marina, speaking with any ship captain he could find. Several sailboats that had left Portobello two days after them had already arrived earlier that morning. After an hour's exploration of the port, Simon found a friendly female captain, Belinda, with a beautiful long yacht, the *Estrela Fugaz,* who was sympathetic to his story and could accommodate Simon, April, Helena and the Danes on board. *Fuck Ron and Avi.*

Belinda's boat was considerably larger and a bit more expensive, but Simon volunteered to pay the difference for all five of them. He had money to spend after all—but his time with April was already running short.

After securing the new deal, Simon charged back to the *Santa Maria* and demanded a full refund from Ricardo. The surly captain refused, scoffing at the idea. But a new incarnation of Simon had begun to form, Simon 2.0, and he wasn't just going to lie down and give in anymore. He stepped hard to the Captain's face and warned, "If you don't give me our money back, *right now*, I will turn this into an international incident, and you will *never* sail this piece of shit boat again."

Captain Ricardo could see in Simon's eyes that he meant it. After a few seconds, he begrudgingly conceded and retrieved the money.

With cash in his pocket, Simon headed down the beach to find the Danes, Helena and April sitting at a table by a local restaurant, trying desperately to get their stomachs about them.

Simon's face was somber as he walked up to the group resting on the beach. "We have to go back on the Santa Maria now," he said.

The group looked up at him with desperate faces as though the world were ending.

He continued. "That is, we have to go grab our things off the Santa Maria and move them onto the new boat I just hired for us. Our new captain, Belinda, needs us to move our bags on board now so she can go purchase fresh seafood at the market for our welcome feast tonight!"

There was a long pause as everyone just stared at him, slowly grasping what he'd just said. Smiles gradually crept over their faces.

"Let's go!" Simon hollered, clapping his hands together and laughing.

At once, the group leapt to their feet and dashed over to the *Santa Maria*. As they marched off the boat with their luggage, the eldest of the group, Helena, had some choice words for Captain Ricardo in German. No one else could understand, but they got the drift of what she was saying.

When the lot arrived at Belinda's immaculate, long wooden yacht, a collective sigh of joy swept over the whole group. Lars put his hand on Simon's shoulder. "Thank you, Simon," he said with a smile.

"You're welcome," Simon replied. "I couldn't leave you good people behind."

Lars smiled wider. "And Avi and Ron?"

"Only room for five," Simon laughed.

Lars laughed as well.

When they reached the deck, Belinda welcomed her new arrivals, explaining the rules of the boat before showing them to their cabins. April and Simon's room was twice the size of their previous one and had wide windows facing the sea. "Good freakin' job, darling!" April said, dropping her bag by her feet and wrapping her arms around Simon, kissing him deeply. Seconds later, she was taking his clothes off again and began to remove hers as well. "Time to christen the new boat," she whispered in his ear.

Amen to that.

A sweaty, fun-filled hour later, they departed the boat for the beach and took a swim in the cool blue ocean. It was euphoric being off the vessel and together in the sunshine at last. Soon, they fell asleep on the beach, wrapped in each other's arms beneath the slowly shifting shade of a palm tree.

Best sleep in days.

***

When they returned to the boat at 5 p.m., Belinda had laid out hors d'oeuvres and sparkling wine on white wooden tables on the deck. Several of the other boat guests had returned, and Simon and April met their new companions. The dozen or so guests drank and ate fresh shrimp as the sky grew amber and golden across the Caribbean before them. When the last sliver of setting sun had disappeared into the ocean, Belinda switched on long strands of lightbulbs, that draped from the mast high over the deck. It was positively enchanting, and Simon, April, Lars, Almeta and Helena, each in their own language, thanked the stars above for their new home.

A delicious seafood dinner was served, prepared by Belinda and her chef Mikael, and the meal was rounded off with fresh tropical fruit and champagne.

After the decadent feast came to a close, the sails were raised on the *Estrella Fugaz,* and the group began the next leg of their journey, pushing on towards the next island. As the large boat moved quietly and smoothly out of the marina, they passed the *Santa Maria,* which was still lashed haphazardly to a nearby dock. Simon and April glanced over, and were delighted to see Captain Ricardo, Avi and Ron on the deck, drinking cans of beer somberly in the dark. The three men looked up at the beautiful yacht sailing past, its strands of lights aglow above its blissful passengers. Simon and April lifted their wine glasses and smiled at the trio with boundless satisfaction. Though Simon wanted so badly to give them the finger, he reasoned that them seeing his happiness was good enough. *The best revenge is to live well.*

Later assholes.

***

That night brought the fulfillment of all the romantic yearnings the two had been waiting for. April brought a bottle of wine to their room, and they stayed up for hours in bed, talking and making love, with the moonlight pouring in through the windows.

When April finally fell asleep in Simon's arms, he stared at her face glowing in the pale blue light. So angelic and peaceful, he thought. Beyond her, through the far window, he could see the moonlit waves rolling over the sea into the distance. And in the liminal state between consciousness and sleep, one solitary thought penetrated his soul.

This *is happiness.*

***

Two and a half months later, Simon would be sitting in the back seat of a taxi, staring through tear soaked, bloodshot eyes at the passing lights of an urban night—his hands and clothes covered with blood—nausea from early stage drug withdrawal twisting through his frail body. Then, as he wished that death would consume him quickly, and bring his pain and anguish to a merciful end, he would remember this moment long ago with April. And he would wonder.

How did it all go so horribly wrong?

CHAPTER 71

The next morning Simon and April awoke from a glorious night's slumber and wandered up to the deck for a breakfast of coffee, scrambled eggs and cold, fresh pineapple. Finding the boat anchored beside a tiny deserted island, they stared in awe at the unblemished mound of white sand amid the turquoise Caribbean water. Untouched and glistening white against the sea, it looked like something out of an exotic postcard.

After breakfast, Simon and April could no longer resist, and dove off the boat into the ocean to swim to the mini paradise.

As they clambered ashore, April declared, "I claim this island in the name of April and Simon!", stomping one foot down beside her and planting an imaginary flag.

Simon laughed. *If I was ever going to be stuck on a deserted island, I sure as hell would want it to be with her.*

After a few hours of snorkeling, sunbathing, and romantic frolicking on the island, the yacht set sail once again. Simon and April sat lackadaisically on the deck, chatting with other passengers and sipping rum punch. It wasn't long before the boat's chef, Mikael, walked curiously past them with snorkeling gear in hand and a large mesh bag hanging from his waist. The passengers' eyes wandered along with the thin, dreadlocked man as he approached the rear of the boat. Slipping on his snorkeling mask and fins, Mikael proceeded to pick up a towrope attached to the stern. Then suddenly, and to everyone's shock, he leapt off the rear of the swiftly moving vessel and out into the water.

"What the hell!'" cried, Simon.

Rising from their seats, the stunned passengers rushed to the boat's rear railings to find Mikael, hands still clinging to the rope, being dragged headfirst along the surface of the water. His face and mask, now submerged in the glistening blue, tilted side to side as if scanning for something.

"He's looking for conch!" Belinda called out from the helm.

What?

Skimming effortlessly above the shallow seafloor, Mikael eventually caught sight of something approaching below and plunged his head deep under the water. In a flash, his body followed—his fins steering him quickly down towards the sandy seabed like an oceanic Tarzan.

Simon and the other passengers could see everything through the crystal-clear water as Mikael darted a hand out and snatched a large conch shell from the seafloor, deftly placed it in his hip bag and swung back up to the surface to breathe.

"Oh my god!" April exclaimed, laughing with delight.

As Mikael dove, again and again, the passengers watched, mesmerized, as the young man swooped down, plucking shell after shell from the sand and collecting them in his bag.

When at last he returned to the boat, it was with a round of applause and a hero's welcome.

"Do you want to try?" he asked Simon, smiling.

"No way!" Simon laughed.

"It's really not that hard, mon... If you think you're about to hit something, just let go of the rope and swim to the surface. We'll come back for you... I promise," he added with a wink and a grin.

Simon quickly realized Mikael wasn't joking. "You're serious?"

"You only live once, right mon?" Mikael replied, handing Simon the snorkel and mask.

Simon looked to Mikael, then to the water behind the ship. Then back to Mikael. "Okay fuck it, I'll try it."

"Seriously?!" April blurted, surprised and simultaneously terrified.

"Yeah, why not?" Simon couldn't believe the words coming out of his own mouth.

"Um... okay. Be safe," she said.

Am I being adventurous or foolhardy here? I guess I'll find out pretty quickly.

Simon slipped on the mask and fins and walked to the back of the boat. He held the towline in his hands and stared down at the water moving swiftly below him.

What are you stu—

Simon jumped in.

When he hit the water at full speed, it felt something akin to falling out of a moving car onto a freeway. Slamming forward and tumbling head over heels chaotically, he bounced across the ocean surface for a good ten feet before landing upside down in the drink. Finally managing to right himself, he breached the surface for air, but had barely inhaled when the towrope snapped taught, yanking him forwards with a twang and launching him across the surface like a rocket. Rolling and flopping and struggling to hold on to the rope, he bounced furiously like a rag doll through the boat's wake.

This was a terrible idea! Foolhardy, definitely foolhardy!

Choking on the spray and writhing like a snake through the churn, Simon somehow managed to roll onto his belly and blow the water from his snorkel. As he took a deep breath and glanced up at the boat ahead of him, he could see April and the other passengers standing on the stern watching him, mortified. April's hands were over her mouth.

That looked bad...really bad.

Abashed from his graceless entry, Simon ducked his face underwater to hide from their watchful eyes. And as he slid beneath the water's surface, his mood transformed instantly, as it had done so many times before.

Serenity.

Ahhhh, that's the stuff.

The ten-foot-deep water was clear and blue as Simon glided smoothly across it now, his arms outstretched over his head, clutching tight to the towrope. Below him, the floor of the ocean was covered with white sand and sprawling fields of undulating green seagrass curling out in every direction. Hundreds of brightly colored tropical fish dotted the waters beneath him, and every fifty feet or so large sea turtles hovered, munching on the green vegetation below. Simon began to breathe calmly through the snorkel, feeling like Superman flying over the azure sea. *This is incredible.*

Glancing back up to the boat, he gave an awkward thumbs-up to April, who offered him a crooked half-smile in return. And as he looked back down, he suddenly spied a field of large conch shells coming into view, peppering the seafloor ahead like drops on a Jackson Pollock painting.

It was time to try his hand at getting one. Super Simon's first attempt, however... didn't go quite as planned. *Down, down and awaaaaaay!* Simon took a deep breath of air and plunged his head underwater. And as he tilted his chest to a precarious angle, the tension on the rope and the hydrodynamics of his kinked body sent him suddenly hurtling straight down towards the seafloor. *Oh shit!*

Instinctively, he pulled back to avoid a collision, over correcting his trajectory upward as he did and launching himself back to the surface. As he burst from the water in a chaos of splash and spray, he nearly completed a full somersault before belly-flopping back into the wake. *Holy shit!* But he dared not look back up to April. He could only imagine the look she was giving him now.

Let's try that again.

Moving more timidly this time, Simon barely managed to dip under the water before resurfacing. *Come on now…gotta find the middle ground.*

He tried again and again, each time coming closer to control. Until finally, he reached a vague level of mastery that allowed him to maintain stability and adjust his up and down movement by tipping his fins.

Ahead, another cluster of conch was approaching. *Here goes something.* Simon pulled as much air into his lungs as he possibly could and dove down again towards the ocean floor. As he reached the field of seagrass below him, he plateaued just above it, the tall vegetation tickling his belly from beneath. Yet he quickly recognized that he'd have to go lower to reach his goal. So down he went.

The green grass whipped across his face and stomach as he charged onward through it. The patch of sand was coming, and Simon prepared himself for action. Suddenly, he burst from the field of grass like a pouncing tiger—just inches above the sand now. Simon could see several conches lined up ahead and coming fast. His lungs craved air, yet he needed to focus harder than ever to keep from slamming into the sandy seafloor. A solitary target came into view ahead. *This is it.*

Simon clutched the towline handle hard with his left hand and released his right hand, dangling it down below him. He stretched out wide, extending his fingers to their limits.

15 feet…10 feet…5 feet…SLAM!

When his hand careened hard off the spiny shell, a blistering pain shot through his entire arm. He lifted his hand to his face to find blood swirling from a large gash on his palm. "Oh shit!" he gurgled through his snorkel as nausea roiled in his stomach. Stunned, Simon prepared to surface in wounded defeat... but then, suddenly... beyond the crimson cloud ahead... he noticed another conch approaching directly below him. *It's now or never.*

Stars had begun to form in Simon's eyes from a lack of oxygen, but something inside of him refused to accept his body's call to surrender. Grabbing the wooden handle with his cut right hand, he lunged with his left, swooping down towards the large shell. The pain was excruciating as the tow rope burned against his wound, but Simon gritted his teeth through it. Determination simmered inside of him unlike any he'd felt before. He was almost there.

As he reached down and scooped the shell from the sand, Simon's fingers slid directly into its open slit and mushed against the soft, slimy mollusk inside. *Jesus!* But he wasn't about to let go. Simon gripped onto his prize tight and launched himself up towards the surface.

Exploding from the water like a Trident missile, Simon flew through the air, tossing the tow rope away, spitting out his snorkel, and ravenously sucking air into his lungs before tumbling back down to earth. When his flailing body eventually came to a stop, his head broke the surface, gasping, and he spied the rear of the vessel, continuing on away from him. April was hanging over the back, staring at him in terrified bewilderment. Simon lifted the large conch shell above his head and watched as she clapped her hands together and smiled.

Man, I have got to look amazingly cool right now.

I think I'm gonna throw up.

A few seconds later, the boat circled around and retrieved him.

"That was amazing!" April gasped, kissing him hard as he climbed wearily aboard. Simon could hardly believe how successful he'd been at impressing her. He was doing a fine job impressing himself as well. *Did I really just do that?*

Once Simon was back on the deck, Belinda and April bandaged his cut hand as he regaled them with his tale of undersea adventure. Mikael, meanwhile, cleaned the conch, and Simon, April and the other passengers gathered to watch him crack open the large shells on a table and then peel the large mollusks from their housing. The dreadlocked boatman chopped the conch up finely, and together with some mango, onion and fresh cilantro, mixed the whole thing together in a large bowl with lime, ginger, garlic and diced chili pepper. Simon and April licked their lips as they watched. *I want to eat this. Oh, yes, it shall be mine.*

When he'd finished, Mikael placed the tangy, spicy concoction on a table with several bowls of tortilla chips. "Conch ceviche!" he yelled with a smile, as the eagerly awaiting passengers pounced like zombies on a cracked skull.

Simon and April scooped up huge bites of the tantalizing creation, and their eyes lit up as the fresh flavor hit their taste buds. "Oh my God, this is good!" April gasped, still chewing.

"I can't even believe it!" Simon mumbled, his words muffled by a full mouth.

The entire bowl was empty in ten minutes.

***

For the next three days, Simon and April enjoyed more of the same. It was paradise.

Island hopping, snorkeling, eating fresh seafood, shopping in small Kuna village markets, sunbathing on the boat deck and reveling in every second of their time together.

On a few occasions, Simon tried to reach Jonah again with Belinda's onboard radio, but all he ever found was static. It worried him.

The couple arrived in Cartagena two days later than expected and checked into a small hotel in the enchanting Old Town neighborhood. As romantic a locale as Simon could have dreamed of, the spectacular, walled colonial gem of Old Town Cartagena is home to countless ornate churches, sprawling, flower and fountain covered plazas and glistening gilded palaces. The narrow, cobblestoned streets are a step back in time, bestrewn with artists, musicians and street performers, bringing a vibrant and festive energy to the town. Spanish era mansions line the charming avenues, each adorned with overhanging balconies that drip ancient flowered vines towards the lively sidewalks below.

With April's flight scheduled to depart the following morning, the pair decided to make one final night of it together, meandering through the enchanting quarter hand in hand, taking in all that makes Cartagena's Old Town so wonderfully distinctive.

With day turning to night, the couple stopped for dinner at a lively restaurant and talked for hours as a *Vallenato* band played melodically on the accordion and the *guacharaca*. Though the evening should have been one of revelry, with every passing second, the pair felt an ache growing inside of them over April's looming departure to Panama.

"Do you really have to go back tomorrow?" Simon asked yet again across the candle-lit table, the band playing a heart-crushing ballad beside them.

April gazed at him with melancholic eyes and a resilient smile on her face. "Yeah, I do. I wish I could stay, but I just can't right now."

Simon tried to think of ways to keep her there. But it was no use.

That night was one of the most heartfelt of their brief time together. They stayed up till sunrise making love, chatting, ordering room service and watching bad Colombian television in bed.

After a solemn breakfast, Simon escorted April in a taxi to the airport and walked her through the terminal to the security entrance. They stopped to embrace. "Will you come visit me on the road again soon?" he asked.

"I'll try, but I only get a few weeks of vacation a year, and I just used most of it," April replied, fighting hard to restrain her emotions. "Thank you for taking me on this trip, Simon."

"Thank you for showing up," he replied, emotion swelling inside him as he recalled the moment he'd found her sitting on the dock in Portobello. "We'll see each other again soon, I'm sure of it," he continued, attempting to somehow remain positive. He leaned in and gave her a final kiss.

In his heart, Simon knew he'd have gone back to Panama with her right then and there if she'd have asked. But she didn't.

After watching April pass through security, he stood waiting for a lengthy spell in the vain hope that maybe, just possibly, she would come running back out to him like in a scene from a sappy, romantic movie. But after several aching minutes, he accepted that it was just a dream. And he wandered outside, head hung, to catch a taxi.

Sitting in the back seat, forlorn, Simon looked over his shoulder at the airport disappearing into the urban sprawl behind him. In that moment, he felt more heartbroken and more alone than he ever had before.

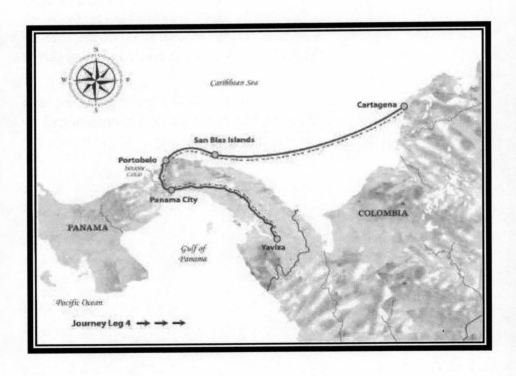

CHAPTER 72

Romance drifted in the air like a stench as Simon walked brokenhearted through Cartagena's old quarter. Strolling across the *Plaza de San Pedro Claver,* he spied a young couple holding each other in an embrace, kissing passionately below a vine cradled veranda. An ache of longing dug deep into his stomach, and he hustled along quickly in retreat.

Yet there was no escaping it. Other couples soon passed by, each one reminding Simon of April and the love he had just so brutally and abruptly lost. The previously joyful lanes of Old Town Cartagena now loomed dark in his eyes, shrouded beneath a mist of pain and regret. He cursed himself for allowing things to end. Self-pity transformed into self-loathing. *I can't believe I let her go. Such a damn fool.*

As Simon wandered back to the hotel, his lonesome mourning was visible for all to see. He unexpectedly found himself propositioned by countless prostitutes and drug dealers along the way. *I guess people see you differently in this town when you're alone.*

At each passing street corner, peddlers he'd never noticed before whispered offers of cocaine, the local drug of choice. And though Simon had never done street drugs in his life, with each new proffer, he found himself growing surprisingly tempted by the thought. *Maybe it would help.*

Unable to retreat into a Zoloft-induced emotional haze, the idea of making a quick mental escape from the anguish he now felt sounded pleasing. It would certainly be an easy way out, he thought. But though he craved a quick fix, the idea of trying cocaine seemed a bit like overkill, and he feared where it might take him. So, instead, he decided rather foolishly to barricade himself inside his hotel room, a misguided attempt to resist temptation and distract himself until he'd had time to heal.

It worked terribly.

After languishing indoors for just over a day, lying in the same bed he'd slept in with April, watching the same TV he'd watched with April and ordering from the same room service menu he'd ordered from with April, Simon had had enough. *I could just do a little... to get me through.*

Desperation driving him, Simon stormed from the hotel at 2 a.m. on a b-line towards Cartagena's infamous *Calle Media Luna* in the rough-and-tumble Getsemani Barrio. If he was going to find a drug dealer at this time of night, it would be here.

Yet when he arrived, Simon was appalled by what lay before him.

The whole abrasive scene was one of depravity and over-indulgence on a grand scale. The narrow street was packed with hundreds of young tourists clamoring about outside of thumping nightclubs, wired on cocaine, drunk on cheap rum, screaming, hollering and vomiting in the streets. Local vendors sold cocktails and beers from rickety bicycle carts that lined the packed road, and it wasn't long before the pressing crowds, the cacophony of competing club music and the wild eyes started to get to Simon. *What am I doing here?*

He was just about to beat a hasty retreat, when he felt a slight tug on his shirt.

"*Co-ca-yayna?*" he heard coming from behind him.

Swiveling around, he peered down to find a young local boy staring at him with glossy, glazed eyes. *My god, how old is this kid? Ten?*

The young boy's nose was running, and he had a white crust around his nostrils. His emaciated frame and dilated pupils made Simon's stomach turn. "*Co-ca-yayna?*" the boy asked again and held out a small plastic bag of powder in plain view of the world.

Simon darted his eyes around and was shocked by the indifference of the public. No one seemed to care. Not the tourists. Not the locals. No one.

"*No, gracias!*" Simon shouted over the sound of the crowds and turned to storm away. Yet as he did, the child grabbed onto his shirt and continued repeating, "*Co-ca-yayna? Co-ca-yayna?*" until Simon finally broke free and took off running.

Dashing down the street and out of Getsemani towards Old Town, Simon's mind flashed with thoughts of the child he'd just left behind. *Who is he? Where are his parents? And who gives a ten-year-old cocaine?!*

When Simon made it back to his hotel, he burst into his room, locked the door behind him and threw himself onto the bed. Overwhelmed with anger, he pressed a pillow to his face and screamed into it. "What the hell am I doing here!" he erupted as tears began to wet the pillowcase.

Simon felt lost. Until this moment, everything on his journey had made some nominal level of sense. For months, he'd chanced upon new comrades at every turn, and the next destination had always seemed to present itself with ease.

But Simon was no longer on the beach of Belize.... and Jack and Alice were now long gone. Nor was he sitting on a dock in Guatemala... and there was no lake nearby for Davis to pop his head out of. The hotel in Old Town had many foreigners... but the likelihood of stumbling onto an adventurous soul like Jonah, making preparations for a date with destiny, was nil.

And he had no reason to visit another consulate, and maybe find another April.

There is no other April.

There was no one, in fact, and Simon felt that weight pressing down on him like a Sisyphean burden. The fortress walls of Cartagena surrounded him on all sides, and he realized just how trapped he now felt within the citadel. He'd been paralyzed by the loss of April, and sedentary for days. But the road was calling to him once again. *I have to get out of here. I have to get free.*

***

The following morning, Simon walked across town to the massive twenty-foot-tall stone wall encircling the city. Built to protect the Spanish colonialists from marauding invaders, the ten-foot thick barricade was daunting in its sheer mass and height. Simon pressed his hands against it with reverence.

As he wandered along the edge of the towering structure, lost in thought, he suddenly stumbled upon an embrasure—a large portal used for firing cannons at approaching ships. Gazing through the hole and down a ten-foot-long tunnel, he could see the turquoise ocean staring back at him. *What is this?*

Throwing caution aside, Simon climbed up into the stone tube and crawled on hands and knees to its far end. When he reached the terminus, he stopped abruptly. "Oh shit!" he muttered, and scuffled back a few inches.

Below him lie a thirty-foot sheer drop, plummeting straight down the flat outer wall to the seashore below. Waves crashed like thunder on the rocky escarpment at its base. Simon carefully turned his body in the tunnel, slid forward to a sitting position, and allowed his feet to dangle over the edge of the portal. The vast Caribbean Sea stretched out before him now, rippling, twinkling in the morning light and seemingly infinite in its enormity.

Simon sat for a long spell, gazing out at the blue horizon. He began to picture the various pieces of land that lay far out to sea beyond the vanishing point. He'd been studying maps of the area for months now and had begun to know the geography well. As he sat there daydreaming, he imagined launching out of the small tunnel like a great seabird and soaring across the ocean into the great expanse straight ahead. On his left, he would first pass by Panama, then Nicaragua, Honduras, Belize and eventually Mexico. On his right, he'd fly by Jamaica, Cuba, and after some time, Florida. Directly in front of him from where he now sat, 4000km across the Caribbean Sea and into the Gulf of Mexico, was the Galveston oil platform where his father had died long ago. Something deep inside him sensed it, and as a gust of wind blew past him, a shiver coursed through his body. *I've come so far, but still, I'm so close.*

His mind wandered back to Belize, and it occurred to him that the water now breaking in waves below his feet was the same water that had lapped on the shore of Sunshine Bay what seemed like a lifetime ago. Simon had now set foot in seven countries, but he had surprisingly remained on the same stretch of ocean for most of it.

The world isn't that big, really, these days, Davis had joked back in Honduras.

Simon disagreed. The world was still a huge place to him, and in the enormity of the earth, he still hadn't really been anywhere. But that still could change.

The name popped back into his head. *Tierra del Fuego.*

Simon had made it the length of Central America, and had now finally arrived on the South American continent. He had clung to this strip of sea for most of his journey so far, but now it was time to move on, further still into the unknown. He resolved, in that moment and with absolute certainty, to continue his journey south towards Argentina. *I've made it this far… I have to keep going.*

For the first time, he believed that he could. *This is my Darien Gap. I won't quit until I get there. No matter what. To the bottom of the world…*

CHAPTER 73

That evening Simon decided to check his social network once again. There were dozens of comments on his last post, many from people Simon didn't even know. A peculiarity which confused him.

Amazing story, man!

Keep going! Can't wait to hear where you end up next!

Wow, what an adventure.

You're inspiring me to travel.

And many more just like them. Simon couldn't believe the response he was getting.

Who are these people, anyway?

Checking his private messages, he again found two waiting for him. Once again, they were from his mother and brother. Unenthusiastic about reading what his brother had to say, he opened the one from his mother first.

Son, your trip sounds like a dream! I'm so proud of you for doing it, and I know that it is taking a lot of courage. As to your question, I've always wanted to go to Central America actually. Or at least since I was in high school. I had planned on doing a semester abroad helping to build homes in rural Guatemala after my senior year. But then as luck would have it, I met your father, and he begged me not to go. So, I stayed in Texas. He promised me every year that he would take me someday, but unfortunately that never happened. I planned an entire family road trip from Mexico to Panama one year, but we never went. Every year your father said he didn't have the time.

I talked often with Gabriela, the Nicaraguan lady at the library about her home country and about Honduras with our neighbor Carlo. When you were twelve your father promised to take us all to Panama City for a week, but when he returned from his "two shift" the three of you ended up going to Utah instead. I never knew why it couldn't wait, but I knew how you boys loved camping with your father, and he loved going with you. I guess we just ran out of time.

Did you ever get to Panama City? If so, was it amazing? I can't wait to hear more about your trip. I hope your travels continue to go well, and I wish I could come meet you somewhere. I just don't have the money, unfortunately. Some day. Be safe and keep us posted on where your adventures take you next. Love you. Mom.

Simon stared at the screen in stunned disbelief. In three paragraphs, he'd just learned more about his mother than in the eighteen years he'd lived with her and the twenty after that. A well of emotions filled him, and a litany of questions pulsed through his mind.

What is she talking about?! Why did she never tell us she wanted to go to Central America? And why did Dad not tell us either? Why the hell did he never take her if she wanted to go so bad? What's a "two shift"? I always thought she was happy being at home...but, then again, I never asked her what she wanted about anything. WHY DID SHE NEVER TELL US?!

Fury filled his heart. Fury at himself, but even more so at his deceased father. It was the first time he'd ever felt any animosity towards the man, but he was realizing just how little he truly knew about him. About both of them. Everything he'd come to believe about his parents' relationship now came into question. His stomach grew raw and ached, and Simon felt enraged and regretful for never having spoken with his mother before. Then he reread what she'd said about the Utah camping trip and felt ashamed. *That trip was my idea.* Young Simon had been the one to push for the trip, and he'd pushed for it hard. It hit him now like a pile of bricks. *It was my fault she never went to Panama.*

Glancing at the note's ending, two blazing words stood out to him beyond all others on the screen. *Love you.*

I can't believe she said she loves me. I don't remember the last time she told me that.

Simon's head swirled, and he felt hopeless to find a worthy response. He began to type and just went with it.

Dear Mom. I honestly had no idea. I'm so sorry we never went to Central America together. If I had known, I wouldn't have pushed Dad to take us to Utah. I would have liked to have traveled with you. It sounds like you had a lot of passion for it.

Did you ever make it out of the country? It is occurring to me now just how little I know about you. I guess that's my fault for never asking. I'm truly sorry we never got to know each other. I don't know whose fault it was, but it doesn't matter, there's still time. I guess I'm more like you than we thought. Panama City was amazing. I think you would have loved it. We'll have to go someday.

Simon sat back in his chair and pondered a moment before continuing. He knew what he had to say, though the thought of it terrified him as he wrote the words: *If you want to come visit me, I could buy you a ticket. I have the money. Let me know if you'd like me to get you one, and we'll make it happen. It would be great to see you. All the best. Love, Simon.*

Simon hit send and took a deep breath. For several minutes he sat there thinking, struggling to imagine what it would be like if his estranged mother came to visit him. He hadn't seen her in more than ten years, and that last occasion had been a horrible experience at Jonathan's wedding. He remembered now how awful he'd been to her that day. The memories tasted like poison. *What a fool I was.*

No amount of remorse could absolve him now, he thought. Not after so many years. Simon fought to put it out of his head and quickly did a web search for *"oil rig two shift."*

As he read, he grew confused.

The standard shift for offshore oil rig workers, known as the two shift, involves 14 days on, followed by 14-21 days off, throughout the year. It equates to roughly 6-8 months a year off, making it a desirable job for people with young families...

Simon immediately recognized the implication and acid crept into his throat. His father had only ever returned for one week at a time... every two months. *Where the* hell *was he the rest of the time?!*

Simon struggled to breathe. The fictitious childhood he remembered suddenly felt as unreal as a children's story. The best moments of his life now lay riddled with deceptions and falsehoods. He stared into space, incapable of understanding. Why had his father, the paterfamilias... the inspirer... the Athos to their Porthos and "Porthos *light"...* deceived them so completely? Simon inhaled deeply yet again and closed his eyes. When, eventually, he reopened them, he checked the message from Jonathan.

Did you just call me? It's Christmas day, and someone just called and hung up before I found out who it was. If it was you, I'm really sorry about that. I've had the phone in my lap the whole day hoping you'd call. Would love to hear your voice, brother. Well, Merry Christmas and call me back if that was you. Jonathan.

Simon already regretted having hung up on his brother Christmas morning, but he'd wanted none of his brother's preaching of irresponsibility. At least this message didn't mention his job, which was a significant improvement. Maybe Jonathan was starting to come around, he thought. He wrote a quick response.

Yes, that was me. Must have gotten disconnected. Will call you when I can.

Then he began to write a new status update.

Since my last dispatch, a great deal has happened. I emerged from the jungles of the Darien and was promptly arrested by Senafront police and brought to the US Consulate in Panama City. Just as an FYI, compared to local chicken busses, the back seat of a Senafront police car was surprisingly comfortable. Though, I don't recommend getting arrested just for the luxury.

While at the consulate, I met the most amazing woman, April, who is unlike anyone I've ever met before. Honestly, she took my breath away the moment I saw her. I asked her out and believe it or not. She said yes!

That evening she and I dined and danced (yes, you read that correctly) to incredible salsa music and had a wonderful night on the town. From Panama City, I then took a historic train along the Panama Canal to Portobello on the Caribbean Sea. April and I boarded a boat bound for Colombia via the San Blas islands expecting a romantic relaxed sea voyage. Boy, were we wrong. A huge storm overtook us at sea in the first few hours. The motor and power went out, and for several terrifying days we found ourselves trapped, adrift on a boat with a drunk captain and a pair of Israeli boys who didn't exactly like us. Okay, I admit it, we didn't like them either. Finally, after a minor mutiny, we made it to safety on one of the San Blas islands and immediately switched boats.

From then on, we had an incredible week island hopping to Cartagena, Colombia. The turquoise sea, the white sand islands and the Kuna villages were unlike anywhere I've ever been. I think I finally have my sea legs which, for someone from Central Texas, is quite the accomplishment. Unfortunately, though, all good things must come to an end. April had to fly back to Panama, leaving me behind here in Cartagena, alone. I've done my fair share of sulking the past week, but finally I've resolved to move on. Which brings me to this moment.

I am alone and feeling it more than I could ever explain. Getting all your comments and support helps, but it doesn't change that fact. In the absence of companionship, I've taken on a new goal. My ultimate destination now is the Lighthouse Inn in the town of Ushuaia in Tierra del Fuego, Argentina. I won't quit until I get there.

I've had a lot of time to think lately and am finding that I have regrets and dreams and love and anger that I never knew were inside me. I guess these are the types of things you're supposed to think about out here. Who I am and what I truly want surprises me almost daily. Also, I think I miss my family. Weird. All the best, and thanks for reading.

Simon hit send and sat back in his seat.

The next phase of his adventure would be his and his alone. His journey was changing, but he felt more confident and more capable on the road than ever. He looked at the map in his guidebook and naively envisioned another month and a half of cruising south towards Ushuaia, Argentina and then possibly returning home after.

He had no idea the incredible obstacles and adventures that still stood in his way. Between Cartagena and Ushuaia lies some of the most hazardous and daunting terrain in the world. The dense jungles of the Amazon rainforest, the staggering peaks of the Andes Mountains, the barren wasteland of the Bolivian Desert and the frozen tundra of Patagonia.

It was still over 4,500 miles to Ushuaia, as the crow flies... and Simon... was no crow.

CHAPTER 74

Nearly a week had passed since Jonah had come upon the river. Consulting his carefully crafted map, it hadn't taken him long to deduce that it was the end of the line. The expanse of brown water flowed for fifty kilometers in either direction, and the current was swift, deep and impassable. Regardless, he'd always known this day would come.

Actually, he'd been ecstatic when it finally arrived. At long last, he'd be free from *The Prison,* as he'd come to call the van. The first few weeks of his journey had been more or less tolerable, but as the heat of the jungle swelled and claustrophobia set in, the steel chamber had begun to feel like a stockade. Or worse yet, a coffin.

After locking the doors to the van, he'd pressed his palms against its faithful walls and given the hot steel a long kiss farewell. "Goodbye, old friend, thanks for everything," he'd said—a scruff of a beard and the sweaty stench of time served in the jungle clinging to Jonah's pale greasy skin.

Moments later, he'd set off, skimming along the water's surface in his orange plastic kayak. Behind him dangled a rope towing an inflatable yellow rubber raft filled with food, water, supplies and, of course…his all-terrain wheelchair.

Finally, free from beneath the jungle canopy, Jonah had felt the warm radiance of sunshine on his face for the first time in well over a month. He'd smiled ear to ear with jubilation, inhaling deeply the fresh air breezing over his body.

In the week since, Jonah had already made significant progress. Forced to backtrack only on rare occasions, he'd managed to make his way south, gravitating ever closer to his Colombian destination. He was well aware that each of the innumerable rivers of the Darien eventually ran into each other or the sea. As long as he kept his compass by his side and his bearings straight, Jonah felt sure he could make it through.

Each evening, he'd pull the kayak over to a shallow shore and set up camp, hidden in the woods near the river's edge. At night, he would roll back out to the riverbank under the cover of darkness, and gaze for hours up at the stars—the first he'd seen in the many weeks since he'd entered the jungle. He'd never considered how much he would miss them.

This is the life, he began to think on more than one occasion.

His confidence grew as the days passed on. Jonah was so proud of his overwater successes, and joyful to once again be in touch with the wild, that he slowly, without even realizing it, began to stop thinking about the little things. But, in a perilous place like the Darien, the little things can be the difference between life or death.

On his eighth day since leaving the van, the current on the river began to grow stronger, and Jonah foolishly embraced his increasing speed as expedited progress. *Now we're moving!*

But it was a fleeting victory. As the pace of the water quickened, Jonah turned a bend, and fear suddenly grew deep in his wide eyes. A mere thirty meters ahead, white-capped rapids spanned the width of the river, roiling violently, crashing and churning with ferocity. In an instant, he knew that entering the roaring cauldron would mean near certain death. Glancing to his left and right, he shuddered upon realizing there was no bank, just a sheer cliff on the left and a field of massive boulders on the right. Between them, they funneled the water ahead swiftly into the rapids. *Shit! A bottleneck!*

In desperation, Jonah quickly swung to reverse his course, turning sharply into the current and nearly rolling his kayak in the process. The raft he towed behind now whipped past him and bucked, causing several items to flip out, splashing into the swiftly moving river.

Jonah paddled frantically against the driving current with all his strength, his muscular arms swinging back and forth, dragging deep through the water, trying desperately to propel himself forward, back upstream. But he was soon to realize that the furious work only served to keep him in place. He would have to paddle harder, the thunderous roar of the raging rapids behind him, giving him all the motivation he needed. Survival.

Digging deep, he directed every ounce of energy into his thrusting torso. Water sprayed across his face and his heart pounded, but slowly, he began to move forward. Centimeter… by aching centimeter. Burning pain throbbed in his arms as the kayak slithered back a few meters, finally reaching the bend in the river. But as he made his way around the blind curve, what appeared on the far side instantly dashed any hope in his heart into dust. Jonah's face dropped. There was nowhere to go.

Having grown so thrilled by his forward progress, Jonah hadn't noticed he'd entered a narrowing canyon more than fifty meters back. There was no bank whatsoever. Just shear rock and earth along either side as far back as he could see.

His arms were failing, and Jonah stopped paddling for just a second to rest and think. Immediately, he started drifting backwards, back around the bend. Back towards the rapids and certain doom. *Fuck! What am I going to do?!*

Swiveling the nose of the kayak around once again, he faced into the rapids, head on. And taking a deep breath of courage, he braced for the inevitable.

Then an idea struck him. *The boulders.* It was his only option.

Though the strength in his arms felt depleted, Jonah hoped he had just enough left to cross the width of the river one last time. He clutched the paddle solidly in his fists, and began to row as hard as he could to the right—angling himself diagonally across the river towards a large, round boulder positioned just a meter before the start of the rapids. Charging forward with everything he had, Jonah launched himself through the water—the boulder dead in his sights and approaching fast. But the current was even stronger than he'd realized. Like a missile, Jonah and the kayak flew towards the massive rock face. *I'm going too fast!*

He tried desperately to slow down. But it was too late.

Turning his body to the right, Jonah braced for impact as the left side of the kayak, and his body, crashed violently into the hard stone. His face whipped to the side and smashed into the rock, breaking the teeth on the left side of his mouth at once and sending piercing needles of pain through his head. Blood from his mouth sprayed across the grey granite, and the stunned Jonah coughed crimson teeth onto the front of his kayak. Water pushed hard against his side as the semi-delirious young man pressed his hands against the boulder, trying desperately to stabilize himself.

Then he felt the pull. In an instant, Jonah realized he was slowly being dragged backwards across the rock face towards the raging river. He glanced over his shoulder and discovered the supply raft he'd been towing hadn't reached the boulders with him. Instead, it had continued around the large stone and was now being churned hard amidst the rapids. The rope was yanking Jonah's kayak backwards closer and closer towards the thundering river. He pressed his hands onto the smooth stone, trying desperately to get some traction. *Fuck!* But there was nothing to grab onto.

Jonah knew what he had to do, but the thought of it terrified him. *I have to, or I'll die.*

In a flash, he reached into his chest pocket, grabbed his pocketknife, leaned over and began cutting the rope frantically. When, finally, it snapped, the line whipped around the boulder out of sight, and Jonah heard a loud crash from beyond it. Though the force of the river continued to push him hard against the rock, the kayak stopped moving, and Jonah exhaled deeply. Pressing his face to the cold stone, he spread his arms out wide against it in a thankful embrace.

It would take him a few seconds to fully grasp the severity of the situation.

My chair... my food... my water.... my tent and supplies.... everything is gone.

But before he could spend too much time worrying about it, he knew he needed to get off the angry river, its water still slamming against him and threatening to push him under. Wearily, he looked up and scanned his surroundings. From his position against the rock, he could see the tops of trees far off, beyond the sprawling field of boulders.

Land.

END PART 1

Made in the USA
Middletown, DE
23 January 2024

48410694R00231